Pynchon's Poetics

Pynchon's Poetics

Interfacing Theory and Text

Hanjo Berressem

University of Illinois Press
Urbana and Chicago

© 1993 by the Board of Trustees of the University of Illinois

Manufactured in the United States of America

1 2 3 4 5 C P 5 4 3 2 1

This book is printed on acid-free paper.

Library of Congress Cataloging-in-Publication Data
Berressem, Hanjo, 1956–
  Pynchon's poetics : interfacing theory and text / Hanjo Berressem.
    p. cm.
  Includes bibliographical references and index.
  ISBN 0-252-01919-9 (cl).—ISBN 0-252-06248-5 (pb)
  1. Pynchon, Thomas—Criticism and interpretation. 2. Subjectivity
in literature. I. Title.
PS3566.Y55Z57 1993
813'.54—dc20   91-43973
                                                         CIP

In memoriam: "Daddy"

Contents

Introduction: Text as World—World as Text   1

Part One: Poststructuralist Poetics

1. Lacan: The Text of the Subject   15
2. Derrida: The Subject of the Text   30
3. Baudrillard: The Subject in the Text   42

Part Two: Textual Analyses

4. *V.:* "V. in Love"   53
5. *The Crying of Lot 49:* Writing the Subject   82
6. *Gravity's Rainbow:* The Real Text   119
7. *Gravity's Rainbow:* Text as Film—Film as Text   151
8. *Gravity's Rainbow:* The Fatal Word   191
9. *Vineland:* Everything under Control   201

Conclusion: Writing the Real   243

Works Cited   247
Index   259

Acknowledgments

If there is a basic lesson to be learned from poststructuralist theory, it may well be that our words are never our own and that we are less "original" than we sometimes like to believe. While there are undeniably certain "discontents" in our inevitable suspension within the field of what Lacan calls "the Other," there are, however, also a great many satisfactions. These have to do with the fact that although many factors that form what we are and what we write are untraceable and anonymous, some are attached to specific "people"—fortunately, still the most convenient and tangible form of discursive network.

It is only fitting for a book that deals to some degree with the "logic of belatedness" that some situations in the history of its conception and realization take on, retrospectively, a special meaning and relevance. In the case of this book, such situations go back a long way:
  · a phone-call from Kach Tölölyan that started the connection with *Pynchon Notes,* the journal that has given me the first opportunities to get a taste of publishing. Indirectly, this phone call also marked the beginning of the continuous support of John Krafft, without whose scrupulous—and entirely unselfish—work on this manuscript (and others) numerous mistakes would have gone unnoticed and even more numerous hints would not have been followed up. From sending me material and letting me browse through the "hog heaven" of his files to reading and rereading multiple versions of the manuscript, he has been an unfailing help. In particular, the textual discussions have profited almost "shamelessly" from his advice.
  · a conversation with Ellie Ragland-Sullivan after an MLA workshop that resulted in a long chain of encouragements and intellectual stimulations. If there is a Lacanian "instance" to which I have always written, it

is her, and in the theoretical arguments in the book her "critical eye" is a constant presence.

- a letter from the DAAD, whose scholarship provided me with the opportunity to prepare the book during a year at Brown University, where Robert Scholes and Michael Silverman introduced me—one gently, the other "with a vengeance"—to the "wonderful world of semiotics."
- a talk at an MLA convention with the University of Illinois Press's Ann Lowry, who was seminal in accepting the manuscript and whose direction has been a crucial help in bringing it into shape; her encouragement during the time that I executed her advice has been equally helpful.
- a phone call from Bruce Bethell, who copyedited the manuscript and whom I thank for his scrupulous work on what at that time, I imagine, was still a very "German" text, as well as for his penetrating comments, which I read as the first real "reader responses," similar to one's own scribblings in the margins of other people's books and which as such came to prefigure the passage of the book from the private realm to the discursive one.

Most of all, however, my thanks go to Richard Martin, who has been both teacher and friend. He has "taught me to read," focused my interest on American literature, and has had the rare gift of bundling all the influences I have been exposed to, directing, supporting, and cautioning me without ever imposing his own views on mine. When in *Slow Learner* Pynchon discusses the various changes he has gone through and the various "personalities" he has been, I am always reminded of the great fortune I had in having someone whom the "various versions of myself" could invariably count on and go to for help and advice. I am convinced that without his unfailing support and guidance none of my work would have reached a stage beyond wishful thinking.

Last but not least I want to thank Jutta Göricke, Christiane Matties, Elke Pacholek, Helmut Göricke, Gregor Wessels, Rüdiger Schreyer, Pete Marsden, and Sahar, my "bebe." They know best why . . .

All translations from foreign sources that are not given in the English version in the bibliography are my own. Chapter 5 has been published in *Pynchon Notes* 18–19 (1986): 5–28 in slightly altered form as "V. in love: From the 'Other Scene' to the 'New Scene.'" In the quotations from Pynchon's work, unadorned ellipses are his; my deletions have been marked by ellipses in square brackets.

Pynchon's Poetics

Introduction:
Text as World—World as Text

"root and rhizome"
Thomas Pynchon, *Gravity's Rainbow*

The creation of a "poststructuralist Pynchon" is long overdue. It is, in fact, one of the major ironies of modern literary criticism that Pynchon should be almost the last contemporary American writer to be fully incorporated into a poststructuralist framework. This, I think, has as much to do with a specific quality of his writing as with the difficulty of finding a sophisticated enough theoretical apparatus into which to fit his work.

Pynchon presently holds a precarious but highly interesting and symptomatic position in literary studies. Primarily Derridean critics have hailed him as a leading deconstructor, yet the ease with which he is read within a Derridean framework is deceptive.[1] In fact, I will argue that one reason why Pynchon has so long and persistently resisted successful "French" readings lies exactly in the critics' insistence on inserting his texts into the framework of only one specific theory. In the case of Pynchon, such exclusive readings are particularly problematic; they almost invariably imply their own deconstruction by a host text that itself continually undercuts stable meanings and readings. This is true even when the critical reading, as in the case of Derridean deconstruction, stabilizes itself only around the very notion of instability.

Critics of the postmodern literary avant-garde, on the other hand, have judged Pynchon as regressive.[2] Interestingly enough, these critics are also informed by Derridean deconstruction. These diverging judgments have to be accounted for, especially because they mirror a duplicity constantly operative in Pynchon's texts themselves.

The failure of poststructuralist literary criticism to come to terms with Pynchon is ultimately the result of an unfortunate development within poststructuralist theory and its use in literary studies. Judging from the polemics of the theoreticians and their followers, it is easy to believe the various theories to be so much at odds that any one necessarily excludes all the rest. Within literary studies, this has led to the development of various hermetic schools of criticism, such as the Derridean and Lacanian.

Instead of proposing such mutually exclusive readings, I maintain that the various theoretical approaches—in the context of this book, those of Jacques Lacan, Jacques Derrida, and Jean Baudrillard—are not competitors but components in a complex grid of complementary systems. Rather than read Pynchon within one specific theoretical framework, therefore, I center my investigation on a notion relevant to all three approaches: subjectivity. This approach facilitates parallel rather than contrary readings, for it centers the discussion on a term that functions as an interface between various frames—psychoanalytical, philosophical, social, and literary—into all of which it is inscribed simultaneously. It is in fact the interplay among these frames that defines the multiple tensions operative in and on the subject.

Lacan's rewriting of Descartes shows in a nutshell what has happened to the notion of subjectivity in recent theory. In the *Discourse on Method*, Descartes bases every kind of knowledge on the knowledge of the self, defining the transcendental, self-reflexive subject (the *cogitans*) as the only truly existing reality. Descartes bases this knowledge on the contention that the subject's thoughts have the status of *intuitions*, which are invariably true. For a long time, especially within the French tradition, Descartes's formula provided the rhetorically most effective definition of an autonomous subject. In his essay "The Agency of the Letter in the Unconscious or Reason since Freud," Lacan stresses this spatial congruity of the subject and its thought by rewriting Descartes's *"cogito, ergo sum"* as *"'cogito ergo sum' ubi cogito, ibi sum"* ["'I think, therefore I am,' where I think, there I am"] (*Écrits* 165). Especially because of the central position of Descartes's statement within the history of philosophy, Lacan's subsequent distortion of its classical topography into the ruptured geometry of "I think where I am not, therefore I am where I do not think" (166) must be read in its fully sacrilegious dimension. Further, as though actually making fun of Descartes, Lacan carries this disruption almost *ad absurdum* linguistically by clothing the further disjunction of the subject and its thought in the convoluted statement "I am not wherever I am the plaything of my thought; I think of what I am where I do not think to think" (166). These disjunctions of the realms of *thinking* and *being* proceed along a parallel disjunction of signifier and signified: "Is the place that I occupy as the subject of a signifier concentric or eccentric, in relation to the place I occupy as subject of the signified?—that is the question" (165).

Lacan's disruption of the unity of the self-reflexive, transparent subject is informed by a general critique of humanistic concepts of subjectivity, a critique that unfortunately has often been read as a full-fledged attack against the notion of subjectivity as such.[3] Rhetorically powerful images such as Michel Foucault's ominous vision of man "erased, like a face drawn in sand at the edge of the sea" (*Order of Things* 387), Roland Barthes's polemical title "The Death of the Author," and Gilles Deleuze and Felix Guattari's joyous celebration of the schizo[4] have all had their share in giving rise to a fear, in both philosophical and literary circles, that the concept of subjectivity was to be dismissed altogether, leaving only the "anonymity of a murmur," which Foucault evokes so emphatically in his article "What Is an Author?" It should be remembered, though, that these erasures are always directed against the strictly Cartesian subject, in whose demise Foucault sees not the end of subjectivity as such but merely the end of a specific way of thinking about the subject, a cancellation that opens up a space "in which it is once more possible to think" (*Order of Things* 342).

Having lost the transparency of self-reflection, the new subject is a highly precarious construct, no longer autonomous, but acutely aware that language (understood as the network of signifiers rather than of the signifieds) is the horizon of representation. Rather than finding its freedom in unhindered self-expression, it is from now on "sentenced to speak" and is defined by language and the various modes and mechanics of representation, a "variable and complex function of discourse" (Foucault, "Author" 158). It is a subject whose world is, therefore, always already "fictional" (Lacan, *Écrits* 2) and whose knowledge can no longer be "perfectly homogeneous." Rather, it is fragmented and "exploded in different directions" (Foucault, *Order of Things* 346).

The development of this notion of subjectivity has gone hand in hand with a redefinition of the human sciences themselves, which can no longer deal with *knowledge* and *representation* as two successive terms that permit uncomplicated translation from one to the other. Instead, in their own dynamics and structure, as well as in their thematics, they have to account for both the complicity of these terms and the gap between them, the "hiatus between what one wishes to say and the articulation in which that aim is invested" (*Order of Things* 352). The awareness of this gap is the main reason for the literariness of much of the discourse employed by recent—especially Derridean—theory. What the human sciences ultimately have to deal with is the inherently problematic position of a subject who, "from within the life to which he entirely belongs and by which he is traversed in his whole being, constitutes representations by means of which he lives, and on the basis of which he possesses that strange capacity of being able to represent to himself precisely that life" (352).

After the "linguistic turn," the representation of the world is no longer the uncomplicated and natural expression of a well-ordered universe and discourse by a self-reflexive subject; reality and life are revealed as having always been fictions that the subject has created and come to believe.

The parallel to literature is especially interesting because the fictionalization of life and the problematization of the subject's function as author have always been major concerns for literature, both modern and otherwise. Acutely aware of the subject's interception by language, however, contemporary literature in particular has provided numerous images of the subject's entanglement within its own strategies of representation. Because of this awareness, Barthes has replaced the notion of the classical Cartesian author with that of the "modern scriptor," a discursive function rather than an inspired genius, "in no way equipped with a being preceding or exceeding the writing" (*Image* 145). This scriptor can no longer draw on the implicitly *natural* translation of his "passions, humours, feelings, [and] impressions" (147) into language and knows that what he calls emotions are always already part of "this immense dictionary from which he draws a writing that can know no halt: life never does more than imitate the book, and the book itself is only a tissue of signs, an imitation that is lost, infinitely deferred" (147).

Between the scriptor and the reader—whose birth is implied by the death of the author—a vast text begins to unfold: the text of the world. Because the subject itself has been completely textualized, strategies for reading this text are invariably literary strategies.

The modern, ontologically problematized and textualized subject has reemerged from the passage through the sign function as a "figure of speech." Its textualization has been carried out mainly in the fields of philosophy and psychoanalysis. Such references are not sufficient to provide a full image of subjectivity, however, if only because, ironically, in this textualization, the textualized subject is given over to a world that, although it has also been textualized, is experienced more and more as an overcoded semiotic wasteland. In fact, many contemporary sociocultural theories see pure fascination as the final, passive relation of the subject to the glitter and flux of the signs.[5] In their whirl, the "incessant sliding of the signified under the signifier" (*Écrits* 154) comes dangerously close to slipping its moorings in the notion of a subject and to disintegrating completely into an anonymous cybernetic scene presided over by the turbulent choreographies of "floating signifiers."

The ontologically and psychoanalytically already decentered subject thus finds itself *doubly* alienated by a society that provides less and less possibility for symbolic anchorings and in which the code *obstructs* rather than *facilitates* the reading of signs. It is exactly because the "literary subject" has always been suspended in all three registers simultaneously that literature holds a privileged position in relation to these developments. After the theoretical textualization of both the subject and society, it can provide a complete dramatization of the subject's radically discursive universe. Jonathan Culler has pointed out this mutual reflection in his preface to *On Deconstruction:* "Since literature takes as its subject all human experience, and particularly the ordering, interpreting, and articulating of experience, it is no accident that the most varied theoretical projects find instruction in literature and that their results are relevant to thinking about literature" (10). Today, then, the textuality of the world and the worldliness of the text meet within the position of a textual subject.

The belief and fear that poststructuralist theories invariably exclude the notion of subjectivity from their investigations are thus based on a number of misunderstandings, many of which originate in the highly controversial term *poststructuralism,* which I myself have used rather indiscriminately until now. Covering the activities of a wide spectrum of theoreticians working within various fields, it often blurs rather than clarifies important demarcations and issues. Because of this indeterminacy, I will not enter into a terminological discussion; instead, I refer the reader to the relevant theoreticians. A detailed reading of their texts will reveal that rather than going beyond the problem of subjectivity, they put it on the agenda with renewed vigor and unprecedented complexity.

Pynchon's works can be read in the light of recent theories of subjectivity because these theories share many of the concerns that underlie Pynchon's texts. The autonomy of the subject is continually and rigorously questioned in both. Furthermore, both investigations develop a new topography in which the dichotomies of artificiality versus naturality, text versus body, and control versus self-regulation are redefined.

The first section of this study introduces these theoretical positions and traces the shifts in the notion of subjectivity from one to the other. The theoretical positions are illustrated by passages from Pynchon's early stories, in which many of the motifs dealt with in detail in the subsequent textual analyses are already present in embryonic form. This preliminary section distills from the theoretical positions it examines complementary views of subjectivity and complementary poetics that can then be employed in the readings of selected passages from Pynchon's novels and that form an arena in which Pynchon's poetics can unfold.

These subsequent readings, rather than giving a general overview of Pynchon's novels, trace some paradigmatically chosen textual instances in detail. Although this forces me to be somewhat overselective, it has the advantage of enabling me to work "as close to the signifier as possible." First, I read chapter 14 of *V.*, "V. in love," putting a special emphasis on Pynchon's rhetorical deconstruction of Freudian psychoanalysis and the critique of the various codifications and modes of control in which the subject is caught within social space. This reading draws on the fetishization and textualization of the body. Second, I delineate the position of the subject in the fully textualized world of *The Crying of Lot 49*. Next, I examine the modes of personal and cultural conditioning portrayed in *Gravity's Rainbow*. This investigation is supplemented by a reading of the Kirghiz Light episode (*Gravity's Rainbow* 336–59), a passage that concentrates on the poetological implications of a completely conditioned, textualized, and simulated world and in which various of Pynchon's key metaphors converge. The further sections on *Gravity's Rainbow* treat Slothrop's quest and the poetological effects of the filmic strategies employed in the book. In the final chapter, on *Vineland,* I concentrate on the fateful complicity between subjectivity, power, and language.

One result of the textualization of the world and the subject is the radical emancipation of the signifier from the signified. It is therefore not surprising that Derridean critics in particular should be fascinated by Pynchon, because the first thing that strikes a reader is indeed the play of the signifier, the almost polymorphously perverse delight in signification, the loving portrayal of always more and more complicated signifying structures and the dissemination of meaning. The description of Slothrop's desk at the beginning of *Gravity's Rainbow* stands metonymically for this investment in the signifier and its proliferation:

> Slothrop's is a godawful mess. It hasn't been cleaned down to the original wood surface since 1942. Things have *fallen* roughly into

layers, over a base of bureaucratic smegma that sifts steadily to the bottom, made up of millions of tiny red and brown curls of rubber eraser, pencil shavings, dried tea or coffee stains, traces of sugar and Household Milk, much cigarette ash, very fine black debris picked and flung from typewriter ribbons, *decomposing* library paste, *broken* aspirins ground to powder. Then comes a scatter of paperclips, Zippo flints, rubber bands, staples, cigarette butts and *crumpled* packs, stray matches, pins, nubs of pens, stubs of pencils of all colors including the hard-to-get heliotrope and raw umber, wooden coffee spoons, Thayer's Slippery Elm Throat Lozenges sent by Slothrop's mother, Naline, all the way from Massachusetts, bits of tape, string, chalk . . . above that a layer of *forgotten* memoranda, *empty* buff ration books, phone numbers, *unanswered* letters, *tattered* sheets of carbon paper, the scribbled ukulele chords [. . .] an empty Kreml hair tonic bottle, *lost* pieces to different jigsaw puzzles showing parts of the amber left eye of a Weimaraner, the green velvet folds of a gown, slate-blue veining in a distant cloud, the orange nimbus of an explosion (perhaps a sunset), rivets in the skin of a Flying Fortress, the pink inner thigh of a pouting pin-up girl . . . a few old Weekly Intelligence Summaries from G-2, a *busted* corkscrewing ukulele string, boxes of gummed paper stars in many colors, pieces of a flashlight, top to a Nugget shoe polish can in which Slothrop now and then studies his blurry brass reflection, any number of reference books out of the ACHTUNG library back down the hall—a dictionary of technical German, an F.O. *Special Handbook* or *Town Plan*—and usually, unless it's been pinched or thrown away, a *News of the World* somewhere too— Slothrop's a faithful reader. (*Gravity's Rainbow* 18; emphases added. Further citations are abbreviated as GR.)

This passage reads almost like a willful parody of Foucault's "table" of representation.[6] In a seemingly random constellation numerous fragmented items are superimposed on one another. Layer on layer of discarded objects and discourses form an irredeemably chaotic heap of ruinous references. Any reading, however, that foregrounds only the delight and desire invested in the representation of these fragmented surfaces invariably misses something. The proliferating mass of details into which the narrative is continually drawn and the *horror vacui* of the passage cover up a carefully arranged structure.

A reading centered on the *signified* rather than the *signifier* reveals the table as a perfectly well-ordered microcosm that provides a precise architectural blueprint for the book and functions as an overture that presents many of its leitmotifs, such as the lovingly detailed refuse of writing itself (the pencil sharpenings, the dirt from typewriter ribbons) and the Thayer's Slippery Elm Throat Lozenges from Massachusetts, which are a reminder of Slothrop's and his family's past in Puritan New England. (Naline, Slothrop's mother, will reappear and write a letter to Joseph P. Kennedy.) The Kreml hair tonic bottle evokes a "historical" hair tonic as well as Russia (*Kreml* being the German word for the Kremlin); the Nugget shoe polish foreshadows the theme of race; and the image of prewar Germany is distilled into the eyes of a Weimaraner, maybe von Thanatz Alpdrucken (GR 142) or generally a citizen of the Germany that preceded the Nazi regime. Ukulele chords refer to the Kirghiz Light episode, and the jigsaw puzzle evokes Slothrop's quest. More general allusions to the culture of pin-up girls, the German rocket,[7] and the bureaucracies of war complete this historical panorama. Apart from thematic references, however, the passage also incorporates the book's main metaphors. The orange explosion evokes the central rocket image and already incorporates its double definition in the ambiguity of weapon or sunset. In a final *mise-en-abîme*, there is the gossip rag whose name could easily have served for the title of the book, the *News of the World*.

As a pile of references, abbreviations, and allusions, the desk becomes a shorthand for the historical panorama into which the book is inscribed and through which Slothrop will stumble in his quest for identity. More than he realizes, history has converged on his desk. A product of the war and its histories, it is as impossible to order as the war itself. If Roger Mexico's map is a replica of the war in London, Slothrop's desk is a replica of the war in general. The introductory *tableau* thus prefigures not only the shape of history but, simultaneously, the shape of the book, highlighting both its indebtedness to the signifier and its investment in the signified.

With the realms of the book and history converging on the common ground of the desk, it becomes a veritable "table of contents," announcing also, for the first time, the interrelatedness of history and historiography. Journals like the *News of the World*, which depict history's factuality "inaccurately accurate," are part of the table and thus added to the field of mere representations. Like Foucault, Pynchon is interested less in these superficial facts than in the project of a general archaeology.

The display of a seemingly chaotic collage of disparate elements thus turns into a legible image comprising a complicated network of overlapping structures, parallels, and inverted contours. Nonetheless, a reading that focuses exclusively on this order is in turn missing something. It is neither the signifier nor the signified alone that presides over the text, but their "complicity." The two approaches are not exclusive; my reading of Pynchon attempts to explain how and why they complement each other and how they themselves ultimately account for their complementarity.

The passage also shows another aspect of Pynchon's writing that is important for my investigation: in Pynchon's texts, the *grammar* of language is continually overlayed with its *lexicon*. The first thing that the reader is confronted with is therefore a world not of relations but of the sheer physicality of objects and the words that describe them, both of which pile up before the reader like clusters of convoluted bodies in mannerist painting. In this respect it is interesting to compare Pynchon's writing to the degree-zero literature, such as Alain Robbe-Grillet's, which has produced quite different tables, as in Robbe-Grillet's *In the Labyrinth:*

> On the polished wood of the table, the dust has marked the places occupied for a while—for a few hours, several days, minutes, weeks—by small objects subsequently removed whose outlines are still distinct for some time, a circle, a square, a rectangle, other less simple shapes, some partly overlapping, already blurred or half obliterated as though by a rag.
>
> When the outline is distinct enough to permit the shape to be identified with certainty, it is easy to find the original object again, nor far away. For example, the circular shape has obviously been left by a glass ashtray which is lying beside it. Similarly, a little farther away, the square occupying the table's left rear corner corresponds to the base of the brass lamp that now stands in the right corner: a square pedestal about one inch high capped by a disk of the same height supporting a fluted column at its center.
>
> The lampshade casts a circle of light on the ceiling, but this circle is not complete: it is intersected by the wall behind the table. (*Two Novels* 141–42)[8]

In this writing, the objects are defined by and represented through their topological positions within the clearly structured geometry of a Renaissance perspective. In contrast, Pynchon's universe resembles a junkyard, a giant pile of unordered, eclectic waste. Whereas Robbe-Grillet's table presents the image of a world without substance, Pynchon's world seems to be all substance, the characteristic "physicality of Pynchon's world" on which Richard Pearce has commented (9). This physicality—both of the world depicted and of the writing itself—opens up two questions: first, what, if anything, do these objects hide, and second, which position do the words—the objects of discourse—hold in this economy of hiding and representation? What, in short, is the relation between *object* and *word*?

The reading of the passage describing Slothrop's desk already shows that Pynchon's writing is filled with potential traps for the reader: either he will be deluded by the glittering surface and the obsession with representation, and carry out the allegory of the horizontal to its very limits, or, antithetically, he will read Pynchon's texts within a strictly structuralist framework, the approach with the longest tradition in Pynchon criticism.[9] Then, of course, there is the referential aspect, the relation of the text to the "reality" and "history" it describes, a question that has been central to a lot of "humanist" approaches to Pynchon. Apart from the occasional recognition of each other's project, however, neither group has attempted a reading of Pynchon's fiction that focuses on the *interrelatedness* of these three approaches, an especially important interrelation because it is also one of the main topics *within* Pynchon's texts and underlies their production. It is one of the characteristics of fiction in general and Pynchon's work in particular to constantly oscillate between various and often seemingly exclusive readings, each word suddenly changing its meaning and frame of reference, as in a figure/ground ambiguity in the visual realm. Rather than being inscribed into one conceptual framework, the text constantly rotates over various theoretical positions. My aim in the following study is to create a site on which this textual polyvalence is described in a series of *complementary* rather than *exclusive* readings that approach Pynchon's texts from various sides and directions, converging on the notion of subjectivity.[10]

Notes

1. A first deconstructive context for Pynchon was provided by *Pynchon Notes* 14 (1984), in a special issue entitled *Deconstructing "Gravity's Rainbow."* Furthermore, Molly Hite in particular has stressed Pynchon's "postmodernism" in "Review of Cooper, Peter L., 'Signs and Symptoms,'" and in *Ideas of Order in the Novels of*

Thomas Pynchon. Gabriele Schwab has dealt with Pynchon's "poststructuralism" in *Entgrenzungen und Entgrenzungsmythen* [*Subjects without Selves*]. Lance Olsen, in "Deconstructing the Enemy of Color," goes so far as to say that for Pynchon "language becomes a meaningless and joyous affirmative freeplay in a world without truth" (81). For the most extensive deconstructive reading of Pynchon see Alec McHoul and David Wills, *Writing Pynchon*.

2. In *The Self-Apparent Word*, Jerome Klinkowitz states that Pynchon writes "dramas of the signified rather than self-referential performances of the signifier" (59). See also Jerome Klinkowitz, *Literary Subversions*.

3. In *Entgrenzungen und Entgrenzungsmythen* Schwab bundles together Foucault, Derrida, Baudrillard, Lyotard, and Deleuze/Guattari, all of whom, she believes, are out to do away with subjectivity altogether. Fredric Jameson detects in Foucault a "left-wing celebration of the 'end of man' . . . some new post-individualistic state of things" (393).

4. *Anti-Oedipus: Capitalism and Schizophrenia*; see also Deleuze and Guattari, *A Thousand Plateaus: Capitalism and Schizophrenia*.

5. See Jean Baudrillard, "Requiem for the Media," *For a Critique of the Political Economy of the Sign*; Neil Postman, *Amusing Ourselves to Death*; Guy Debord, *The Society of the Spectacle*; Arthur Kroker and David Cook, eds., *The Postmodern Scene*; and Daniel Bell, *The Coming of Post-Industrial Society*.

6. Foucault uses the term "table of signs" (*Order of Things* 66) to describe a field of knowledge and representation defined by an "absolutely transparent language" (62) with a "binary organization" (64), a language in which there is "no meaning exterior or anterior to the sign . . . no opacity intervening between the sign and its content" (66).

7. Although Pynchon sometimes capitalizes the word ROCKET, I give it as lowercase throughout my text.

8. Robbe-Grillet delineates these "poetics of the surface" in *Snapshots and Notes toward a New Novel*. See also Roland Barthes, "Objective Literature: Alain Robbe-Grillet."

9. "Pynchon's poststructuralist, deconstructionist readers . . . tend to come out swinging against virtually any hint that a particular signifier might totalize one's reading of the novel" (Weisenburger 3). Charles Hohmann, in *Thomas Pynchon's "Gravity's Rainbow,"* actually differentiates between poststructuralists and postmodernists. In the introduction to his collection *Approaches to "Gravity's Rainbow,"* Charles Clerc asks "whether Pynchon is ultimately a diabolic prophet of doom or a humanistic visionary" (24). See also David Cowart, who maintains in *Thomas Pynchon* that Pynchon "may in fact take a relatively sanguine view of things" (4). Most recently, Kathryn Hume, in *Pynchon's Mythography*, presents a balanced image of Pynchon as both a "postmodernist writer by most definitions of that term" (221) and a mythographer, but she takes recourse to a mythical author image to congeal

these two aspects, which, I maintain, implicate each other much more than Hume realizes. For a discussion of Hume's relation to modern literary theory see Thomas Schaub's review "Mythologies New and Old: Hume and Current Theory."

10. This is a project sketched out in Khachig Tölölyan, "Criticism as Symptom." See also his "Seven on Pynchon," in which he opts for a semiotic and deconstructive reading of Pynchon, balancing, however, his use of the "deferral characteristic of the Derridian signifier" (166) with an "increase of sorrow caused by an excess of proliferating, contending orders in contemporary narrative" (167).

Part One
Poststructuralist Poetics

Chapter 1 **Lacan:
The Text of the Subject**

> "la lettre, l'être et l'autre"
> Jacques Lacan, *Écrits*

> "I would call this 'linguisterics.'"
> Jacques Lacan, *Encore*

What makes Lacan's theory especially relevant to literary studies, and in particular to my study of Pynchon, is that it combines the fields of psychoanalysis and modern linguistics—and thus those of subjectivity and writing—in one theoretical project. Unlike Freud, who for obvious reasons could only "anticipate its [linguistics'] formulas" (Lacan, *Écrits* 284), Lacan centers his theories on them: "[The] passion of the signifier now becomes a new dimension of the human condition in that it is not only man who speaks, but that in man and through man *it* speaks *(ça parle),* that his nature is woven by effects in which is to be found the structure of language, of which he becomes the material, and that therefore there resounds in him . . . the relation of speech" (284).

This subversion of the subject by the signifier provides a model of a radically decentered subject defined as a function of the signifier—the materiality as well as structure of language. Because this structure pervades the whole subject, which is strictly speaking only its effect, the unconscious is also *"structured like a language"* (Lacan, *Fundamental Concepts* 20). In language, the law and structure of the signifier regulate the movement and production of the signified. In fact, for Lacan the subject becomes so radically a function of the signifier that he defines a signifier as that which "represents the subject for another signifier" (*Écrits* 316). In semiotic terms, the intervention of the signifier in the subject yields a twofold effect: it continually bars the subject from a stable relation to a signified, while, insofar as it represents language in general, the intervention simultaneously bars the subject from the referent. Instigating the breach between *being* and *thinking* I discussed in the introduction, it marks the subject with a "lack-of-being"[1]—which is why Lacan writes the subject as $—and inserts it inextricably into a signifying chain, the recursive succession of signifiers referring to other signifiers.[2]

Because of the intervention of the signifier in the signified, and the fact that language inevitably positions the subject in a discursive and thus intersubjective realm, the language according to which the unconscious is structured is not an ideal "discourse of the Self" but the "discourse of the Other" (*Écrits* 193), a definition in which the Other stands for language as "the locus of the signifier" (310). Again, the signifier is responsible for the fact that the subject has a *barred* rather than a *direct* relation to this Other. Like the subject, in fact, language is barred. In Lacan's terminology, this appears as "S(ø) . . . signifier of a lack in the Other, inherent in its very function as the treasure of the signifier" (316). There can thus be no objective metalanguage, for there is no position outside the discursive and intersubjective space, no "outside" of the signifier: "no Other of the Other" (311).

These effects of the signifier pervade all of human reality, even and especially the realm of sexuality, which is commonly considered the most natural aspect of human existence. Through the intervention of the signifier, this field, too, is constantly barred. Lacan, in fact, proceeds from the premise that "there is no sexual rapport" (*Encore* 131).

From the very beginning, Pynchon's writing describes a similarly closed discursive universe, in which even the sexual scene is inevitably experienced as a textual one. In "Entropy," for instance, Saul, whose wife has just left him—ironically, because of a fight about communications theory—comes to feel the effects of the signifier in a quite painful way: "Tell a girl: 'I love you.' No trouble with two-thirds of that, it's a closed circuit. Just you and she. But that nasty four-letter word in the middle, *that's* the one you have to look out for. Ambiguity. Redundancy. Irrelevance, even. Leakage. All this is noise. Noise screws up your signal, makes for disorganization in the circuit" (*Slow Learner* 90–91; further citations are abbreviated as SL).

It is exactly because Pynchon's metaphor is taken from communications theory that it can be read as an example of the lack-of-being that pervades language. Although language is the only means to communicate, "real" communication is impossible because the textual machine does not allow for a direct and complete transfer of an ideal and stable meaning: "You never run at top efficiency, usually all you have is a minimum basis for a workable thing. I believe the phrase is Togetherness" (SL 91). Although Pynchon evokes love—Togetherness—as the concept in which a relation between subjects becomes possible even within the constant failures of language, the passage ultimately shows the impossibility of a sexual union to be caused by the "defiles of the signifier" (Lacan, *Fundamental Concepts* 149), so that from the start, Pynchon ironically undercuts the vision of unity he evokes. Meatball's answer, "Aarrgghh" (SL 91), may be seen as a first hint at the deconstructions of promises of such visions in Pynchon's later work.

Another aspect of Lacanian theory that touches on a leitmotif of Pynchon's writing—in fact, probably the best known—is that Lacan, like Pynchon, sees human reality and knowledge as inevitably paranoiac. This paranoiac nature of reality results from the specific formation of the ego during the "mirror stage,"[3] which defines, on a visual, prelinguistic level (the imaginary), the phantasmatic and libidinal character of the human perception of both *self* and *others*. After the subject's entry into language (the symbolic), this imaginary realm continues to pervade the symbolic one, through which, however, all further imaginary encounters are filtered. As Ellie Ragland-Sullivan states, the logic of the imaginary is an "identificatory, fusional" one (*Philosophy of Psychoanalysis* 131) that aims at covering up the lack-of-being. The "other side" of its "demand" for fusion and unity, however, is aggressivity and confrontation. In contrast, the logic of the symbolic is a "differential" one (131) that, in acknowledging the lack-of-being (castration), makes mediation possible. The complex interplay of these two realms defines human perception and creates the subject's reality. Finally, a third realm, one that designates what is neither imaginary nor symbolic, affects this reality by relating it to the problematic, "impossible" realm "beyond" representation: "the real, that's the impossible" (Lacan, *Séminaire XVII* 143). Lacan symbolizes the interrelatedness of these realms through the Borromean knot.

The real denotes on the one hand the underlying material that makes any imaginary or symbolic structuration possible, opening up the very "possibility of the order of presence and absence" (*Seminar II* 323), which is the basic dualism in which language is defined. On the other hand, as the "im-monde,"[4] which can only be reconstituted retroactively within the imaginary and the symbolic, the "pure real" (Juranville 41) becomes identical to the unconscious itself. Like the unconscious, it can be apprehended only as a cut and a void. It is the thing experienced as (no)thing, "*la chose*" experienced as "*l'achose*" (*Séminaire XVII* 186),[5] a paradox solved in the structure of "belatedness" (*Nachträglichkeit*).[6] The unconscious is thus defined in three frames: "On the one hand, the unconscious is . . . something negative, something ideally inaccessible. On the other hand, it is something quasi real. Finally, it is something which will be realized in the symbolic . . . something which . . . *will have been*" (*Seminar I* 158).

The real produces effects because, simply by being excluded from representation, it inscribes representation into a specific topography and gives it a direction: "There is an orientation. But this orientation is not a meaning" (Lacan, "Le Sinthome" 9:33). Whereas meaning can originate only from within the imaginary and the symbolic, the real is that which *underlies* meaning, *subverts* it, and *insists* within it. As *Waiting for Godot* evokes, "something is there waiting [*en attendant*], for better or worse, but waiting" (*Séminaire VII* 65). It is this insistence of the real within signification with which the poetics of both Lacan and Pynchon are ultimately concerned.

The real is "without fissure . . . we have no means of apprehending this real . . . except via the go-between of the symbolic" (*Seminar II* 97). Although language aims at re-creating the real *within* representation, the symbol "manifests itself first of all as the murder of the thing" (*Écrits* 104). This twofold orientation fundamentally problematizes the relation of language to the real. Language, especially in its function of naming, "is both destructive of the thing and allows the passage of the thing onto the symbolic plane, thanks to which the truly human register comes into its own" (*Seminar I* 219).

It is ultimately the speaking subject's negative relation to the real, as that which "resists symbolization absolutely" (*Seminar I* 66), that makes for the specifically fractured and distorted character of human reality, defining its imaginary, visual topography and its linguistics as *anamorphotic* and *libidinal*.

These distortions are related to the effects of desire in the registers of the imaginary and the symbolic. Desire, which "begins to take shape in the margin in which demand becomes separated from need" (*Écrits* 311), is the "product" of the subject's separation from the real and its entry into language. Whereas need, which denotes the minimum of the subject's necessities, is situated on the level of the real, demand, which denotes the maximum of the subject's claims, is situated on the imaginary level. Desire, which denotes the surplus in relation to need and the shortage in relation to demand, is situated on the symbolic level: "Thus desire is neither the appetite for satisfaction, nor the demand for love, but the difference that results from the subtraction of the first from the second, the phenomenon of their splitting [*Spaltung*]" (287).

Unlike demand, which creates "the phantom of the Omnipotence . . . of the Other" (311), as the agency that promises the fulfillment of the subject's demands, desire acknowledges the lack-of-being. Although in my textual discussions I do not always differentiate between desire and demand when I talk about a "desire for the real," in the strictly Lacanian sense it is always in this margin between demand and desire that Pynchon's protagonists are defined.

Desire thus regulates the movements of the subject within the imaginary and the symbolic and defines its broken and barred position in relation to both its own being and the world of objects, which is why its world is neither "a world of things . . . [nor] a world of being, it is a world of desire as such" (*Seminar II* 222). Through the separation from the real, which is defined negatively as "the lack of a lack" (Grosz 34), the human condition from the very beginning presupposes an inevitable lack-of-being. It is this lack that desire constantly attempts to fill: "Desire is a relation of being to lack. This lack is the lack of being properly speaking" (*Seminar II* 223). This lack is the "motor of the structural [symbolic] system" (Leclaire 96) because its "negativity" is why desire is forced to take the detour of discourse. Because of this inevitable detour through the "battery of signifiers," the subject's desire is always already the "desire of the Other" (*Écrits* 312) and comes to mark the lack in and of language.

All objects, in that they are reconstituted in and through language, are "objects in desire" and can only partly substitute for a "lost object," which strictly speaking is not an object at all but the promise of a unity that lies well before the split into subject and object: "The human object always constitutes itself through the intermediary of a first loss . . . the subject has to reconstitute the object, he tries to find its totality again starting from I know not what unity lost at the origin" (*Seminar II* 136). This loss, which traverses language, turns it into the subject's ultimate exile and from the start inevitably amalgamates it with desire: "The moment in which desire becomes human is also that in which the child is born into language" (*Écrits* 103). All objects then are invariably

> structured around the wandering shadow of his [the subject's] own ego. They will all have a fundamentally anthropomorphic character, even egomorphic we could say. Man's ideal unity, which is never at-

tained as such and escapes him at every moment, is evoked at every moment in this perception. The object is never for him definitively *the final object,* except in exceptional experiences. But it thus appears in the guise of an object from which man is irremediably separated, and which shows him the very figure of his dehiscence within the world. . . . It is in the nature of desire to be radically torn . . . this experience either alienates man from himself, or else ends in a destruction, a negation of the object. (*Seminar II* 166; emphasis added)

This final object Lacan calls "the Thing" (*la Chose*). Like the real, this "eternally lacking" object (*Fundamental Concepts* 180) is "not nothing, but literally not—it distinguishes itself as absent" (*Séminaire VII* 78). Strictly speaking, it is only "the presence of a hollow, a void, which can be occupied . . . by any object" (*Fundamental Concepts* 180). Because of that, it is always "represented by something else [*par autre chose*]" (*Séminaire VII* 143).[7] This lost object as retroactively [*nachträglich*] reconstituted in the imaginary and the symbolic is the "object *o*[ther],"[8] the object in desire, which, like desire itself, has a fundamentally chiasmatic character. In its double definition as both

the illusion of being
X
the being of illusion

its negativity as the mere "illusion of being [*semblant d'être*]" (*Encore* 87) is countered by the fact that it sustains the "being of illusion."

Again, Lacan uses "the sigla ($\$ \Diamond o$), . . . introduced in the form of an algorithm" (*Écrits* 313), to denote the subject's relation to this lost object, which is represented by various objects, the nonidentity between them being the reason why reality is inevitably phantasmatic and fictional: "The phantasm is defined in the most general form which it receives through an algebra constructed by us . . . the formula ($\$ \Diamond o$), in which the rhomb $\Diamond$ should be read as 'desire for'" (*Écrits*, French ed., 774).

Although it is located outside representational space, the real has a number of privileged positions in relation to the symbolic and the imaginary: sex, death, madness, and violence.[9] The first two are especially important for my discussion. In a sexual register, the real is "represented" by what Lacan calls *jouissance:* sexual (en)joy(ment), with its connotation of "orgasm." As "real enjoyment," this *jouissance* partakes in and shares the impossibility of the real (as well as, in extension, that of the unconscious and the body). In its fundamental negativity, however, it recapitulates the insistence of the real in the imaginary and symbolic. Like its separation from the real, the subject's separation from *jouissance* is what "propels" desire and makes it "eternal." Lacan, in fact, proposes to give the drive [*Trieb*] as the "drift of *jouissance* [*dérive de la jouissance*]" (*Encore* 102).[10] *Jouissance* is thus situated at "the point where psyche and soma become intertwined" (Ragland-Sullivan, *Philosophy of Psychoanalysis* 80–81). As "real," *jouissance* is related to the pure pleasure principle, polymorphous perversity and its aggressivity, the primary process and the body.

In the imaginary register, the libidinal agency of the ego aims at a reconstitution of real *jouissance*, which, however, remains phantasmatic and thus illusory. In this project, *jouissance* is related to the imaginary motifs of narcissism, the demand for a precastration unity, and the transgression of the (phallic) law of desire. Like the economy of demand, however, which terminates in the positing of the "omnipotence of the Other"—as well as, more directly, the other—the economy of the imaginary re-creation of *jouissance* does not find its solution in a "real" *jouissance* but in "the *jouissance* of the other" (Lacan, *Écrits* 42).

In the symbolic, the agency of the subject sets desire—in its conjunction with castration and the law—against the illusion of *jouissance*. Here the phallus, in its embodiment of "*jouissance* in the dialectic of desire" (*Écrits* 319), becomes the symbol and measure of the subject's alienation from its *jouissance*. Through the phallus, desire is related to "the prohibition of *jouissance*" (320). Lacan, in fact, sees desire as a defense "against going beyond a certain limit in *jouissance* (322).[11] In the symbolic, the sexual scene is treated as a textual one. It is through this conjunction that Lacan aligns a "sexual" and a "textual" *jouissance* that he calls—in opposition to the imaginary *jouissance* of the other—"the *jouissance* of the Other" ("Radiophonie" 70).

Although pure *jouissance*—like the unconscious—is always of the real, because of its different connotations in the various psychic registers, I will differentiate, for the sake of terminological clarity, between a real, an imaginary, and a symbolic *jouissance*, as well as—especially in the discussion of Derrida—a textual one.

Whereas sexuality is linked to the birth of the subject, its death, although it is "never experienced as such, . . . never real" (*Seminar I* 223),[12] denotes the border that reintroduces the subject into the real and "heals" the split between the subject and the real that birth (especially the "second birth" into language) initiates. The subject is thus defined within two brackets or points of perspective: "Death and sex participate in the real, at this locus of the irreconcilable, between the lack and the word" (Leclaire 23). This inextricable entanglement of sex (*jouissance*) and death—Eros and Thanatos—becomes obvious in the designation of the orgasm as a "*petite mort*."[13] In my textual discussions, I will refer to the effect evoked in the descriptions of moments of the impossible meeting of the subject with the real, in which unity and death (Eros and Thanatos) implode, as a "*jouissance* effect." In the reader, these *jouissance* effects—which are situated at the junction of the symbolic and the real in that they are *real* within the textual scenario but symbolic through their textualization—cause the specifically ambiguous affect that constitutes the fantastic. Through the violent replacements of subject and language with death and silence, death (like real *jouissance*) is linked to the ineffable, the "negativity of language": "Behind what is named, there is the unnameable. It is in fact because it is unnameable, with all the resonances you can give to this name, that it is akin to the quintessential unnameable, that is to say to death" (*Seminar II* 211).[14]

This relation between language, silence, and death is a further link between Pynchon's poetics and a possible Lacanian one, because Pynchon's work is always concerned with death—one might even say obsessed with it—so much so that if one were to talk of a teleology in Pynchon's texts, it would have to be a "teleology of death."[15] This preoccupation is explicitly stated in the introduction to *Slow Learner:* "When we speak of 'seriousness' in fiction ultimately we are talking about an attitude towards death" (SL 5). Although in retrospect Pynchon feels it was wrong to have the characters of his first published story, "The Small Rain," "hook it [death] up with sex" (SL 5), the story opens up the question of the position of the real in relation to these two registers. When little Buttercup and Levine sleep together surrounded by the widespread death following a hurricane disaster, they perform a sterile, clichéd act, "he puffing occasionally at the cigar throughout the performance [. . .] she evoking a casually protective feeling, a never totally violated Pasiphae [. . .] 'In the midst of great death,' Levine said, 'the little death.' And later, 'Ha. It sounds like a caption in *Life*. In the midst of *Life*. We are in death. Oh god' " (SL 50).

Although Levine connects sex and death, he becomes aware of the cliché when he imagines it as a headline in *Life,* an association that highlights the scene's careful arrangement and artificiality. There is thus a shift within the passage from the clichéd relation between sex and death to a more important relation—their common impossibility. Both real sex (*jouissance*) and real death are inaccessible, especially for Levine, but also generally, because they are always already mediated. In the evocation of the two people "acting out" the sexual act and the reference to cultural clichés and mediations, for which the magazine is a metonymic stand-in, the passage stages the "impossibility" of the real and its immediate symbolization in the imaginary and the symbolic, of which it is only a belated retro-effect.[16] When, in his introduction to *Slow Learner,* Pynchon retrospectively describes the language of the scene as "too fancy to read" (SL 6), the negativity of this "silence *in* language" mirrors perfectly the effect of symbolization described *by* it.

It is the agency of the ego that functions as an intermediary between the subject and the real. It is the "mechanism of regulation, of adaptation to the real, which enables the organism to refer the hallucination . . . to what is happening at the level of the perceptual apparatus" (*Seminar II* 144). Sometimes, however—although certainly not for Levine—the real is experienced without this mediation, in what Pynchon would call an "epiphany": "this real Medusa's head, . . . the revelation of that which is least penetrable in the real, of the real lacking any possible mediation, of the ultimate real, of the essential object which isn't an object any longer, but this something faced with which all words cease and all categories fail, the object of anxiety *par excellence*" (164).

This encounter is captured in the primary process and in hallucinations. It forms the navel of the dream with its "abyssal relation to that which is most unknown, which is the hallmark of an exceptional, privileged experience, in which the real is apprehended beyond all mediation, be it imaginary or symbolic" (176–77).[17] The basic paradox is that such a direct meeting entails the complete fading of the subject and thus the *negation* of subjectivity and the signifier, for instance, as in Slothrop's disintegration in *Gravity's Rainbow.* As a rule, this meeting is immediately translated into the realm of representation via the secondary processes—the dream content—so that it is always already inscribed into the apparatus of "infinite displacements" (177), metaphorically, into fiction, the artistic "apparatus of infinite displacements." This always deferred and thus inevitably "missed encounter" (*Fundamental Concepts* 55) is another literally central concern of Pynchon's writing, because all his works describe the failure and promise of such an encounter in constant evocations of threshold experiences between language and the real. In the recurrent motif of an impending, apocalyptic message intruding into representational space from an "impossible" outside, these "encounter[s] with the real" (52) are linked to language. For Lacan, as for Pynchon, the meeting is impossible exactly because it must by necessity take place *within* the symbolic, which can never map onto the real directly. Because the referent is excluded from representational space, "the signified misses it [the real/referent]. The collimator does not function" (*Encore* 23). As a result, language is forever "beside the referent" (44), a fact constantly thematized by Pynchon. In *Gravity's Rainbow,* for instance, he continually highlights the small but unbreachable gap between language and the real, with "words [. . .] only an eye-twitch away from the things they stand for" (GR 100) and "pencil words [. . .] only Δt from the things they stand for" (GR 510). An ideal encounter with the real would have to take place in a silent and instantaneous identification, yet such an identification would also denote the end of desire, the text, and, ironically, writing itself.

Because of the real's insistence in the text and in (the text of) desire, discourse, "in so far as . . . it constitutes, all by itself, a full universe," has at the same time "something irreducibly discordant about it, in every one of its parts" (*Seminar II* 130). It can never produce a complete message, only a message that is "interrupted, but insistent" (125) within "the furrows opened up by the signifier in the real world" (*Écrits* 194).

The subject's (and especially the ego's) always unsuccessful attempts to achieve unity within systems of representation, especially language, foreground the fact that the phonemes, or the signifiers—"one sound as opposed to another sound, within a set of oppositions" (*Seminar I* 248)— are always separated by a void. Its incessant desire to bridge this void—the Δt—defines the subject's fundamental relation to language.

It is the real, being strictly outside the representational realm, that prevents the closure of the symbolic within itself. Because the symbolic is the means through which the subject comes to terms with the loss of the real, the impossibility of integrating the real into its systematics makes out the ontological failure of the symbolic. In that the real denotes the borders of the symbolic—in Freudian terminology, the primal scene and the repressed—it becomes the aim of all psychoanalytic (and, I argue, fictional) (re)search. It is what lies beyond language but what language constantly tries to represent: "The real is beyond the *automaton,* the return, the coming-back, the insistence of the signs . . . The real is that which always lies behind the automaton" (*Fundamental Concepts* 53–54). It is the excluded *"upokeimenon"* (*Seminar II* 323) of language and literature.

Although the discursive universe, and certainly "serious literature," is set against the real, it is inevitably implicated in it: "The text is related to the real like the spider-web to the space which it orders and in which it places its trap" (Leclaire 22). What it does is to transform the *real* into *reality:* "And what is transmitted and tends to get constituted is an immense message into which the entire real is little by little retransplanted, recreated, remade. The symbolization of the real tends to be equivalent to the universe, and the subjects are only relays, supports in it" (*Seminar II* 322).

Because of the impossibility of transgressing or escaping the symbolic, the automaton—"and we know, at the present stage of modern mathematics, that it is the network of the signifiers" (*Fundamental Concepts* 52)— relegates the subject to both *repetition* and *compulsion,* the combination of which defines the quests of Pynchon's characters and their endless detours through real as well as symbolic space. Through this repetition compulsion, these quests are linked to the concept of entropy, because it is the subject's relation to homeostasis within which the dynamics of the repetition compulsion are defined. In "Entropy," the first story in which Pynchon uses this concept, he deals with it by means of a *spatial* metaphor, with Callisto's apartment standing for a "high-energy" environment and Meatball Mulligan's for a "low-energy" one. Unlike Pynchon's later work, this is still a rather static and abstract approach to the topic. Although Tony Tanner has read the house as already "some sort of paradigm for modern consciousness" (*City of Words* 154), the notion is still related to a *general,* cosmic heat death rather than an *individual* one. Pynchon actually comments on this shift of emphasis in the introduction to *Slow Learner:* "When I think about the property [entropy] nowadays, it is more and more in connection with time, that human one-way time we're all stuck with locally here, and which terminates, it is said, in death" (SL 14–15).

In the structure of the repetition compulsion, the historicity and *finality* of the subject are linked to the *eternity,* or rather atemporality, of the text: the mortal subject to the eternal/atemporal symbolic machine. In the dynamics of the repetition compulsion, repetition refers to the historicity of the subject and its re-staging and re-presenting of specific traumata, the most basic of which is the symbolic one itself, the fall into language. In its repetitive games, especially as exemplified by the game of "Fort-Da," the subject "brings together mastery of its dereliction and the birth of the symbol" (*Écrits* 103). The structure of repetition is grounded in the laws of language—the dynamics of metaphor and metonymy—whose interplay defines every repetition as a difference. Repetition "is only introduced by the register of language, by the function of the symbol, by the problematic of the question within the human order" (*Seminar II* 90). Whereas repetition is thus aligned with *metaphor* and *meaning,* compulsion is related to *metonymy* and *lack* and the structure and force of desire. As these two registers are amalgamated in language, the repetition compulsion "finds its basis in what we have called the *insistence* of the signifying chain" ("Purloined Poe" 28).[18]

The symbolic and imaginary registers aim at re-creating the real, but they can do so only as a fiction, which is the hinge between the psychic structuration and literature. This re-created real "has nothing to do with what has been carried by traditional knowledge [the mapping of nous and soul], and which is not what this thinks, reality, but exactly a phantasy" (*Encore* 118).

It is in this "impossible" space between the real and the fantasy that a Lacanian poetics operates. On the one hand, repetition, "demand[ing] the new . . . the ludic" (*Fundamental Concepts* 61), opens up the free zone of artistic production. On the other, however, although it promises diversity, it is equally important for a Lacanian poetics that every investment in repetition *as* difference only masks the initial impossibility of successfully recovering the object/real as such: "The adult . . . demands something new in his activities, in his games. But this 'sliding-away' (*glissement*) conceals what is the true secret of the ludic, namely, the most radical diversity constituted by repetition in itself" (61). This twofold movement is perfectly captured in *Gravity's Rainbow* in the dynamics of the "Zone," which unfold between a concentric movement of "Holy-Center-Approaching" (GR 508) and an eccentric one in which "each alternative Zone speeds away from all the others, in fated acceleration, red-shifting, fleeing the center" (GR 519).[19]

Unlike the symbolic and the imaginary, the real itself remains beyond formalization, because any project to delineate the "real as real" would have to "show it as subsisting by itself, solely by itself, as the language of Being" (*Encore* 108). As a result, every signification is shot through by an "ontological enigma": "There is something real, a given. This given is structured in a specific manner. In particular natural asymmetries exist . . . are we going to get to the bottom of their mysterious meaning? . . . It never gets very far. It leads to completely ineffable things, which moreover soon peter out—except if one wants to carry on regardless, ending up with what is commonly called a delirium" (*Seminar II* 35).

Because it always foregrounds the enigma of the real, Pynchon's prose, especially in its fantastic aspects, is certainly "delirious," yet "all of art is characterized by a specific mode of organization around that lack [of the real]" (*Séminaire VII* 155). This "mode of organization" is ultimately what *distinguishes* the theoretical and the fictional project. Whereas the former tries to elucidate the structural position of the object *o* within human reality, the latter tries "*to make visible* the sublime object Lacan named the *objet a*" (Ragland-Sullivan, "Logical Time" 29; emphasis added). In this impossible project the object *o* is sublime "because it 'drives' reader and author . . . just beyond the level of understanding, at the place of missed encounters" ("Logical Time" 43).[20] The sublimity of art lies in the paradoxical project to bring to light this inevitably veiled object, which is why Pynchon's works constantly de-*scribe* the border to a direct apprehension of the real, where subjectivity, and with it writing, negates itself: a space in which consciousness and writing dream of a state in which they are absent.

Because it denotes the split between *being* (body) and *thinking* (consciousness), the real falls into the gap between these two registers. It remains the "mystery of the speaking body . . . the mystery of the unconscious" (*Encore* 118). As the discussion of Slothrop's dispersal will show, the tensions that define writing become most obvious when writing (the text) is aligned with the body, because in the same way in which writing is always both symbolic (as a network of significations) and real (as material markings), the body oscillates between being a (real) object and a (symbolic) nexus of signifiers.

For Lacan, the symbolic and imaginary structurations are *not* mysterious. What is outside them, however, what affects them from that outside and insists within them, can be read only as a *trace* of an absence, something lost and enigmatic that forever escapes representation, and thus as a *writing-effect*. Because of this, Leclaire defines writing as "an attempt to reproduce or to represent the unconscious text; an attempt whose necessary failure itself must fix the true rules for the use of writing" (Leclaire 68). Ultimately, this failure is related to the interplay of life and death:

> That is what life is—a detour, a dogged detour, . . . deprived of any significance. Why . . . does something happen, which insists throughout this life, which is called a meaning? . . . A meaning is an order which . . . suddenly emerges. A life insists on entering into it, but it expresses something which is perhaps completely beyond this life, since when we get to the root of this life . . . we find nothing besides life conjoined to death. (*Seminar II* 232)

This image of life as a detour introduces the difference between a Lacanian and a Derridean poetics. Whereas the detour is always related to and read within the reference to an "originary" lack and loss in Lacan, Derrida sees its inevitability as opening up a free space in which the subject can invest its desire in a freeplay of signification.

Notes

1. Although Lacan himself has proposed to translate "Manque-à-être" as "Want-to-be" (*Écrits* 323), for reasons of clarity I will refer to it as "lack-of-being."
2. "The subject is nothing else—whether it is conscious or not of which signifier it is the effect—than what glides in a signifying-chain" (Lacan, *Encore* 48).
3. For more on this notion, see Lacan, "The Mirror Stage as Formative of the Function of the I," *Écrits* 4–7. I discuss the mirror stage in more detail in the chapter on *Lot 49*.
4. Quoted in Alain Juranville, *Lacan et la philosophie* 6. Meaning originally "base" or "vile," the word also puns with "unworldly."
5. See also Lacan's use of the experiment with the convex mirror to show how an image is reflected from a "real," inaccessible space into the imaginary and the symbolic (*Seminar I* 73–159).
6. Because "deferred action" is too closely connected to Derrida's "deferral" in my discussion, I will use "belatedness" to designate the Freudian *"Nachträglichkeit."*
7. Within the imaginary and the symbolic, this "hors signifié" [outside-of-the signified] (*Séminaire VII* 67) is re-presented by the thing [*Sache*], which is *"the word of the Ding* [Thing]" (78). Lacan thus differentiates between three terms: *"Sache* and *Wort* [word] are . . . inextricably linked, form a pair. *Das Ding* situates itself somewhere else" (58). This elsewhere is a point intimately related to the inaccessible: "What is in *das Ding* is the true enigma" (58).
8. I will write the French "*objet a*" as "object *o*." I will retain it only if a secondary source gives the original French version.
9. "The borders of discourse are given as death, violence, madness, the sexual act, *jouissance*. In all of these cases the real, which punctures the symbolic . . . is present in a pure form" (Lipowatz, *Diskurs und Macht* 126).
10. For discussion of this term see Ragland-Sullivan, *Philosophy of Psychoanalysis* 75.
11. In "God and the Jouissance of the Woman," Lacan relates the "impossible" possibility of a "jouissance beyond the phallus" (*Encore* 69) to women, especially the mystics: "a jouissance which is beyond. That is what one calls the mystics" (70). Revealingly, however, he adds—through a pun with his christian name—his own writings, "these mystic e/jaculations" (71), to the "mystical canon."
12. See also, "each death, up till the moment of our own, is miraculous" (Pynchon, *The Crying of Lot 49* 14; further citations are abbreviated as *Lot 49*).
13. "Is it surprising that its [the drive's] final term should be death, when the presence of sex in the living being is bound up with death?" (Lacan, *Fundamental Concepts* 177). This intermixing always lies at the center of Pynchon's texts and constitutes their fantastic aspect. See in this regard the following statement by Lacan, which links the orgasm to the fantastic, uncannily echoing Pynchon's evocations

of the subject's meeting with the real: "It is possible not to want to ejaculate . . . in so far as it involves terrible promises, by the approach of *jouissance* as such" (234).

14. In "Desire and the Interpretation of Desire in *Hamlet*" (in Felman, ed., *Literature and Psychoanalysis*), Lacan retraces the meeting of the subject with death, which he describes as a hole in the real: "Indeed, there is nothing of significance that can fill that hole in the real, except the totality of the signifier" (38), with death standing for "that greater *béance,* the point *x,* the symbolic lack" (40). As such, it is the perspective point of the human scene: "human life could be defined as a calculus in which zero was irrational" (28).

15. Symptomatically, in his introduction to a reprint of Richard Fariña's *Been Down So Long It Looks Like Up to Me,* Pynchon singles out the motif of death, stating that an "awareness of mortality blows through every chapter" (vii) and comments on the fact that "undergraduate consciousness rests in part on a set of careless assumptions about being immortal [. . .] this belief in one's own Exemption, not only from time and death, but somehow from the demands of life as well" (vii-viii).

16. "The 'body' of meaning predates any causality . . . one can attribute to the organism *qua* biological material" (Ragland-Sullivan, "Logical Time" 32).

17. "There is a sort of immediate external world, of manifestations perceived in what I will call a primitive real, a non-symbolised real, despite the symbolic form . . . that this phenomenon takes" (*Seminar I* 58).

18. See also: "The presence of the signifier in the Other . . . usually persists in a state of repression . . . from there it insists on representing itself in the signified by means of its repetition compulsion" (*Écrits* 200).

19. From a Lacanian perspective, then, the movement of writing is never that of a pure dissemination. Writing "does not so much open possibilities as confront the human with the real, the impossible in which he is *always already* caught" (Juranville 291; emphasis added). As such, "writing calls to the human [subject] to 'install' itself in the lack of the Other, which is the lack of the self" (291). On the other hand, its movement is never merely a pure expression of lack. In fact, only writing allows for a pure, symbolic *jouissance* through and in the replacement of the real body with the symbolic one. The passion of the signifier is "*jouissance* of the Other because it [the passion of the signifier] is delighted by a body, which, through that, becomes the space of the Other" (Lacan, "Radiophonie" 70). This space is a decidedly positive one: "The *jouissance* of the verbal signifier is thus pure *jouissance,* while the phallic *jouissance* is inmixed with suffering, because the phallus is a signifier which implies the negativity (as the death-drive)" (Juranville 336). To enjoy, therefore, is ultimately "to posit the signifier as signifier" (221).

20. On the "terrible" and "fantastic" aspect of this sublime object, which is captured in Lacan's evocation of the "head of the Medusa," see Edmund Burke, *Philosophical Enquiry.* For a further discussion, see the chapter on *Vineland.*

Chapter 2 **Derrida:
The Subject of the Text**

"L'être à la limite"
Jacques Derrida, *Marges de la philosophie*

In *Writing Pynchon,* Alec McHoul and David Wills ask "how . . . Pynchon [can] be read outside the logocentric tradition" (*Writing Pynchon* 10; further citations are abbreviated as WP). Their study, although it is written from within a purely Derridean framework, can be used to show how a Derridean and a Lacanian poetics complement each other in Pynchon's work.[1] Their argument proceeds from Derrida's critique of philosophy's symptomatic differentiation between *full speech* and *empty writing,* which had come to stand metonymically for the difference between a self-reflexive subject and a "merely" discursive one. With Derrida, they argue against the philosophical tradition that idealizes speech as an instance of natural self-presence, reading Pynchon's work not so much as the expression of a (presumably self-present) authorial voice but as a "writing practice" (WP 1). For this project, they draw on Derrida's basic assumption that speech, and by extension the voice—understood as the *incarnation* of this self-presence—always necessarily presupposes writing(s), systems of notation, a very broad term that for Derrida encompasses "all that gives rise to an inscription in general" (*Of Grammatology* 9).[2] This writing is not a secondary effect—the mere inscription of an originary, spoken signifier—but the very mode of the signified itself: " 'Signifier of the signifier' no longer defines accidental doubling and fallen secondarity. 'Signifier of the signifier' describes on the contrary the movement of language" (7). The metaphysical idea(l) that an act of inscription simply reifies a more initial intuition is thus replaced by the contention that intuition is always already a function of and embedded within a system of notation—the system of signifiers—and as such is never ideal, initial, or originary.

McHoul and Wills deal with this closed-off textual space in their readings of Pynchon, using the term *material typonomy* to describe the continual folding back of the text onto itself: "A material equivalence between the signifiers replaces a rhetorical difference between them. This equivalence we should like to call *material typonomy*" (WP 53). The difference between two "meanings" is thus not *canceled (aufgehoben)* in a third "meaning" that combines the first two, but "a relationship of duality . . . is undercut/rewritten/overruled by another term, which as a result sets up a *second duality . . .* between it and the first two terms" (WP 57).[3] The important fact is that "the order of the third term in no way transcends or embraces the order of the first two terms" (WP 57). Rather than being a hierarchical model, which would synthesize differences until reaching an ultimate term in which all differences are canceled (Hegel's "absolute knowledge"), this model is a horizontal one, in which every third term can again function as the first in another duality, so that an origin is forever deferred. It differs from Hegel's system also in that it is not so much a *signified* that presides over the combination of the first two terms but a pure *object* that holds them together, the final object being the signifier, the written mark itself. A dualism is thus "over-ridden . . . by an object or person (at least something of material substance, no matter how mysterious). Substance, that is, supplants rhetoric—though all this . . . is accomplished within and *as* the play of signs, in themselves, of course, nothing but material points" (WP 61).

In their discussion of *Gravity's Rainbow*, McHoul and Wills see, among others, the "parabola" of the V-2's flight—the *"rocket trajectory"* (WP 60)—as well as *"Imipolex"* (WP 61) as such material objects.[4] Rather than viewing them as Lacanian objects *o*, however, which are pervaded with desire, they see them as *neutral* textual markings through which every meaning is referred back to the text and to the writing out of which it has produced itself. Any meaning is thus caught up in a structure of *différance*, "an economic concept designating the production of differing/deferring" (Derrida, *Grammatology* 23).[5]

It is here that Derridean theory and Lacanian theory differ. Although they are very similar over long stretches, especially on an ontological level,[6] the difference between them is linked to the term or law that they substitute for the transcendental position they both exclude and question.[7]

Against the oedipal and triadic law of the phallus and its relation to lack and castration around which Lacan centers his theory, Derrida posits the binary, oppositional law of *différance:* "Derrida wants to read and write in an aleatory mode, by means of dissemination rather than the gathering and collecting and division of dialectics and conceptual thinking" (Ulmer, *Glossary* 119). Whereas Lacan stresses the lacuna between two signifiers, Derrida stresses the difference between them and the resulting dissemination of meaning.[8] From this dissemination, McHoul and Wills develop what they call a "prosthetic" reading strategy, which stands in striking contrast to Lacan's image of life as a dogged detour: "Whereas a more traditional reading might work at recovery to compensate loss, the prosthetic might profit from detachability, reversibility. . . . Whereas the humanist might strive for integrity, the prosthetic might encourage radical intervention and radical detour" (WP 81–82).

In "Structure, Sign, and Play in the Discourse of the Human Sciences," Derrida shows the *différance* between these two readings:

> There are thus two interpretations of interpretation, of structure, of sign, of play. The one seeks to decipher, dreams of deciphering a truth or an origin which escapes play and the order of the sign, and which lives the necessity of interpretation as an exile. The other, which is no longer turned toward the origin, affirms play and tries to pass beyond man and humanism, the name of man being the name of that being who, throughout the history of metaphysics or of ontotheology . . . has dreamed of full presence, the reassuring foundation, the origin and the end of play. (*Writing and Difference* 292)

Although this might seem to imply that Derrida favors the second mode of interpretation, he states, strictly according to the structure of *différance,* that he does not "believe that today there is any question of *choosing* . . . because we must first try to conceive of the common ground, and the *différance* of this irreducible difference" (*Writing and Difference* 293).[9] In fact, Derrida acknowledges the inevitability of this "irrepressible desire for such a [transcendental] signified" (*Of Grammatology* 49), stating that "the desire to restrict play is . . . irresistible" (59). Within the *différance* of life and death, Derrida links play to life and death to the absence of play:

> Can one not affirm the nonreferral to the center, rather than bemoan the absence of the center? Why would one mourn for the center? Is not the center, the absence of play and difference, another name for

death.... But is not the desire for a center, as a function of play itself, the indestructible itself? And in the repetition or return of play, how could the phantom of the center not call to us? It is here that the hesitation between writing as decentering and writing as an affirmation of play is infinite. This hesitation is part of play and links it to death. (*Writing and Difference* 297)

The utopia of an originary unity thus reenters the realm of textual play as a function of a subject's desire—"us." In fact, the terms *phantom* and *repetition* are very reminiscent of the Lacanian terms *phantasm* and *repetition compulsion*. Yet for Derrida, it is ultimately the signifier itself that links the free-play of dissemination to the complementary desire for the termination of this play: because they can never represent life directly, "all graphemes are of a testamentary essence" (*Of Grammatology* 69). At this point, however, the questions arise of whether and how one can speak of a "textual desire." Does something like a repetition compulsion operate within a purely textual universe?

Like Lacan, Derrida sees repetition as the prerequisite for both *différance* and representation, because it is only within repetition that legibility becomes possible: "A signifier is from the very beginning the possibility of its own repetition, of its own image or resemblance" (*Of Grammatology* 91). In fact, what is tragic is "not the impossibility but the necessity of repetition" (*Writing and Difference* 248).[10] To be within a text is always already to be caught within a play of *différance*. Both Derrida and Lacan, then, proceed from the subject's immersion in the signifier. Without wanting to cover up unduly the differences between Lacan and Derrida, it seems at this point to be a difference of *perspective* rather than *structure* that opens up the oscillations between Lacanian and Derridean readings. A Lacanian desire of the subject is staked against a Derridean desire for and of the signifier. Derrida does for the "body of the text" exactly what Lacan does for the "body of the subject." This investment in the "text(uality) of the body" can be followed everywhere in Derrida's writing.[11] Although both see the body as a text, for Lacan every text is grounded in a subject, whereas for Derrida every subject is grounded in a text.

Because a "thesis would be the death sentence... of *différance*" (*Post Card* 285), Derrida thinks of a deconstructionist writing/text as "athetic" (268). Providing a parallel to this athetic text, McHoul and Wills introduce an "athetical ethics" (WP 90) in their readings that situates the subject in a medial position, "refraining from the hope for a definite origin and refraining equally from the hopelessness of an absent origin" (WP 95). For them, this subjectivity is one we have not yet learned to realize, a fact that already foreshadows a utopian aspect in Derridean theory: "We have come to accept the sliding around of meaning.... But we have not yet learned ... to find our way with this new signifier" (WP 102). To acknowledge the workings of this signifier would mean to "think of meaning as other than 'the meaning' ... as an activity, like bathing and so forth" (WP 102). Although this is certainly an inviting idea, it implies that the subject might also come to think, for instance, of its own death as it would about "bathing and so forth," which is possible only when subjectivity as such is negated. And it is in fact this dissemination of the subject in the movement(s) of the text that McHoul and Wills stake against the centering tendencies of thematic and characterological readings of Pynchon.

If "the destination is death" (Derrida, *Post Card* 33) and *"différance ... does not arrive"* (192), the "adestination" (222) of the text and symbolization is life itself. From a Lacanian perspective, therefore, *différance* could ultimately be seen as a "trompe-la-mort" (Juranville 107). Lacan, in contrast, constantly stresses the presence of death in the text, the "surplus of the Real over every symbolization" (Žižek, *Sublime Object* 3) [12]

I argue that Pynchon's texts cannot be "contained" in the structure of *différance*, although they are doubtlessly implicated in and thematize it. Today, the proof that every text disseminates may almost be taken for granted, and projects that attempt to prove the dissemination operative in a text often run in open doors. What remains to be investigated by literary studies is the *différance* between the economy of radical dissemination and the signifying economy of the text under discussion.

Only in this space are the questions of desire and death opened up again. Unlike a subject, a text does not die, except for a very metaphorical death. It cannot commit suicide, or stop to produce itself, because it *is* signification as such. If the text is treated as a subject, therefore, the only act that cannot be thought is the destruction *of* the text *by* the text, because without the text—the materiality of the signifier—*différance* cannot operate. Although Lacan and Derrida would agree that there is no escape from the text, Derrida, when he theorizes the tragedy of a literary text that cannot abolish itself, is *blind* to the effects that the "subject's desire" (born from the disruption of the human from the real) has on the text into which it both is inscribed and inscribes itself. Rather, what he *sees* is a writing that, as the *materiality* of language, is its own "material typonomy": its own real. Ultimately, for Derrida writing is its own signification, *as well as* its own real. The final constant in the Derridean system is therefore discourse as production of itself, discourse as representation folding back onto itself even within its constant displacements. As a result, for Derrida a purely textual desire is not retrogressive and implicated by a beginning and an end. Rather, it is an endless, expansive desire to fill more and more discursive space, to indulge in "radical detour." This trajectory is always in opposition to that of the mortal subject, although both operate within representational space. Because of this common ground, Foucault can criticize both psychoanalysis and semiotics from a position of complete transgression: "the poor technicians of desire—psychoanalysts and semiologists of every sign and symptom—who could subjugate the multiplicity of desire to the twofold law of structure and lack" (*Anti-Oedipus* xiii).

In strict accordance to the inclusion of the text's auto-negation into the economy of the play of differences, Derrida defines silence *within* and as a function of discourse. It is a mere hesitation, which implies an immediate *commencement* rather than a final *termination* (as, for instance, in the subject's death, the moment in which the subject falls out of the text).[13] Lacan relates this pure silence to the real as the ultimate horizon of discourse, and although Derrida acknowledges this "worst violence, the violence of primitive and prelogical silence, of an unimaginable night" (*Writing and Difference* 130), he is more concerned with the economy of violence *within* discourse: "There is war only after the opening of discourse, and war dies out only at the end of discourse" (117).

What Derrida excludes by continually folding the text onto itself is the insistence of the real in it. As a result, Lacan's and Derrida's theories are coupled *and* separated by a diverging interpretation of the concept of desire: in Lacan, desire is born from a fundamentally lost object and is defined in a subjective, sexual arena; in Derrida, it is basically a desire for the signifier, originating not from a *lack* but from an originary *plenitude*—that of discourse—and operative in the coupling of the language material itself, resulting in an "erotics of the text," or, even more drastically, a "textual *jouissance*." A Lacanian stress on the *text of the subject* is thus countered by a Derridean stress on the *subject of the text,* and whereas Lacan centers his theory on how the real affects the subject, Derrida concentrates on the affirmation of the endless dissemination of meaning within a textual universe that excludes the real as an agency affecting this play. Although they are not taking issue with the Lacanian real, McIIoul and Wills express this idea when they characterize writing as not simply a means of expression that "maps on to something more important or *central* in the world—the real, for example" (WP 7). Finally, whereas Lacan knots the texts around the nucleus of the real in concentric movements, Derrida's disseminations involve an eccentric movement that defers and disperses meaning in a multiplicity of texts for which even a hermeneutic polysemy is too centered an approach: "The text is no longer the expression or representation ... of any *truth* that would come to diffract or assemble itself in the polysemy of literature. It is this hermeneutic concept of *polysemy* that must be replaced by *dissemination*" (*Dissemination* 262).

A Derridean poetics thus operates on the reverse side of a Lacanian one and *vice versa,* in a once-twisted space in which they cannot be separated. Indeed, a Derridean perspective would in fact suggest Derrida and Lacan to be the representatives of two modes of interpretation whose *différance* has to be questioned. This *différance* should not be the one between a Derridean, purely textual writing strategy and a self-reflexive subject; rather, it should be lodged between this writing strategy and the writing of the Lacanian $. Although McHoul and Wills are informed by the Derridean mode of interpretation (which implies that they play out Pynchon's writing against a "self-reflexive Pynchon") and in their reading of Pynchon's introduction to *Slow Learner* come to see Pynchon's text as "almost but not quite grammatological" (WP 157), I want to read Pynchon's texts as the "material typonomy" that overrides the binarism of a purely Derridean or a purely Lacanian reading. Ironically, this might be an ultimately more Derridean gesture than that of McHoul and Wills.

It might be less rewarding to identify the Lacanian text with the modern and the Derridean with the postmodern one in a binary system than to read the effects of both trajectories within a single text. This requires combining the psychoanalytic subject and the philosophical subject within a literary scenario, a scenario in which both subjects are transposed into a fictional one.

This brings me back to my introduction: the seemingly mutually exclusive assessment of Thomas Pynchon as *both* regressive (Lacanian) and deconstructionist (Derridean) suggests that both Lacanian and Derridean contentions operate in his texts, something that I touched on already in my discussion of Slothrop's desk. Pynchon's texts, whose production stands temporally at the threshold from the modern to the postmodern era, in fact provides a textual site on which to follow the spectacle of the convergence and interaction of both positions.

Such an investigation, however, is made especially difficult by the fact that Derrida's theses have had a number of problematic effects within literary studies, although Derrida himself doubts that they can be appropriated: "Deconstruction is not a method and cannot be transformed into one. . . . It is true that in certain circles (university or cultural, especially in the United States) the technical and methodological 'metaphor' that seems necessarily attached to the very word 'deconstruction' has been able to seduce or lead astray" ("Letter to a Japanese Friend" 5).

Apart from having introduced a specific style of criticism, American deconstruction sets up a strict program: "Deconstruction emphasizes the self-referential moments of a text in order to reveal the surprising effects of employing a portion of a text to analyze the whole or the uncanny relationships between one textual level and another or one discourse and another" (Culler 205). Its topics are "presence and absence, origin, marginality, representation, indeterminacy" (206). As concerns reading, "one could . . . identify deconstruction with the twin principles of the contextual determination of meaning and the infinite extendibility of context" (215). Finally, it should reveal the "uncanny irrationality of texts and their ability to confute or subvert every system or position they are thought to manifest" (220).[14]

Unfortunately, the problematics of the subject are carefully evaded within all these approaches. Either it is neglected, as in the question about the relation between one discourse and another, or it is implied, as in the notion of interpretation. The unsatisfactory result is that in American deconstruction, the notion of subjectivity remains undefined. And, in fact, the translation of Derrida's philosophical project onto literature involves a number of problematic substitutions. Within the philosophical arena, the rigorous centeredness of Derrida's texts around an always identical motif of self-presence causes a violently ex-clusive reading of the host texts. This is the main reason for his constant and inevitable misreadings, which Paul de Man has diagnosed and among which his misreading of Lacan certainly has to be counted as prominent.[15] Yet these misreadings are the strategy of a specific philosophical project. In the realm of literary theory, this approach favors readings that deal with how literary texts can be deconstructed in terms of self-presence and how they "unwittingly" dismantle their own meaning(s). What is often neglected in these investigations is the text's relation toward this deconstruction. Literary deconstruction thus falls into the danger of attempting to prove something that—within the structure of the specific text—is not a metaphysical *a priori* but a result of the text's own literary and rhetorical mode.

Paul de Man's version of Derridean deconstruction accounts for this very rhetoricity. In *Allegories of Reading* he shows how literary texts inevitably deconstruct themselves, so that rather than *prove* a logocentric motif, the critic need only follow the deconstructive tendencies that constitute them in the first place. Especially in literary texts, de Man maintains, positions that are at first sight logocentric have to be read as *rhetorical* rather than *declarative:* "The unwarranted separation between the way of reading and interpreting 'literary' as opposed to 'philosophical' or discursive texts . . . deprives the reading of philosophical texts of elementary refinements that are taken for granted in literary interpretation" (226).

What also separates de Man from Derridean deconstruction and enables one to see him as a hinge between Lacan and Derrida is that he constantly emphasizes the referential aspect of (not only literary) language, the "persistence of the referential moment" (208), a moment that makes for its basic aporia. Language "*has to be* referential but can never signify its actual referent" (160).

For de Man, fiction operates not only in the intertextual realm but also in the "margin between text and external referent" (203), denoting, however—as with Lacan—not so much their mapping as their inevitable failure to map: "Fiction has nothing to do with representation but is the absence of any link between utterance and a referent" (292). As a result, every fiction—and Pynchon's is a prime example—ultimately tells of its failure.[16] This margin between text and referent creates a space in which logocentric and deconstructive positions, as well as subjective and textual ones, form an undecidably rhetorical and figural system, in which the fundamentally rhetorical nature of language allows two mutually exclusive readings to persist at the same time,[17] a system in which text and subject constantly oscillate: "By calling the subject a text, the text calls itself, to some extent, a subject" (112).[18]

This rhetorical space stands in contrast to McHoul and Wills's replacement of rhetorical difference by material equivalence based on their leveling of the logocentric distinction between "the mental and the real" (WP 50), or "form . . . [and] matter" (WP 58), which is overridden by a material typonomy. In their opinion, this flattening of "rhetorical depths" (the realm of the signified) by the material (the signifier) invalidates readings dealing with the distinction between *text* and *real world,* or *text* and *logocentric subject.* Such readings, they argue, are impossible in "post-rhetorical" (WP 50) textual spaces like those in *Gravity's Rainbow.* Yet by arguing against a logocentric subject (and a logocentric reading) that still believes in "some confused—but really existing—universe" (WP 51), they evade the problems of the relation between the text and a fully textualized subject (such as Lacan's or de Man's), for which, similarly, "reality . . . is only ever and always already a discursive/rhetorical one" (WP 52). Though they have rightfully gotten rid of the notion of a "real world" (in the sense of an "objective reality"), they have not escaped the question of the *impossibility* but *insistence* of the real, or de Man's "external referent," in the text. In their world, in which signifiers rule over signifieds and, as a result, "substance . . . supplants rhetoric" (WP 61), they exclude the problem of *signification*, the way meaning operates in a fully textualized subject. I maintain instead that, as a figure rather than a substance, the subject inevitably (re)figures material typonomies, so that, after substance has supplanted (logocentric) rhetorics, a rhetoric again supplants a substance that has by now become an inevitable function in its figurative system and has turned it into a project operating "in the shadow of the real."[19]

Whereas de Man still centers his interpretations on the motif of deconstruction proper, however, the subject—certainly the one portrayed by Pynchon—has to be related to a third, social reference. Baudrillard's theory is especially useful in this respect, because its highly rhetorical character makes it a perfect hinge between theory and literature.

Notes

1. Apart from Derrida himself, Gregory L. Ulmer's *Applied Grammatology* is certainly McHoul and Wills's most important reference.

2. Derrida's notion of writing is a very general one: "cinematography, choreography . . . but also pictorial, musical, sculptural 'writing'" (*Of Grammatology* 9)—thus in fact any semiotic structuration, provided it "creates meaning by enregistering it, by entrusting it to an engraving, a groove, a relief" (*Writing and Difference* 12).

3. The German term *aufheben*—a key term in Hegelian dialectics—has the triple meaning of "to cancel," "to conserve," and "to lift up."

4. See also Madsen's treatment of the rocket as allegorical "*figura*" in *The Postmodern Allegories of Thomas Pynchon* 106.

5. See also Derrida, "Différance," in *Margins of Philosophy* 1–27.

6. In fact, Lacan's definition of the subject as "a signifier representing the subject for another signifier" might well have been Derrida's model for his definition of writing: "a signifier referring in general to a signifier signified by it" (*Of Grammatology* 46). Both Lacan and Derrida aim at the emancipation of the signifier in relation to the signified, the term in which philosophy had always grounded the simple, unquestioned, undisrupted and undisruptable link between the subject

and its thought, "the unique experience of the signified producing itself spontaneously, from within the self, and nevertheless, as signified concept, in the element of ideality and universality" (*Of Grammatology* 20). Both show that the subject is a function of language and reveal the notion of stable, transcendental signifieds as illusory. Both subjects, in fact, the philosophical as well as the psychoanalytic, are similarly decentered and disrupted. For a discussion of the similarities between Lacan and Derrida see Ulmer, *Applied Grammatology,* 189–224; for a discussion of their differences, see Slavoj Žižek, "Why Lacan Is Not a 'Post-Structuralist.'" For a discussion of their relation see also David Fisher, "Introduction: Framing Lacan," and Patrick Colm Hogan, "Introduction: The Repression of Lacan."

7. This substitution forms the backdrop of Derrida's critique in the controversy about Lacan's "Seminar on 'The Purloined Letter.'"

8. "The lack, the void, the break . . . have been given the value of a signified or . . . a transcendental signifier: the self-presentation of truth . . . as *Logos*" (Derrida, *Dissemination* 26).

9. Jonathan Culler reads this passage within the framework of authorial intention and reader response: "one cannot simply or effectively choose to make meaning either the original meaning of an author or the creative experience of the reader" (Culler 132). Gerald Graff, in *Literature Against Itself,* stresses Derrida's joyful Nietzschean affirmation, the "enterprise of doing without a truth and an origin as anchoring points outside the infinite play of linguistic differences" (62). Dwight Eddins, in *The Gnostic Pynchon,* states that in this passage, "Derrida is anxious to jettison the humanistic baby along with the epistemic bathwater. He seeks to 'pass beyond' the human in order to negate the transcendental" (17). The rhetorical implications of Derrida's *Post Card* take up the topos of a message without addressee in a more general framework.

10. See especially his discussion of Artaud in "La Parole soufflée," in *Writing and Difference*. Artaud's text actually forces Derrida to the limits of his own theory, to the paradox of a self-presence as *différance:* "In this sense the theater of cruelty would be the art of difference and of expenditure without economy, without reserve, without return, without history. Pure presence as pure difference" (247).

11. In *The Post Card,* for instance, Derrida calls his signature "the body of my name" (73) and states that "this is my body, at work, love me, analyze the corpus that I tender to you, that I extend here on this bed of paper" (99).

12. In this respect see also the "shadow of death" that hangs over Derrida's "Pour l'amour de Lacan." For Derrida, "that thinking of the destination is inextricably bound . . . to the thinking of death, destination as death" ("Pour l'amour" 417). In his meetings with Lacan, the question of death was always present, and "it was he alone who spoke of it" (417). In contrast, he says, "as a conclusion of an analysis of 'a lack which never lacks [in its place],' I clarified what seemed to me to show adequately the difference 'with' Lacan: 'The difference which interests me here is that . . . the lack does not have its place in dissemination'" (418).

13. See also McHoul and Wills's discussion of Derrida's "No Apocalypse, Not Now" in *Writing Pynchon*.

14. See also J. Hillis Miller, "The Critic as Host."

15. See especially de Man's "Rhetoric of Blindness."

16. In *Postmodern Allegories,* Deborah L. Madsen employs the concept of allegory and the "relentless way in which it pursues an ultimate referent that would bridge the rift between sign and signification" (9) to delineate the double movement of "express[ing] a dissemination of signs and a desire for semantic unity" (9). Yet, she argues, because the pretext in postmodern allegory is "a tissue of competing discourses" (76) rather than an unambiguous master-text, "*figurae* become *écriture,* [and] the pretext becomes an intertext" (78). As a result, postmodern allegory discovers "Absense" rather than "Presence" (20). For a discussion of de Man see especially pages 7–9.

17. "There can be no text without grammar: the logic of grammar generates texts only in the absence of referential meaning, but every text generates a referent that subverts the grammatical principle to which it owed its constitution" (de Man, *Allegories* 269).

18. In one of his few references to psychoanalysis, de Man sketches a linguistic psychoanalysis that is comparable to Lacan's description of the symbolic as a machinic system and implies a similar subversion of meaning: "The text as body, with all its implications of substitutive tropes ultimately always retraceable to metaphor, is displaced by the text as machine and, in the process, it suffers the loss of the illusion of meaning" (*Allegories* 298). As in Lacan, language is seen as constitutive of the subject and naturality rather than *vice versa:* "Far from seeing language as an instrument in the service of a psychic energy, the possibility now arises that the entire construction of drives, substitutions, repressions, and representations is the aberrant, metaphorical correlative of the absolute randomness of language, prior to any figuration or meaning" (299).

19. In this context, see also Lacan's statement that metaphor (condensation) is the limit from where "the category of the real installs itself through the symbolic" ("Radiophonie" 69), while metonymy (displacement) plays its part from the point of "jouissance in which the subject produces itself as a cut" (70). These dynamics of language testify to the logical and temporal primacy of the figure over substance. The definition of the status of "materiality," in fact, lies at the center of the debate between Lacan and Derrida.

Chapter 3 **Baudrillard:
The Subject in the Text**

> "'Why bring her back? Why try? It's only the difference between the real boxtop and the one you draw for Them.' [. . .] No difference between a boxtop and its image, all right, their whole economy is based on *that* [. . .] but she must be more than an image, a product, a promise to pay."
> Thomas Pynchon, *Gravity's Rainbow*

Baudrillard's critique of subjectivity defines the subject within sociopolitical references, the subject "thought in economic terms, rethought, simplified and abstracted by the economy" (*Critique* 133). Of course, because both Lacan and Derrida see society as a textual construct, it functions as a determining factor of subjectivity for them as well. Lacan, for instance, posits the "Name-of-the-Father" (*Écrits* 310) as the agency by means of which the subject is inscribed into social space through oedipal subjugation, the acceptance of castration, and the mediations within the symbolic. Derrida, in turn, works toward a deconstruction and redefinition of the hierarchical structure of the binarisms defining sociopolitical systems in the light of a "playful" and just dissemination.[1] Baudrillard's critique, however, goes deeper than that: the polemic disputes between Lacan and Derrida are in fact overridden by Baudrillard, because whereas both Lacan and Derrida base their theories on a specific view of the structure of language, Baudrillard aims at a fundamental critique of this very structure and its effects on the subject in sociopolitical space.

Taking a view opposed to that of Marxist theorists, Baudrillard maintains that "ideology can no longer be understood as an infra-superstructural relation between a material production . . . and a production of signs"

(*Critique* 143). Today, the fields of semiotics and political economy can no longer be separated, because they have been subjected to the same underlying law, that of operational simulation. Any critical position grounded on semiotics cannot therefore act as more than "a description of the . . . circulation and structural functioning [of signs]" (148). Although this description can be very complex, it can never "violat[e] the logic of the sign" (149), because it operates in the same simulatory space in which the levels of sign and economy are continually conflated, in which "everything, even artistic, intellectual, and scientific production, even innovation and transgression, is immediately produced as sign and exchange value" (87). In a simulatory society, the movements of both the *sign* and *value* are based on two premises: the exclusion of the referent and the rigid "exclusion and annihilation of all symbolic ambivalence on behalf of a fixed and equational structure" (149).[2]

Baudrillard agrees with both Lacan and Derrida in believing that "the process of signification is, at bottom, nothing but a gigantic *simulation model of meaning*" (*Critique* 160). It is the growing *operational* simulation of reality, instigated by the identification of the *real* with the *rational* (especially in and since the Enlightenment), within which Baudrillard theorizes the closure of the political field. Both Pynchon's and Baudrillard's antirational rhetorics are ultimately directed against this equation.[3]

The result of operational simulation is that "the very definition of the real becomes: *that of which it is possible to give an equivalent reproduction*" (*Simulations* 146). This implies that the "actual" real is abolished and replaced by "the generation by models of a real without origin or reality: a hyperreal" (2). On the level of the code, this results in the "liquidation of all referentials . . . their artificial resurrection in systems of signs" (4).

According to the various historical stages in the history of simulation, the concept of subjectivity passes from a magical to a psychoanalytic level, and finally, to a fully simulatory one: "In the beginning was the secret, and this was the rule of the game of appearance. Then there was the repressed, and this was the rule of the game of depth. Finally comes the obscene, and this is the rule of the game of a world without appearance or depth—a transparent universe" (*Fatal Strategies* 65).

Pynchon stages this final shift from a psychoanalytic to a fully simulatory level in "Under the Rose," in which Porpentine feels himself at the threshold between a universe of subjective interiority and "depth" and a purely operational one: "It was no longer single combat [. . .] like a bright hallucination against Cairo's night-sky he saw [. . .] a bell-shaped curve.

[...] Only statistical odds. When had he stopped facing an adversary and taken on a Force, a Quantity?" (SL 134–35).

This bell-shaped curve is the "curve for a normal or Gaussian distribution" (SL 135), which will become important again in *Gravity's Rainbow*. The statistical universe it evokes is one in which history is made no longer "through the *virtù* of single princes but rather by man in the mass; by trends and tendencies and impersonal curves on a lattice of pale blue lines" (SL 107). Fittingly, it is under the wings of the Sphinx, with its Freudian connotations, that Porpentine's final, deadly confrontation takes place. In its shadow, his individual death comes to stand symbolically for the death of psychoanalysis and that of subjectivity in general.

The simulation of both the real and the subjective turns language into a purely operational tool in a final conflation of real and symbolic machinery. The operational transparency of the sign is one of pure horizontality, an "immanent surface of the development of operations, smooth surface, operational, of communication" (Baudrillard, *Fatal Strategies* 66). Ultimately, the implosion of language and the real entails the "liquidation of metaphor, th[e] precipitation of the sign into brute, senseless matter" (121).[4] Although there is a proliferation of language, it is language without mystery and without depths, consisting of "signs that do not let meanings filter through" (60). In a psychoanalytic register, the abolition of the real implies the abolition of repression as well; what remains is merely the *simulation* of repression. This replacement is ultimately what renders the position of the subject untenable for Baudrillard.

Within sociopolitical and economic simulation, the Lacanian real becomes identical to the structure of political economy because all objects are invariably simulated within operative models: "From now on political economy is the *real* for us" (Baudrillard, *L'Échange symbolique* 53). This is the fundamental shift between Lacanian and Baudrillardian theory. Baudrillard proceeds from the "(science) fiction"[5] that the subject's relation to the real—which defines psychoanalysis in its most basic assumptions—has been made impossible by sociopolitical simulation, which implies the production *of* the real *by* the imaginary, not its—ultimately impossible—reproduction within it: "The real, *therefore* the imaginary. Because these formerly separated categories have merged and [now] branch off [*dérivent*] together" (*L'Échange symbolique* 53).[6] Whereas for Lacan the relation of discourse to the real implies its fundamentally torn character and the impossibility of closure, from Baudrillard's perspective discourse *is* finally closed in itself, because everything is always already a simulation originating from within its own parameters.[7] For the politically and economically defined subject, this means that every image it interiorizes is always an image already *produced* according to an earlier imaginary projection based on the structure of operational and economic simulation. Unlike the subject in Lacan's system, the subject in Baudrillard's interiorizes images originating not from a real to which they refer but from a real that is only the exteriorized version of its own imaginary scene, so that the real and the objects *o* are conflated to become simulated "objects *o[perational]*": "Today . . . the real and the imaginary are confused in the same operational totality" (*Simulations* 150). In his introduction to *Slow Learner,* Pynchon comments on this dissociation of experience and reality through sociopolitical mediations, the replacement of that part of the subject related to *being*—its "real-ity"—with *mediation:* "We were onlookers: the parade had gone by and we were already getting everything secondhand, consumers of what the media of the time were supplying us" (SL 9).

This replacement of reality by operational mediations also entails the end of the mirror stage: "No more mirror of being and appearances, of the real and its concept" (Baudrillard, *Simulations* 3). Because reality "has been confused with its own image" (152), the unconscious itself becomes the mere symptom of a more primary simulation. It has "lost its own reality-principle and has turned into an operational simulacrum" (*L'Échange symbolique* 10). Because of this closure, "psychoanalysis in its entirety as a model of simulation . . . must be questioned" (*Forget Foucault* 31). Because simulation prohibits the insistence of the real within the psychic apparatus, it is necessary to add the *hyperreal* to the categories of the real, the symbolic, and the imaginary, the new term being the one that "captures and obstructs the functioning of the three orders" (*Simulations* 157).

Whereas in Lacanian theory the (imaginary) ego mediates between the (real) organism and the (symbolic) subject, for Baudrillard an always already simulated—and thus imaginary—real disperses or "diffracts" the subject into countless imaginary spaces, producing "a multitude of identical miniaturized egos" (*Ecstasy* 40). This psychic dissemination leads to an endless differentiation, as if Derridean *différance* had invaded and were operative in psychic space, without the instance of an ego—albeit a hallucinated entity—regulating and centering the various perceptions. Whereas Derrida stresses the freedom opened up by dissemination, however, Baudrillard evokes the horror of an operationally grounded dissemination in which the simulated real comes to operate completely without a subject: "The forms play with one another, exchanging one another without passing through the psychological imaginary of a subject" (48).

For Baudrillard, only radical ambivalence, a space that negates both operational and binary structures, reopens the possibility of a critical theory and, by extension, of subjectivity. This ambivalence links Baudrillard's theoretical critique of rationality to Pynchon's fictional one. Both Baudrillard and Pynchon aim to free language from its operational and rational determinations within a culture of simulation, the former from the position of a rhetorical theory and the latter from that of a theoretical rhetorics. A semiotics based on an unequivocal, binary structure of differentiations, which today forms the law of the signifier, cannot promise such a critical theory: "Only ambivalence . . . as a *rupture* of value, of another side or beyond of sign value . . . sustains a challenge to the legibility, the false transparency of the sign" (*Critique* 150).

In that it operates in a symbolic space that it simultaneously disrupts, fiction can become once again a valid mode of political criticism because "one will never destroy the system by a direct, dialectical revolution of the economical or political infrastructure. . . . One will never win out against it via its own logic . . . the most fatal mistake of all our revolutionary strategies is to believe to be able to end the system on the *real* level" (*L'Échange symbolique* 62). Like Pynchon, Baudrillard poses a rhetorical, ironic, and catastrophic theory in which "one has to carry the things to their limit" (11).

This critique ultimately must be directed against the code itself, for "only total revolution, theoretical and practical, can restore the symbolic in the demise of the sign and of value. Even signs must burn" (*Critique* 163).[8] In this most direct expression of Baudrillard's poetics Pynchon's and Baudrillard's rhetorics converge.

Baudrillard therefore questions the structure of the code itself—especially in his later works—trying to save the "impossible object" that is excluded by it, because it is exactly this object that "returns the subject to its mortal transparency. So if it can fascinate or seduce the subject, it is because it radiates no substance or meaning of its own. The pure object is sovereign, because it is what breaks up the sovereignty of the other and catches it in its own trap" (*Fatal Strategies* 113–14).

In this structure, the concept of the Lacanian "Thing" and its transcriptions into the object *o,* as well as Baudrillard's own earlier simulatory "object operational," are replaced by the idea of an object that has its own enigmatic strategy, so that the play of meaning unfolds no longer within the relation between subject and "humanized object" but between subject and an enigmatic other. The notion that "we need to be respectful of the inhuman" (*Fatal Strategies* 183) evokes again the delirious and sublime aspect of Pynchon's writing, because in a fictional register this inhuman [*im-monde*] marks exactly the register of the fantastic, which, as the gap or hesitation between the (unknown) real and reality, functions as the threshold between the human and the inhuman. Baudrillard's rhetorical theory draws on the fantastic—in fact, it becomes a "fantastic theory"—because in a simulatory society the fantastic mode becomes the most valid means of artistic rebellion and expression: "What we call art, theatre, language have worked for centuries to save illusion in this sense, that is, to maintain the tiny distance that makes the real play with its own reality, that plays with the disappearance of the real while exalting its appearance, and to rescue this ironic rule of the game" (173).

In a simulatory society, there is no more paranoiac, fantastic, delirious, and thus artistic space. There is "no more . . . projective paranoia as such, but a state of terror which is characteristic of the schizophrenic the absolute proximity to and total instantaneousness with things. . . . He [the subject] becomes a pure screen, a pure absorption and resorption surface of the influent networks" (*Ecstasy* 27). Pynchon's universes are situated exactly at this junction between paranoia—"the onset, the leading edge, of the discovery that *everything is connected* (GR 703)—and schizophrenia; projection and the immediacy of the object. In *Gravity's Rainbow*, for instance,

> Slothrop perceives that he is losing his mind. If there is something comforting—religious, if you want—about paranoia, there is still also anti-paranoia, where nothing is connected to anything, a condition not many of us can bear for long. Well right now Slothrop feels himself sliding onto the anti-paranoid part of his cycle, feels the whole city around him going back roofless, vulnerable, uncentered as he is, and only pasteboard images. (GR 434)

In the light of the previous chapters, the cycle that Pynchon evokes is a curiously twisted one, a fact to which Joseph W. Slade has drawn attention: "Pynchon . . . gives discontinuity a half-twist and makes of it a metaphysical Möbius strip" ("Thomas Pynchon" 59). This twisting is most directly illustrated by Kevin Spectro, who does not differentiate "between Outside and Inside. He saw the cortex as an interface organ, mediating between the two, but *part of them both*" (GR 141–42). Although one might wonder whether this discontinuity is really a *metaphysical* Möbius strip, the initial question remains: "Was Spectro right? Could Outside and Inside be part of the same field?" (GR 144). Apart from the question of its metaphysical nature, it is therefore certainly correct to state that in Pynchon, "the discontinuity between... [humankind's] world and nature's has been twisted into a Möbius strip, so that in a sense the paranoid may be right: the universe may have only one edge after all" (Slade, "Pynchon" 72).

Pynchon continually evokes scenarios in which "Inside is Outside" (GR 373), and his dualisms are defined in such a topography.⁹ It is ultimately within and along this "new space" that he can be aligned with Lacan, Derrida, and Baudrillard, who all question the separation of inside and outside within Cartesian space. Derrida's statement that *"there is nothing outside of the text* [. . . il n'y a pas de hors-texte]" (*Of Grammatology* 158), for instance, has to be read in the light of this new topography. In fact, the idea that "the Outside *is* the Inside" (44) is a fundamental figure of thought for contemporary theory.

For Lacan, similarly, the passage from nature to culture implies a break not between inside and outside but *within* representational space, and as such within the realm of the signifier, in a paradoxical space Lacan calls extimacy (*"L'extimité"*).¹⁰ In this space, for instance, the materials of the body are not only biological givens but, within the half-twist of the strip, "on the other side" always already signifiers, a fact that will be of importance in the discussion of Slothrop's scattering. For Baudrillard, finally, the real is always already a simulation as the result of the implosion of real and imaginary space.

The reference of all three to the "logic of the always already" is a second parallel, related to the fact that the new topography also distributes time in a new way.¹¹ It replaces the realm of cause and effect with a temporal space of belatedness, the retroactive staging of an impossible "event," a dynamics that continually operates in Pynchon's texts and has often been misread as his logocentrism. In Lacan, this belatedness defines the status of the real as a phantasm, because the birth of the repressed takes place exactly between the real and the constitution of the phantasm, which is already a reflection of it. "In the sense that the object *o* plays . . . the role of that which takes the place of the missing partner, the thing constitutes itself which we are used to see emerge also at the place of the real, namely the phantasm" (*Encore* 58). This belatedness is mirrored in Derrida's idea of the trace or the chora, which "'is' nothing but the sum or the process of that which will gradually inscribe itself 'on' it . . . but it is not the *subject* or the *self-present bearer* of all of these interpretations, although it can nevertheless not be reduced to them" (*Chôra* 273). Similarly, Baudrillard's hyperreal shows everything to be a retroactive result of imaginary, operative processes.

Although these similarities warrant the parallelization of the respective theories, their differences become obvious in the way they structure the space on the strip. Their "ontological" similarities are set off by "epistemological" differences—although these, too, should be seen as "two sides of the same plane"—which makes for the prismatic effect of their simultaneous application. There are at least as many different "perspectives" in the new topography as there are in the old.

Critical discourse necessarily inhabits the same topological space, and every critical reading is caught in its structure. How, then, to regulate and valorize the various perspectives? One approach—and this is where my valorization of Lacan as "central" finds its legitimation—is to take the writing strategy of the text under discussion as a guideline. This, of course, implies identification, which in turn implies misidentification and misreading, resulting in what Leo Bersani has called a "paranoid criticism," whose result is only yet another "model of unreadability" ("Pynchon" 118).[12] That such a reading should, therefore, retrospectively show the critic's own proclivities is inevitable. For better or worse, the critic takes out only what he or she has put in.

Notes

1. See especially Derrida, "Deconstruction and the Possibility of Justice." For a discussion of a Derridean politics see also my "Digging for the Truth: Archaeology and the End of History."

2. For a more detailed discussion of Baudrillard's theory and poetics see my "Even Signs Must Burn. Jean Baudrillard and the Reemergence of the Object."

3. See also Lacan's critique of the "paradoxical and absurd equivalent of *Everything real is rational*" (*Seminar II* 168).

4. See also Theodor Adorno and Max Horkheimer's *Dialectic of Enlightenment*, in which they show that the enlightened "man without qualities" uses "signs without qualities": "The more completely language is lost in the announcement, the more words are debased as substantial vehicles of meaning and become signs devoid of quality; the more purely and transparently words communicate what is intended, the more impenetrable they become" (164).

5. In *Jean Baudrillard: From Marxism to Postmodernism and Beyond*, Douglas Kellner comments on this aspect of Baudrillard's theory: "While Baudrillard's texts are arguably quite good science fiction, they are rather problematical as models of social theory" (203). Although Kellner gives a good introduction to Baudrillard's theory, his critique of Baudrillard as a "sign fetishist" (199) falls back exactly into the semiotic frame Baudrillard himself criticizes.

6. See also Anthony Wilden, *System and Structure,* lvii: "The result of the dominance of the Imaginary relation in our present world is that . . . the Imaginary becomes the Real."

7. This closure is reminiscent of the closure Lacan detected in Hegel: "And the thing with absolute knowledge . . . is that discourse closes in on itself, whether or not it is in complete disagreement with itself, whether or not everything which can be expressed in the discourse is coherent or justified" (*Seminar II* 71). It is in fact "reason" that presides over both the notion of absolute knowledge and that of simulation.

8. "The only revolution in things is today no longer in their dialectical transcendence (*Aufhebung*), but in their potentialization, in their elevation to the second power, in their elevation to the nth power . . . no longer . . . dialectics, but . . . ecstasy" (*Fatal Strategies* 41). The end-result is the auto-abolition of culture by a self-induced implosion. Many misunderstandings concerning Baudrillard's theory are based on such "apocalyptic" statements, which have been read much too often as being *declarative* rather than *rhetorical* in the de Manian sense. A similar rhetoric, however, is already operative in the works of Adorno and Horkheimer, and Baudrillard might well be read as an updated, modified follower of the Frankfurt school.

9. "This topography is not a "description or representation of a structure but it is the structure itself, in the same way in which the Möbius strip does not represent a cut, but is the cut itself" (Gondek, *Angst, Einbildungskraft, Sprache* 246).

10. Quoted in Slavoj Žižek, *The Sublime Object of Ideology* 132. Compare Jacques-Alain Miller, "*A* and *a* in Clinical Structures." For Lacan's use of the Möbius strip see especially *The Four Fundamental Concepts* (270) and "La Science et la vérité" (*Écrits,* French ed., 855–77).

11. See especially Lacan's "Le Temps logique et l'assertion de certitude anticipée" (*Écrits,* French ed., 197–213).

12. For the development of a Lacanian poetics see especially Ragland-Sullivan, "The Magnetism between Reader and Text," and Ragland-Sullivan, *Jacques Lacan and the Philosophy of Psychoanalysis,* as well as, very much in her footsteps, James M. Mellard, *Using Lacan.* In my use of Lacanian theory, I consciously play down this "reader response" aspect of Lacanian theory, which deals with the ego as "the identificatory construct the reader exchanges with the literary text" (Mellard 44), although I agree that "all interpretation is Imaginary" (53). Furthermore, I believe that in the future, a Lacanian poetics will have to supplement such "characterological" readings as Mellard's by readings of the "lines of desire" that constitute the structure of the literary text across characterological borders—especially, to trace the struggle of the "textual imaginary" with the "textual symbolic" and their relation to the "atextual real."

Part Two
Textual Analyses

Chapter 4   **V.:**
                  "V. in Love"

> "Love is love. It shows up in strange displacements."
> Thomas Pynchon, *V.*

> "Le textile est d'abord un texte."
> Jacques Lacan, *L'Envers de la Psychanalyse*

In *V.*, Pynchon fictionalizes Baudrillard's vision of a fully simulated subject, doing so within the parameters of a simulatory society in which the subject is defined as both a *real* and a *symbolic* robot.

Published in 1963, *V.* takes up the motif of the twentieth century's growing decadence, which Pynchon had already used as the backdrop to "Under the Rose." In its historiographic project, which aligns theories of history, their sociopolitical implications, and the growing mechanization of modern culture, Benny Profane and Herbert Stencil symbolize two extreme positions. Stencil is obsessed with origins and the search for the plot or cabal that would reveal the organizing principle behind his identity, as well as his time's. This is a *vertical*, metaphorical search into history, which he "stencilizes" according to parallels with his own past and identity, an implosion of personal and general history that is symbolized by his own identity's purely generic nature; accordingly, he speaks of himself only in the third person: "This helped 'Stencil' appear as only one among a repertoire of identities" (*V.* 62).[1] This search for a unifying principle in history is ultimately unsuccessful. Toward the end of the book, "Stencil [. . .] had left pieces of himself—and V.—all over the western world. V. by this time was a remarkably scattered concept" (*V.* 389).

A similar scattering process defines Benny Profane's purely *horizontal*, metonymic driftings through the mechanical and inanimate landscape of contemporary society, a world in which "millions of inanimate objects [are] being produced brand-new every week" (*V.* 148). His scattering process, however, is not historical but decidedly individual. Whereas Stencil ceaselessly projects his ego onto history, Profane, the schlemiel, fights a continuous battle against the world of dead, uncaring objects, and, because he invariably fails to establish a relation between himself and his environment, he is in constant danger of losing his ego. His dissolution, which mirrors V.'s literal and conceptual one, corresponds precisely to Lacan's image of the "fragmented body" (*Écrits* 4), which defines the extreme position of the experience of the self at the beginning of the mirror stage. (The other extreme is the "anticipation" [4] of a never achieved totality and unity— exactly the logocentric promise that defines Stencil's search. Consequently, between the two of them, Profane and Stencil run almost the whole trajectory of the mirror stage; as individuals, however, both fail to achieve the "alienating identity" [4] that concludes it, each separately following his trajectory into phantasm and disintegration, respectively.) Although the mirror stage should function to overcome these images, images of the fragmented body can reappear later in connection with psychic "disintegration[s] in the individual" (4), such as occur in Profane's case: "Maybe he was looking for something [. . .] to make the fact of his own disassembly plausible as that of any machine [. . .] if he kept going down that street, not only his ass but also his arms, legs, sponge brain and clock of a heart must be left behind to litter the pavement, be scattered among manhole covers" (*V.* 40).

Profane and Stencil thus come to symbolize two sides of contemporary culture, *chaos* and *order:* "V.'s is a country of coincidence [Profane's world], ruled by a ministry of myth [Stencil's world]" (*V.* 450). *V.*'s main theme is the inability to align these extremes, in textual terms, to align metonymy and metaphor. If one were to chart a graph—a gesture warranted by Pynchon's use of the catenary (*V.* 326)—Stencil would represent the vertical axis and Profane the horizontal. McHoul and Wills stress this aspect in their reading of *V.*, seeing the text as the copula that makes "accident and intention" (WP 182) inseparable. Although this evokes an almost peaceful scenario, for Pynchon the result is a schizophrenic, dual personality and society, because there is no mediation between the two: "We carry on the business of this century with an *intolerable* double vision [. . .] the hothouse and the street" (*V.* 468; emphasis added).

Pynchon aligns this general duplicity with a growing social entropy, the fact that "the world [had] started to run more and more afoul of the inanimate" (*V.* 290), the frightening promise of pentecostal apocalypse and the imminent intrusion of an (un)holy ghost.

In a panorama reminiscent of Foucault's *Discipline and Punish*,[2] Pynchon shows how in the twentieth century, the political arena has declined from the Father, "the Prince [. . .] the single leader, the dynamic figure whose virtù used to be a determinant of history" (*V.* 472), to the Son, "genius of the liberal love-feast which had produced 1848" (*V.* 472), a change that has brought about the shift of politics into "engineering" (*V.* 242) and, with it, the abolition of subjectivity,[3] an abolition Pynchon links to the destruction of the realm of dreams and thus "interiority." The personal confrontation with death and the real that Porpentine still remembers in "Under the Rose," which Godolphin can still experience with Vheissu and Rafael Mantissa could still sense when viewing the Venus of Botticelli, the "gaudy [. .] *dream* of annihilation" (*V.* 210; emphasis added), has been replaced by an impersonal, anonymous war machine: "That war destroyed a kind of privacy, perhaps the privacy of *dream* [. . .] our Vheissus are no longer our own [. . .] they're public property" (*V.* 248; emphasis added).[4]

In *V.*, Pynchon describes culture and reality as a complex coating of the (void of the) real: "we [. . .] paint the side of some Peri or other [. . . .] We call it society. A new coat of paint [. . . .] She can't change her own color" (*V.* 461). Godolphin's experience in Vheissu implies that it is only the coats of color that hold culture together and that to scrape off this color would only expose the void of the real, which cannot be included in a symbolic or logical framework: "The inert universe may have a quality we can call logic. But logic is a human attribute after all [. . . .] What are real are the cross-purposes" (*V.* 484).[5] It is not possible to assimilate the mysterious structure of the inert universe into culture, whose self-reflexive structure is best exemplified by Mondaugen's paradoxical message from outer space stating that "the world is all that the case is." In this culture, the only way out is a way in, a medial position in which one can "keep cool, but care" (*V.* 366), a state of grace facilitated by a "feminine principle" (*V.* 209) that permeates the book and whose most prominent representatives are Paola and Rachel. Yet it is exactly the destruction and conversion of this female principle into male machines and technologies that underlies the universe portrayed in *V.*

When Jacques Lacan describes the brain as a "dream machine" (*Seminar II* 76),[6] this definition testifies to the fact that after having invaded its garden, the machine has finally invaded the subject itself. Freud's and certainly Lacan's theories are already constructed from systems of interlocking optical, symbolic, and sexual machines, whereas for Derrida, the network of signifiers in general works like a machine.[7] The machine figures most drastically, however, in the theories of Deleuze and Guattari. For them, its entry into the unconscious as *the* pattern of unconscious registration ("the unconscious itself is no more structural than personal, it does not symbolize any more than it imagines or represents; it engineers, it is machinic" [*Anti-Oedipus* 53]) heralds a possible breakup of old, corroded oedipal structures and a release of culturally unregulated and unmediated flows of pure desire and energy, with a generally liberating effect. Their *molecular* "desiring machines" are machines without operational use, "formative machines, whose very misfirings are functional" (286). Like the machinic sculptures of Jean Tinguely, these desiring machines are in fact defined by their very unproductiveness and their aesthetics of pure motion, flows, passages, and movements. They are *"system[s] of interruptions* or breaks" (36), completely free of functional parameters. In this uselessness, they actually come to evoke a kind of "machinic *jouissance.*" These machines, however, which in their dynamics are also reminiscent of the Futurists' spectacles of pure speed and energy, find their dark doubles in the cold, mechanical robot of the factory—or of any purely operational endeavor, for that matter.[8] Even within this promise, then, the machine carries more sinister connotations that serve as backdrops within Deleuze and Guattari's study. Borrowing their terminology from physics, they write of *molar* machines, great machinic networks following certain well-defined parameters, in which all flows are directed toward a particular project (e.g., the oedipal machine, the social machine, or the capitalist machine). Against the utopian liberation and the dispersion of the subject within the molecular machine, and against the objectification of desire,[9] molar machines insert the subject into, and define the subject through, preset structural patterns, within which—as a living extension of this machine—the subject is defined, much as is Charlie Chaplin's character in the *"Modern Times* machine."

This meeting of the machine and the subject is carried out within both psychoanalytic and cultural registers and figures as a constant trope within modern consciousness. It pervades all discursive practices, either as formal structuration or as direct content, and gives each discursive instance a specific marking. Postmodern society has borne witness to this meeting in all its various manifestations, from projects of artificial intelligence to worldwide computer networks, from Ballard's postindustrial science fiction to the whole complex of political and technological simulation, most recently, "cyberspace." Lacan's psychic machine is thus only one in a series of machinizations. In fact, psychoanalysis, in that it combines the dream and the machine, functions as a border between the logocentric ideal of a "natural" human and the vision of a completely artificial and dreamless automaton, which is why it can become the rhetorical and topological site on which these extremes can be played out against each other.

As early as "Under the Rose," Pynchon described a character—Bongo-Shaftsbury—as part automaton: physically, because he has a "knife-switch [. . .] fastened to [his] arm" (SL 123), and psychically, because he is a member of the new breed of spies with a "faith in nothing but the perfection of their own internal machinery" (SL 123). In fact, Bongo-Shaftsbury has a special fondness for automata, "dolls that walk, or speak, or are able to jump rope. [. . .] Such lovely dolls, and clockwork inside. Dolls that do everything perfectly, because of the machinery. Not like real little boys and girls at all. Real children cry, and act sullen, and won't behave. These dolls are much nicer" (SL 120).

This landscape of automata and their "mechanical brides" also defines the scenario of *V.*, an overall investigation of the inanimate's growing invasion into the animate. The dark vision of modern society that Pynchon sketches also functions as a critique of humanistic illusions concerning the status of the subject. The text describes the infiltrations of the inanimate as parallel to the growing mechanization of V., who stands metonymically for the growing usurpation of the human and the human body by the various scientific and cultural simulacra.

The replacement of the human by the machine and the effects of mechanization on what used to be called love are exemplified most concisely by the fate of Mélanie L'Heuremaudit in a chapter that brings together most of the book's leitmotifs. In chapter 14, entitled "V. in love," Pynchon stages the disruption of Freudian psychoanalysis and posits, from within its own concepts, if not the invalidity of its theoretical framework, then at least its inapplicability to a "new scene." His rhetorical reading of psychoanalysis against itself revolves around notions of the *subject* and the *fetish*.

Freudian psychoanalysis is based on specific assumptions concerning the status of the subject. Pynchon questions these assumptions by applying Freudian concepts to a subject that has turned into a purely operational object. Beginning with the Freudian concept of the primarily oedipal determination of the subject, Pynchon quickly moves to reveal and confront the problems generated when Freudian analysis is made to address a completely simulated subject. This kind of critique is analogous to Baudrillard's, which enters the Lacanian scene at an angle comparable to the one at which Pynchon's enters the Freudian. Baudrillard voices his critique of psychoanalysis from within Lacanian theory, but he aims at a complete rearrangement and disruption of its positions via the concept of simulation.[10] Pynchon's critique of Freudian psychoanalysis, I claim, is isomorphic to Baudrillard's. The latter enters the Freudian scene in its second, Lacanian generation, and Pynchon's concept of "complete determination" may well be read as an early, narrativized version of Baudrillard's simulation.

For his deconstruction of psychoanalysis, Pynchon, like Baudrillard, creates a rhetorical/fictional scenario in which the death of the subject has already happened and from which it is possible to comment retrospectively on the state of the subject today. It is in this respect that both Baudrillard's theory of simulation and the story of "V. in love" are science *fictions*, the science in the latter case being psychoanalysis. The new scene that is evoked in both is one in which psychoanalysis is put under erasure. By focusing on the replacement of the *body* by the *automaton,* Pynchon creates a figure of the more general and basic replacement of the *real* by *simulation*. In the same way in which the automaton puts the body under erasure—b̶o̶d̶y̶—the chapter describes an erased real—r̶e̶a̶l̶. Because of this strategy, the chapter, which at first sight seems to invalidate psychoanalysis, should be read *with* rather than *against* Freudian or Lacanian theory. In fact, the chapter perfectly hollows out the space in which Lacanian theory operates.

Chapter 14 describes the final days in the life of Mélanie L'Heuremaudit, a fifteen-year-old dancer who comes to Paris to perform in an avant-garde ballet.[11] It describes her relations with a mysterious woman, V., and culminates in her death during the premiere of the ballet, in which she dies the very death she was supposed only to act out on stage. Right away, the first sentence of the chapter develops these tropes and defines Mélanie in her first "interpellation": her last name translates as "the cursed hour," a time that denotes both a historical and a cultural framework—for Pynchon, a growing decadence.[12] Accordingly, Mélanie's exact time of arrival in Paris is not *her* time and can be extrapolated only by its relation to various official time-systems operating simultaneously: "The clock inside the Gare du Nord read 11:17: Paris time minus five minutes, Belgian railway time plus four minutes, mid-Europe time minus 56 minutes" (*V.* 393). Her arrival is defined as an interface of various paradigms and is from the beginning colonized by differing forces and determinations that align her with a specific historical moment: "By the cover of Le Soleil [. . .] it was 24 July 1913" (*V.* 393). Against these geographically, culturally, and politically mediated times, Mélanie's time, as well as she herself, is explicitly undefined: "To Mélanie, who had forgotten her traveling clock—who had forgotten everything—the hands might have stood anywhere" (*V.* 393). Another such interface, this one not temporal but psychological, defines her personality, which is neither logocentrically *unified* nor *dispersed* (as are Deleuze and Guattari's utopias of the schizophrenic), but defined within specific functions and thus fully *operational:* apart from being Mélanie L'Heuremaudit, she is also "La Jarretière" (her stage name, "The Garter") and "Su Feng" (the persona she plays on stage).

The psychoanalytic concept within and against which the whole chapter must be read is that of fetishism, introduced early on by Itague's welcome to Mélanie: "Come, fétiche, inside" (*V.* 395). For Freud and Lacan, fetishism is related to the fear of castration. For the male, it serves to circumvent the fear of castration. It "re-creates" the woman's (missing) phallus, the lack of which grounds his fear of castration by presenting him with an absence that, he fantasizes, may come to be his own as well. It thus re-creates a missing phallus from a material, inanimate object associated with women's bodies. For Freud, then, the fetish is the male's way of giving female nature something that it initially lacks, if this "lack" is viewed from within the phallic position; it functions as a conceptual crutch that supplements an initial lack. The fetish object is thus always a supplement and a simulation. It stands for and signifies the phallus, inscribing its presence at the very place of its absence, via a semiotic substitution—signifier for signified/referent.[13] The initial lack is reified in a chain of replacements. It is Freud's contention that fetishism becomes pathological only when it loses this function of supplementarity and becomes a signified itself.[14] The fetish, however, is a supplement only from within the phallic position: "And if women are not fetishists, then this is because they apply this constant fetishwork to themselves, turning themselves into *dolls*" (Baudrillard, *L'Échange symbolique* 169).[15] In other words, a woman can use the inanimate to add to and to shape her body in ways congruent with male desire, so that the missing phallus is not equated with a single fetish (her shoe, her underwear) but is spread out over her entire body as phallic object. From both the female and the male position, it is the phallus that defines the fetish, so that women ultimately become their "own as well as the other's fetish" (169). From the male perspective, the fetish replaces the absence of the female phallus—itself a virtual, imaginary term—with an inanimate object; from the female perspective, the absence of the "female phallus" causes the fetishization of the "real thing"—the male phallus—and the power it signifies. This economy is inaugurated and guarded by the "phallocratic" structure of psychoanalysis. As Lacan says,

> I am saying that it is in order to be the phallus, that is to say, the signifier of the desire of the Other, that a woman will reject an essential part of femininity, namely, all her attributes in the masquerade. It is for that which she is not that she wishes to be desired as well as loved. But she finds the signifier of her own desire in the body of him to whom she addresses her demand for love. Perhaps it should not be forgotten that the organ that assumes this signifying function takes on the value of a fetish. (*Écrits* 289–90)

Lacan writes from the Freudian position that "there is only one *libido*, his [Freud's] text showing that he conceives it as masculine in nature" (*Écrits* 291), which implies that "the problem of her [the woman's] condition is fundamentally that of accepting herself as an object of desire for the man" ("Intervention" 68). In order for the woman to make the phallus her own, she can either make the male phallus into her fetish or turn her own body into a phallus, a gesture facilitated by the complementary male desire to turn the female body into a phallus. Lacan clearly situates her in this position when he says that "such is the woman concealed behind her veil: it is the absence of the penis that turns her into the phallus, the object of desire" (*Écrits* 322). Both men, who have the phallus but fear its lack, and women, who lack it, desire (to be) the phallus.[16] Woman's lack of a phallus makes her stand in for the lack she also represents for the male position. She does not need an inanimate fetish object, because the phallus—as a function—is either in the place of the male or projected and spread out over her own body. For her, the inanimateness of the male fetish is thus paralleled by the inanimateness of herself as phallic object or by the real phallus. These positionings of woman within the phallic theater designate to her the role that she has to act out within this double choreography of her own desire, which in turn firmly grounds male desire. The question is "that of woman's own desire for her position as fetish . . . woman is taken to desire herself but only through the term which precludes her" (Rose 212).[17]

Mélanie's first autoerotic scene soon after her arrival starts with a daydream triggered by her image in an overhead mirror and continues after she has undressed and put on the costume she is to wear as Su Feng, including now a discarded lay figure. The scene shows her insertion into the phallic mode and proceeds precisely along these two positionings. In the beginning, she watches *herself* in the mirror and moves her legs "till the hem of the blue skirt had worked high above the tops of the stockings. And lay gazing at the black and tender white" (*V.* 397). The route of her desire is already lodged according to a male perspective and is grafted onto her own body: she sees herself in the mirror as the object of male—her father's—desire: "Papa had said, 'How pretty your legs are: the legs of a dancer'" (*V.* 397). In taking the perspective of her father's desire in relation to herself, she already inserts herself firmly into a fetish function.

After this initial contemplation in the mirror, which already stresses the relation between body and cloth, she immediately goes on to "disguise" herself. The broken relation to her *own* sexual attributes, which Lacan diagnoses in woman, is highlighted by the emphasis placed on her being dressed up for her encounter with the lay figure, rejecting and concealing quite literally "all her attributes in the masquerade" and thus all natural relation to her own body. This need for *concealment* as well as *addition* marks her involvement with her own body.

> She rose, in a near-frenzy, removed blouse, skirt and undergarments [. . . .] Back in the hot room she quickly removed shoes and stockings, keeping her eyes closed tight until she had fastened her hair in back with the spangled amber comb. She was not pretty unless she wore something. The sight of her nude body repelled her. Until she had drawn on the blonde silk tights, embroidered up each leg with a long, slender dragon; stepped into the slippers with the cut steel buckles, and intricate straps which writhed up halfway to her knees. Nothing to restrain her breasts: she wrapped the underskirt tightly around her hips. It fastened with thirty hooks and eyes from waist to thigh-top, leaving a fur-trimmed slit so that she could dance. And finally, the kimono, translucent and dyed rainbowlike with sunbursts and concentric rings of cerise, amethyst, gold and jungly green. (*V.* 397)

In this intricate phallic masquerade, in which the objects themselves already come to life—the inventory includes blonde tights, writhing straps, and underskirts with eyes—she "lay back once more [. . .] breath taken by her own beauty. If Papa could see her" (*V.* 398). This transformation of her body into a phallic simulation also entails her body's submission under somebody else's language and code:

> The whole contemporary history of the body is that of its demarcation, of the matrix of marks and signs that cover it with a network and partition it, that negate it in its difference and its radical ambivalence . . . [in order to create] a sexuality that is seen as the determining instance—a phallic instance, which is organized entirely around the fetishization of the phallus as the general equivalent. (Baudrillard, *L'Échange symbolique* 155)

Within this "phallic grammar," the female body itself is strictly excluded and banned from representation. All the signs that cover it are male signs, so that a male erotics ultimately has to detach itself from the body proper and affix itself to the overlying signs themselves, the endpoint of which process is the "body *as* sign," defined within and dominated by a "phallic code."[18] In this code,

> a marking that gets the power of a sign and by way of this a perverse erotic function [turns into] a line of demarcation that represents castration. . . . In this basic scheme, which is analogous to that of the linguistic sign, castration is *signified* . . . and thus misunderstood. The naked and the non-naked stand in a *structural* opposition and work toward the *representation* of the fetish. As for instance the border of stocking and thigh . . . because the naked thigh and metonymically the whole body have turned into the *phallic image* [*effigie*] through this demarcation, the fetish-object of contemplation and manipulation. (*L'Échange symbolique* 155–56)

By the *mise-en-scène* of the female body as a fetish-repertoire, the fear of castration is canceled, and the lack is caught up by the fetish (which is now the *code*) to which it is immediately linked.

It is within the juxtaposition of skin and clothing (for example, "La Jarretière, or "garter") that the phallocratic erotic element is lodged. These eroticized divisions make lace the ultimate(ly) erotic fabric; it is the "délire"[19] of the polarity between body and fetish. It is the bar as such that opens up the play of the juxtapositions of body and fetish within which male desire is lodged, providing them with a structural framework, an oppositionality based on a system of digitalized differences. This line also always functions as a demarcation between the animate—skin—and the inanimate—cloth. The demarcation of clothing and body, of black stockings and white skin, which was so important for Mélanie in her first mirror reflection, denotes exactly the part of the structure in which the phallus is spread out over her *own* body, turning it into a fetish (without her having to take the detour of a male figure in a fake "narcissism"[20]). Another route determines her relation to the mannequin, which functions as a replacement of the desired phallus: her father's. The lay figure, in its oscillation between ideas of the automaton and the mannequin, is in this sense not a pathological fetish, because it *represents* the desired real phallus, denoting a *real*—temporal or spatial—lack rather than a *structural* one. It is an aid in the attempt to hallucinate the presence of the real being, and the lay figure, in its lifelikeness, is of course the perfect surrogate and substitute, especially because it is "without a head" (*V.* 396) and thus has no identity of its own. It is the truly phallic and already machinic body. "The ideal body . . . is that of the mannequin. The mannequin is the model for this complete phallic instrumentalization of the body" (*L'Échange symbolique* 168). This body-as-mannequin refers primarily to the female body and to women, who are quite literally the mannequins of phallocratic fashions: "The unveiled body of the woman . . . denotes quite obviously the appearance of the phallus, the fetish-object, it is a gigantic work of the phallic simulation" (159). It can, in this scene, however, take on a complementary function for the woman, who is herself already a fetish object. In her fantasy, Mélanie transposes the phallic body of her father onto the mannequin and actually "plays back" the becoming-phallus of her own body with the help of the image of the phallus she desires.

Both parts of the initial encounter are performed within a phallocratic perspective and denote the two ways in which woman has to lodge *her* desire: in the first structure, she emerges as the object desired *by* the phallus; in the second, as the object desiring the phallus. The scene shows the supplementarities and dynamics of this economy, the result of which is that in both dimensions Mélanie can relate to herself only within an externalization. Active or passive, her desire is ultimately the desire of the phallus, and she is the product of her father's fantasy: "He gave her all that. Or was he giving it all to himself, by way of her?" (*V.* 399).

Within the chapter's literary structure, the scene also figures as an overture, presaging its "automatic" ending and from the beginning establishing, via the lay figure, a connection between Mélanie's father and the automata. Just before the scene, Itague tells Mélanie about the inclusion of automata in the ballet, and the connotations of this permeate the entire scene: "What was he saying? Automata . . ." (*V.* 396). Her "lovemaking," which ends the scene, is, in this sense, also already a prefiguration of her final dance.

> The lay figure in the corner was light and carried easily to the bed. She raised her knees high and—interested—saw her calves in the mirror crisscross over the small of its plaster back. Felt the coolness of the figure's flanks against the nude-colored silk, high on her thighs, hugged it tight. The neck top, jagged and flaking off, came to her breasts. She pointed her toes, began to dance horizontal, thinking of how her handmaidens would be. (*V.* 398)

From the beginning of the chapter, various motifs serve to establish a Freudian connection for Mélanie: her very first word, the screamed "'Papa!'" (*V.* 394), triggered, revealingly, by a statue of Apollo; the images of the incestuous relation with her father in the past ("Mélanie lay on the wide bed beside him, while he touched her in many places, and she squirmed and fought not to make a sound. It was their game" [*V.* 394]); and a remembered daydream of herself sliding down the roof of the family mansion—a thinly disguised dream about incestuous sexual intercourse. Mélanie's dream about the German engineer, however, which follows her dance with the lay figure, is the most revealingly Freudian one, and also the one in which psychoanalysis itself is thematized along Mélanie's shift from *psychoanalytic* to *real* object. In this dream, she equates the engineer of the automata with her father, so that the phallic instance turns into an *engineer* who "built her."

> The German stood over the bed watching her. He was Papa, but also a German.
> "You must turn over," he repeated insistently. She was too embarrassed to ask why. Her eyes—which somehow she was able to see, as if she were disembodied and floating above the bed, perhaps somewhere behind the quicksilver of the mirror—her eyes were slanted Oriental: long lashes, spangled on the upper lids with tiny fragments of gold leaf. She glanced sideways at the lay figure. It had grown a head, she thought. The face was turned away. "To reach between your shoulderblades," said the German. What does he look for there, she wondered.
> "Between my thighs," she whispered, moving on the bed. [...] The Mélanie in the mirror watched sure fingers move to the center of her back, search, find a small key, which he began to wind.
> "I got you in time," he breathed. "You would have stopped, had I not..."

The face of the lay figure had been turned toward her, all the time. There was no face.
She woke up, not screaming, but moaning as if sexually aroused. (*V.* 401–2)

The mechanical arousal of the automaton (Mélanie) by the winding of the key between its (her) shoulder blades figures here as a displacement of a more direct sexual arousal; her whispered "between my thighs" denotes her desire to change the place of arousal from her back to her genitals. Constructed directly according to Freudian concepts of displacement and condensation, the dream contains much of the latent wish within its dream material and is in this sense a direct quotation of psychoanalytic theory. Because of this equivalency, it can be read from a "postpsychoanalytic," simulatory perspective not only as Mélanie's dream but also as the dream of psychoanalysis about its own subject. Mélanie's desire to be a phallic automaton mirrors the desire of psychoanalysis itself for *its* latent wish, the implied phallic structuration behind the scenarios of the dream work; Mélanie dreaming is thus simultaneously psychoanalysis dreaming the "nostalgic" dream of the (phallic) subject. In this reading the dream is dreamed by psychoanalysis and results from a retroprojection of psychoanalytic structures into the unconscious, which conveniently takes on the structure of its science. The ghostlike structure of this dream, as well as the complicity it establishes between sex and the inanimate, is expressed by Mélanie's final reaction, which is not, as one might have expected, *horror* but rather *arousal*. Already, Pynchon's final project emerges here: a critique not only of the subject within psychoanalysis but of the subject of psychoanalysis itself.

Yet the Freudian episteme is not the only one within which Mélanie is defined. She is also the object of a specifically *modern* love, which is—like psychoanalysis itself—a cultural and historical phenomenon. As such, she is a *cultural* object. Within phallocratic society, a society mirrored in Freudian and Lacanian concepts, woman has to turn herself into a doll[21] to fit the phallic scene, which is exactly how V. describes Mélanie: "What are you like unclothed? A chaos of flesh. But as Su Feng, lit by hydrogen, oxygen, a cylinder of lime, moving doll-like in the confines of your costume . . . You will drive Paris mad. Women and Men alike" (*V.* 404).

The repressed image of the female body as a chaos of flesh is transformed into a phallic fantasy by an artificial light show and costumes. As its doll, the inanimate representation of a human, Mélanie becomes the inanimate object of phallic desire itself. Within male society, woman seems to lend herself "naturally" to such an object function, her role as cultural object having been instituted via a long historical process. Within Pynchon's setup, however, the fetish object—not shoes, garter belts, etc., but the one to which the fetish is linked as a supplement, that is to say, the subject—turns it-/herself into an object by becoming a fetish in her *entirety*. Woman thus crosses the border from being a cultural object, but still human and *animate*, to being an *inanimate* fetish object. Within the shift, Pynchon also implies that from now on both victim and victimizer—female and male—will be victimized, because in the new scene sexual differences will be annulled altogether. In this shift, the *code* takes the position of the *phallus*, not in the Lacanian and Freudian sense as always already implicated by castration but as a simulation of "fullness," a simulation that by necessity excludes the real—in this case, the real as/of the body.

In what follows, Pynchon explores the mechanics of this new "erotic stage" along the split between subject and object *within* the new fetish object (the inanimate female). This separation has to be reestablished *within* the fetish/object, for otherwise, both subject and object functions would be combined in an unstable union. The line of demarcation, the bar that separates the fetish (the fetish as human) from the object (the human as fetish), is the plane of the mirror. It takes over the function of the "bar" within fetishism, the plane on which differences can be inscribed. But by now, this line is no longer directly connected to the body of the subject but instead marks the complete exteriorization of the fetish in relation to itself.

Symptomatically, mirrors mark the topography of the whole chapter. Mélanie herself "functions as a mirror" (*V.* 399). In Lacanian terms, her investment in the imaginary can be observed in her inability to express herself within the symbolic. The only words she speaks within the whole chapter are "Papa!" (*V.* 394), "I have nowhere to stay" (396), "Move?" (396) "I . . ." (404) and, within her dream, "Between my thighs" (401). Twice, her silences are commented on from the outside: "Mélanie could not speak," and "The girl didn't answer" (*V.* 404; 406). In a space quite unlike that charted by Lacanian topography, in which the imaginary and the symbolic constantly interact once the mirror stage has been passed, Mélanie is firmly caught within a specular scenario, less a *subject* than an *object*—namely, the mirror-plane, reflecting the presence of her father, who has modeled her after his own wishes. She has become the embodiment of this phallic dream, its *"fétiche."* But because the phallic scene has itself

V.: "V. in Love"   67

been revealed as a mere ghost (a male hallucination), she can, as its mirror image, only mirror "the reflection of a ghost" (*V.* 399).

The initial reason for Mélanie's obsession with mirrors and her double is that she herself, being a pure object/fetish, can relate only to a double of this object and can "love" only other fetishes, who thus become fetishes of a fetish. To any other than such a "virtual reality" she is emotionally immune: "The eyes would not respond. Not with fear, desire, anticipation. Only the Mélanie in the mirror could make them do that" (*V.* 404).

Her first mirror encounter is performed still under the aegis of the male, the memory of her father and her incestuous relationship with him. But although in this instance the mirror performs a bringing-to-life, an identification of the inanimate object (the lay figure as phallus) with the animate one (the desired father as phallus), in her later mirror encounters, the audience she at first hallucinated in order to fill the gap between inanimate and animate, loved object becomes real. It is exactly here that Pynchon finally overthrows the psychoanalytic scene: whereas Mélanie's first encounters still take place within a phallocratic scenario, and Mélanie, as a male hallucination, remains a *metaphorical* object, her later relation to V. defines her as a *real* object. The textual nodal point along which this change is established is another of Pynchon's "low puns" (*Lot 49* 129). Like Mélanie, who completely internalizes her fetish function, Pynchon takes psychoanalysis at its word; taking the word *object* literally, he can redefine the Freudian setup and project this new scene back onto the old one. Once the fetish function has completely colonized the female body (here still to be thought of within psychoanalytical parameters), Pynchon can in a next step treat this body as a completely objectified site. This shift from *human body* to *automaton* is linked to V., with whom Mélanie enters into a "lesbian" relationship. Pynchon thus disrupts the male/female dichotomy not only by letting Mélanie become the fetish for a woman but also by making this woman at the same time a "machine," an automaton who sees in Mélanie the perfect fetish: "'You are not real.' [. . .] 'Do you know what a fetish is? Something of a woman which gives pleasure but is not a woman. A shoe, a locket . . . une jarretière. You are the same, not real but an object of pleasure'" (*V.* 404).[22] Their meeting is from the beginning a meeting of two variously defined objects that are mirrored and grafted onto each other.

Even before she meets Mélanie, V. has worked within parameters of fetishism, and again, it is the juxtaposition of cloth and skin, inanimate object and body, into which the fetish function is quite literally inscribed. During a "Black Mass," V. is "absorbed in burning tiny holes with the tip of her cigarette, through the skirt of the young girl. [. . .] She was writing ma fétiche, in black-rimmed holes. The sculptress wore no lingerie. So that when the lady finished the words would be spelled out by the young sheen of the girl's thighs" (*V.* 403).

Soon after their introduction, Mélanie and the woman enter into a complicated *ménage à trois* in which the concepts of subject and fetish are imploded and constantly oscillate. V. leads Mélanie to her loft outside Paris in "a landscape of factories, chemical works, iron foundries" (*V.* 406). Within this ambience of industrial robots and molar machines, she has created a secret chamber of mirrors: "As for Mélanie, her lover had provided her with mirrors, dozens of them. Mirrors with handles, with ornate frames, full-length and pocket mirrors came to adorn the loft wherever one turned to look" (*V.* 408). In this landscape of the imaginary and its multiple diffractions, Mélanie derives pleasure from contemplating her mirror image (her double), which can function as audience (as "other") because it is violently split along the mirror plane and thus completely separated from her. Its voyeuristic position (which is actually the mirror image of *her* voyeurism) enables her to enact the internal split of subject and object functions within herself and to re-create her own image for herself as her own (though "other") fetish. She uses the presence of a real "other" (V.) whose virtual as well as real images are present to amplify this separation of herself from herself. The presence of V. strengthens the voyeuristic position of the mirror-Mélanie by the introduction of a *real* voyeur, equating herself-as-audience with the other-as-audience in the space defined by mirrorings in which the plane of the mirror(s) marks an even more basic split: "She needs, it seems, a real voyeur to complete the illusion that her reflections are, in fact, this audience. With the addition of this other—multiplied also, perhaps, by mirrors—comes consummation: for the other is also her own double" (*V.* 410).

Within the complicated geometries of the virtual spaces, the multiple and diffracted images constantly ricochet and are lost in the depths and dispersions of the mirror planes as such.[23] V.'s virtual mirror image, her real image, and her voyeuristic function objectify V. for Mélanie in the same ratio in which her own image is objectified by the reflection, a step that puts the self-as-audience into a similarly distant position as the other-as-audience. The separation of virtual fetish from real fetish is carried out within these substitutions.

In the position of the real voyeur, V.—herself a fetish—occupies a position parallel to that which the fetish (Mélanie) has to itself: "As for V., she recognized—perhaps aware of her own progression toward inanimateness—the fetish of Mélanie and the fetish of herself to be one" (*V.* 410). Within these multiple identifications, the scenario is closed into a symbiotic triadic function, because from V.'s perspective the fetish (Mélanie) is also doubled and amplified in the mirror(s) in a similar equation of mirror image and original. In this complex grid of fetish functions, the tableau freezes into inanimateness. No submission, no oppression: "No movement but a minimum friction" (*V.* 409). In fact, gazes are the only carriers of this structure.[24] The scopic structuration of this tableau evokes Lacan's definition of the gaze as an object *o:* "The gaze may contain in itself the *objet a* of the Lacanian algebra" (*Fundamental Concepts* 76). The subject and the "other" are simultaneously connected and separated via the structure of the gaze, and the lack (of being) is made visible.[25] Yet here, with each image already a mirror image, the other as well as the self, the gazes can no longer affix themselves to an ego, even a permanently decentered one, but bounce from fetish to fetish in an endless doubling and redoubling. Instead of the "alienating identity," which ends the mirror stage, there is a complete dispersion, what Baudrillard calls an "endlessly reflected vision" (*Simulations* 144), without "anchoring points" (Lacan, *Écrits* 154) that might throw the subject out of its paralyzed passivity within the imaginary. Of course, the minimum friction also evokes death, and it is precisely at this point that Pynchon introduces the "master of the inanimate" as the final equivocator of the fetish function: "Dead at last, they would be one with the inanimate universe and with each other. Love-play until then thus becomes an impersonation of the inanimate, a transvestism not between sexes but between quick and dead; human and fetish" (*V.* 410)

The fetish posing as human and the human functioning as a fetish are the final transmutations within this scenario, which violently disrupts psychoanalysis in relation to its field of investigation. It can no longer be the science of a subject, because the line of demarcation runs no longer between subject and subject or subject and object but between two objects.

Pynchon thus displaces the Freudian concept of fetishism on various levels. First, he disconnects it from the male perspective and interlocks it with the system of lesbianism,[26] and, via V., with the machinic. He thus undermines one of Freud's basic contentions, the relation of fetishism to the fear of castration, although a shadow of this relation does persist and is taken up again within V. as the "braid cutter," hence castratrix, and an "androgynous" and hence partly male Mélanie: "One day the girl arrived at Le Nerf accompanied by the woman and wearing schoolboys' clothing.

[. . .] Moreover, her head—all her thick buttock-length hair—had been shorn. She was nearly bald [. . .] she might have been a young lad playing hooky" (*V*. 407).

In a second step Pynchon disrupts the level of relations between fetish and loved object, declaring, like Baudrillard, the loved object to be a fetish *in her entirety*. He takes elements of the Freudian system and leaving the basic definitions such as fetishism and homosexuality intact, but aligning them along different lines so that the initial displacements trigger and thus reveal a number of other displacements. What Pynchon disrupts in the first step is the internal structuration of the Freudian setup. That he also has his fun with Freud can be seen in the lovingly detailed speculations about the "64 different sets of roles" (*V*. 408) Mélanie and V. could enact in their triangular scenario.

In this second step, however—the equation of subject and fetish—Pynchon breaks open the difference between animate being, formerly the "loved object," and inanimate object, formerly "the fetish." From the male perspective, Freud's fetish object is an inanimate object that has a supplementary relation to the animate one. Pynchon's concept of the fetish describes instead the implosion of the animate object into the inanimate, thus blurring the initial difference between subject and object on which the Freudian binarism is based.

Only two of Mélanie's "interpellations" however, have been brought into play by now: "L'Heuremaudit," "the cursed hour," denoting the atemporality of Mélanie as an object, and "La Jarretière," "the garter belt," denoting her function as fetish object but also meaning, in a revealing twist of the French language, "conductor-wire." This "sexualization of science," and "scientization of sexuality," defines Mélanie in her role as Su Feng, the raped virgin in "L'Enlèvement des Vierges Chinoises."

Mélanie's final mirror stage, as depicted in this role, also differs in an important respect from Lacan's concept. Whereas a constant displacement underlies Lacan's mirror stage, a continuous and basic misapprehension that gets carried over into the symbolic, Pynchon defines this stage as an even more complete disruption. In Lacan, the "self" and "the other" constantly oscillate yet despite this oscillation, the notion of subjectivity, even if violently decentered, is still valid and in operation. In Pynchon's setup, these terms implode into each other, with the subject becoming an object in its totality. This "new scene," as differentiated from the psychoanalytic "other scene" of Freud, is adapted for the stage by Porcépic and Satin. Within it, all elements of the new triad are present: it is populated not only by male and female dancers but also—and this is the addition that disrupts the basic Freudian binarism—by automata. In this scene, the final implosion of "fetish and human, dead and quick," is acted out.

The climax of the ballet, depicting the rape of the virgin by Mongols, shows how Mélanie is impaled by the "entire male part of the company" (*V.* 413) while the women lament.[27] The phallic and psychoanalytic connotations are unmistakable here, and Pynchon is still working within the psychoanalytic structure he then sets out to deconstruct. Nonetheless, although this part of the drama directly implies the Freudian and Lacanian concept of the phallic signifier and contains in a nutshell the female position within Freudian and Lacanian theory, Pynchon provides the scene with yet another twist; the death that should have been only theatrically simulated becomes real: Mélanie "forgets" to wear her protective belt, "the one inanimate object that would have saved her" (*V.* 414). Because Mélanie is in her entirety a fetish, however, this real death is also one in which only a simulated human—a fetish—dies. Orchestrating this final disruption in an ironic sideshow, one of the automata on stage, whose lifelikeness had been so stunning—"But they move so gracefully! Not like machines at all" (*V.* 396)—runs amok and commits, apparently out of some sort of machinic solidarity with Mélanie, a symbolic suicide.

Within the growing chaos of the music, automaton and human finally merge in a modern *homme-machine*. The automaton acts human, while the human is revealed as having always already been an automaton, and it is only in death, within the final passage from animate to inanimate, that "the expression on the normally dead face" (*V.* 414) becomes haunting. The phallic and operational machine and the automaton switch places, taking on each other's characteristics within the chaos of the climactic music: "all tonal location had been lost, notes screamed out simultaneous and random like fragments of a bomb" (*V.* 414). While the automaton actively "toss[es] itself about the stage" (*V.* 413), Mélanie's movements get more passive, uncontrolled and "more spastic" (*V.* 414). Within this catastrophic moment the inanimate and the animate implode, and the scene tumbles out of the psychoanalytic framework into a machinic one, which can be read no longer in human parameters, Lacanian or otherwise, but only in machinic ones, and in which the "Name-of-the-Father"—the phallic instance of control and authority—is replaced by the "Name-" or "Law-of-the-Machine."

In *V.*, this "Law-of-the-Machine" takes over both the individual and the cultural field, annexing the body in both dimensions. The fetish, all workforce or all sign, is the signifier by which the culturally determined, sexual economy is inscribed onto the body via the semiotic code. It is the relay by which Baudrillard's "symbolic ambivalence" is replaced by a digital, phallic economy. The fetish as a signifier finally comes to designate the desire of the semiotic code itself: "Something like a desire, a perverse desire, the desire of the code is brought to light here" (Baudrillard, *Critique* 92). This transfer of desire onto the code replaces the body and the subject with the sign and the code, which becomes its own simulated real and relates back to the importance of objects (signs) and their oppositional structure: "It is the sign in this beauty, the mark . . . which fascinates; *it is the artifact that is the object of desire*" (*L'Échange symbolique* 94). In the same way as this exclusion of the subject creates for Mélanie the space for the display of all her clothes, which "take her place," for the text itself this exclusion creates a space in which Pynchon can stage "orgies of the signifier," which, in analogy, "take the place" of meaning, creating fetish countries of increasing complexity, which is where language is in complicity with fetishization.

Mélanie marks the nodal point between psychoanalysis and a purely simulatory phallic economy. In a simulatory society, the human body is split into two functions: an "economic" one (the robot) or—as in the case of Mélanie—an "ego-nomic" one (the mannequin). Within both spheres, however, it is a dead body that serves as the model.

In other parts of *V.*, Pynchon follows the sexually dead body into its equally dead culture. Like SHROUD and SHOCK, two more automata in *V.*, Mélanie and V., whose whole history describes her mechanization into a pure object, enter the inanimate and death-time. The deceptively idyllic, private scenery in which their love drama is acted out is embedded within a greater cultural analysis of tourism and its "colonial machine," which Pynchon calls "perhaps the most absolute communion we know on earth" (*V.* 409). This machine has the same relation to the cultures visited as man has to the fetish, so that fetishism is ultimately a *tourisme-à-deux*. It replaces and thus simulates the "other" within the self's own parameters, much in the same way in which the fetish replaces and thus simulates the phallus within the parameters of castration: "For as tourists bring into the world as it has evolved part of another, and eventually create a parallel society of their own in every city, so the Kingdom of Death is served by fetish-constructions like V.'s, which represent a kind of infiltration" (*V.* 411). The concept defining both movements is that of psychic and cultural colonization. It implies a gesture that radically alters and redefines objects according to specific operational parameters, a gesture that invades the "other," whom it redefines as a pure object.

V.: "V. in Love" 73

In *V.*, Pynchon carries this tendency to its two logical conclusions, at the end of which invariably lies a dead object.

> [V.] might have [. . .] come to establish eventually so many controls over herself that she became—to Freudian, behaviorist, man of religion, no matter—a purely determined organism, an automaton, constructed, only quaintly, of human flesh. Or by contrast, might have reacted against the above, which we have come to call Puritan, by journeying even deeper into a fetish-country until she became entirely and in reality—not merely as a love-game with any Mélanie—an inanimate object of desire. (*V.* 411)

Both trajectories, the *robot* of puritanism and the *fetish* of psychoanalysis, are defined by inanimateness, once in the change from subject to economic simulation within the social order, and once in the change from subject to fetish object, in which desire is dead because it is invariably implicated in the deadness of its object. Together, these two determinations insert the body inextricably into an operational grid, an ultimate molar machine, a purely operational Metropolis in which even the operators are machines: an industry of robots building other robots. Max Weber's critique and analysis in *The Protestant Ethic and the Spirit of Capitalism* is, of course, the early key text for Pynchon, but Baudrillard provides a later, parallel text:

> For the system of political economy, the *robot* is the ideal type of body. The robot is the ultimate model of the functional "liberation" of the body as work-force. It is the extrapolation of the absolutely rational, asexual productivity. . . . For the system of the political economy of the sign, the reference-model of the body is the *mannequin*. . . . As a contemporary of the robot, . . . the mannequin also represents a fully functionalized body. . . . What is produced is no longer the work-force but *sexuality itself as a model*. (*L'Échange symbolique* 177)

Similar perspectives open up for Profane and Stencil. What is at stake is the transformation of psychoanalysis into mechanics and simulation.[28] The limit of fetishism, and also the limit of psychoanalysis, is the individual as fetish and pure object. It is from this new perspective, presided over by the engineer, that Pynchon deconstructs psychoanalytic constellations. He exposes the inadequacy of psychoanalysis and its field, a field based on outdated assumptions, in the light of a new cultural arena. In a radical critique of humanistic patterns of explication, psychoanalysis is the first to fall. Appropriately, in the last extended image of V. in chapter 14, she stands metonymically for the new scene:

> at age seventy-six: skin radiant with the bloom of some new plastic; both eyes glass but now containing photoelectric cells, connected by silver electrodes to optic nerves of purest copper wire and leading to a brain exquisitely wrought as a diode matrix could ever be. Solenoid relays would be her ganglia, servo-actuators move her flawless nylon limbs, hydraulic fluid be sent by a platinum heartpump through butyrate veins and arteries. Perhaps [. . .] even a complex system of pressure transducers located in a marvelous vagina of polyethylene; the variable arms of their Wheatstone bridges all leading to a single silver cable which fed pleasure-voltages direct to the correct register of the *digital machine* in her skull. (*V.* 411–12; emphasis added)

The specter of simulation and the fetish weaves not only through this chapter but through the whole of *V.* At every conceivable and investigable angle, inanimate simulation enters and "replaces" the real. Profane's losing battle against his inanimate universe; Rachel's sexual relation with her sports car, which defines her as a part of the machine, with Profane "trying to find the key to her own ignition behind the hooded eyes" (*V.* 27); Fergus, the extension of the TV set; Esther's nose, which shows the passage from psychoanalysis into body engineering; Eigenvalue's dentures; the "inanimate buddies from Detroit" (*V.* 357); Profane's dream about an all-electronic woman ("Any problems with her, you could look it up in the maintenance manual. Module concept: fingers' weight, heart's temperature, mouth's size out of tolerance? Remove and replace, was all" [*V.* 385])—these all add up to a universe streaked through with the mechanical and the machinic. The female body, however, is a privileged site for this mutation. Being simultaneously the direct phallic object and the ultimately "other" of the phallic scene, woman is the first, but also the last, to fall prey to this mechanization.

Like the stage-setting *within* "V. in love," the text itself stages this invasion on the field of the signifier, the ultimate fetish and the ultimate (Derridean and Lacanian) "machine." It is this machine that McHoul and Wills evoke when they read Mélanie's fetishization (carefully excluding any Freudian or Lacanian reference) as her "becom[ing] part of a larger machine" (WP 182). Nonetheless, although they conclude with the Derridean argument that the fact of fetishization retroactively invalidates any idea(l) of naturality—because where should fetishization come from in a purely natural universe?—Pynchon, who has never claimed a purely natural realm, laments the shift from a human level to that of completely operational simulation, a shift related not so much to McHoul and Wills's optimistic idea that the fetish opens up "the possibility of transfer, ad infinitum" (WP 182) but to the death of desire and dream, the demise of the human and the advent of the dreamless machine. These losses are theorized and textually recovered within the text's desire, its thrust into signification, and the momentum that loads the signifiers with desire within the infinitesimal line of demarcation between reality and the real.

In another context, Roland Barthes has commented on this double movement and definition of the text as both *promise* and *denial,* linking it, as Pynchon does, to the female body. On the one hand, the text overcomes fetishization: "The subject . . . knows the female body only as a division and dissemination of partial objects: leg, breast, shoulder, neck, hands. . . . Divided, anatomized, she is merely a kind of dictionary of fetish objects. This sundered, dissected body . . . is reassembled by the artist . . . into a whole body, the body of love . . . in which fetishism is abolished" (*S/Z* 112). On the other hand, in that it is part of the code, the text itself is a fetish: "*The spitefulness of language:* once reassembled, in order to *utter* itself, the total body must revert to the dust of words, to the listing of details, to a monotonous inventory of parts, to crumbling: language undoes the body, returns it to the fetish . . . it accumulates in order to totalize, multiplies fetishes in order to obtain a total, defetishised body" (113–14).

In *The Pleasure of the Text,* Barthes further extends this function to the reader: "The text is a fetish object, and *this fetish desires me*" (27). Pynchon's poetics are defined within these dynamics. Aware that the text is always already this supplement, Pynchon constantly carries it to its own limit, to the limits of reading as well as writing.[29] What remains for the text is to be a site on which to voice the *desire* for the "real" and the "whole body." That it is always already implicated within writing, and never quite "real" itself, however, opens up the question of its desire for its own termination within its desire to signify.

Through this fetishistic aspect of the text, the *real* machines *in* the text are aligned with the *symbolic* machine *of* the text. It is in their fateful and tragic complicity, rather than in the idea of a liberating, endless detour, that *V.* and V.—writing and the written-about—finally merge.

Notes

1. Compare also the character of Callisto in "Entropy." Pynchon's device ultimately derives from Henry Adams's *Education of Henry Adams*.

2. In *Discipline and Punish* Foucault presents a broad panorama of the history of political power hinged on its penal technologies, a panorama that mirrors the development from virtù to simulation in *V*. Foucault proceeds from a Bakhtinian and Machiavellian "carnival" (61) of power and then traces the shift from a power that operates directly on the physical body to one that "insert[s itself] . . . more deeply into the social body" (82), a shift that makes it necessary to "define a strategy and techniques of punishment in which an economy of continuity and permanence would replace that of expenditure and excess" (87). This power is depersonalized, directed against not only the guilty person but "all the potentially guilty" (108). It is "a modest, suspicious power, which functions as a calculated, but permanent economy" (170) encompassing even those who work within its structure. The development of this anonymous power goes hand in hand with the emergence of a vast apparatus and network of control, which on a visual level is defined by an apparatus of surveillance, the panopticon. On the other hand, the surveillance is a written one, "an immense police text . . . [that covers] society by means of a complex documentary organization" (214). Ultimately, power—as punishment—is completely separated from the specific crime and becomes synonymous with the individual who does not follow the norms of society (183). What forms "the case" is not a specific criminal action but rather the subject in its totality—and by extension, the world itself.

3. See also my "Short Note on Pynchon's Sources for 'The Firm,'" *Pynchon Notes* 15 (1984): 77–79.

4. See also my "Godolphin, Goodolphin, Goodol'phin, Goodol'Pyn, Good ol' Pym: A Question of Integration."

5. Compare Lacan's statement that "it is man who introduces the notion of asymmetry. Asymmetry in nature is neither symmetrical, nor asymmetrical—it is what it is" (*Seminar II* 38).

6. Lacan links the machinic to the structure of the *symbolic:* "In as much as he is committed to a play of symbols . . . man is a decentered subject. Well, it is with this same play, this same world, that the machine is built. The most complicated machines are made only with words" (*Seminar II* 47). The difference between a subject and a machine, however, is that the subject has a specific—even if violently decentered—relation to itself. Two machines, each constructed so as to react only to each other's intervention, still cannot function as subjects. The messages within the machine operate on a binary level ("What is a message inside a machine? Something which proceeds by opening and not opening" [89]) and thus are congruent with the neuronic structure of the brain, as well as with the differential nature of language. Yet "for something to become established, it would require the presence

of a third, placed inside the machine . . . pronouncing an *I*. . . . This third party is what we find in the unconscious" (52). The prerequisite is thus that the machine be able "to count itself" (56). On another level, Lacan uses the machinic in opposition to the visual and links it to a specific verbal syntax: "Cybernetics is a science of syntax, and it is in a good position to help us perceive that the exact sciences do nothing other than tie the real to a syntax" (305). Although the machine is especially apt for dealing with symbolic structures, its imaginary use is more difficult because the machine lacks the ability to relate to images: "With the machine, we never produce an effect founded on a simplicity of the same order—it is always through the most complex, the most artificial compositions, by a point-by-point sweeping of space, a scanning" (316).

7. In his discussion of Hegel in "The Pit and the Pyramid" (in *Margins of Philosophy*), Derrida uses the field of mathematics and arithmetic, as a science of pure differences, to play a counterpoint to Hegelian dialectics. Against the Hegelian ideal of the play of signifieds and its moral and didactic implications, Derrida sets the play of the signifiers themselves. To do so, he evokes the image of a "pure machine" as a system whose parts cannot be "canceled" within a higher unity: "a machine, perhaps, and one which would function. A machine defined in its pure functioning, and not in its final utility, its meaning, its result, its work. . . . What Hegel . . . *could never think* is a machine that would work. That would work without, to this extent, being governed by an order of reappropriation" (107). Within such a machine, no synthesis could reappropriate the pure movement of the signifieds *as* signifiers in a self-referential production machine.

8. Deleuze and Guattari see the molar machines as a conglomeration of molecular machines under determinate—one could also say operational—conditions: "By 'determinate conditions' we mean those statistical forms into which the machines enter as so many stable forms, unifying, structuring, and proceeding by means of large, heavy aggregates; the selective pressures that group the parts retain some of them and exclude others. . . . These are therefore the same machines, but not at all the same régime. . . . It is only at the submicroscopic level of desiring-machines that there exists a functionalism—machinic arrangements, an engineering of desire. . . . Only what is not produced in the same way it functions has a meaning, and also a purpose, an intention. The desiring-machines on the contrary represent nothing, signify nothing, mean nothing" (*Anti-Oedipus* 287–88). In both molar and molecular machines, the subject is the excluded term. In the former it is defined as a pure machine; in the latter, as a pure body.

9. "Desire does not lack anything; it does not lack its object. It is, rather, the *subject* that is missing in desire, or desire that lacks a fixed subject; there is no fixed subject unless there is repression" (Guattari and Deleuze, *Anti-Oedipus* 26). For Felix Guattari, this elision of the subject entails a replacement of the Lacanian "*objet petit a* [the object *o*]" by an "*objet-machine petit 'a'*" (*Molecular Revolution* 115) and of Lacan's definition of the signifier as "that which represents the subject for

another signifier" (*Écrits* 316) by "a pure signifying space where the machine would represent the subject for another machine" (*Molecular Revolution* 117–18).

10. The *raison d'être* of operational simulation is to gain complete control. In a simulated universe, analogous to fetish constructions, the simulated real becomes a supplement and a signifier. "It becomes the real for the real, fetish of the lost object [the real]—no longer object of representation, but ecstasy of denegation and of its own ritual extermination: the hyperreal" (Baudrillard, *Simulations* 142). The result is a merely *"hallucinatory resemblance of the real with itself"* (142).

11. The whole chapter is a pastiche of the éclat surrounding the premiere of Stravinsky's *Le Sacre du printemps* in Paris in 1913, which provides the chapter's constant subtext. Porcépic, Satin, and Itague represent Stravinsky, Nijinsky, and Diaghilev, respectively. While Stravinsky was working on *Le Sacre du printemps*—a ballet about the sacrifice of a young girl to the god of spring—he was also working on *Petruschka,* a ballet about an automaton inspired by a "vision of a mannequin, which suddenly comes to life and tests the patience of the orchestra through the diabolic arpeggio of its jumps, so much that it [the orchestra] finally threatens it with fanfares" (Stravinsky, quoted in Burde, *Strawinsky* 68). In "Entropy," Pynchon again uses Stravinsky as a reference. This time he refers to his *L'Histoire du Soldat* (SL 93).

12. "'A decadence,' Itague put in, 'is a falling-away from what is human, and the further we fall the less human we become. Because we are less human, we foist off the humanity we have lost on inanimate objects and abstract theories'" (*V.* 405).

13. In almost every theoretical field the fetish has come to stand for something lifeless and immobile. Victor Burgin describes its characteristics of "petrification, ossification, glaciation" (*The End of Art Theory* 106). In *Psychoanalysis and Cinema,* Christian Metz sees the apparatus itself, "the cinema in its *physical* state" (75), as the cinematographic fetish.

14. "The situation only becomes pathological when the longing for the fetish ... actually *takes the place* of the normal aim, and, further, when the fetish becomes detached from a particular individual and becomes the *sole* sexual object" ("Three Essays on the Theory of Sexuality," *The Standard Edition* 7:154).

15. Lacan's statement that "a letter always arrives at its destination" ("Purloined Letter" 53) actually "returns" the signifier to its position of subversion/castration *in* and *to* the woman. As a *signifier of lack,* woman becomes the support of male writing, the enigmatic surface onto which male writing is projected.

16. Lacan links the sexual to the textual scene by defining the phallus as "the signifier intended to designate as a whole the effects of the signified, in that the signifier conditions them by its presence as a signifier" (*Écrits* 285). As such, it is "the bar which ... strikes the signified" (288). Both males and females are affected by its function. For the male, for example, "to have" the phallus does not mean "to be" the phallus, it merely means "to seem" (289) to be the phallus in an attempt to "protect it ... and to mask its lack" (289). For a detailed discussion of these

relations see Ragland-Sullivan, "The Sexual Masquerade," in Ragland-Sullivan and Mark Bracher, eds., *Lacan and the Subject of Language* 49–80.

17. The phallic alienation of woman from herself is carried to its limit within striptease, the scenario in which the complete woman, and not only some of her attributes, is turned into a fetish object. In ratio to the gradual discarding of her clothes and the corresponding uncovering of her body, the female subject vanishes completely while a purely male hallucination takes its place, her autoerotic caresses becoming caresses of herself as phallus within the two basic positions of striptease: voyeurism and fetishism.

18. In *The Medium Is the Massage,* Marshall McLuhan comments on a photograph of two crossed female legs in net stockings: "When information is brushed against information . . . ," showing the double definition of the erotics of the code and the code of erotics. Baudrillard sees a similar convergence: "Within the general equivalent of the phallus-cult, the body has become a total sign-system, organized by operative models" (*L'Échange symbolique* 173).

19. The pun on the French *délire* ("delirium," but also suggesting *de lire,* "of reading") is especially apt here. Lace indeed produces an intricately woven "erotic text."

20. In his analysis of "Little Hans" ("Analysis of a Phobia in a Five-Year-Old Boy," *Standard Edition* 10:1–147), Freud had already stressed the fact that the phallus served the child as a clue to the problem of the animateness/inanimateness of objects. The shift from the human to object to machine can thus proceed especially well along these lines.

21. For Lacan, both the male and the female narcissistic object is a "heteroclite mannequin, a baroque doll, a trophy of limbs" (*Schriften II* 69). Relating directly to his notion of the mirror stage, these artifacts are "statues" in everybody's psychic landscape. It is only from the female perspective, however, that this doll overlaps with the phallic doll that she herself becomes within the sexual arena.

22. "La Jarretière" evokes again the scene in which Mélanie contemplates her body in the overhead mirror and is related to the line between thigh and nylon constituted by the garter belt.

23. This image is reminiscent of the mirror gallery shootout scene from Orson Welles's *Lady from Shanghai,* its play with differing planes of reality and the emphasis it places on the difficulty of shooting at the right image, the real object.

24. Pynchon gives the Freudian reference himself: "Had they [. . .] read [. . .] in the new science of the mind, they would have known that certain fetishes never have to be touched or handled at all; only seen, for there to be complete fulfillment" (*V.* 408). The immediate reference here is to the famous "*Glanz auf der Nase* [*shine* on the nose]," which really was a "*glance* at the nose" (Freud, "Fetishism," *Standard Edition* 21:152).

25. Lacan uses the anamorphosis in Holbein's painting *The Ambassadors* to illustrate the difference between the *eye* and the *gaze.* The eye denotes the abstract

geometrical structure of visual space and its visualization by the laws of the central perspective. The subject functions as a mere perspective point and thus comes to symbolize the "Cartesian subject" (*Fundamental Concepts* 86), that "punctiform being" (96) *outside* the image system from which the image is projected. What is at issue in geometrical perspective is "simply the mapping of space, not sight" (86). In *The Ambassadors,* both the image and the anamorphosis are structured according to the rules of the eye. The important thing is that in the painting two points of perspective are superimposed on the canvas so that the two images are not legible simultaneously. For the eye, the painting is a paradox: it sees either the image (and the skull as a stain) *or* the skull (and the image as a stain). This paradox can be solved only by the gaze, which denotes the subject's position and movements *within* visual space and its perception, "the depths of field, with all its ambiguity and variability, which is in no way mastered by [it]" (96). In the last "gaze" that the subject casts back at the painting—an effect carefully engineered by the specific position of the painting in the room in which it was originally hung—it can *solve* the riddle of the painting. The gaze, while it subverts the clarity of the system of the central perspective, allows the subject to come into being, the subject *within* the image system, which denotes the position of desire, in which the images are not purely geometrical forms but objects *o,* and as such representatives of the lack-of-being, for which the skull is a worthy *memento.*

26. Again, Pynchon gives the Freudian reference himself: "Lesbianism, we are prone to think in this Freudian period of history, stems from self-love projected on to some other human object" (*V.* 407). He might be referring to any one or several of Freud's texts, for example, "On Narcissism: An Introduction": "perverts and homosexuals . . . have taken as their model not the mother but their own selves" (*Standard Edition* 14:88). In "Leonardo da Vinci and a Memory of His Childhood," Freud makes a similar statement: "and he takes his own person as a model in whose likeness he chooses the new object of his love . . . he finds the objects of his love along the path of *narcissism*" (*Standard Edition* 11:100). Freud combines this theme with two others that are also important in Pynchon's chapter, the fetishistic adoration of the female foot or shoe and the motif of the braid-cutter: "Fetishistic reverence for a woman's foot and shoe appears to take the foot merely as a substitutive symbol for the woman's penis which was once revered and later missed; without knowing it, . . . [the 'braid-cutters'] play the part of people who carry out an action of castration on the female genital organ" (*Standard Edition* 11:96).

27. Pynchon provides a similarly "harsh" image of this relation in *Gravity's Rainbow.* During an orgy on the *Anubis,* "a girl with an enormous glass dildo inside which baby piranhas are swimming in some kind of decadent lavender medium amuses herself between the buttocks of a stout transvestite in lace stockings and a dyed sable coat" (GR 468).

28. In chapter 11 of *V.,* the "Confessions of Fausto Maijstral," Pynchon shows the relation of the engineer not to psychoanalysis but to poetics. Dnubietna, the

poet, "reverses" into "Anteibund(t)" (Latin for "they will progress"), the engineer of empty progress who ends up building roads in America. The counterweight is Fausto, the fragmented humanist who tries to re-create the lost unity in his poetry.

29. In this respect see also Madsen: "The dual function of V as both *figura* and allegoric pretext prevents the totalization of meaning because V represents only fragmentary aspects of a total pretextual discourse" (52).

Chapter 5   *The Crying of Lot 49:*
            Writing the Subject

"In the beginning, in principle, was the post."
Jacques Derrida, *The Post Card*

"On errands of life, these letters speed to death."
Herman Melville, "Bartleby the Scrivener"

In *The Crying of Lot 49,* Pynchon shifts from the "science fiction" of *V.* to a more direct "writing of the subject"—from the fantastic scenarios of *V.* to the description of the phantasmatic quality of reality itself.[1]

Although chronologically correct, the passage from *V.* to *The Crying of Lot 49* is in many aspects more difficult than a direct move ahead to *Gravity's Rainbow,* because *Lot 49* differs in some important aspects from the two other books. Most obviously, it does not present vast historical panoramas but provides a specific and detailed view of the California of the sixties, although this proves to be a continually punctured surface into which history seeps. To use an image from the movies, Pynchon's strategy resembles the procedure of Deckart in *Blade Runner* or Tommy in *Blow Up,* who both take a snapshot of a scene and reveal the seemingly invisible by scanning, probing, and enlarging the image, and in the case of *Blade Runner,* actually entering photographic space.

A second difference is that Oedipa Maas is without doubt Pynchon's "roundest" character prior to those in *Vineland*. This roundness, however, does not diminish her "textuality" (a fact that makes her especially interesting for a complementary reading). Oed, her nickname, is—probably not accidentally—the acronym of the *Oxford English Dictionary,* as well as the German word for sad and lonely *(öd)*, the word T. S. Eliot quotes from *Tristan and Isolde* in *The Waste Land*. In fact, Pynchon's California is a postmodern, cybernetic wasteland. In my reading, I trace Pynchon's portrayal of the gradual decomposition of this cybernetic space—a process that entails the dissemination of its inhabitants—as well as the multiple entropies at work in it. On the other hand, I am also concerned with the protagonist's desire for a metaphysical intrusion into this cyberspace and Pynchon's sociopolitical dissection of a binary, and thus imaginary, universe.

One of the most important models for *Lot 49*, a book that deals at length with the subject of cultural iconicity, is Orson Welles's film *Citizen Kane*, a work of art that has itself become a cultural icon (not the least by making cultural iconicity its main subject). There is, however, one main difference between *Citizen Kane* and *Lot 49,* a difference that might well be decisive. The solution to "Rosebud," Welles's "mystery signifier," is singled out for the camera, and thus for the spectator, in the epilogue. This gesture completes the *thematic* cycle of Freudian references in the movie, which starts with a scene from Kane's youth in which his mother is singled out as the primary "lost object." In the closing shot, Welles takes up this thematic completion on the formal level, ending the film with the camera "revers[ing] the path it took at the beginning of the picture" (Mankiewicz and Welles 299). Welles thus has it both ways. Within the frame of the story the mystery remains, while outside it, it is solved. This oscillation is sustained by Welles's reliance on the camera as a diegetic device. When everybody has left Xanadu, and the only gaze is that of the spectator of the movie, the camera, or "omniscient recorder"—smoother and more unobtrusive than an omniscient narrator could ever be—zooms in on the one detail that solves the puzzle of Kane's life and thus provides a frame of reading.

In contrast, although Pynchon follows this model on the *formal* level by circling back to the book's title in the last sentence, he resists such a closure on the level of *content;* unlike "Rosebud," the question of the "Trystero" remains open even beyond the termination of the text.

The radicality with which *Lot 49* withholds an interpretative frame calls for a parallel radicalization of reading. The text, in which several frames of reference constantly overlap, invites ontological, epistemological, and sociocultural readings equally. Rather than focus on one specific angle, I will therefore read *Lot 49* as a textual site on which various readings intersect.

Like *Citizen Kane, Lot 49* is heavily invested in the cultural background from which it emerges and contains countless references to aspects of both high and low culture. As in *Citizen Kane,* however, the selection of these cultural images is anything but eclectic. Almost all of them, as Tanner has pointed out, are "concerned with . . . aspects of communication—voices, postal systems, postage stamps, newspapers, books, radio, TV, telephones, signs on walls, acronyms, drawings, doodlings" (*Pynchon* 63), which provides another parallel to *Citizen Kane.* Although Pynchon's main theoretical reference is doubtlessly McLuhan, this indebtedness to almost every conceivable network of communication[2] also opens up *Lot 49* to a Baudrillardian reading, because for Baudrillard as well, it is in the realm of the media that the subject and simulation collide most forcefully. The media are the main carriers of simulation and (in their growing expansion, which entails that an ever-increasing amount of the real *becomes* the media) the main area in which the real is reconstituted as a simulation. The shift from an industrial to a postindustrial, cybernetic society implies a shift from alienation to the "ecstasy of communication" (Baudrillard, *Fatal Strategies* 67). In fact, although they describe the same symptoms, Baudrillard's theory implies a radical critique of McLuhan's "cybernetic idealism," the "blind faith in radiating information, [and the] mystique of information services and the media (*Critique* 199).[3]

For Baudrillard, media simulation affects the subject on various levels. One main interface between them is the subject's body: "we no longer exist as playwrights or actors but as terminals of multiple networks" (*Ecstasy* 16). If in the second order of simulacra the body had already turned into a *"metaphor,"* now, with the modern media, it has become a screen, a fact already noted by McLuhan: "With TV, the viewer is the screen" (*Understanding Media* 334).

This insertion into various networks of communication makes the "real" body as obsolete as the entire real, so that Baudrillard can, in fact, equate these two fields: "The real itself appears as a large, futile body" (*Ecstasy* 18). The experience of reality is no longer grounded in a passage from objects to their representation. Via the media, the objects are "object images" from the very start. As part of the greater simulation structure, the media are no longer mimetic. The relation between "the image and its referent, the supposed real" (*Evil Demon* 13), has in fact been reversed. In the same way in which economic simulation creates objects that originate in *models,* the media images produce *models* of events and thus "precede the real to the extent that they invert the causal and logical order of the real and its reproduction" (13). Like economic objects, events no longer have any inherent meaning, because "they have been preceded by models with which their own process can only coincide" (22). Ultimately, "images become more real than the real" (30).

Pynchon's most powerful symbol of this reversal is television. In a manner similar to the way that *V.* traces how simulation destroys the realm of dreams on a *machinic* level, *Lot 49* follows the colonization and contamination of the subject's dreams via the *media*, especially television, which not only constantly intrudes into "real life" but also "comes into your *dreams*, you know. Filthy machine" (*Lot 49* 91; emphasis added). In fact, television not only *intrudes* into dreams, it actually *produces* and *simulates* them, in a feedback that ultimately conflates psychic and televised space.

Whereas *Citizen Kane* is still set in a "theatrical" universe, Pynchon's choice of television as a metaphor of simulation mirrors Baudrillard's differentiation between television and film. Although the cinematic image is still "something that belongs to the sphere of the double, the phantasm, the mirror, the dream" (*Evil Demon* 25), television is "only a screen" (25). On one hand, this differentiation is based on the differing spaces of television and film. Unlike film, which still has its own "theatrical" space in the cinema, television has become so much a part of everyday reality that it is always already in the position of reality. On the other hand, the differentiation lies in the quality of the produced images. Whereas film images are based on an *analog* structure, the television image has passed through a process of *digitalization*, producing an image of reality that has been decomposed and then artificially recomposed according to digital operations. This specter of digitality, which had already defined the fully mechanical version of V., underlies all of *Lot 49*. When a spray can flies through the room, for instance, Oedipa thinks that only "God or a digital machine" (*Lot 49* 37) could measure its erratic path.

The mingling of reality and simulation, or real and televised space, finds its most convoluted staging in the scene in which Oedipa and Metzger make love with and in front of the television, the apparatus McLuhan had already understood as "the most recent and spectacular electric extension of our central nervous system" (*Understanding Media* 338). Pynchon seems to draw on this implosion when, in a libidinal short-circuiting of television and reality, he stages what Baudrillard calls the ultimate "collusion between images and life, between the screen and daily life" (*Evil Demon* 27). Oedipa's and Metzger's "Strip Botticelli"—itself a game based on a digital yes/no structure—is "tuned to" the fragmented reels of a television film that stars Metzger as a boy-actor: "So it went: the succession of film fragments on the tube, the progressive removal of clothing"

(*Lot 49* 41). The scene ends with the complete "implosion of image and reality" (*Evil Demon* 27); their orgasms coincide with that of the electronic image machine. In this meeting of human and machinic *jouissance*, human and electronic levels are conflated within a sexual agenda: "Her climax and Metzger's, when it came, coincided with every light in the place, including the TV tube, suddenly going out, dead, black" (*Lot 49* 42).

In fact, the scene might well be read the other way around, because in humankind's use of technologies to supplement bodily functions, any invention or technology can be understood as "an extension or self-amputation of our physical bodies" (McLuhan, *Understanding Media* 55), so that humanity "becomes, as it were, the sex organs of the machine world" (56). Technological development has created a space in which inside and outside have become reversible and in which the subject's psychic space is constantly endangered by the conflation of a simulated and therefore imaginary real and the "true" imaginary.

Baudrillard's theory of simulation is also relevant to Pynchon's description of San Narciso, the city that stands metonymically for postmodern cyberspace. Pynchon's fictional city is, like Los Angeles for Baudrillard, a town "whose mystery is precisely that it is nothing more than a network of endless, unreal circulation" (Baudrillard, *Simulations* 26). For both, the modern city is no longer "a space of the production and the distribution [*réalisation*] of merchandise." Rather, it is—in both senses of the word— "a space of the *execution* of the sign" (*L'Échange symbolique* 119; emphasis added). As such, its decentralized pattern becomes a cipher for and comes to reflect the discursive space of differentiating signs. The city becomes an endlessly disseminating text. San Narciso is in the first instance just such a complex agglomeration of multiple networks of sign systems, whose interweaving results in a complicated grid of superimposed levels of reality. This moiré is mirrored in the discursive maze of *Lot 49*, in which discourses are constantly grafted onto each other, as in the summary of the *Courier's Tragedy*, which is "related near to unintelligible by eight memories unlooping progressively" (*Lot 49* 64).

Appropriately, in *Lot 49*, visual/imaginary and textual/symbolic simulation constantly overlap. Pynchon describes the symbolic aspect of *Lot 49* and the simulations operative in it by using the postal system—the official institution of the displacement of signs—as its main structural metaphor. Along this motif, which stresses the disseminating power of the play of differences, *Lot 49* can be linked up with Derrida, which is what McHoul and Wills do in *Writing Pynchon*. If, as Derrida claims, "the signified is originarily and essentially . . . *always already in the position of the signifier*" (*Of Grammatology* 73), the possibility of an infinite play of the signifier is opened up within discourse,[4] because no signification can be returned to the level of a stable and natural signified but glides endlessly within the passage from signifier to signifier. Whereas the signified had always functioned as a point of origin that stopped the regression of meaning through the signifier, recuperating the originary unity on which thought could double back onto itself, Derridean *différance* refers the idea of a stable signified both to the (synchronic) differences between the signifiers as well as to the temporal (diachronic) deferral of the origin. It "simultaneously splits and defers presence, by submitting it in one stroke to the originary division and the originary delay" (*La Voix* 98). On one level, then, the cyberspace of *Lot 49* could be understood as a symbol of dissemination and could become a textual space in which "poetic language" can unfold:

> Th[e] revelatory power of true literary language as poetry is indeed the access to free speech, speech unburdened of its signalizing functions by the word "Being." . . . It is when that which is written is *deceased* as a sign-signal that it is born as language; for then it says what is, thereby referring only to itself, a sign without signification, a game or pure functioning, since it ceased to be *utilized* as natural, biological, or technical information, or as the transition from one existent to another, from a signifier to a signified. (Derrida, *Writing and Difference* 12)

By thus closing off poetic language from any relation to an outside determination, be it social, biological, natural or cultural, Derrida can define poetic language as a nonpragmatic "writing-machine," a purely self-reflexive system of notation that refers only to itself in its function of signifier and that arouses speech "from its slumber as sign" (*Writing and Difference* 12): writing restored to its "original" vocation. This polymorphously perverse language again evokes a purely textual *jouissance*. Poetic language becomes a (utopian) space in which signifiers and signifieds (the constantly deferred "functions of the signifier") can operate without the interference of a stable meaning in a constant play of differences, in which the "anthropomorphized phoneme" does not search for presence but finds its arena in the horizontality of re-presentation, the experience of "the endless derivation of the signs, which wander about and change their scenes (*Verwandlung*), chaining the representations together (*Vergegenwärtigungen*), without beginning or end" (*La Voix* 116).

In this context, Derrida's *Post Card* is a perfect parallel text to *Lot 49*, because in it, Derrida juxtaposes poetic language with the language of power in a "conceit" parallel to the one Pynchon uses in *Lot 49*. As does *Lot 49*, *The Post Card* uses the notion of the postal system to symbolize culture and its various modes of exchange: "All kinds of cultural, that is postal, relays" (100). Like Pynchon, Derrida sees in the postal system the privileged site of the system of power, especially in the light of a growing uniformity and de-individualization, which Derrida compares to the disappearance of individual messages in an increasingly anonymous, corporate network: "The progressive disappearance of private mail and . . . [the] terror before the 'collective' envelope" (105). In fact, Derrida links the "postal technology" (104) to the same forces that underlie *Lot 49:* "The conjoint development of capitalism, Protestantism, and postal rationalism . . . are necessarily linked. The post is a banking agency" (138–39). This aspect of *The Post Card* allows for a complementary reading with *Lot 49*, but Derrida's idea of the postcard as the deconstruction of this mailing system and his vision of a culture with a completely free and thus poetic circulation of signs, "post-psychoanalytic and post-postal" (123) constitute a utopia that finds its dark double in the "Inamorati Anonymous" of *Lot 49*. In a culture of telecommunications, questions of power, control, and the flow of information are certainly too closely connected to allow belief in the disseminating power of postcards. Whereas Derrida counters the postal language of power with the postcard (of which his book is, of course, one example), the use of the postal system in *Lot 49* brings Pynchon to the very center of these complex relations.

Rather than just show the dissemination of the (inter)text, Pynchon stages the confrontation of the mortal subject with the immortal, atemporal, and disseminating text. The framework of inheritance is especially apt for this project because it is the system of inheritance that regulates the passing on of cultural material—as well as, metaphorically, the signifying chain—from one subject to the next, ensuring that each new subject is never originary but only the trace of former subjects, in the same way in which a signifier is defined within a network of traces of other signifiers. From the start, Pierce's "last will" links writing not only to dissemination but also to death.[5]

Fittingly, *Lot 49* starts with a reference to communication, the letter and the voice and their respective links to death. "One summer afternoon" (*Lot 49* 9), Oedipa receives a letter from the lawyers of Pierce Inverarity informing her that she has been named executrix of his estate. The last she had heard of her former lover was a phone call whose "origin, intention, extension—all are insolubly ambiguous" (Tanner, *Pynchon* 57) and that sounds like the result of an erratic switching between several telephone lines: "a voice beginning in heavy Slavic tones as second secretary at the Transylvanian Consulate, looking for an escaped bat; modulated to comic-Negro, then on into hostile Pachuco dialect, full of chingas and maricones; then a Gestapo officer asking her in shrieks did she have relatives in Germany and finally his Lamont Cranston voice" (*Lot 49* 11).

This call already defines Pierce, the originator of Oedipa's quest, as a mere compound and reflection of various cultural icons and a switchboard of various discursive frameworks. His constant shifting of voices hides a more basic void and exposes his personality as being always already an impersonation.

This phone call is simultaneously a first clue that any attempt to order Pierce's legacy will be doomed to fail. Pierce is not an original person but a cultural simulacrum, an extension of culture in the same way in which the cars that Mucho's customers exchange are "dented, malfunctioning version[s]" of their owners and, as such, "automotive projection[s] of somebody else's li[ves]" (*Lot 49* 14). A return to a real Pierce is not possible; every approach to his personality entails a deflection into cultural space, a dynamics that in a very Derridean gesture puts every utopia of a return to a stable origin under erasure, because every meaning one might want to attach to Pierce is endlessly—and hopelessly—deferred. But Pierce is not the only one defined as a cultural matrix; Oedipa herself is the result of a similar inscription into and encoding by culture. It is, therefore, highly ironic that her affair with Pierce had been an attempt to escape this very inscription, her existence as a "prisoner among the pines and salt fogs of Kinneret" (*Lot 49* 20).

In an important strategic gesture, Pynchon shifts Oedipa's first revelation to a time *before* the actual story starts, describing her *present* situation as the result of an "insulation" (*Lot 49* 20) against this more primary revelation. Pierce's death triggers memories of this initial, repressed scene—mainly, his failed attempt to free her from her own ego, the instance along which this inscription is regulated and in which Oedipa felt caught, like Rapunzel in her tower: "All that had then gone on between them had really never escaped the confinement of that tower" (*Lot 49* 20).

Because Pynchon describes Oedipa's ego as an *effect* rather than an originary unity and entity in this scene, Lacan's topography of the mirror stage provides once again a useful reference. In fact, whereas Mélanie, Profane, and Stencil can be defined only "against" the mirror stage, Oedipa is defined "within" it. For Lacan, the ego is the set of forces that forms the identity of the subject and around which the subject stabilizes itself.[6] Nevertheless, this ego is not an originary core of the subject; not a prereflexive entity but the result of a reflection. It is constructed during the narcissistic identifications and confrontations of the infant with its own mirror image, as well as with the images of others. Through the concept of the mirror stage, Lacan describes the visual structure within which the (preverbal) infant develops the instance of the ego—the image it has of itself. The concept describes the formation of the ego and defines it as an essentially fragmented, hallucinated entity connected to a *"function of méconnaissance* [misrecognition] that characterizes . . . [it] in all its structures" (*Écrits* 6).

Because of a specifically human *"prematurity of birth"* (*Écrits* 4), the infant's confrontation with its mirror image can never lead to a perfect mapping. It results rather in an always "alienating identification" (128) that simultaneously inaugurates the *double* and the *ego*. In fact, it inaugurates the ego *as* the double, a twofold dynamics that is the reason for a specific "ontological structure of the human world that accords with . . . [Lacan's] reflections on paranoiac knowledge" (2). For Lacan, every perception, and therefore human reality, is invariably a distortion or anamorphosis of the real and thus paranoiac in nature: reality is the "grimace of the real" (*Television* 6). Clinical paranoia is only an extreme case of this paranoia of perception. For Lacan, the ego is ontologically ruptured and split. Within the imaginary, the mirror functions as the plane along which this split is executed.

Lacan provides another structuration of this visual field in his *Seminar I*, in which he focuses on the way in which instinctual/bodily agencies are translated into and represented within the perceptual apparatus developed during the mirror stage. He furthermore conceptualizes how libidinal forces affect the visual arena and the extent to which visual space is itself invariably libidinal. The interplay of the real objects and their imaginary images engineers the more or less successful optical mapping of the external images of the world and *our* internal images of this world.

> Think of the mirror as a plane of glass. You'll see yourself in the glass and you'll see the objects beyond it. That's exactly how it is—it's a coincidence between certain images and the real . . . a specific relation between our images and images. . . . This is nothing other than the images of the human body, and the hominisation of the world,

its perception in terms of images linked to the structuration of the body. The real objects, which pass via the mirror, and through it, are in the same place as the imaginary object. The essence of the image is to be invested by the libido. (*Seminar I* 141)

Lacan's objective is twofold. On the one hand, he wants to prove the impossibility of the unity of the subject, which results from its inscription into a specific visual structure; on the other hand, he wants to show the impossibility of a prereflexive ego, which results from the fact that it is a reflection that inaugurates the ego in the first place. It is not the ego that structures the visual scene; rather, it is the visual scene that structures the ego. This scene is the matrix in whose structure the "*I* is precipitated in a primordial form" (*Écrits* 2).

The mirror stage thus has two important results. The first is that every kind of knowledge, whether of oneself, others, or objects, is inevitably "paranoiac" (*Écrits* 2) because it originates in a projection of narcissistically and therefore libidinously charged and structured images onto the original object. "The specular image is the channel taken by the transfusion of the body's libido towards the object" (319). Second, the ego is "originarily" split along the axis of the "mirror of perception."

Oedipa's first revelation takes place exactly within these parameters. During her affair with Inverarity, Oedipa is confronted with the ontological impossibility of escape from (the tower of) her ego. While in Mexico with him, standing in front of a painting, she has a first revelation, maybe the most important one:

> In the central painting of a triptych, titled "Bordando el Manto Terrestre," were a number of frail girls with heart-shaped faces, huge eyes, spun-gold hair, prisoners in the top room of a circular tower, embroidering a kind of tapestry which spilled out the slit windows and into a void, seeking hopelessly to fill the void: for all the other buildings and creatures, all the waves, ships and forests of the earth were contained in this tapestry, and the tapestry was the world. (*Lot 49* 21)

Oedipa suddenly sees the scene as an allegorical mirror of herself. *She* is one of the frail girls, and the tower the ego that imprisons her. The structure of the painting, which is itself another "allegory of belatedness," reveals her as one of the girls, as always already a part of the tapestry she is weaving. She sits in a tower and weaves a tapestry that is the world. The tower in which she sits, however, is itself a part of this world, so that she is always already woven into the world she is weaving. Weaving the world, she weaves herself. The painting thus becomes a perfect allegory of the reflexive space and the "symbolic matrix" (*Écrits* 2) in which Lacan describes the construction of the ego, as well as, in extension, the symbolic space of the subject, whose nature, Lacan had said, "is woven by effects in which is to be found the structure of language." In the "prison-house of language," the subject who is itself a function of the signifier weaves a world of signifiers. But, always already, the signifiers have intercepted the subject from behind.

In her first mirror encounter, Oedipa realizes three things: (1) the structural matrix of her ego; (2) the fact that she will never be able to escape this ego, that whatever she perceives is by necessity refracted through it; and (3) the fact that, as a result of this, there is no objective reality, a premise that also underlies the poetics of *Lot 49*, in which there is also, contrary to what Cooper says, *no* "objective reality" (*Signs* 140). Because the ego is not a prereflexive, originary entity but rather the result of an inscription into cultural space, her perceptions are her own only to the extent to which they are ultimately *not* her own. Like Pierce, she herself is a merely accidental cultural crossroad: "She had [. . .] known, then, [. . .] that what she stood on had only been woven together a couple thousand miles away in her own tower, was only by accident known as Mexico, and so Pierce had taken her away from nothing, there'd been no escape. [. . .] Her tower, its height and architecture, are like her ego only incidental" (*Lot 49* 21).

Realizing for the first time the impossibility of escaping the phantasmatic and paranoiac nature of reality, Oedipa also becomes aware of the question of the real, the outside of reality and representation—that which insists within it but is structurally excluded from it—and the most important nodal points connecting the real to the imaginary and the symbolic: *death, silence,* and the *phantasm*. Symptomatically, it is a combination of exactly those three that provides the parameters of Oedipa's subsequent quest.

During the first "encounter with the real" in front of the painting, Oedipa experiences and subsequently imagines the real as something "magic, anonymous and malignant, visited on her from outside and for no reason at all" (*Lot 49* 21). Nonetheless, she finds ways to integrate and domesticate it by investing herself completely into cultural registers, relegating the experience to "superstition" (*Lot 49* 22) and taking up "a useful hobby like embroidery" (*Lot 49* 22), which, although it repeats the symbolic covering of the real by the girls in the tower, brings with it a sadness that permeates every perception, so that the world is always seen "refracted through [. . .] tears" (*Lot 49* 21). Another evasion is the flight into suburbia and her "marry[ing] a disk jockey" (*Lot 49* 22). Only her involvement in Pierce's legacy will introduce Oedipa to a fourth possibility, the fact that she may "go mad" (*Lot 49* 22). It will also ultimately lead to her confrontation with her own death, a reality that Oedipa realizes much later she "had been steadfastly refusing to look at [. . .] directly" (*Lot 49* 167).

Even before the actual story starts, Oedipa's paranoia has thus been revealed as an ontological one that is linked to the paranoiac nature of knowledge and perception as such. This is important, because it is exactly along this motif that Pynchon's "deconstruction" of the genre of the detective story—another link to *Citizen Kane,* and another of its models—has to be read. What *Lot 49* puts under erasure are the assumptions about knowledge on which the classic detective novel rests, assumptions that Poe had from the beginning of the genre canonized in his theory of ratiocination. In Dupin's "game theory," the initial identification of the detective with the opponent/criminal is an imaginary, visual one. It is based on the analyst's imitation of the opponent's visual expression: "I fashion the expression of my face, as accurately as possible, in accordance with the expression of his, and then wait to see what thoughts or sentiments arise in my mind or heart" ("Purloined Letter" 216).

For Poe, such an ideal and complete mapping on the imaginary level, in which the analyst's face becomes the exact mirror image of the opponent's, invariably and necessarily results in a symbolic identification with the opponent's intellect: "The analyst throws himself into the spirit of his opponent . . . [and] identifies himself therewith" ("Murders" 142). A combination of these two levels makes out the "*thorough* identification" ("Purloined Letter" 215) that combines the imaginary and symbolic levels, "observation and ad-measurement" (215).

Because this "mirror stage" is a logocentric one, which permits the immediate translation from signified to signified without the interference of the signifier, it results in an "absolute" knowledge. In Poe's theory, this complete identification with the opponent decides between success and failure. Although the method expressly does not include any element of intuition, Dupin's invariably exact identifications make intuition superfluous because they are themselves intuitive and logocentric.

Lacan and Pynchon both counter this ideal mapping by contending that all knowledge is always already paranoiac. Oedipa's inability to project herself onto Pierce leads therefore to a dissolution rather than a solution. Tony Tanner's question of whether, at the end of the story, Oedipa "has emerged from 'narcissism' . . . only to enter into 'paranoia'" (*Pynchon* 71) would therefore have to be rephrased into the question of how Oedipa deals with a knowledge that is always already paranoiac. Like Tanner, most critics of *Lot 49* have interpreted Oedipa's paranoia as a case of a distorted perception of reality, which was then played out against a "more objective" perception of reality. An objective perception of reality, however, does not exist in *Lot 49*.[7] In fact, the story traces Oedipa's journey from a secure space *within* cultural networks, part of whose function is exactly to *cover up* the originary paranoiac origin of reality and with it their own paranoiac roots, to the Lacanian realization that culture and the symbolic are only a "network . . . over the entirety of things, over the totality of the real," and that language "inscribes on the plane of the real this other plane, which we here call the plane of the symbolic" (*Seminar I* 262). Lacanian theory stresses the *construction* of symbolic space, however, whereas *Lot 49* follows in detail what happens when this network begins to disintegrate, ultimately revealing the void it is made to cover up.

At the beginning of the story, then, although she has already passed through a "primal scene," Oedipa has more or less successfully repressed all its implications and is completely submerged within culture, a culture that is in turn completely submerged within itself. San Narciso serves Pynchon as a symbol of this "culture of narcissism," which is locked in the paralyzing confrontation of an eternal mirror stage. At the time the book was written, McLuhan already had linked Narcissus to such an entropic deadlock. Narcissus, and in extension all of culture, has become "the servomechanism of his own extended or repeated image," and as such forms an entropic, "closed system" (*Understanding Media* 51). In fact, the myth of Narcissus figurizes perfectly how the exclusion of death in the psychic register leads to real death. When Oedipa stops in San Narciso at a motel called "Echo Courts," she sees a "representation in painted sheet metal of a nymph holding a white blossom tower[ing] thirty feet into the air; the sign, lit up despite the sun, said 'Echo Courts.' The face of the nymph was much like Oedipa's [. . . .] She was smiling a lipsticked and public smile, not quite a hooker's but nowhere near that of any nymph pining away with love either" (*Lot 49* 26–27).

The fact that the figure of Echo in the advertisement for the "Echo Courts" has degenerated into a profane and degraded version of her former self already points to the corruption of love and a general secularization that permeate all of *Lot 49*. Her resemblance to Oedipa implies that, like Echo with Narcissus, Oedipa is in love with the narcissistic culture of which she herself is so much a part. Carrying the parallel even further, it also implies that as for Echo, who can only repeat other people's words, Oedipa's language is never her own but consists of cultural fragments she merely reflects. The myth, and with it Pynchon, thus ingeniously combines the realms of the imaginary and the symbolic, because in the same way in which the image of Narcissus is reflected in the water, the echo reflects fragmented pieces of discourse from the planes of the stones and rocks. It is this very parallel that defines the passage from the imaginary to the symbolic. In speech directed to another subject, whose ego is constituted via a similar imaginary reflection, the two mirror planes meet in a reciprocal reflection, which is now mediated by language. In this realm, the imaginary split is repeated along the axis of the signifier and the signified. Although the symbolic, as a third term, allows for mediation, the failures of identification are also preprogrammed within it because of the bar between signifier and signified. Whereas the imaginary leads to an "alienating identification," in relation to the speaking subject, Lacan talks about the impossibility of pinning a signified to a signifier once and for all. "The subject is always punctual and fading, because it is a subject only because of another signifier and for another signifier" (*Encore* 130). In the same way in which the ego is a mirror effect, the subject is an "effect of the signifier."

This contention, which is the common denominator of Lacan's, Derrida's, and Baudrillard's theories, is a premise that underlies all of *Lot 49*, in which the whole world is textualized.[8] In the place of a fictional world, Pynchon installs the fictionality of the world as such. From the beginning, the tears (with a possibly unintended pun on "Oedipa's tears") in the order of things are textual, and events from "real life," such as Pierce's alleged involvement in experiments with human bones, are constantly reflected in texts.

It is therefore programmatic that Oedipa detects the first break in the symbolic universe by shifting her attention from the *signified* to the *signifier*. When she receives a letter from her husband, she has a closer look at its material aspects: "It may have been an intuition that the letter would be newsless inside that made Oedipa look more closely at its outside" (*Lot 49* 46). Because the signifier generally envelops the signified, it is only fitting that the letter's envelope should reveal a first irregularity in the text of the world, a "blurb put on by the government" that carries the inscription "REPORT ALL OBSCENE MAIL TO YOUR POTSMASTER" (*Lot 49* 46). The error is based on the smallest form of linguistic disorder, the displacement of two phonemes, yet this minimal mistake is the first instance at which the tissue of the complex and vast discursive network that makes up Oedipa's reality begins to give way. This happens invariably at its weakest points, either in the form of such inconspicuous and seemingly innocent reversals or, even more often, along the fissures of discourse, its ambiguities and homonyms. In *Lot 49* it is almost invariably by way of puns that Oedipa shifts from one revelation to the next. This is important, because the pun is in the first instance a game the language material plays with itself, stressing the effect of the *signifier* within signification rather than that of the *signified*, a "supremacy" (Lacan, "Purloined Letter" 36) Lacan emblematizes by writing their relation as $\frac{S}{s}$: "the signifier over the signified, 'over' corresponding to the bar separating the two stages" (*Écrits* 149).

Whereas the metaphor sustains any attempt to create a mapping of *concepts* on the ideal level of the signified (or the level of an ideal signified) without the interference of the language material, the pun proceeds from a *material* or *phonological* similarity of two or more signifiers. And whereas the metaphor *fuses* two seemingly dissimilar concepts, amalgamating them into one identity and so connecting the discursive network, the pun *proceeds* from an identity that it unmasks as always already split and duplicitous, and so disintegrates the symbolic network. This gradual disintegration of discourse becomes especially obvious in the *Courier's Tragedy*, which is also the nodal point of the endless reflections of *text* and *world*, and which, because it is in many ways comparable to *Lot 49* itself, creates an extra *mise-en-abîme* of the text. Like *Lot 49*, it is centered on an inheritance. Within its endless schemes and counterschemes—themselves reminiscent of the convoluted plot of *Lot 49*—a secret power suddenly intervenes, and, again as in *Lot 49*, the introduction of mystery—the Trystero—is marked by the spot where the discourse of the play begins to fall apart: "Heretofore the naming of names has gone on either literally or as metaphor. But now [. . .] a new mode of expression takes over. It can only be called a kind of ritual reluctance" (*Lot 49* 71).[9] In the performance of the play, the only mention of the Trystero occurs in the following line: *"No hallowed skein of stars can ward, I trow, / Who's once been set his tryst with Trystero"* (*Lot 49* 75). The subsequent burglarizations of this line underscore the unreliability of the signifying chain. When Oedipa buys the text of the tragedy to find out more about the Trystero, she finds another version at the specific passage: *"No hallowed skein of stars can ward, I trow [. . .] Who once has crossed the lusts of Angelo"* (*Lot 49* 101–2). And in a footnote, based on the "Whitechapel version," yet another one: "This tryst or odious awry, O Niccolò"

(*Lot 49* 102), "odious awry" being a "low" pun on "O dies irae." In this constantly shifting signifying chain, it is indeed impossible to "pin a signifier to a signified." *Lot 49* thus presents a universe in which texts and sources constantly recede into each other.

The disorder of the world, then, is a direct result of its textuality and its dependence on the very materiality of language. Pynchon again and again exemplifies this subversion and the effects it has on subjectivity. The tendency of signs to evaporate and disseminate is symbolized by what happens to Randolph Driblette, the actor/director of the *Courier's Tragedy*, whom Oedipa questions after she has attended a performance of the play. Driblette is very skeptical about the value of signs: "'Why,' Driblette said at last, 'is everybody so interested in texts?'" (*Lot 49* 78). The text of the play, he tells her "'doesn't mean anything'" (*Lot 49* 77). It is the performance that gives it its meaning: "To give the spirit flesh. The words, who cares?" (*Lot 49* 79). The motif of giving the spirit flesh seems to point to the possibility of representing a pure spirit. Especially in its biblical connotation, it implies the intrusion of metaphysics into the physical world and the possibility of reaching a truth *behind* language. It thus functions as a logocentric utopia: "You can put together clues, develop a thesis, or several [. . . .] You could waste your life that way and never touch the truth" (*Lot 49* 80). McHoul and Wills even see in it a position "blatant in its own contradictions" (WP 69). Yet one should bear in mind that within the structural matrix of the book this truth is always a promise not kept. In this case, the truth is not metaphysical but only that of a specific subject, the result of the projection of Driblette's psychic images into reality: "I'm the projector at the planetarium" (*Lot 49* 79). In Pynchon's texts these moments of logocentricity are, in de Man's use of the term, invariably "rhetorical."

In this respect, Oedipa is comparable to Driblette. Like him, she feels she has to bring to life the legacy of a dead person, although in her case it is not a fictional text but the "fictional" world itself: "Part of her duty [. . . was] to bestow life on what had persisted, to try to be what Driblette was, the dark machine in the center of the planetarium, to bring the estate into pulsing, stelliferous meaning" (*Lot 49* 82). Like Driblette, the ultimate question she has to face is, *"Shall I project a world?"* (*Lot 49* 82), whether, as in the Freudian concept of projection—especially in its relation to paranoia—she should become the center from which the world is structured.

It seems that although the text of the world itself is endlessly disseminating, subjects can—and hope to—ground significations. Yet ironically, these very subjects in turn disseminate. Driblette drowns himself in the "primal blood the Pacific" (*Lot 49* 162) and thus, true to his name, which derives from *driblet,* merges into the "nautical unity" of the Pacific. His metaphorical dissemination aligns the *text's* dissemination with that of the *subject* along the motif of death, the subject's reentry into the real.

Oedipa's problem is that because "man's desire is the desire of the Other," the vanishing of the "other" (in the sense of "other person," as well as in the more strictly Lacanian sense of the imaginary "alter ego") implies the vanishing of the "Other" (again in the sense of "other person," but now in relation to the symbolic "Other": language). These losses within the imaginary and symbolic realms in turn imply the fading of the self. Driblette warns her of this: "If I were to dissolve in here [. . .] be washed down the drain into the Pacific, what you saw tonight would vanish too. You, that part of you so concerned, God knows how, with that little world, would also vanish" (*Lot 49* 79–80).

If Driblette's dissemination is linked primarily to *death,* Mucho's is linked to the motif of the *phantasm*. Where other people hear harmonies, he hears only single notes: "Spectrum analysis, in my head. I can break down chords, and timbres, and words too into all the basic frequencies and harmonics [. . .] and listen to them, each pure tone, but all at once" (*Lot 49* 142). Sending out this "arche-sound," Mucho aims at creating a mystical union of sound spectra and spectra of subjectivity: "Everybody who says the same words is the same person if the spectra are the same only they happen differently in time, you dig?" (*Lot 49* 142). He tries to overcome and redeem the accidental nature of single egos by aligning them along similar signifiers and chains of signifiers, thus making them identical and congruent for short periods of time. In this attempt he evokes the innocence of the sixties through a reference to a Beatles song: "When those kids sing about 'She loves you,' yeah well, you know, she does, she's any number of people [. . . .] And the 'you' is everybody. And herself" (*Lot 49* 143). It is to this generic subjectivity that he is linked when he broadcasts—and thus also projects—his "pattern out across a million lives a night" (*Lot 49* 144). Yet, although he tries to reverse the dissemination of words by his "vision of consensus" (*Lot 49* 143), his Jungian mysticism of unity also implies his dissemination: "'Behind his back,' Funch was whining, 'they're calling him the Brothers N. He's losing his identity [. . . .] Day by day, Wendell is less himself and more generic'" (*Lot 49* 140). Ironically, as Mucho enters more and more into the sonic space of his "archetypal" phantasm, communication with him becomes more and more impossible because "so much of him already had dissipated" (*Lot 49* 144).

Oedipa's quest for the Trystero is punctured by such losses. Throughout the novel, the anchor points of her symbolic network vanish. Pierce and Driblette die (as she knows the sailor will and suspects Mr. Thoth has), Hilarious goes mad, Mucho retreats into his phantasm, and Metzger runs off with a nymphet. Arnold Snarb, finally, simply hangs up the phone on her, a gesture that ironically reflects the beginning of her quest and underlines once more its basic circularity. With all of these losses, more and more of Oedipa herself vanishes. At the end of this process, she has to face a void, the void (of the real) that is both around and within her.

Before she comes to this void, however, she is faced with the problem of ordering Pierce's legacy. In relation to this search, most critics have concentrated on Pynchon's use of entropy and its relation to information theory, arguing that Oedipa's perception of information actually increases the entropy, or disorder, around her.[10] Yet entropy is not only an informational metaphor. It also has, for instance, a close link to the subject's body and death. Ultimately, John Nefastis's demonic machine, which promises to reverse entropic processes, is a machine intended to turn the subject into a *perpetuum mobile* and thus to reverse even death, the most "irreversible process" (*Lot 49* 128).

Nefastis's machine works on the principle that by looking intently at a portrait of James Clerk Maxwell, sensitives (that is, people with "the gift" [*Lot 49* 87]) can bring a piston into motion and so intervene and bring about a change in the physical universe (the real) through a direct, logocentric transfer of *mental* to *physical* energy. It is important to realize that from the start the machine is implicated in the "network of signifiers," because it is based on the principle of a "mathematical pun":

> She did gather that there were two distinct kinds of this entropy. One having to do with heat-engines, the other to do with communication. The equation for one, back in the '30's, had looked very like the equation for the other. It was a coincidence. The two fields were entirely unconnected, except at one point: Maxwell's Demon. As the Demon sat and sorted his molecules into hot and cold, the system was said to lose entropy. But somehow the loss was offset by the information the Demon gained about what molecules were where. (*Lot 49* 105)[11]

It is by supplementing the initial pun with a metaphorical meaning that Nefastis has "made his mere coincidence respectable" (*Lot 49* 109).[12] The question, in Lacanian terms, is whether it is he who makes the metaphor *exist*, or whether it can *subsist* by itself.

Via the demon, a closed system loses entropy because the demon produces order. In terms of information theory, this means that although the system loses some of its virtual information content, this loss is countered by the transfer of virtual *information content* into real *information/knowledge:* "Mathematicians . . . locate information as that which moves in the opposite direction to entropy" (Lacan, *Seminar II* 83). In information theory, a code actually takes over the position and function of the demon.[13] Because the demon/code is only a "fiction," however, any encoding entails an inevitable loss of virtual information. Transmitting all the virtual information would require overcoming the inherent structure of language itself, abolishing the workings of the signifier within the transfer of the signifier into the signified, what McHoul and Wills call a "mythically pure transfer" (WP 150). Any codification, because it entails a loss of virtual information, destroys the utopia of this direct, integral transfer. Without the insertion of a code, the transfer of information is impossible—because too complicated—although one would, hypothetically, gain the full information about the system. Such an uncoded transfer would imply the elimination and exclusion of the system of signifiers. Apart from denying the problem within logocentrism, the only possibility of such a transfer—because the subject is inevitably inscribed into the network of signifiers—would be a magic intrusion of a signified from *outside* the system. It would have to come from a space outside the symbolic—in Nefastis's case, from the dead Maxwell. Having recourse to a message from "the other side," then, is the only way to escape or circumvent the subversion of the signified by the signifier. In *Lot 49,* Oedipa is constantly looking for such a metaphysical intrusion, but her attempts to call up ghosts—to communicate with the real—constantly fail. Neither Maxwell, Pierce, nor Driblette can be contacted. Her problem is that this does not prove the impossibility of metaphysics; there is still a binary choice: "Either she could not communicate, or he did not exist" (*Lot 49* 162).

In this respect, Oedipa's quest is a mirror image of Nefastis's dilemma: like him, she is faced with the problem of creating metaphors from puns, signifieds from signifiers, while what she would like to do is to find an ideal order that will show itself without the interference and intervention of the signifier, a Wittgensteinian paradox Pynchon had already treated in Mondaugen's story in *V.* Furthermore, in her case it is even more difficult because she is faced not with a simple binary relation but "with a metaphor of God knew how many parts; more than two, anyway" (*Lot 49* 109). All of them are held together by the Trystero, which as Hite has rightly stressed is itself a signifier.

In the sense that it makes a direct/ideal transfer impossible, then, language is inevitably entropic. Early critics especially read this as the realization that order is impossible and that the universe is irredeemably chaotic. The resulting options for the subject were either a retreat into paranoia or the acceptance of "radical detour," an option advanced by McHoul and Wills, who read *Lot 49* "against itself" within a Derridean framework. Writing about the scene when, after the death of Driblette, Oedipa wonders whether "someday she might replace whatever of her had gone away by some prosthetic device" (*Lot 49* 161), McHoul and Wills state that, "whereas the humanist might strive for integrality, the prosthetic might encourage radical intervention and radical detour" (WP 81–82). What they do not take into consideration is the originary loss on which this prosthetic device or structure is based, the paradoxical "presence of the loss" in the object *o* that haunts the subject: the "phantom limb" (*Lot 49* 161). In its "absent presence," this phantom limb and the phantom pain become metaphors of "mourning . . . the lost bodily totality" (Grosz 44). Seen as a metaphor for the void of the real, it is a perfect image of the "retrospective," phantasmatic reconstruction of a lost unity, what Lacan has called, in reference to *The Merchant of Venice*, "that self-sacrifice, that pound of flesh which is mortgaged . . . in his [the subject's] relationship to the signifier" ("Desire" 28). Oedipa's hope that one day she will be able to replace it with something else, "a dress of a certain color, a phrase in a letter, another lover" (*Lot 49* 161) shows that she experiences this lack as a fundamental one. What the "loss" of Driblette makes her recognize is that she is inevitably inscribed into the field of the "other"—as well as that of the "Other."

The fact that Oedipa chooses neither paranoia nor free-play—although of course a Derridean reader might—implies that her relation to entropy is more complex. It is therefore necessary to widen the range of the entropic references operative in the novel. Language sets up a complex dynamics between entropic and negentropic tendencies, because although it is inevitably entropic, it is negentropic in that it opens up the possibility of communication in the first place. It is in this twofold structure that desire is defined: "desire can never be satisfied. . . . Such satisfaction would be equivalent to total information, or to death" (Wilden, *System* 454–55).

The first level on which entropy operates on the subject is the organic, material level and its relation to death and homeostasis, which for Lacan is based on the fact that "the organism already conceived by Freud as a machine . . . has a tendency to return to its state of equilibrium—this is what the pleasure principle states" (*Seminar II* 79). This tendency operates because life "is only caught up in the symbolic piece-meal, decomposed. The human being himself is in part outside life, he partakes of the death instinct. Only from there can he engage in the register of life" (90).[14] Insofar as the subject is an effect of the signifier, however, and participates in the entropy of language—understood as a closed system and a binary machine—this homeostatic tendency of the organic machine is linked to the entropy at work in the textual machine. In this respect, it is certainly symptomatic that the initial analogy between entropy and the death of a culture is based on the idea of culture as an organism. The biological relation to death is always filtered through language and operative in it.[15] The implications of entropy thus reverberate constantly within the subject's (textual) reality: "The minimum tension can mean one of two things . . . according to whether it is a matter of the minimum given a certain definition of the equilibrium of the system, or of the minimum purely and simply, that is to say, with respect to the living being, death" (80). It is within this double inscription of language and death, merging in the concept of the death drive, that entropy should be read. The important point in this analogy between "the death instinct and entropy" (115) is the realization that the death drive does not lead to immediate death, but that the relation to death makes out a constitutive and permanent part of life, regulating its dynamics in a specific way: "The principle which brings the living being back to death is situated . . . behind the necessity it experiences to take the roads of life" (80–81). The question is how, and why, although it is implicated by a desire for death and homeostasis, the human machine holds and "looks after itself" (81). Paradoxically, in that it is mediating between life and death, the death drive is ultimately more related to the symbolic than to the imaginary, to the reality principle rather than the pleasure principle, and to the secondary processes rather than the primary processes. It takes on concrete form in the work with and in the signifier.

> This is the point where we open out into the symbolic order, which isn't the libidinal order in which the ego is inscribed, along with all the drives. It tends beyond the pleasure principle, beyond the limits of life, and that is why Freud identifies it with the death instinct. . . . The symbolic order is rejected by the libidinal order, which includes the whole of the domain of the imaginary, including the structure of the ego. And the death instinct is only the mask of the symbolic order. . . . The symbolic order is simultaneously non-being and in-

sisting to be, that is what Freud has in mind when he talks about the death instinct as being what is most fundamental—a symbolic order in travail, in the process of coming, insisting on being realized. (*Seminar II* 326)

The death drive is "the basic mode, according to which the negativity implied by the signifier is manifested in the human" (Juranville 228).

To complicate matters even more, there is a third, social form of entropy that intervenes in these dynamics, an entropy concerning the information that *has* been generated out of chaos. In a simulatory society, in which information is everywhere, information itself becomes entropic, a realization on which Baudrillard rests his *reversal* of the second law of thermodynamics: "The fundamental thesis would have it that information would be synonymous with negentropy, the resistance to entropy. . . . But it would be fitting to pose the opposite hypothesis: INFORMATION = ENTROPY" (*In the Shadow* 109). Information breeds entropy, because it is always implicated by a surplus of information. A second facet of this socio-informational entropy has to do with the social subject itself, the tendency to make individuals uniform and equal and to insert them into "the lowest form of social energy: . . . behavioural utility . . . [the social's] entropic form" (77).

Oedipa is a nodal point among these three systems of entropy—biological, informational, and social—which constantly overlap in the text. All have to do with the relation between the body/death, as well as between language and the symbolic/social. It is therefore not surprising that the relation between the subject, reality, and death lies at the center of *Lot 49* and that everywhere in the novel, as in the illustration of the *Courier's Tragedy,* "the figure of Death hovers in the background" (*Lot 49* 155).[16] For Oedipa, this relation comes to a climax in her nighttime journey through San Narciso. In a passage saturated with an explicit death wish, Oedipa suddenly feels that it would be "lovely beyond dreams" (*Lot 49* 118) simply to merge with the city's image systems: "The city was hers, as, made up and sleeked so with the customary words and images (cosmopolitan, culture, cable cars) it had not been before" (*Lot 49* 117). Even death, "gravity's pull, laws of ballistics, feral ravening" could not "promise [. . .] more delight" (*Lot 49* 118). At this moment, her desire to lose herself in the *jouissance* of the text of the city and her surrender to the pleasure principle (which would imply the transgression of the symbolic law and the foreclosure of death) actually become identical. This surrender, however, would ultimately imply her real death, because—to rewrite Lacan—"if death is rejected from the symbolic register (the signifier), it will reappear in the real." This relation of real *jouissance* to death is highlighted when Pynchon writes that Oedipa faces the possibility of complete merging "as she might [. . .] any death-wish that can be consummated by some minimum gesture" (*Lot 49* 118).

But there is the "beyond the pleasure principle." It is the death drive's "conservative" tendency that stops Oedipa from giving in to the desire to lose herself completely.[17] What she realizes is that every investment in language and culture results from a more initial loss, and as such is only a compensation—what McHoul and Wills call a prosthesis. To give in to the movement(s) of clues, drifting freely within the signifying chain without hold and desire to ground her movements in a kind of Derridean dissemination, would mean to deny this loss: "She tested it, shivering: I am meant to remember. Each clue that comes is *supposed* to have its own clarity, its fine chances for permanence. But then she wondered if the gemlike 'clues' were only some kind of compensation. To make up for her having lost the direct, epileptic Word, the cry that might abolish the night" (*Lot 49* 118).

This realization inaugurates another round in her search. The reality principle takes over again, instigating repetition because it "consists in making the game last . . . ensuring that pleasure is renewed . . . these pleasures whose aim is precisely to end in cessation" (Lacan, *Seminar II* 84). It is always this oscillation between an investment in the process of ordering and the failure of this process that defines Oedipa's quest, the constant oscillation between language and the promise of an integral transfer of information. All of Oedipa's "hierophan[ies]" (*Lot 49* 31) are promises of such a break into discourse.

The epileptic attack, for instance, serves as the promise of such an intrusion: "She could, at this stage of things, recognize signals like that, as the epileptic is said to—an odor, color, pure piercing grace note announcing his seizure" (*Lot 49* 95). Yet only this trigger, and never the "central truth itself" (*Lot 49* 95), is all the epileptic—and she herself, she fears—can remember of the attack: "Oedipa wondered whether, at the end of this (if it were supposed to end), she too might not be left with only compiled memories of clues, announcements, intimations, but never the central truth itself, which must somehow each time be too bright for her memory to hold; which must always blaze out, destroying its own message irreversibly, leaving an overexposed blank when the ordinary world came back" (*Lot 49* 95).

It is always the paradoxical promise of a message outside language, the "battery of signifiers," that marks the borders of the symbolic, the promise of "another world's intrusion into this one" (*Lot 49* 120). Elsewhere, Oedipa describes these messages "as if, on some other frequency, or out of the eye of some whirlwind rotating too slow for her heated skin even to feel the centrifugal coolness of, words were being spoken" (*Lot 49* 24–25). On the level of writing, "hieroglyphics" (*Lot 49* 52) promise these revelations. In this discussion, the hieroglyph functions as both the promise and the denial of a less abstract and more direct mediation between the real and the symbolic.

The concept of the hieroglyph or of hieroglyphic script is especially apt, as it has always haunted the theory of language. Starting from Leibniz's and Humboldt's unease about the Chinese language and continuing to Hegel's[18] and Saussure's arguments for the preference of alphabetical script, the hieroglyph has always resisted inclusion within linguistic theory, and, although classical linguistics seemed to have domesticated and tamed the term quite successfully, it has (at least since Freud) regained some of its importance and relevance, haunting again the more recent theories of Derrida and Lacan, as well as McLuhan, who states that "all non-phonetic forms of writing are . . . artistic modes that retain much variety of sensuous orchestration. Phonetic writing, alone, has the power of separating and fragmenting the senses and of sloughing off the semantic complexities . . . of implementing continuity and lineality by fragmented repetition" (*Understanding Media* 356–57).[19]

In his treatment of the problem, Derrida argues against the idea of ideogrammatic script as a natural mode of registration: "The history of the voice and its writing is comprehended between two mute writings, between two poles of universality relating to each other as the natural and the artificial: the pictogram and algebra" (*Of Grammatology* 302).

Against these extreme positions (themselves the result of logocentric separation) he sets their inevitable *complicity:* "Each graphic form may have a *double value*—ideographic and phonetic" (*Of Grammatology* 89). Because the hieroglyph holds such a medial position, it could become the promise (what he calls a "European hallucination" [80]) of a "universal language." Yet the hieroglyph has always functioned as a greater promise, a more radical and holy revelation. Derrida's "economy of writing" does not account for the force of this seemingly logocentric utopian promise and the desire attached to it.

Interestingly, Lacan's discussion of the hieroglyph is also suspended between Derrida's extremes of "the pictogram and algebra" and the analog and the digital: the imaginary and the symbolic.[20] It is at the threshold between the imaginary and the symbolic that the hieroglyph holds the position of a hinge, mediating between the immediacy of the image and the mediating, self-regulative system of language.

In *Lot 49,* however, the hieroglyph stands *rhetorically* for a more radical, romantic promise, a writing of the real/referent. As a "prose of the real," it promises a direct expression of the world, such as the natural or metaphysical (two similarly logocentric ideals) characters written *with* and *into* the landscape of Tsalal in Poe's *Narrative of Arthur Gordon Pym*—another important model for *Lot 49,* especially in relation to the motif of suspended revelation and the fantastic. Yet, because the subject's reality is formed like a Möbius strip, every structural pattern is always already cultural rather than natural or metaphysical.

Already at the beginning of her journey, before she enters San Narciso, Oedipa looks down at suburbia and compares the view, "less an identifiable city than a grouping of concepts" (*Lot 49* 24), to a printed circuit: "There were to both outward patterns a hieroglyphic sense of concealed meaning, of an intent to communicate [. . .] a revelation also trembled just past the threshold of her understanding [. . .] she and the Chevy seemed parked at the centre of an odd, religious instant" (*Lot 49* 24). Any hope of revelation, however, is immediately deconstructed by the very text in which it is evoked. As with Nefastis's machine, natural or metaphysical signs remain a fiction, and the question whether "behind the hieroglyphic streets there would be either a transcendent meaning, or only the earth" (*Lot 49* 181) remains open until the end of the text. Invariably, the net of signifiers is interposed between the subject and a possible revelation. Pynchon's rhetorical deconstructions, however, are never simply playful, because they try to account for the desire bound up with the logocentric promise.

In all of Pynchon's texts, a *choice* between either transcendental revelation or materialistic explanation is exactly what is to be avoided. In this hesitation, the linguistic aspect of the hieroglyph as the imaginary promise of the direct, unmediated representation of an "impossible," real referent is linked to the Lacanian idea of desire, or, more specifically, the margin between symbolic desire and imaginary demand.

In both linguistic and psychic registers, however, the promises are never kept, because the hieroglyph is subjected to the law of the signifier, which refers the subject to the symbolic—in the first case in the sense of the "symbolic signifier," in the second in the sense of "symbolic desire." Although

Oedipa wants to, she cannot (as in the Nefastis passage) escape her medial position. This realization begins with Oedipa's confrontation with the sailor who suffers from delirium tremens:

> Behind the initials was a metaphor, a delirium tremens, a trembling unfurrowing of the mind's plowshare. The saint whose water can light lamps, the clairvoyant whose lapse in recall is the breath of God, the true paranoid for whom all is organized in spheres joyful or threatening about the central pulse of himself, the dreamer whose puns probe ancient fetid shafts and tunnels of truth all act in the same special relevance to the word, or whatever it is the word is there, buffering, to protect us from. The act of metaphor then was a thrust at truth and a lie, depending where you were: inside, safe, or outside, lost. Oedipa did not know where she was. Trembling, unfurrowed, she slipped sideways. (*Lot 49* 128–29)

In contrast to the sailor's delirium (which is "real"), Oedipa's is a decidedly symbolic one, although the gap between the two can be infinitesimal, like a Duchampian "infra-thin" or Dali's differentiation between himself and a madman, when he states that "the only difference between me and a madman is that I am not mad." Her delirium denotes a *medial* position. Pynchon actually uses the same word to describe it that Lacan uses to describe the symbolic, "the furrows opened up by the signifier in the real world" (Lacan, *Écrits* 194). Both Lacan and Pynchon base their idea on the fact that *delirium* literally means "to unfurrow."[21] The saint, the clairvoyant, the paranoiac, and the dreamer have all transcended the realm and laws of discourse. They are outside language and the metaphorical construction of reality. Whereas the sane person is always within the field of metaphor,[22] by which he or she constructs meaning, these others are completely outside the symbolic. Yet it is only from Oedipa's medial position that the question about truth can be put: "Truth hollows out its way into the real thanks to the dimension of speech. There is neither true nor false prior to speech. Truth is introduced along with it, and so is the lie. . . . And then, what else?—ambiguity, to which, by its very nature, speech is doomed. Because the very act of speech, which founds the dimension of truth, always remains, by this fact, behind, beyond" (Lacan, *Seminar I* 228).

Oedipa is *within* the symbolic, but she is constantly drifting toward its borders, so that her position is exactly that of the Lacanian subject. Lacan's mapping of the Freudian terms *condensation* and *displacement* onto *metaphor* and *metonymy,* whose combined dynamics had made out the self's radical eccentricity to itself, delineates exactly the double dynamics of metaphor as both "a thrust at truth and a lie." Although "metaphor occurs at the precise point at which sense emerges from non-sense" (*Écrits* 158), this sense is invariably subverted, because it is a signification that can be sustained only by a "reference to another signification" (150). The simultaneous sustenance and subversion within a system of references caused by the structure of discourse are described by metonymy, which denotes that every meaning is always missing or lacking something and is only "a part for the whole." Lacan links metonymy to desire, because the desire to create meaning is forever displaced from one metaphor to the next via the lack opened up by metonymy. The positive aspect of metaphor, its "truth," is thus always countered by its failure to denote a signified once and for all (to pin a signified to a signifier), which is why it is always also a lie: "Meaning only shows the direction in which it falters" (*Encore* 74).

Metaphor and metonymy thus refer the subject simultaneously to sense and nonsense, being and lack—"what links metaphor to the question of being and metonymy to its lack" (*Écrits* 175)—and shape the subject's desire. They cause the incessant gliding of the subject in the signifying chain, a double movement that describes Oedipa's position. Without "anchoring points," she drifts through discourse in a constant movement of flight. Every metaphor can bring about only an *approximation* of signifieds and is itself implicated by the instability of discourse, so that the only way to the "repressed" is through the materiality of language itself, the "high magic to low puns" (*Lot 49* 129), an especially apt definition, as it is itself based on a pun. This basic senselessness of the net of signifiers is expressed in Lacan's statement that "the signifier is stupid" (*Encore* 24). The subject's only possibility to create metaphors out of puns—as with Nefastis—is paralleled by Pynchon in his own text, in which he in turn weaves a vast metaphor out of a system of puns. As such, the programmatic openness of his text turns it into an "allegory of its own textuality" and of textuality in general, showing that the signifying chain is the only thread by which the subject can find its way through the discursive labyrinth. *The Crying of Lot 49* shows that it is a very fragile thread, which is "woven with allusions, quotations, puns, and equivocations" (*Écrits* 169–70). Because the subject depends on this very thread, "the slightest alteration in the relation between man and the signifier [like a switching of two phonemes] . . . changes the whole cause of history by modifying the moorings that anchor his being" (174).

Pynchon, however, carries the metaphor behind the DTs even further. It also

> meant [. . .] a time differential, a vanishingly small instant in which change had to be confronted at last for what it was, where it could no longer disguise itself as something innocuous like an average rate; where velocity dwelled in the projectile though the projectile be frozen in midflight, where death dwelled in the cell though the cell be looked in on at its most quick. [. . .] DT's must give access to dt's of spectra beyond the known sun, music made purely of Antarctic loneliness and fright. (*Lot 49* 129)

In this final pun, Pynchon shows the ultimate tearing of the signifying chain, the moment at which the subject, who is usually gliding through the chain, comes to a halt and is suspended in the void between the signifiers. This stopping of the signifying chain is comparable to the freezing of the projectile in flight and to the freezing of life through death, in that all reveal natural movement as a system of artificial phases. Symptomatically, it is just before this passage that Oedipa feels "as if she had just discovered the irreversible process" (*Lot 49* 128). This aspect of the DTs shows how much the subject depends on the simulations of the system of representation. In that it denotes the moment in which the subject is "outside" this representational space, however, it is also one of the most "fantastic" moments in *Lot 49*.

The ending of *Lot 49*, however, implies that Oedipa has found a way to cope with her situation and is thus not clinically or pathologically "paranoiac," although still ontologically so. As Schaub has pointed out, Oedipa's paranoia is "more protective than psychotic" (*Pynchon* 41). If in the beginning of her quest she had been "curious," at the end she is beginning "to feel reluctant about following up anything" (*Lot 49* 166), with the decided aim not to let paranoia engulf her whole being: "Anxious that her revelation not expand beyond a certain point. Lest, possibly, it grow larger than she and assume her to itself" (*Lot 49* 166). In this realization, the other aspect of language becomes important. It is a buffer that protects the subject from the fantastic, hallucinatory confrontation with the real, as in the "cold and sweatless meathooks of a psychosis" (*Lot 49* 132) of which Oedipa is so afraid and in schizophrenia, with the absolute proximity and immediacy of the objects, which Baudrillard sees as a sign of modern simulatory society. Against this terrifying proximity, which entails the "*foreclosure* of the signifier" (Lacan, *Écrits* 201), Pynchon sets the paranoia of interpretation.

At the end of her quest, Oedipa's "isolation [is] complete" (*Lot 49* 177). This absence of love and sexuality, implying also the absence of language, brings about despair, "as it will when nobody around has any sexual relevance to you" (*Lot 49* 116). Symptomatically, in this state, all her dreams center on revelations and psychotically hallucinated voices that speak to her: "She dreamed of disembodied voices from whose malignance there was no appeal, the soft dusk of mirrors out of which something was about to walk" (*Lot 49* 175). At the end of this isolation, "San Narciso [. . .] lost [. . .] gave up its residue of uniqueness for her; became a name again [. . .] an incident among our climatic records of dreams [. . .] storm-systems of group suffering and need, prevailing winds of affluence" (*Lot 49* 177–78).

Yet Oedipa escapes psychosis. Her realization that everything is the void, and the void is in everything, however, is followed by the realization that she is caught in a mirror structure. Either the Trystero is real, or she is hallucinating it. Either it is a plot, or she is fantasizing such a plot: "Those symmetrical four. She didn't like any of them, but hoped she was mentally ill; that that's all it was. That night she sat for hours . . . teaching herself to breathe in a vacuum. For this, oh God, was the void. There was nobody who could help her. Nobody in the world. They were all on something, mad, possible enemies, dead" (*Lot 49* 171).

At this point, a sociopolitical reading has to supplement the ontological and epistemological ones, because although Oedipa has accepted the paranoiac structure of her ego, she is still caught up in questions of simulation. This is important, because the sociopolitical reading constantly destabilizes the (already destabilized) ontological and epistemological ones and renders them undecidably ambiguous. The realization that order is always already simulated by the perceptual apparatus does not solve the problem of reality, because it implies that reality is the space of conflicting and competing projections of various simulatory systems. "Citizen Inverarity" himself is of course the most extensive projector, representing America *in toto*. Like "Citizen Kane," he is a "founding father" (*Lot 49* 26) whose legacy is all of America: "She had dedicated herself, weeks ago, to making sense of what Inverarity had left behind, never suspecting that the legacy was America" (*Lot 49* 178). To find out about the reality of America therefore entails finding out about Pierce, who during his lifetime has projected himself continuously into the real: "His need to possess, to alter the land, to bring new skylines, personal antagonisms, growth rates into being" (*Lot 49* 178). As a result of this externalization, America cannot be decoded until Pierce's personal motives can be decoded. The openness of *Lot 49* is based on the fact that this is impossible, because it is impossible to separate private and public life, as there is neither an extratextual subject nor an extratextual reality. All one can say about these motives in the text is that they are again linked to the subject's relation to death—"He must have known, writing the will, facing the spectre, how the bouncing would stop" (*Lot 49* 178)— and its relation to desire and society, in whose interplay Oedipa had already searched for the unfathomable motives of Driblette's insertion of the lines about the Trystero into the play, which might have been the result of "a hundred hangups, permuted, combined—sex, money, illness, despair with the history of his time and place, who knew. Changing the script had no clearer motive than his suicide. There was the same whimsy to both [. . .] perhaps [. . .] adding those two lines had [. . .] served him as a rehearsal for his night's walk away into that vast sink of the primal blood the Pacific" (*Lot 49* 162).

Pierce might have wanted only to "harass" (*Lot 49* 178) her, "so cynically sure of being wiped out he could throw away all hope of anything more" (*Lot 49* 179). He might actually have "discovered" (*Lot 49* 179) the Trystero. Another possibility is that "he might even have tried to survive death, as a paranoia" (*Lot 49* 179), and thus beat death by creating a plot "too elaborate for the dark Angel to hold at once, in his humorless vice-president's head, all the possibilities of" (*Lot 49* 179).

The ultimate question, then, is whether reality is a simulation originating from one source, or whether "Inverarity had only died, nothing else" (*Lot 49* 179). In the latter case, there exists an America that does *not* belong to Inverarity: "What was left to inherit? That America coded in Inverarity's testament, whose was that?" (*Lot 49* 180).

It is here that the motif of the narcissistic capture of American culture becomes relevant, as well as the inevitable relation of power to paranoia and the imaginary scene. According to Baudrillard, power ultimately wishes to become part of the real, which is of course impossible: "Power shares all the illusions of the real and of production; it wants to belong to the order of the real and so falls over into the imaginary and into self-superstition" (*Forget Foucault* 45). This imaginary capture underlies all the binary separations into rich and poor, elect and preterite, that define America and American life, although America had once functioned as the utopia of a *tabula rasa*: "How had it ever happened here, with the chances once so good for diversity?" (*Lot 49* 181). The narcissistic system is based on the fact that *one* system sets out by force to project only its own image into the outside. The other subjects can either submit to this image and insert themselves into it, like Oedipa in the beginning of the novel, or they can create an equally narcissistic mirror structure, a black on white negative of the more initial projection. This is why the Trystero, as society's "other" and the symbol of a counterhistory, reverts ultimately to the same strategies as the ruling culture, a development symbolized by Bortz's "mirror-image theory" (*Lot 49* 162). In fact, the position of the Trystero is a highly complex and ambivalent one. From the clues given, its origin lies in yet another tale of disinheritance. Hernando Joaquín de Tristero y Calavera, "perhaps a madman, perhaps an honest rebel, according to some only a con artist" (*Lot 49* 159), intervenes as "The Disinherited" (*Lot 49* 160) into the fight for the postal monopoly between the Thurn and Taxis family and that of J. Hinkart, justifying both the intervention and the epithet by his claim to be the rightful heir of the Hinkart family. Rather than provide an uncontaminated origin, Pynchon creates a tale of infinite regression congruous with the infinite line of inheritance.

Tristero, apart from waging guerilla warfare against the ruling monopoly, sets up his own countersystem. Beyond the question of moral *right* or *wrong*, therefore, the Trystero is in the position of the "difference" within the structure of binary opposition—the inevitable result of a binary structure. In the tale of the Scurvhamites, Pynchon carries this opposition to an extreme, for their Puritan philosophy (an allegory of America) distinguishes absolutely between a good God and the "brute Other" (*Lot 49* 150), or "anti-God" (*Lot 49* 165), symbolized by the Trystero.

This binary structure is played out allegorically in three incidents. The first is that recounted by Diocletian Blobb, telling of the Trystero's attack on the Thurn and Taxis coach in which he was a passenger at the "Lake of Piety" (*Lot 49* 157). This scene is mirrored in the scene in the *Courier's Tragedy* in which the Trystero kill Niccolò, who poses as a Thurn and Taxis courier (and who is himself disinherited), at the lake where Faggio's Lost Guard were murdered by Angelo. The "miracle" (*Lot 49* 74) that results from the mingling of *"innocence with innocence"* (*Lot 49* 74) is the unveiling of truth in the play, *"a life's base lie, rewritten into truth"* (*Lot 49* 74); although it still bears Angelo's seal, the message of the "purloined letter" is reversed. Pynchon arranges this miracle around the motif of "piety," not so much in the sense of compassion as of awe in the face of a metaphysical intervention.

This scene is again reflected in the killing of the GIs at the "Lago di Pietà" (*Lot 49* 61) by Germans and Italians, with America standing for Faggio, Germany and Italy for Squamuglia, and the cynicism of the messages written by Angelo to Faggio with the bones of the Lost Guard, which were "made into charcoal, and the charcoal into ink" (*Lot 49* 74), mirrored (via the Cosa Nostra connection) in Tony Jaguar's "message" to America, which ends up "smoking" its own soldiers. *Lot 49* is ultimately about the impossibility of "writing Pierce's life into truth" in a secular, profane universe.

It is thus certainly not true that an inevitably imaginary paranoia is a viable solution within *Lot 49*, as Cooper has stated: "If it [paranoia] becomes truly 'creative' it progresses beyond a 'They-system' to posit a 'We-system'" (Cooper 77). Neither is the Trystero a purely positive force that, "as *The Crying of Lot 49* unfolds . . . looks more and more like a positive counterforce to the prevalent grotesque and entropic forces that desecrate contemporary America" (93).

In the concept of the mirror stage, Lacan has already shown that the imaginary, narcissistic confrontation leads to an aggressivity that can be mediated only by language. In order for the system of imaginary capture not to amount to "a more and more paralysing, vast concentric hallucination, so that it works, the intervention of a regulatory third party was necessary, which would put . . . the distance of a certain prescribed order . . . between them" (Lacan, *Seminar II* 169). This is what is excluded by mirror systems. In *Lot 49*, they have in fact been coexisting without direct mediation throughout history, resulting in an "800-year tradition of postal fraud" (*Lot 49* 98). In this context, the use of the mail is an apt metaphor, because, as Baudrillard states, "the basic ideology does not function anymore on the level of the political signifieds, but on the level of the signifiers—and . . . it is here that the system is vulnerable and must be dismantled" (*L'Échange symbolique* 123). The Trystero covers the town with a subtext, a parallel production of signs, yet its very secrecy is a sign of its ultimate ineffectiveness.

In his essay "Aggressivity in Psychoanalysis," Lacan follows aggressivity to its roots in the imaginary capture of the ego and its images: "The ego appears to be marked from its very origin by this aggressive relativity" (*Écrits* 19). It is defined by narcissistic tendencies and misrecognition, "the narcissistic relation and to the structures of systematic *méconnaissance* [misrecognition] and objectification that characterize the formation of the ego" (21). It finds its outlet exactly in projection, which defines Pierce: "The passionate desire peculiar to man to impress his image in reality" (22).

Lacan's reasons for "the pre-eminence of aggressivity in our civilization"

(*Écrits* 25) mirror Pynchon's. The first is society's failure to give a sense of community to *all* its members, a failure that stems from its definition by operational simulation and "the increasing absence of all those saturations of the superego and the ego ideal that are realized in all kinds of organic forms in traditional societies" (26). The second is linked to the debasement of love and the implosion of the sexual scene, to "abolishing the cosmic polarity of the male and female principles" (26). The third is the promotion of the ego and individuality, especially pertinent in capitalist entrepreneurship. This tendency "today culminates, in conformity with the utilitarian conception of man that reinforces it, in an ever more advanced realization of man as individual, that is to say, in an isolation of the soul ever more akin to its original dereliction" (27). This very utilitarian isolation presides, for instance, over the tale of the founding of the "Inamorati Anonymous" (*Lot 49* 112), a support group for "isolates" (*Lot 49* 113) that uses the "once knotted horn" as its logo.

Oedipa's fantasy of all the other telephone calls that might have run through the telephone lines parallel to her last call from Pierce shows this dereliction, highlighting the desperate search through the networks of communication and the desire to break through the net of signifiers in the hope of picking up the message of the other: "And the voices before and after the dead man's that had phoned at random during the darkest, slowest hours, searching ceaseless among the dial's ten million possibilities for that magical Other who would reveal herself out of the roar of relays, monotone litanies of insult, filth, fantasy, love whose brute repetition must someday call into being the trigger for the unnameable act, the recognition, the Word" (*Lot 49* 180).

All these developments lead (and have led) to the "derealization[s] of others and of the world" (*Écrits* 28). Oedipa's quest is defined in these parameters. Pynchon offers no way out of this deadlock, only a desire to escape. This desire is always linked to the motifs of *revelation* and *death*. It is for this reason that the final, "fantastic" scene of the book, in which the auctioneer Passerine celebrates the transubstantiation of the stamp, is full of apocalyptic hints. But the immense expectation of revelation is balanced and checked by a similarly immense letdown. As always with Pynchon—as with Lovecraft, to whom he alludes—the revelation is forever "trembling just past the threshold of understanding."[23] The apocalypse is not a final cataclysm, it is *inherent* in every sign. It is not their destruction that is apocalyptic, but their growth and continuation. Although Oedipa expects further revelations from the buyer of the lot, it becomes clear that revelation will again be suspended and deferred by language, because although the mysterious bidder "decided to attend the auction in person" (*Lot 49* 182), the agent who represents him is called *Schrift*—German for *writing*—implying that the future developments will involve further disseminations of texts, significations, and interpretations. The subject can be reached only *through* the "agency of the letter."

Notes

1. At first sight, a psychoanalytic background for *Lot 49* might seem unwarranted, because Pynchon (as in *V.*) continually reads psychoanalysis against itself. In *Lot 49* Hilarious is the center of Pynchon's criticism, yet Hilarious is exactly one of the ego psychologists against whom Lacan continually polemicizes for trying to reinstall the autonomy of the ego: "And part of me must have really wanted to believe—like a child hearing, in perfect safety, a tale of horror—that the unconscious would be like any other room, once the light was let in. That the dark shapes would resolve only into toy horses and Biedermeyer furniture. That therapy could tame it after all" (*Lot 49* 134–35). As such, ego psychology belongs to the systems that veil the truth about the subject.

2. For a discussion of this aspect see especially John O. Stark, *Pynchon's Fictions*.

3. In "Requiem for the Media," Baudrillard states that "the 'media revolution' has remained empirical and mystical, as much in the work of McLuhan as with his opponents" (*Critique* 164). His point of critique is that McLuhan "exalts the media and their global message with a delirious tribal optimism" (172). In *Understanding Media,* McLuhan himself calls this "a faith that concerns the ultimate harmony of all being" (13), yet it suffices to read the first page of that book to see how much Baudrillard draws on McLuhan's theories: "After three thousand years of explosion . . . the Western world is imploding. . . . Rapidly, we approach the final phase of the extensions of man—the technological simulation of consciousness" (11).

4. "One could call *play* the absence of the transcendental signified as limitlessness of play" (Derrida, *Of Grammatology* 50).

5. The motif of the letter and writing thus inscribes *Lot 49* into the very framework of the controversy between Lacan's and Derrida's definitions of subjectivity in their discussion of Poe's "Purloined Letter." The question of whether in *Lot 49* the letters ultimately arrive at their destination and whether *Lot 49*, like "The Purloined Letter" in Lacan's reading, can ultimately be read as an "allegory of the signifier" might well be crucial in a reading of the novel.

6. "In short, we call ego that nucleus given to consciousness, but opaque to reflexion, marked by all the ambiguities which . . . structure the experience of the passions in the human subject" (Lacan, *Écrits* 15).

7. In *Ideas of Order,* Molly Hite states, "As Oedipa comes to suspect, such projection is equivalent to paranoia and at her stage amounts to cosmic error" (77). John O. Stark comments that "the dominant dichotomy is paranoia and not-paranoia" (82). In *The Grim Phoenix,* William M. Plater also gives a rather bleak outlook: "In the meantime she can only wait, consumed by her own paranoia" (213). Bersani's "Pynchon, Paranoia, and Literature" comes closest to my reading. For him, "paranoia is a necessary and desired structure of thought" (103).

8. "In the symbolic order the totality is called a universe. The symbolic order from the first takes on its universal character. . . . As soon as the symbol arrives, there is a universe of symbols" (Lacan, *Seminar II* 29).

9. Driblette repeats precisely this reluctance in "real life": "He had managed to create around it the same aura of ritual reluctance here, offstage, as he had on" (*Lot 49* 79).

10. See Anne Mangel, "Maxwell's Demon, Entropy, Information." For other "entropic" readings see John P. Leland, "Pynchon's Linguistic Demon," and Peter Abernethy, "Entropy in Pynchon's *The Crying of Lot 49.*" See also Hite: "She [Oedipa] has failed all along as a sorting demon because she has persistently rejected the elements of her experience that signal meaning and value in her own world" (*Ideas of Order* 85); Seed: "The communication process breaks down entropically towards total disorder" (*Fictional Labyrinths* 146); and Plater: "The world as it is presents a frightening prospect: entropy increases, accident and chance are everywhere, and nothing is certain" (xv).

11. In a nice coincidence, it was the Bell Telephone Company that first worked out the informational angle of this equation. For a discussion of this fact see Lacan, *Seminar II,* 82.

12. For Maxwell, Nefastis tells Oedipa, the Demon existed "long before the days of the metaphor" (*Lot 49* 106). Yet Oedipa herself is not so sure whether "Clerk Maxwell [had] been such a fanatic about his Demon's reality" (*Lot 49* 106).

13. "I have been able to establish an order (that is, a code) as a system of probability within an original disorder" (Umberto Eco, *The Open Work,* 58). A code is thus a system of probabilities that is superimposed on the disorder (equal probability) of the initial system in order to master it communicatively.

14. Although it is sometimes given as "death instinct," I will use Lacan's "death drive": "'Drive' would seem to translate the German word quite well in English" (*Écrits* 301). Consider also his comment that "beyond the pleasure-principle, there appears to us that opaque face . . . which calls itself death-drive" (*Séminaire VII* 29) and that "on the level of the material systems considered as lifeless, up to and including that which intervenes as the form of material organization within the living organisms, the entry into a function of an irreversible tendency . . . a state of terminal equilibrium, is that which is, properly speaking, articulated in the field of energetics as entropy" (250).

15. Schaub refers to Norbert Wiener: "Organisms are viewed by him as mes-

sages, since they are 'opposed to chaos, to disintegration, to death, as message is to noise'" (*Pynchon* 39). Yet it is not so simple to turn man into a cybernetic concept. Although it denotes the subject's "consistence," the organism is on the other hand exactly what links it to death.

16. See Marie-Claude Profit, "The Rhetoric of Death in *The Crying of Lot 49*," as well as Seed, *The Fictional Labyrinths of Thomas Pynchon,* and Plater: "Most of Pynchon's principal closed systems will be sorted out subsequently. However, the one that subsumes all others is the world, and it is only moving in one direction— toward death" (3).

17. In these dynamics, the repetition tendency stresses the psychoanalytic, sexual field and denotes a regressive movement, whereas the metonymical and metaphorical structurations stress the symbolic field and denote a progressive movement. The interplay of these two movements forms the specific structure of human time: "The coalescing of at least two series of motivations is necessary to the production of any symptomatic form. One is sexual, the other is . . . symbolic" (Lacan, *Seminar II* 137). Lacan, like Derrida, posits the ultimate impossibility of the return of the repressed via a recursive model: "What can the memory . . . of something so erased be, a memory of a memory?" (125).

18. Hegel's depreciation of hieroglyphic script as less ideal than alphabetical script is ultimately the result of this need for a completely logical, abstract, and arbitrary code that ensures that intuitions (which are, strictly speaking, "before the sign") can be *translated* into representations without any loss or interference. Alphabetical script is the system that best brings about this complete effacement of the signifier. It "erases its own spacing better than any other" (Derrida, *Margins* 95).

19. For William Burroughs, whose work is in many ways comparable to Pynchon's and also influenced by McLuhan, the hieroglyph also functions as a utopia, which is why he sees Chinese language as the promise of a "total language closer to the multi-level structure of experience, with a script derived from hieroglyphs, more closely related to the objects and areas described. . . . The aim of this project is to build a language in which certain falsifications inherent in all existing Western languages will be made incapable of formulation" (*The Job,* 199). As they do with Pynchon, these falsifications touch the very core of subjectivity, language, and signification: the "IS *of Identity,*" the "*definite article* THE," and the "*whole concept of* EITHER/OR" (200).

20. Lacan compares Freud to Champollion, the first European to decipher the Egyptian hieroglyphs, because it was Freud who first succeeded in reading the dream, this "stone covered with hieroglyphics" (*Fundamental Concepts* 199) found in the desert of the human arena. In Lacan's view, Freud succeeded because he was the first to read these hieroglyphs within a specific symbolic system, showing "how speech . . . can get itself recognized through anything, provided that this anything be organized in a symbolic system. There we have the source of what was

118   Textual Analyses

for so long the indecipherable character of the dream. And it is for the same reason that for a long time no one knew how to understand hieroglyphics—they were not set up in their own symbolic system" (*Seminar I* 244). Throughout his theory, Lacan subjects the image quality of the dream to its symbolic structure, seeing the ideogram predominantly in its function of a letter, stressing its arbitrariness: "The image as signifier has nothing to do with its signification, giving as an example Egyptian hieroglyphics" (*Écrits* 159) and its syntactical functions: "The dream has the structure of a sentence, or, rather, ... of a rebus; ... it has the structure of a form of writing, of which the child's dream represents the primordial ideography, and which, in the adult, reproduces the simultaneously phonetic and symbolic use of signifying elements, which can also be found both in the hieroglyphs of ancient Egypt and in the characters still used in China" (57). Wilden links the analog, which he also links to the primary process, to Chinese epistemology, which "emphasize[s] totality, homeostasis, natural and social context ... and wisdom rather than analysis, pure knowledge ... 'reason' or 'rationality,' and the various separations and dichotomies which underlie all western epistemology" (166).

21. In *Of Grammatology*, Derrida also links writing to ploughing: "It is a matter of *writing by furrows*. The furrow is the line, as the ploughman traces it. . . . The furrow of agriculture . . . opens nature to culture" (287).

22. In *V.*, Fausto realizes that "metaphor has no value apart from its function; that it is a device, an artifice. [. . .] Fausto's kind are alone with the task of living in a universe of things which simply are, and cloaking that innate mindlessness with comfortable and pious metaphor [. . . .] It is the 'role' of the poet, this 20th Century. To lie" (*V.* 326).

23. On Lovecraft and Pynchon see Jeffrey L. Meikle, "'Other Frequencies.'"

Chapter 6 *Gravity's Rainbow:*
The Real Text

"In the Zone, in these days, there is endless simulation."

"it's a plot it's a plot it's *Pavlovian conditioning!* or something"

"The War has been reconfiguring time and space into its own image. The track runs in different networks now. What appears to be destruction is really the shaping of railroad spaces to other purposes, intentions he can only [. . .] begin to feel the leading edges of . . ."

Thomas Pynchon, *Gravity's Rainbow*

In *Lot 49* Pynchon depicts the oscillating spaces in which a textual subject drifts through the "text of the world." This space finds its correlative in the book's similarly oscillating, and therefore open, rhetorical structure. In such a scenario, in which every subject is "sentenced" to use language, the story can indeed be only a "Courier's Tragedy." In this chapter I investigate the problematics of language in terms of conditionings and s(t)imulations, first at the personal level and then at the cultural.

One of the important shifts from *Lot 49* to *Gravity's Rainbow* is in Pynchon's mode of characterization. Unlike *Lot 49*, *Gravity's Rainbow* makes use of a more schematic and abstract characterization reminiscent of *V.* Yet unlike *V.,* the main aporias are linked not to a dialectical pair but to only one person, Slothrop (who, however, constantly shifts personalities). He is Max Schlepzig, alias Ian Scuffling (GR 256), alias Rocketman (GR 359), alias the Schwarzknabe (GR 286), alias "Plechazunga" (GR 567).

Despite this shift, however, *Gravity's Rainbow* takes up most of the themes developed in *V.* and *Lot 49,* developing them in a more complex "network of [. . .] plots" (GR 603).¹ In particular, the positions of the Trystero and V. as "mystery signifiers" are taken over by the V-2, and the "Counterforce," which with its "ad hoc arrangements" (GR 620) shares some characteristics with Deleuze and Guattari's idea of "de-territorialization" (Guattari 83), is, like the Trystero, caught in a mirror structure with "Them": "Dialectically, sooner or later, some counterforce would have had to arise" (GR 536). Although Pynchon portrays the Counterforce in more positive terms than he does the Trystero, he questions—as he does in *Lot 49*—any concept of "creative paranoia" (GR 638), stating that the Counterforce's members ultimately might be nothing more than "doomed pet freaks" (GR 713) who are in constant danger of co-optation and thus complicity with "Them": "They are as schizoid, as double-minded in the massive presence of money, as any of the rest of us, and that's the hard fact" (GR 712; this topic is developed in more detail in the chapter on *Vineland*).

In a further parallel, like Stencil and Oedipa, Slothrop is looking for his identity, which for him means trying to uncover the mysterious connection of his libido to the V-2. As in the other books, this search takes place in a fully cybernetic universe in which "information [has] come to be the only real medium of exchange" (GR 258) and in which there is an "overabundance of signifier" (Tanner, *Pynchon* 76). As he does in *Lot 49,* Pynchon singles out exactly this aspect for his investigation, centering his depiction of the war on the informational universe of spies, counterspies, and intelligence operations.

Finally, in *Gravity's Rainbow,* the concepts of "Them" and "The Firm" are worked out in more detail and linked to the issues of "synthesis and control" (GR 661). In the internal thematic structure of the novel, control is related to the realm of Pavlovian conditioning, whereas synthesis is related to that of chemistry and simulation. In the following, I center my discussion on these two aspects, dealing first with Slothrop's conditioning, then with that of the Zone, and finally, in a reading of the chemical imagery in the Kirghiz Light episode, with an example of the "conditioning" of a whole culture through the imposition of a completely digital language.

Before dealing with the various modes of conditioning, however, it is necessary to sketch out the topography of the landscapes of *Gravity's Rainbow,* which not only provide the arena in which these conditionings proceed but are themselves "conditioned."

The ambiguous character of the landscapes of *Gravity's Rainbow* is evoked, for instance, when Slothrop dreams of Bianca at some point during his journey through postwar Germany, the Zone into which he has been sent by "forces unknown" in order to "be present at his own assembly—perhaps, heavily paranoid voices have whispered, *his time's assembly*" (GR 738). In this dream "Bianca comes to snuggle in under his blanket with him. 'You're really in that Europe now,' she grins, hugging him" (GR 492–93). This passage, and many other similar ones, shows that in his treatment of the historic scene as a psychopathological one, Pynchon understands Europe not so much as a mere grouping of geopolitical units but more as both a real and a mental territory, a "state of mind" in which psychic and geographic space are conflated.

In such a topography, as I mentioned at the end of part 1, classical space and the distinction between inside and outside are replaced by a new kind of space, one that is represented by the Möbius strip. In this space, the cut is no longer between inside and outside; rather, the space itself is now *in toto* defined by a cut that is *internal* to the structure, so that inside and outside are inextricably aligned in a "one-sided," convoluted space.

This redefinition of space simultaneously entails one of time, because at the same time that it represents the *spatial*, the Möbius strip also represents a *temporal* loop in which past, present, and future are no longer defined along a straight line but constantly fold back onto each other. As Jeanne Granon-Lafont states, with a Möbius strip the dichotomy between the two terms *front* and *back*—as well as, I argue, in extension, *inside* and *outside*— appears only through "the intervention of a new dimension: that of time" (30). Such temporal loops also define the concept of belatedness, which describes the fact that a real, unconscious, and repressed trauma, one that is "experienced" when the perceptual apparatus is not yet developed, can be dealt with only belatedly, in its symbolic and imaginary transcriptions. Finally, the looping of these "categorical" terms also brings about a loop in the *logical* universe. Pynchon's frequent use of the trope of *hysteron proteron*, which Weisenburger notes, reveals that almost every aspect of the book is implicated by such loops.

The psychic landscapes—and those of *Gravity's Rainbow* are always partly psychic—are defined by such spatiotemporal and logical loops. As such, the landscapes of *Gravity's Rainbow* become more than backgrounds to the story. Like dream-landscapes, they are belated representations of repressed mental territories. The wrecked, wasted landscapes of postwar Germany, however, represent not only a *personal* repressed but also a *cultural* one. Slothrop, alias Rocketman, is searching not merely for his *own* past: "Rocketman has just landed here to tour the ruins, the high-desert traces of an ancient European order . . ." (GR 436).

Already in the beginning of the book, the evacuation from the V-2–ravaged London deeper into the city is both a spatial *and* a psychic event, a movement toward the "navel of the city" as well as toward the "navel of the dream." It is not an escape, but a journey toward a more atavistic center, "not a disentanglement from, but a progressive *knotting into*" (GR 3). Pynchon condenses the atmosphere of this ruinous, derelict world, its hopelessness and lovelessness, into (often ironically undercut) images in which destruction and death, Thanatos, are inextricably amalgamated with love, Eros: "Back in the wreckage a brass bedpost winks; and twined there someone's brassiere, a white, prewar confection of lace and satin, simply left tangled . . ." (GR 43). It is in these ambiguous spaces that Slothrop's conditioning is both anchored and prefigured.

In *Gravity's Rainbow,* the theme of conditioning is treated in reference to a number of juxtaposed concepts. Similar to *Lot 49,* in which Oedipa is confronted with the binary choice between one and zero, "either a transcendent meaning or only the earth," *Gravity's Rainbow* revolves around the binary positions of a metaphysics, although this is again a metaphysics under erasure—m̶e̶t̶a̶p̶h̶y̶s̶i̶c̶s̶—and a pure physics. Yet this dualism is supplemented and thus complicated by a third position, that of a physics turned metaphysics, all of which Pynchon aligns in an intricate rhetorical matrix. The physics turned metaphysics is represented by Pavlovian conditioning, the Pavlovian scientists Laszlo Jamf and Ned Pointsman, and the part of the plot that revolves around them.

At the beginning of the book, while he is still in London, Slothrop has a map on which he marks the sites of his sexual encounters, whereas the statistician Roger Mexico—who represents the world of pure physics and is therefore the "Antipointsman" (GR 55) and ultimately Pointsman's repressed—keeps a map of the sites of the V-2 strikes on London. His map follows a statistical model, the Poisson distribution: "Each hit is independent of all the others. Bombs are not dogs. No link. No memory. No conditioning" (GR 56). The mysterious thing, however, is that "the slides that Teddy Bloat's been taking of Slothrop's map have been projected onto Roger's, and the two images, girl-stars and rocket-strike circles, demonstrated to coincide" (GR 85–86).[2] Throughout the book, Pointsman tries to account for this superimposition of Eros and Thanatos and to answer the implicit question, whether there is a mutual or reciprocal induction of these two forces—in short, whether "desire grow[s] directly or inversely as the real chance of sudden death" (GR 86). His main question is, "what *does* make the little doxies do it for free? Are there fluctuations in the sexual market [. . .] that we clean-living lot know nothing about? Does news from the front affect the itch between their pretty thighs?" (GR 86). For Mexico, these questions are irrelevant, because his map does not represent a structure based on the law of cause and effect. It is merely the belated representation of a universe of pure contingency and reconstructs not a logical *sequence* but a mere *series* of random events. Pointsman, however, the champion of cause and effect, is terrified by such a universe and wonders whether postwar will also be a *post-histoire,* with "nothing but 'events,' newly created one moment to the next? No links? Is it the end of history?" (GR 56). Yet he, like Mexico, cannot account for Slothrop's (psychosexual) connection to the V-2. Being a Pavlovian, he searches for the ominous "Mystery Stimulus" (GR 84) that supposedly brings about what he calls Slothrop's "hardon reflex" (GR 84), which in turn "brings about" or "accompanies" Slothrop's meetings with women.

Although Pynchon "quotes" Pavlov at some length in his presentation of conditioning, he also modifies him in a crucial manner. Unlike Pavlov, who used food as a stimulus and salivation as a measure of the animal's response, thus allowing exact measurement of response level, Pointsman is after another sort of "drooling": "a hardon, that's either there, or it isn't. Binary, elegant" (GR 84). Apart from transferring conditioning from real to sexual hunger, this replacement implies a shift to a purely binary realm.

Finally, there is the realm of metaphysics under erasure. It is evoked, for instance, after a passage in which Slothrop, in bed with Darlene, hears a rocket fall, and his "penis [springs] erect, aching" (GR 120). This is followed by a "hint of revelation," when an unattributed and thus anonymous narrative voice asks, "And who's that, through the crack in the orange shade, breathing carefully? Watching? And where, keepers of maps, specialists at surveillance, would you say the next one will fall?" (GR 120).

Pynchon introduces the first time loop at this point; although the similarity of the maps "proves" a connection between Slothrop and the V-2, the *rendez-vous* with the women take place *before* the rocket strikes at the place of the *rendez-vous*. The stimulus, or cause, therefore cannot be simply "auditory" (GR 52), such as the slowly growing noise of the V-1; rather, it is related to the new era of the V-2, whose most terrifying characteristic is precisely that it travels faster than sound. Accordingly, "Slothrop [. . .] gets erections when this sequence happens *in reverse*. Explosion first, then the sound of approach: the V-2" (GR 86). According to this new logic, the reason for his "premature" erections must be something "in the air" (GR 86) *before* the actual rocket strike, but already connected to it, a "precursor wraith" (GR 86) or a (fantastic or phantasmatic) "double" (GR 86).

Already, the sequence of cause (stimulus) and effect (response) is looped, or reversed. In a second step, Pynchon links up the fields of *conditioning* and *paranoia*. This happens through Slothrop, who is a model paranoiac. Again, this link is established along an instance of a reversal. According to Pavlov, the brain functions, like a computer, as a mosaic of neurons that are either *on* or *off,* and mental illnesses, such as paranoia, are the result of a state in which brain cells—through the collision of a process of excitation with one of inhibition—get so excited that the ideas of opposites get lost and the area around them becomes "inhibited" (GR 90).[3] In such a state, which Pavlov termed "transmarginal" (GR 49),[4] there is no more flux. All that is left is "one bright, burning point, surrounded by darkness" (GR 90), a "point of pathological *inertia*" (GR 90; emphasis added). To describe this state Pynchon paraphrases Pavlov's "open letter" to Pierre Janet when Pointsman states, "you weaken this idea of the opposite, and here all at once is the paranoid patient who would be master, yet now feels himself a slave . . . who would be loved, but suffers his world's indifference [. . . .] Our madmen, our paranoid, maniac, schizoid, morally imbecile—" (GR 48–49).[5]

These transmarginal states are brought about by "reciprocal *induction*" (GR 90; emphasis added), a term that—through Pointsman—is also related to the dynamics between Eros and Thanatos: "And how much of the pretty victim straining against her bonds does Ned Pointsman see in each dog that visits his test stands . . . and aren't scalpel and probe as decorative, as fine extensions as whip and cane?" (GR 88). Reciprocal induction is a term used in a number of frameworks, such as biology, philosophy, and magnetism, denoting in all of them different shades of "to lead to" or "to bring about"; in Pavlovian conditioning, it denotes the intensification of one process by another, specifically, the fact that the effect of an excitatory stimulus increases when it is applied immediately or soon after an inhibitory one. This reciprocal induction is in turn closely linked to the *"ultraparadoxical phase"* (GR 49) of conditioning, the phase in which a stimulus operates precisely when it is *absent,* and the patient "seek[s], in the silence, for the stimulus that is not there" (GR 90). This, then, is one possible explanation of Slothrop's sexual encounters, which would have to be understood as frustrated searches for the "silent" stimulus that links him to the rocket.

This stimulus might actually be olfactory rather than auditory. In one passage, Slothrop wonders whether the "Mystery Stimulus" might be Imipolex G, which is also, as Drohne suggests, closely connected to the Schwarzgerät: "A smell, a forbidden room, at the bottom edge of his memory. [. . .] He knows what the smell has to be: though according to these papers it would have been too early for it [. . .] he knows that what's haunting him now will prove to be the smell of Imipolex G" (GR 286). Although it might well make sense within a concept of belatedness, this temporal problem, which is never resolved logically in the text, actually prefigures the difficulties surrounding any attempt at a critical *"Imipolectique"* (GR 490).[6] Actually, Imipolex G[ottfried] is used only once as the insulation device of the 00000, with the final marriage of man and machine—Gottfried and the rocket—taking place in a "shroud" (GR 754) of Imipolex G.

Whether the stimulus is indeed Imipolex G or something else remains an open question, but it is certain that it cannot be the rocket itself. Nonetheless, according to Pavlov, a trivial or vague precursor can become the stimulus; sometimes merely the entry into the laboratory, "some cue we might never pin down would be enough to send him [generally the dog, but in this case Slothrop] over, send him transmarginal" (GR 49). This is why Pointsman comes to think of "the war itself as a *laboratory*" (GR 49) and sends Slothrop into the Zone, hoping that he will lead them to the "missing link" or clue. This "laboratory," however, is again defined as a Möbius-like, ambivalent space. It is exactly here that Pynchon evokes Spectro's idea that the universe "might have one edge after all":

> the symmetry [. . .] assuming that a mechanism must imply its mirror image—"irradiation," for example, and "reciprocal induction" . . . and who'd ever said that either had to exist? [. . .] But how it haunts him, the symmetry of these two secret weapons, Outside [. . .] the sounds of V-1 and V-2, one the reverse of the other. Pavlov showed how mirror-images Inside could be confused. Ideas of the opposite. But what new pathology lies Outside now? What sickness to events—to History itself—can create symmetrical opposites like these robot weapons?
>
> Sign and Symptoms. Was Spectro right? *Could Outside and Inside be part of the same field?* (GR 144; emphasis added)

Pointsman's objective is to find the experimental setup *behind* the war and thus to prove the "stone determinacy of everything, of every soul" (GR 86); to do this would be to realize Pavlov's dream, the proof for the "true mechanical explanation [. . .] a pure physiological basis for the life of the psyche" (GR 89). This is why Pointsman, like Slothrop himself, is constantly trying to read the Zone.

The epigraph to part three—"In the Zone"—of *Gravity's Rainbow*, "Toto, I have a feeling we're not in Kansas any more," designates the Zone as a dream-space, while the statement that "there are no zones [. . .] no zones but the Zone" (GR 333) shows that Pynchon thinks of it as ultimately identical to the space of "human reality" itself. Its main characteristic is that, because of the war's destructions, "categories have been blurred badly" (GR 303). There is "never a clear sense of nationality anywhere, nor even of belligerent sides, only the War, a single damaged landscape" (GR 257). In this respect, the destroyed landscape of Germany serves as a metaphor for a state of disorder. It is a landscape stripped of meanings, a purely material surface: the utopia of a *tabula rasa*, a free, unhierarchical, anarchic space without cultural—symbolic and imaginary—inscriptions, which is why Geli Tripping, a witch and another of Slothrop's part-time lovers, can tell him to "forget frontiers now. Forget subdivisions" (GR 294). As in Guattari's dynamics of de- and re-territorialization, the Zone is an "interregnum" (294), the "timeless" moment of the cut or pulse that separates *de*struction from *con*struction and *de*centralization from centralization: "In ordinary times [. . .] the center always wins. [. . .] Decentralizing, back towards anarchism, needs extraordinary times . . . this War [. . .] has wiped out the proliferation of little states that's prevailed in Germany for a thousand years. Wiped it clean. *Opened it*" (GR 264–65).

Although he realizes that this open space "won't last" except "for a few months [. . .] for a moment of spring, perhaps" (GR 265), maybe only for "the warm, romantic summer of '45" (GR 445), the Argentine anarchist Squalidozzi hopes for a change for the better: "In the openness of the German Zone, our hope is limitless" (GR 265). Yet, he also realizes, "so is our danger" (GR 265). Similarly, Slothrop dreams about a possible new beginning:

> It seems [. . .] that there might be a route back—maybe that anarchist he met in Zürich was right, maybe for a little while all the fences are down [. . .] the whole space of the Zone cleared, depolarized, and somewhere inside the waste of it a single *set of coordinates* from which to proceed, without elect, without preterite, without even nationality to fuck it up . . ." (GR 556; emphasis added)

Pynchon uses one of his many scientific metaphors to define the dynamics of the Zone, especially its promise that "the people will find the Center

Figure 1.

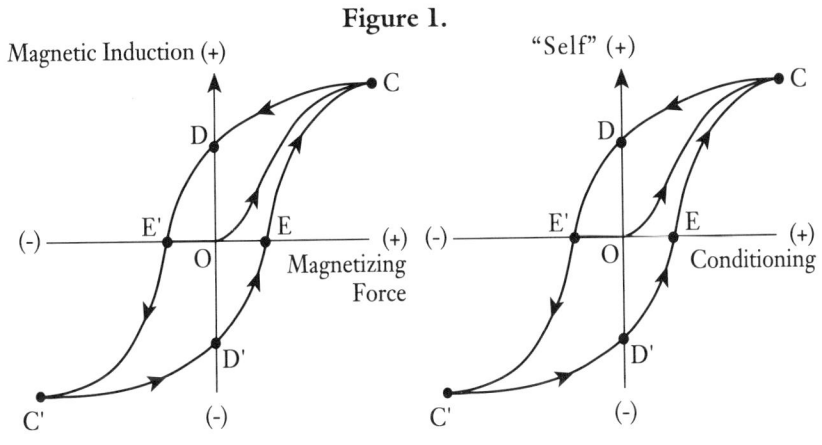

Magnetic Induction (+) ... **Magnetizing Force** (with points C, D, E, O, E', D', C')

"Self" (+) ... **Conditioning** (with points C, D, E, O, E', D', C')

again, the Center without time" (GR 319). Pynchon describes such a logocentric, utopian journey toward the center as a "journey without hysteresis, where every departure is a return to the same place, the only place . . ." (GR 319).[7] Such a journey, however, would have to exclude both the pathological *psychic* (mental) and the *physical* (material) inertia, thus touching both sides—or actually the Möbius-like "one side"—of subjectivity: *mind* and *body, consciousness* and *unconsciousness*. Pynchon hinges his argument precisely on these two kinds of "inertia," which adds a whole new dimension to the name *Sloth*rop and the *Gravity* in the book's title.[8] Whereas the pathological, psychic inertia is dealt with in terms of Pavlovian conditioning, the parallel problem of physical inertia is appropriately dealt with in physical terms through the concept of hysteresis, which denotes the tendency of inert, physical materials to lag in response to changing forces.[9] A ferromagnetic material, for example, that is put into a growing magnetic field up to the point of saturation (O-C) will not return by itself to its former state after the field has been removed but will remain to some degree magnetized (C-D), a rest called *remanence,* or *residual induction* (see figure 1). This process can be reversed only through the application of a "negative" magnetic field, with a complete demagnetization reached at E'. The amount of negative induction needed to reduce the magnetization of the material to zero is called *coercive force*.[10] The application of a negative field up to the point of saturation yields the curve D-C'. A *decrease* of the negative field yields the curve C'-D'; the subsequent *re*application of a positive field, D'-C. The important thing is that this loop—itself comparable in some aspects to a Möbius strip—will never bring the magnetized material back to the initial point O. Because of the inherent physical inertia of the material, the curves from C to C′ and back to C take different paths, and both differ from the initial curve O to C, which denotes a point of departure to which no return is possible.

Pynchon uses this scientific fact to create a complex metaphor and allegory of the "human condition"(ing) and of "life as a detour."[11] If O—the state of complete chaos and entropy, in which electrons are randomly oriented—is seen as the moment of the "birth of subjectivity," and the magnetic fields are seen as various (cultural) conditionings (with complete saturation, the state in which the electrons are completely aligned in either direction, denoting the complete conditioning of the subject), the metaphor ultimately shows the impossibility of a return to the origin. The Zone is such an ambivalent space because, although it is on the one hand the utopia of an origin—which would imply a logocentric innocence and presence—Pynchon simultaneously uses it to stage the impossibility of such a return. Once innocence has been lost—in electromagnetic terms, the first curve, O-C, is appropriately called the "virgin curve"—it cannot be regained without completely demagnetizing the metal, a process analogous in Pavlovian conditioning to a complete deconditioning. As Pointsman notes, "ordinarily [. . .] the little sucker would have been de-conditioned" (GR 84). Yet even with such a deconditioning—and parallel with a complete demagnetization, especially if one considers the world as a "mind-body" (GR 590)—a return to a completely unconditioned state might be impossible. Again, Pynchon quotes Pavlov directly: "we must [. . .] realize that extinction can proceed *beyond* the point of reducing a reflex to zero [. . .] there can still be a *silent extinction beyond the zero*" (GR 84–85). This silent extinction, which one might actually see in analogy with the "negative coercive force," might be the ultimate reason for and clue to Slothrop's link to the V-2.

What links physics and hysteresis with conditioning is that Pavlov understands the human body as a purely physiological apparatus, a complicated cybernetic machine. In fact, Lacan singles out this very concept, especially in relation to its foreclosure of the signifier, in his critique of Pavlovian conditioning. He develops this critique within a discussion of the difference between the purely biological function of *need*, which operates on the level of the real, and those of *desire* and *demand*, which operate on that of the symbolic and the imaginary. Conditioned stimuli do not function as signifiers for the animal because in the conditioned reflex it is merely a "need" (*Fundamental Concepts* 228) that is broken down, not a desire. For the stimuli to become signifiers, what is needed is "an internal apparatus which reflects not only the stimuli of the external world, but also, in a manner of speaking, its structure" (*Seminar II* 107).¹² Unlike in the story of the mice that "use" the experimenters to get food, Pavlov's dogs never enter the "intersubjective" level of the signifier: "The experiment may cause in him [the dog] all sorts of disorders, all sorts of disturbances, but, not yet being a speaking creature, he is not called to put in question the desire of the experimenter" (*Fundamental Concepts* 237). Thus, the conditioned reflex functions merely at the level of a purely biological perception. As a result, "even the supposed effects of neurosis that are obtained are not effects of neurosis, for one simple reason—they cannot be analysed by speech" (228). Interestingly, the level of the signifier adds a third kind of inertia to the discussion, the "considerable inertia" (*Encore* 100) of language, whose entropic tendencies are also of such importance to Oedipa in *Lot 49* and will become equally important in the discussion of the Kirghiz Light episode.

It is not surprising that during the course of his odyssey, Slothrop learns that he has indeed been conditioned from his birth onward: "Once something was done to him, in a room, while he lay helpless . . ." (GR 285). His father had sold him to IG Farben "like a side of beef" (GR 286).¹³ In return, they paid for his education at Harvard, so that Slothrop becomes a preterite version of Citizen Kane. His main question (and that of the book) is thus how what he has always thought of as *his* subjectivity is implicated in the "cultural" inscriptions and conditionings of a specifically "Western" civilization, for which the scientist and IG Farben employee Jamf (the acronym of a black insult: Jive-ass motherfucker) and Pointsman are the "personifications."¹⁴ Ultimately, as does *Lot 49*, the book opens up the question of the relation between the individual and culture, "the coupling of 'Jamf' and 'I' in the primal dream" (GR 623).¹⁵ Yet again, the search for this connection is a belated one. It is not Slothrop who is following the S-Gerät, but the other way around: "it's the S-Gerät after all that's following him, it and the plastic ubiquity of Laszlo Jamf. [. . .] Looks like there are sub-Slothrop needs They know about, and he doesn't: this is humiliating on the face of it, but now there's also the even more annoying question. *What do I need that badly?*" (GR 490).

On an individual level, Pynchon deals with the impossibility of a return to a state of zero via Slothrop's conditioning. In fact, retrospectively, "famous analyst" Mickey Wuxtry-Wuxtry states that "Jamf [as a person/personification] was only a fiction, to help him explain what he felt so terribly, so immediately in his genitals for those rockets each time exploding in the sky . . . to help him deny what he could not possibly admit: that he might be in love, in sexual love, with his, and his race's, death" (GR 738). Here, Slothrop's "perverse" sexual trauma is directly equated with Pavlovian conditioning by a culture that links *sex* and *death* in a perverse combination.[16]

On a more general cultural level—and from the perspective of the material, real world rather than of the subject—the Zone symbolizes the impossibility of a return to innocence, because from the beginning, its "anarchy"—and thus its real-ity—is a utopia under erasure. Because of the numerous substories to the war and its destructions, the state of zero it promises is always already encoded, belated, and never real. Also on this level, the zero point of total randomness is a "conditional" one, and the disorder only *appears* to be the true zero. Through the Zone, then, Pynchon restates the question of Slothrop's conditioning on a more generally cultural level: like the subject's, the "history of the real" is always already a "chronic experiment" (Pavlov XIX),[17] and Slothrop's terrible realization that he "has been under their observation—m-maybe since he was *born*? Yaahhh . . ." (GR 286) is mirrored in the question whether the history of the real is nothing more than the random events of a "real history" or is also controlled by a mysterious "Them" or "The Firm." In this light, the Zone is not a free space but a similarly "erogenous Zone," a merely "*synthetic wastefield*" (GR 523; emphasis added) that is the result of an "incalculable plot" (GR 521). One possible substory to the war and its destruction is, as Katje Borghesius learns, that "the real business of the War is buying and selling. The murdering and the violence are self-policing, and can be entrusted to non-professionals. [. . .] It serves as spectacle, as diversion from the real movements of the War" (GR 105). Although the *apparent* war has resulted in sinister destructions, "the true war is a celebration of markets" (GR 105) that extend beyond national borders: "Perhaps it's theater, but they *seem* no longer to be Allies . . . though the history they have invented for themselves conditions us to *expect* 'postwar rivalries,' when in fact it may all be a giant cartel including winners and losers both, in an amiable agreement to share what is there to be shared . . ." (GR 326).

In this respect, the Zone is treated as a space of hidden cultural and, ultimately, psychosexual inscriptions that one can read only if one finds their *grammar*. The main candidate for this grammar is, Enzian realizes, the V-2: "say we *are* supposed to be the Kabbalists out here [. . .] the scholar-magicians of the Zone, with somewhere in it a Text, to be picked to pieces, annotated, explicated, and masturbated [. . .] well we assumed—natürlich!—that this holy Text had to be the Rocket" (GR 520).

Although the landscape *seems* real, in the Schwarzkommando's search for the "True Text" (GR 525)—the "incalculable plot"—it becomes a "Real Text" (GR 520), an ambivalent, even paradoxical territory in which, as in the human body, real and symbolic registers constantly oscillate. Again and again, Pynchon highlights this textual quality of the real, which is also why everyone in the Zone is or feels so "unreal." Again, however, Pynchon does not choose either side: the shift from real to symbolic registers is not from one side to the other but happens—as on a Möbius strip—on the same "field" and thus the *same side*.

Yet it never becomes clear *who* is behind the various encodings and simulations, the "incalculable plot." It might be "a conspiracy between human beings and techniques" (GR 521); it might also be the enigmatic "Firm," the "IG Raketen" (GR 566), or a combination of all these, which might also ultimately be identical. In any case, it is something intimately related to the V-2, "a State that spans oceans and surface politics [. . .] and the Rocket is its soul" (GR 566). This is why in *Gravity's Rainbow,* one way or another, everyone tries to *assemble* the secret message spelled out by the landscape, and everyone is forever "decoding the Text, thus coding, recoding, redecoding the holy Text . . ." (GR 520–21), a movement that parallels the "assembly" of the 00001, the "repressed" counter-rocket to the 00000, the two terms that together form the book's most comprehensive binarism (00000/00001). The direction of this attempt is toward the center and thus counter to "centrifugal History" (GR 737). It is, "in a geographical way, a Diaspora running backwards, seeds of exile flying inward in a modest preview of gravitational collapse" (GR 737), a movement that evokes once again a "fearful," revelatory implosion. Nonetheless, during this very attempt, things fall apart, a movement reminiscent of the loose ending of *V.,* in which V. at the end is a "remarkably scattered concept." In *Gravity's Rainbow,* similarly, Pointsman is "abandoned," "restricted to one small office [. . .] the rest of the space having been taken over by an agency studying options for nationalizing coal and steel" (GR 615), and Slothrop disintegrates. Toward the end, in fact, the whole narration loses what surface coherence it had, fracturing into multiple fragments and changing more and more from real, "geographical" space to the mental space of "comic books" (GR 379). The text, like the landscape and the rocket, can be read only as a belated effect, never as the true, real message—the signal zero itself. Accordingly, the quotation that states that Slothrop has been sent into the Zone to witness "his time's assembly," continues "—and there ought to be a punch line to it, but there isn't. The plan went wrong. He is being broken down instead, and scattered" (GR 738). Yet even this explanation is "twice removed" from the truth, for it is only a "story" (GR 738) both within the book and within the book's overall rhetorical matrix. Pynchon ultimately refuses to answer or even unravel the questions he has raised, so that it is indeed a "knotting into" rather than a "disentanglement from." By doing so, he shows three things: that the struggle between Eros and Thanatos is still going on; that it is possible only to show the "state of the battle," not to predict a winner; and that as long as the struggle goes on, the simulations and conditionings described in the text also inhabit writing itself, which is forever and tragically linked to the conditions of the culture out of which it emerges.[18] As Lacan maintains, there is no metalanguage that can be spoken. Because there is no metaphysical position from which to write, the text must *by necessity* disintegrate, or self-destruct. One cannot "reach" the German soul any more than one can "reach" the repressed. In fact, Slothrop's quest becomes an allegory of reading as well as of the human condition in general: "he keeps pushing aside gauze after wavy gauze but there's always still the one, the impenetrable . . ." (GR 359). This inpenetrability also defines the V-2, which, like Jamf, turns out to be just another "symbol," whereas the "Real Text" is written on an impossible "other scene": "Its symmetries, its latencies, the *cuteness* of it enchanted and seduced us while the real Text persisted, somewhere else, in its darkness, our darkness . . ." (GR 520).[19] As yet another distortion of the impossible unconscious text, the V-2 is inextricably linked to the Herero's "ancient tragedy of lost messages" (GR 520). Rather than a "real space," or a space of "true, final meaning," the Zone is a landscape of multiple mental projections in which dreams, fears, and images of the repressed create a kaleidoscopic space, as kaleidoscopic as the text itself—and ultimately the brain, if one thinks back to Pavlov.

This is one reason why it is difficult to delineate a general poetics operative in *Gravity's Rainbow,* which with its multiple focalizations, points of view, and voices is a true polylogue.[20] The kaleidoscopic effect forestalls a univocal allocation of the various and often contradictory approaches to questions of language, because the reader is confronted with a complex moiré of contexts in which questions of language and communication are dealt with both directly and indirectly. Nonetheless, a number of leitmotifs and tropes link most of these scattered references. They are worked out in greatest detail in the analeptic Kirghiz Light episode, one of the many relatively isolated and autonomous substories in the book, a passage that supplements the themes of Slothrop's and the Zone's conditioning with a treatment of cultural conditioning and colonialization on both a historic and a linguistic level. Slothrop had already felt this connection: "His erection hums from a certain distance, like an instrument installed, wired by Them into his body as a colonial outpost here in our raw and clamorous world, another office representing Their white Metropolis far away . . ." (GR 285).

The protagonist of the Kirghiz Light episode is Vaslav Tchitcherine, a soviet army officer, who in the novel's present is in the Zone looking for his half brother Enzian, the leader of the Schwarzkommando, whom he wants to kill, for he sees in him the black *doppelgänger* of his own Western, white soul: "He thinks of Enzian as . . . another *part* of him—a black version of something inside *himself*. A something he needs to . . . liquidate" (GR 499). Tchitcherine's partly metallic body, reminiscent of V. and Bongo-Shaftsbury, as well as of Evan Godolphin, evokes once again the growing mechanization of Western subjectivity: "The mad scavenger Tchitcherine, who is more metal than anything else. Steel teeth wink as he talks. Under his pompadour is a silver plate. Gold wirework threads in three-dimensional tattoo among the fine wreckage of cartilage and bone inside his right knee joint" (GR 337).

For reasons that never become fully clear, earlier in his career Tchitcherine was sent out into the wilderness of the Kirghiz to supervise the process of establishing an alphabet in an illiterate culture, a first step in the integration of the Kirghiz people into a greater "linguistic state." Apart from providing yet another scenario of the politics of conditioning and colonization[21]—what Pynchon described in a letter to Thomas F. Hirsch as the "imposition of a culture valuing analysis and differentiation on a culture that valued unity and integration" (*Fictional Labyrinths* 241)—this process serves Pynchon to fuse a number of problems that revolve around language and in which the question of linguistic oppositionality, and, as in Pavlovian conditioning, oppositionality itself, figures centrally.[22] The imposition of the alphabet in fact forms the brackets within which all other determinations within the section—historical, economic, chemical, and political—unfold. Tchitcherine has "come to give the tribesmen out here, this far out, an alphabet: it was purely speech, gesture, touch among them, not even an Arabic script to replace" (GR 338).

Before commenting on the directly linguistic aspects of the episode, however, it is necessary to deal with the problems of chemical synthesis, control, and addiction, which are the terms on which Pynchon hinges his discussion. One of the reasons for Tchitcherine's mission, for instance, might have been his former involvement with Wimpe, the "head salesman for Ostarzneikunde GmbH, a subsidiary of the IG" (GR 344). Wimpe, possibly a German spy, allegedly has been trying to develop a *synthetic* anodyne that "can kill intense pain without causing addiction" (GR 348) and with which it would be possible to control pain rationally: "Think of what it would mean to find such a drug—to abolish pain rationally [. . . .] We know how to produce real pain. [. . .] But 'addiction'? [. . .] A rational economy cannot depend on psychological quirks. We could not *plan* . . ." (GR 348).

The elimination of the *irrational* side effect of addiction in the structure of pain and relief, in which addiction is ultimately a symptom of the "pain of existence [Freud's *Not des Lebens*]" (Juranville 229), would allow the inauguration of a stable, *rational* control system, an economy in which a market for relief could be accurately controlled by the production of specific amounts of pain and vice versa.[23] Pain, however, and inversely the desire for its absence, cannot be rationalized: "We seem up against a dilemma built into Nature, much like the Heisenberg situation. There is nearly complete parallelism between analgesia and addiction" (GR 348). Wimpe, like Pointsman, is thus confronted with the situation that something in nature resists rationalization. This resistance can be overcome only by abolishing nature through synthetically realigning its natural components to produce its operational simulation. In his dream of a world of such synthesized chemicals and drugs, Wimpe links the concepts of chemical simulation and chess: "'Think of chess,' [. . .] how each molecule ha[s] so many possibilities open to it, possibilities for bonding, bonds of different strengths, from carbon the most versatile, the queen, [. . .] down to the little hydrogens numerous and single-moving as pawns . . . and the brute opposition of the chessboard yielding, in this chemical game, to dance-figures in three dimensions" (GR 344).

In this passage, the "brute opposition of the chessboard" is constituted by the laws of nature, which Wimpe wants to transcend in his romantic attempt to inaugurate a completely artificial space of chemical simulation,[24] a step that abolishes nature as a referent and replaces it by operational models. The chemical processes underlying Wimpe's project actively synthesize molecular structures and fabricate compounds in the same way in which new nouns are created by linguistic compounding. The results are either synthetically re-created products or newly invented ones. In this context, the invention of plastics marks the exact point at which a truly generic substance is created that is itself nothing but the pure and endless possibility of formed matter: "An announcement of Plasticity's central canon: that chemists were no longer to be at the mercy of Nature" (GR 249).[25]

Resinification, whose chemical formula was "dreamt up" by Kekulé, is a combinatory process based on the principle of cyclization. This chemical compounding also serves Baudrillard as a main metaphor for simulation. In fact, he parallels three orders of simulacra with three stages in the development of the simulation of matter. The first is a mimesis of nature, in which stucco "exorcizes the unlikely confusion of matter into a single new substance, a sort of equivalent of all the others" (Baudrillard, *Simulations* 88). Although it operates predominantly in a theatrical and thus fictional space in which the project is to play with the gap between nature and artifact, it is a first step in the technological project to create "an ideal counterfeit of the world, expressed in the invention of a universal substance and of a universal amalgam of substances" (89). Already with stucco, the real is substituted by a generic substance, whose production can be perfectly controlled because it is completely synthetic. Reinforced concrete—already defined predominantly in economic terms—is the second step toward unification and complete control, although "the counterfeit is [still] working, so far, only on substance and form, not yet on relations and structures. But it is aiming already, on this level, at the control of a pacified society, ground up into a synthetic, deathless substance: an indestructible artifact that will guarantee an eternity of power" (91).

Although in both of these stages there is a development toward the replacement of nature by artificial substitutes, they still retain nature or the real as a referent that is only in a second step reproduced either artistically or mechanically. The third stage, however, Baudrillard's "third order simulacra" (*Simulations* 100), presents a more complex and convoluted scene, because it *creates* its own real according to models developed from within its own structure.

This third and final stage is defined and illustrated by the invention of plastics. Pynchon's text perfectly illustrates how the relations between plastics, simulation, death, and control are based on the premise that simulation operates on the real, as well as on the subject. With plastics, a synthetic substance "freezes" the animation of both the world and the subject, creating a static scene in which power can operate at will. For Baudrillard, as for Pynchon, the invention of plastics is thus the final stage in the attempt to control any physical as well as psychic, mental substance: matter *and* subjectivity. The impossibility of chemically breaking down the plastic simulacra and the consequent break in the cycle of life and death and the metamorphoses in it symbolize the completely lifeless stability of power relations. Symptomatically, Jamf, in whose figure the fields of conditioning, control, and simulation are aligned, has

> a hostility, a strangely *personal* hatred, for the covalent bond. [...] That something so mutable, so *soft,* as a sharing of electrons by atoms of carbon should lie at the core of life, *his* life, struck Jamf as a cosmic humiliation—*Sharing?* How much stronger, how everlasting was the *ionic* bond—where electrons are not shared, but *captured. Seized!* and held! polarized plus and minus, these atoms, no ambiguities ... how he came to love that clarity: how stable it was. (GR 577)

Yet this alleged triumph over death through the installation of a "deathless" code is deceptive, for it is based on an initial execution and abolition of life. During a seance, Walter Rathenau tells Smaragd, the Generaldirektor of the IG Farben, that the creation of plastics is only an "impersonation of life. The real movement is not from death to any rebirth. It is from death to death-transfigured. The best you can do is to polymerize a few dead molecules. But polymerizing is not resurrection" (GR 166). Ultimately, the creation of synthetic substances gives rise to "structures favoring death. Death converted into more death" (GR 167). The synthetic dream and illusion of a deathless world thus create a completely lifeless world: "Plastic, a non-degradable material, interrupting thus the cycle which, by corruption and death, turns all the earth's substances ceaselessly one into another ... [a] substance out-of-the-cycle (Baudrillard, *Simulations* 91).

The description of Kekulé's dream in *Gravity's Rainbow* mirrors this disruption exactly. Originally, like paranoia, a revelation that *"everything is connected"* (GR 703), the dream is immediately perverted by operational projects that bring about the destruction of the cycle: "Kekulé dreams the Great Serpent holding its own tail in its mouth, the dreaming Serpent which surrounds the World. But the meanness, the cynicism with which this dream is to be used. The Serpent that announces, 'The World is a closed thing, cyclical, resonant, eternally-returning,' is to be delivered into a system whose only aim is to *violate* the Cycle" (GR 412). As the result of this violation, "not only most of humanity—most of the World, animal, vegetable and mineral, is laid waste" (GR 412). Yet the violators themselves do not recognize this, for they are deluded by visions of grandeur, their dream(s) of absolute freedom in the creation of models and of absolute control in the process of synthesizing various components: absolute freedom *within* absolute control.

Wimpe symbolizes this paranoiac system with its dependence on and complicity with the rational laws of logic and scientific reasoning, which according to Baudrillard "give . . . the[ir] *models* their forcefulness. But also it is this which only leaves them, as truth, the paranoid projection tests of . . . a group which dreams of a miraculous correspondence of the real to their models, and therefore of an absolute manipulation" (*Simulations* 127), a passage comparable to Roland Feldspath's message that "for the first time it [control] was *inside* [. . . .] A market needed no longer be run by the Invisible Hand, but now could *create itself* [. . .] from *inside*. Putting the control inside was ratifying what de facto had happened—that you had dispensed with God. But you had taken on a greater, and more harmful, illusion. The illusion of control" (GR 30).

In *Gravity's Rainbow*, the most perfidious and advanced agent by which the simulation of matter is inextricably linked to the simulation of the subject is the plastic Imipolex G, a more advanced form of *V.*'s concepts of artificiality in that it simulates—that is, *implodes* rather than mechanically *replaces*—the animate with the inanimate. Imipolex G is an "aromatic heterocyclic polymer" (GR 249) that is not surprisingly developed by Jamf for IG Farben at the "Psychochemie AG" (GR 250), a firm whose name itself already evokes the invasion of the human psyche by chemical simulation and the implosion of nature and simulation, human and fetish, a motif familiar from "V. in love." As a combination of synthesized and "more 'natural' benzene or aromatic rings" (GR 250), Imipolex G marks exactly the threshold between nature and simulation, by way of that between skin and plastics, within a reference to sexuality and its replacement by or shift into simulation, because Imipolex G is used as a sexual stimulus that transfers libido from the human to the fetish, and thus from the living organism to dead simulation: "Imipolex G is the first plastic that is actually *erectile*. Under suitable *stimuli*, the chains grow cross-links, which stiffen the molecule and increase intermolecular attraction so that this Peculiar Polymer runs [. . .] from limp rubbery amorphous to amazing perfect tessellation, hardness, brilliant transparency, high resistance to temperature, weather, vacuum, shock" (GR 699; last emphasis added).

With the help of Imipolex G it becomes possible to create a perfect simulation of the human: a plastic organism that can be stimulated and thus controlled and conditioned electronically, either by "a thin matrix of wires" (GR 699), a "beam-scanning system," (GR 700) or a "projection, *onto* the Surface, of an electronic 'image,' analogous to a motion picture" (GR 700). Greta Erdmann is the first to see it, in a scientific seance in "The Castle" (GR 486): "It was gray, plastic, shining [. . . .] It looked to me like an ectoplasm—something they had forced, by their joint will, to materialize on the table" (GR 487). She is also the first to feel its effects, in a scene that illustrates the sexual replacement of the human by the fetish/ simulation through the merging of skin and plastics. Pynchon expresses the effects of this replacement by a pun. When someone says "butadiene" (a hydrocarbon that is a major constituent of synthetic rubber, first produced commercially by Germany during WW I), Greta understands *"beauty dying"* (GR 487), a shift that evokes Baudrillard's contention that within a simulatory society, the space between the real and reality in which art— and with it beauty and sexuality—unfolds is abolished:

> They took away my clothes and dressed me in an exotic costume of some black polymer, very tight at the waist, open at the crotch. It felt alive on me. "Forget leather, forget satin," shivered Drohne. "This is Imipolex, the material of the future." [. . .] Nothing I ever wore, before or since, aroused me quite as much as Imipolex. [. . .] Drohne had strapped on a gigantic Imipolex penis over his own. I rubbed my face against it, it was so delicious. . . . (GR 488)

The relation of Imipolex G to the V-2 further underlines its deadly character.

Like Baudrillard, who detects in the simulation of material substances a parallel "ambition of a universal semiotic . . . of a closed *mental* substance" (*Simulations* 92; emphasis added), Pynchon links the respective structures of chemical simulation and language. He does so via the image of chess, which also serves Saussure as a model for the structure of language and the arbitrariness of the signifier:

> A game of chess is like an artificial realization of what language offers in a natural form. . . . The respective value of the pieces depends on their position on the chessboard just as each linguistic term derives its value from its opposition to all the other terms . . . values depend above all else on an unchangeable convention, the set of rules that exists before a game begins and persists after each move. Rules that are agreed upon once and for all exist in language too; they are the constant principles of semiology. (*General Linguistics* 88)

Like molecules in chemistry, the letters in the alphabet function as the material that can be compounded endlessly and that provides the network of digital differences in which meaning is constructed. At this stage the need is again for complementary readings of *Gravity's Rainbow* in which—as in *Lot 49*—*ontological* and *social* aspects are aligned. On the one hand, Pynchon thematizes the basic digitality on which language rests, a binarism operative in both Derridean *différance* and Lacan's symbolic. In fact, Lacan takes recourse specifically to a combination of (real) positive and negative elements (presence/absence) as the binary opposition to which every symbolic structure or code can be reduced.[26]

This basic binarism—exemplified in a psychic register by the game of "Fort-Da"—defines language as a cybernetic machine. Lacan's objective is in fact to show that any symbolic system *by necessity* develops its own regulative parameters[27] and syntax that define its operations regardless of any subjective position, so that "the chain of possible combinations of the encounter can be studied as such, as an order which subsists in its rigour, independently of all subjectivity" (*Seminar II* 304).[28] The subject, which is defined by these symbolic laws, is thus inserted into a transsubjective, digital, and self-regulative structure.[29] This digital structure of the symbolic is both inevitable and tragic. It defines the relation between the symbolic and the real, which has just that property of lacking any such parameters.[30] Ontologically, then, an escape from digitality is impossible. On the other hand, the subject cannot—except in simulation—be reduced to this digitality, a reduction that denies its status as a human being as well as the reality of desire.

Apart from the fact that a "nostalgia," or desire, for a real, predigital state pervades the Kirghiz Light passage—as it does all of Pynchon's texts—Pynchon's and Baudrillard's critique is directed more specifically against the dream that sees this digital realm as a system closed in on itself. In Pynchon's text, the nostalgia resulting from the inevitable tragedy of the loss of unity in the passage from nature to culture and language is always supplemented by a critique of the code's growing fascination with its own digitality and the foreclosure of nature, the real, and death as its other within a purely operational project—in this passage, a political one. Ultimately, this foreclosure entails the reduction of life to a system of stimulus/response, as with Jamf's conditioning of Slothrop by a "binary stimulus."

The attempt to negate the insistence of nature within the rational code is similar to the manner in which addiction is negated in a synthetic chemical universe. The simulation of natural speech—which is not only a logocentric ideal but also one of an unoperational, irrational speech—within an operational alphabet leads to a "plastic-symbolic": "The German mania for name-giving, dividing the Creation finer and finer, analyzing, setting namer more hopelessly apart from named, even to bringing in the mathematics of combination, tacking together established nouns to get new ones, the insanely, endlessly diddling play of a chemist whose molecules are words . . ." (GR 391). Because chemical synthesis mirrors language, whose "words are molecules," the development of plastics is comparable to the creation of a completely artificial and empty code that is closed in on itself and creates its own operational real. Engineers and bureaucrats (and chemists) are all "children at the threshold of language with these words they make up" (GR 487).

On an ontological level, the fall into language denotes the birth of human consciousness and the first manifestation of the death drive in humanity's separation from nature. A passage focalized through Geli Tripping comments on this birth of consciousness as the introduction of the concept of death, in what LeClair has called, surprisingly, "one of Pynchon's most ironic lines" (38): "Human consciousness, that poor cripple, that deformed and doomed thing, is about to be born. This is the World just before men. Too violently pitched alive in constant flow ever to be seen by men directly. They are meant only to look at it dead, in still strata [. . . .] *It is our mission to promote death*" (GR 720).

It is *within* the dilemma of a subject that is always already separated from nature/the real, and thus never fully alive, that Pynchon comments on the fact that the growing digitalization of signification—the process of chaining and rechaining linguistic molecules—implies a more and more decadent, ultimately purely synthetic and simulated language. At this point, various theoretical positions converge. Derrida's idea of textual dissemination is linked with Lacan's textualization of the subject and Baudrillard's theory of simulation when the textual subject is put into relation to a completely textualized and simulated real. Symptomatically, Baudrillard, like Pynchon, envisions this project as that of an anonymous and amorphous "they": "They have already tested 'reality,' . . . They have broken down reality into simple elements that they have reassembled into scenarios of regulated oppositions" (*Simulations* 120). This digitalization of the analog defines a purely operational language:

> How alphabetic is the nature of molecules [. . .] one finds Committees on molecular structure which are very similar to those back at

the NTA plenary session. "See: how they are taken out from the coarse flow—shaped, cleaned, rectified, just as you once redeemed your letters from the lawless, the mortal streaming of human speech. . . . These are our letters, our words: they too can be modulated, broken, recoupled, redefined, copolymerized one to the other in worldwide chains that will surface now and then over long molecular silences, like the seen parts of a tapestry. (GR 355)

The ultimate passage is toward a completely simulated universe expressed in a completely digital code. The double movement in this passage first separates the letters from the lawless, mortal streaming of human speech and thus digitalizes them: "The sounds of speech are analog; [whereas] phonology and the alphabet are digital" (Wilden 169). This digitalization is comparable to the isolation of various molecules. In a second step, these digitalized letters/molecules are realigned according to the laws of rational—and more importantly, operational—encodings. Their *natural* flow is thus replaced by the *rational,* "digital space" (Baudrillard, *Simulations* 138) of the code. This digitality is just what haunts Oedipa in *Lot 49,* the "mystic elegance of the binary system, of the zero and the one" (106). In a truly Baudrillardian fashion, *Gravity's Rainbow* highlights this relation of digitality to systems of power, conditioning, and control: "Digitality is with us. It is that which haunts all the messages, all the signs of our societies. The most concrete form you see it in is that of the test . . . the *stimulus/ response*" (*Simulations* 115; emphasis added). Because language has become a purely rational simulation machine, it has infiltrated every human subject, tying them into a machine that, as in *Lot 49,* can no longer be thought of in Freudian or Lacanian categories: "The cool universe of digitality has absorbed the world of *metaphor and metonymy.* The principle of simulation wins out over the reality principle just as over the principle of pleasure" (152; emphasis added). Pynchon uses the story of the insertion of a "natural society" into alphabetical language as an allegory of its insertion into a digital framework: the birth of digital, "electric voices" (GR 720).

Wimpe's desire to transcend the laws of nature thus mirrors directly the Committee's desire to transcend the "irrationality" and "naturality" of spoken language by inserting it into the system of the alphabet. In the same way that addiction is the *rest* that cannot be integrated into the rational model of economic theory, speech, gesture, and touch, as well as silence, remain the analog *rest* that a purely digital language or code cannot encompass.

Like Oedipa in *Lot 49*, Tchitcherine is in a medial position, forever "drifting sideways" and forever "held at the edge . . ." (GR 703). As Oedipa holds a medial position between everyday language and that of "the saint, the clairvoyant, the paranoid and the dreamer," Tchitcherine, caught between chemical and linguistic control, is the hinge between the language of the Kirghiz and that of the Committees.

The differences between the two modes of language are also developed by way of the motif of silence and its relation to the real. Throughout the passage, it figures as a backdrop to the universe of discourse. It denotes the forced "retreats of sound" (GR 336) and pervades the whole landscape, as well as its inhabitants. Within the Russian cadre, only "desperate" Luba, who is symptomatically described in animal terms when she is compared to and even equated with "a pretty hawk" (GR 339), is able to fully enter this silence: "But it's only Luba who flies, who knows the verst-long dive, the talon-shock and the blood, while her lean owner must stay below in the schoolroom, shut in by words, drifts and frost-patterns of white words" (GR 339).

Although Galina also has a special relation to silence, hers is a more Derridean one, forever implicated by discourse: "Here she has become a connoisseuse of silences. The great silences of Seven Rivers have not yet been alphabetized, and perhaps never will be. [. . .] They are silences NTA cannot fill, cannot liquidate, immense and frightening as the elements in this bear's corner—scaled to a larger Earth, a planet wilder and more distant from the sun . . ." (GR 340–41).

This silence, which Derrida would call "unimaginable," is the silence of the real, whose "gaps" the alphabet tries to "word [. . .] over" (GR 589) in its desire for the signifier. By anchoring language firmly in the laws of cause and effect, as well as in rationality, it creates the illusion of continuity.

Like Pierce's projection of himself onto America in *Lot 49*, the alphabetization is a colonization that brings about the complete textualization of the victims. Because culture is a symbolic system, Pynchon can describe in detail how cultural and political determinations are prefigured in the structure of the alphabet and how power relations span the whole range from the initial Committees to the people alphabetized.[31] Printing and, more generally, writing are the initial structures that carry the possibility of both cultural production and counterproduction within them:

> And print just goes marching on without him. Copy boys go running down the rows of desks trailing smeared galleys in the air. Native

printers get crash courses from experts [. . .] on how to set up that NTA. Printed posters go up in the cities [. . . .] On sidewalks and walls the very first printed slogans start to show up, the first Central Asian fuck you signs, the first kill-the-police-commissioner signs (and somebody does! this alphabet is really something!) and so the magic that the shamans, out in the wind, have always known, begins to operate now in a political way. (GR 355–56)

Lévi-Strauss describes how writing causes a shift from a *magical* to a *political* society in "A Writing Lesson."[32] In a magical society, one or various (metaphysical) powers imagined to exist outside the symbolic system are inscribed into a specific representational system. In contrast to this intrusion of power from *without*, written, political language creates power from *within* the system of signification. The insertion of a magical culture, which exists with nature as a constant—although mysterious—referent, into a political and, in Pynchon's case, ultimately simulatory system entails its radical destruction, because it destroys its most basic assumptions. Maureen Quilligan sees Pynchon's evocation of such a natural society as logocentric: "Derrida is . . . trying to find a rhetoric of writing which will allow him to go beyond the epistemology of Presence, while Pynchon is firmly mired in the problems of Presence" (117). Yet this "logocentrism" is always an ironic and never an "innocent" one. This ironization can be seen, for instance, in the vignette of Eddie Pensiero, who is told by his sergeant, "Howard *('Slow') Lerner*" (GR 641; emphasis added) to cut his colonel's hair. During the procedure, an anonymous narrative voice comments on hair as "yet another kind of modulated frequency. Assume a state of grace in which all hairs were once distributed perfectly even, *a time of innocence* when they fell perfectly straight, all over the colonel's head" (GR 643; emphasis added).

Similarly, in the Kirghiz Light episode, the utopia of a preliterate society functions only as a rhetorical perspective point and, as a result, is a utopia "under erasure." It is evoked from within the framework of a specifically Western philosophy of language—symbolized by Tchitcherine—out of which a return to a natural origin is impossible. The idea of a natural society and language therefore neither underlies nor legitimates Pynchon's poetics, it merely functions as its utopian other. It is a lost origin that cannot be re-created or reached within discourse. Pynchon thematizes exactly this *impossibility* of a return in the song of the aqyn, who holds a similar position to language in *Gravity's Rainbow* as do "the saint, the clairvoyant, the paranoid, and the dreamer" in *Lot 49*. Like Galina, Tchitcherine is interested in the old culture, but unlike her he is an outsider caught between the two cultures. Although he wants to experience the old, magical Kirghiz Light, the subject of the aqyn's song, the experience is inaccessible for him because it is beyond rational signification. The only thing the singer can do is to try to re-create in language the ultimately unspeakable experience of the light. He does so by taking language to its limits in paradoxes and silence:[33] "The roar of Its voice is deafness, / The flash of Its light is blindness" (GR 358). The scene he evokes is a mythical, precultural state before the advent of signification, "in a place where words are unknown, [. . .] And the face of God is a presence / Behind the mask of the sky—" (GR 358). Every return to it is simultaneously a step outside culture and signification and a return to one's birth and fall into language. When Tchitcherine takes down the song in stenography—a metaphorical shorthand for the mere recording agency of (not only) written language—he is able to record the geographical information about the occurrence of the light; once there, however, he cannot experience it, because, for one thing, by "taking shorthand" he strips language of its analog qualities:

> The digital . . . relationship to "reality" is rudimentary similar to language itself. In fact, we can say that in human communication all non-conventionalized "gesture language," posture, facial expression, inflection, sequence, rhythm . . . is a kind of analog or iconic communication in which the signal or sign has a necessary relation to what it "re-presents," whereas all denotative, linguistic communication is arbitrary and digital. (Wilden 163)

Yet whereas Wilden believes that the analog can be regained, Pynchon expressly relates it to a time that is irretrievably lost.[34] What Tchitcherine cannot return to is his birth, the ambiguous moment that marks both the separation from and, in retrospect, the regaining of the real: "Tchitcherine will reach the Kirghiz Light, but not his birth. He is no aqyn, and his heart was never ready. He will see It just before dawn. He will spend 12 hours then, face-up on the desert [. . . .] But someday, [. . .] he will hardly be able to remember It" (GR 359).[35]

The *rest* left in Tchitcherine's shorthand representation is on the one hand the analog characteristics of language, yet on the other hand silence, which, like death, marks the border of semiosis and links the rest to the real—the residue of the symbolic: a space without language, time, culture, or the subject. The childlike stage the aqyn reenters lies outside the symbolic.

Such "missed encounters" are staged everywhere in *Gravity's Rainbow*. Although Weissmann is "in love with language" (GR 99) and in the desert feels that "words are only an eye-twitch away from the things they stand for" (GR 100), he can never make sign and referent map completely. Similarly, for the Schwarzkommando, the rocket is only the promise of a "Real Text," while an anonymous narrative voice again seems to suggest that the "real rocket" or a "true revelation" is forever missed: "Is it, then, really never to find you again? Not even in your worst times of night, with pencil words on your page only Δt from the things they stand for? [. . .] Will it really never come to take you, now?" (GR 510).[36] Both Slothrop and the Schwarzkommando are constantly looking for the way out of the simulation of which (as it turns out) they themselves are so much a part. The paradox of a "Real Text" here functions as the perspective point of this search and delineates their impossible hope that "somewhere, among the wastes of the World, is the key that will bring us back, restore us to our Earth and to our freedom" (GR 525). This hope against all odds encompasses also the "ancient tragedy of lost messages," which "began in mythical times, when the sly hare who nests in the Moon brought death among men, instead of the Moon's true message. The true message has never come. Perhaps the Rocket is meant to take us there someday, and then the Moon will tell us its truth at last" (GR 322). This hope, however, is always countered by the realization that the territory of simulation is forever growing: "Will our new Edge, our new Deathkingdom, be the Moon? I dream of a great glass sphere, hollow and very high and far away . . . the colonists have learned to do without air, it's vacuum inside and out. [. . .] There are ways for getting back, but so complicated, so at the mercy of language, that presence back on Earth is only temporary, and never 'real'" (GR 723).

Pynchon's text, then, has a twofold momentum. It is caught in the double bind of the will to terminate and the will to express—paradoxically, to express this very termination. In this respect, the terms *silence* and *nature* occupy similar positions in the Kirghiz Light episode. Nature is silent. To return to this silence, the subject has to give up language. In giving up language, however, it also gives up the self and the ego. The subject's expression of the desire for the extermination of this ego constitutes "the desire of the text."

Notes

1. I do not think, as does Brian McHale, that there are decisive differences between *V., Lot 49,* and *Gravity's Rainbow:* "Oedipa does not break through the closed circle of her solipsism . . . nor does Pynchon break through here to a mode of fiction beyond modernism and its epistemological premises. . . . The breakthrough will not come until Pynchon's next novel, *Gravity's Rainbow,* where, no longer constrained by the limits of modernism, he will freely exploit the artistic possibilities of the plurality of worlds" (*Postmodernism* 24–25).

2. In this superimposition, they form another of the many mandalas in *Gravity's Rainbow,* for instance, "Der Raketen-Stadt" (GR 725), which is "built in mandalic form like a Herero village" (GR 725).

3. For exact identifications of Pavlov's texts in the book see Weisenburger.

4. The word means "beyond the margin of normal consciousness, subliminal."

5. Pavlov in fact singles out persecution mania as a physiological manifestation of the ultraparadoxical phase.

6. For a discussion of some irregularities in the concept of Imipolex G see Douglas Fowler, *A Reader's Guide to "Gravity's Rainbow"* 273–74.

7. Compare: "Once he [Enzian] could not imagine a life without return. *Before his conscious memories began,* something took him, in and out of his mother's circular village [. . .] at the borders of the land of death, a departure and a return" (GR 322–23; emphasis added).

8. See also Freud's concept of "psychic inertia," the "inertia of the libido . . . its disinclination to give up an old position for a new one" ("Civilization and Its Discontents," *Standard Edition* 21:108).

9. In the double definition of "retardation," it again links the psychic and the physical realms.

10. It is symptomatic of the intricately woven texture of the narration that—as with the "low pun" on inertia—a reference to "negative induction" has already popped up in the discussion between Pointsman and Mexico about the extinction of the stimulus in Pavlovian conditioning, in which Pointsman ponders the "fearful consequences" of the possibility that "there *is* nothing to link the rocket strikes—no reflex arc, no Law of Negative Induction" (GR 56)—to Slothrop's mysterious hardons.

11. Interestingly, magnetic induction is the quantity that denotes the flux density in a material. This may be another link to the "flux density" that designates the ratio of paranoia in the brain.

12. Compare also Lacan's discussion of the subject and machine provided in chapter 4. For more on Freud's treatment of the reflex arc see Lacan, *Seminar II* 106–13. See also Pynchon's description of the rocket: "radio signals [. . .] would enter the Rocket body, and by reflex—literally by electric signal traveling a reflex arc—the control surfaces twitch" (GR 517).

13. For a detailed account of the IG Farben background see Khachig Tölölyan, "War as Background in Gravity's Rainbow."

14. See also Stuart Moulthorpe, "Strobe's Stimulus."

15. Slothrop dreams that he "had found a very old dictionary of technical German. It fell open to a certain page [. . . .] Reading down the page, he would come to JAMF. The definition would read: I" (GR 287).

16. Read in the light of Freud's statement that "the evolution of civilization . . . must present the struggle between *Eros* and *Death,* between the instinct of life and the instinct of destruction, as it works itself out in the human species" ("Civilization and Its Discontents," *Standard Edition* 21:122), this "family affair" clearly favors death. Pynchon also comments on the "family affair" created by Pavlovian conditioning: "The Oedipal situation in the Zone these days is terrible [. . . .] The mothers have been masculinized [. . . .] The fathers have no power today and never did, but because 40 years ago we could not kill them, we are condemned now to the same passivity, the same masochist fantasies *they cherished in secret*" (GR 747).

17. Quoted in Gerhard Baader, "Das Leben Iwan Petrovitch Pawlows" [The Life of Ivan Petrovitch Pavlov].

18. See especially the discussion around the "phallocratic" aspects of Pynchon's writing. In fact, *Vineland* takes up exactly this complicity. Symptomatically, the quote continues after the missing punchline with the fact that the cards point not to change but to "a long and *scuffling* [a pun with Ian Scuffling, one of Slothrop's many "identities"] future, to mediocrity (not only in his life but also, heh, heh, in his chroniclers too [. . .])" (GR 738; emphasis added).

19. Compare: "the spot where tradition sez Enzian had his Illumination, in the course of a wet dream where he coupled with a slender white rocket" (GR 297).

20. See Mikhail Bakhtin.

21. The motif of colonization is connected to the Herero scenario by the description of Enzian's birth, which in turn is related to issues of language. Tchitcherine's father went AWOL in Lüderitzbucht and lived with a Herero girl for a couple of days, during which time Enzian was conceived; the two people found "a few words in the respective languages—afraid, happy, sleep, love . . . the beginnings of a new tongue, a pidgin which they were perhaps the only two speakers of in the world" (GR 351). This promise of a utopian (because "private") language, however, is immediately destroyed. For a further discussion of the passage see Seed, "The Central Asian Uprising of 1916," and Qazi.

22. Fowler comments on the passage's fragmentary character, seeing in it "a ménage of red herrings, discarded characters, and anti-climax. It would be hard to find two dozen pages in any other novel where more is promised and less accomplished" (*Reader's Guide* 65). He states that "Pynchon's work seems to be nothing more than the squirming fragments of a dozen bright ideas until we read it *as poetry,* as images and ideas worked for meaning rather than as narrative investigating

personality" (66). Although this is perhaps partially true, the situation is further complicated by the fact that the poetic meaning of the passage deals precisely with the fragmentation of personality and the promises and aporias of language.

23. The sort of mastery the drug would serve is shown in the tableau that introduces one of the minor characters, Chu Piang, a "living monument to the success of British trade policy back during the last century" (GR 346). He is a monument to the introduction of opium, the creation of a demand, its proscription, and the subsequent wars for the monopoly of the English to sell it. "Nowadays whole tourist caravans come through to look at him" (GR 346). Tourism, of course, again functions as the last, most "refined" mode of colonization.

24. Pynchon aligns the two seemingly contrary terms of *rationality* and *romanticism* to show how rationality and the pursuit of logic can themselves constitute a romantic endeavor. Wimpe with his "Schwärmerei" (GR 344), the "foolish and romantic" (GR 344) Tchitcherine, as well as Blicero and other "romantic villains"—as in the film *Metropolis*—use the energies and dreams of a romantic for megalomanic endeavors.

25. For a discussion playing off the negative, artificial aspects of plastic against its positive potential for transformation, see Meikle, "The Culture of Plasticity." He concludes that *Gravity's Rainbow* "exuberantly posits the liberating potential inherent in the decentering of post-modern consciousness" (218). For background information, see Michael V. Adams. It is symptomatic that the term *plastics* is derived from the Greek *plastikos,* which means "to form"; as such, it is itself already a commercial classification—the chemical term is *resinification*.

26. The game of odd and even in "The Purloined Letter" serves Lacan to describe these laws. It is played out in all three arenas in a temporal succession. The first throw marks the *real* arena, the second throw the *imaginary,* and the third, as well as all successors to the third, the *symbolic*. The first throw is "real" because it results from the arbitrary dichotomy of symmetry and asymmetry (presence and absence), the basic scansion of matter that defines the real: "In the real, at each go, you have as many chances of winning or of losing as on the preceding go" (*Seminar II* 182). The second throw is "timeless" (being actually the first throw, the opening, and based on an identification with the opposite player, who should be unknown before the game starts) and inaugurates the phonetic structure of difference. The third throw constitutes the syntax of the chain's formalizations and is the reason why Lacan carries out this formalization in triadic parameters. The initial triadic function is thus inherent in the game. It is Lacan's *second* formalization, the introduction of "a certain significant unity" (193), in which the triadic function becomes an arbitrary choice. He defines it in terms of triadic groups so that it is the triadic function itself that determines their symbolic structure. This second formalization is the node at which Lacan's Freudian disposition structures his own discourse.

27. "From the start, and independently of any attachment to some supposedly causal bond, the symbol already plays, and produces by itself, its necessities, its structures, its organizations" (*Seminar II* 193).

28. Symptomatically, it is cybernetics, the "science of empty places, of encounters in and of themselves" (*Seminar II* 300), which once it has started "function[s] all by itself" (300), that serves Lacan as an example of the attempt of a soft science to "tie the real to a syntax" (305).

29. "I am giving you a possible definition of subjectivity, by formulating it as an organized system of symbols, aiming to cover the whole of an experience, to animate it, to give it its meaning" (*Seminar II* 40–41).

30. "For we do not pretend . . . to retrieve more from the real . . . than we have presupposed by its existence, that means here, nothing" (*Écrits* 43, French ed.).

31. In a cynical sideshow, Pynchon stages miniwars between committees for specific letters. "Most distressing of all is the power struggle he has somehow been suckered into with one Igor Blobadjian, a party representative on the prestigious G Committee. Blobadjian is fanatically attempting to steal Ч from Tchitcherine's Committee, and change them to Gs, using loan-words as an entering wedge" (GR 353).

32. See Lévi-Strauss, *Tristes Tropiques*. See also Schaub: "The primary function of written communication is to facilitate slavery" (*Pynchon* 54). For a general discussion of the scene see Edward Mendelson, "Gravity's Encyclopedia."

33. Paradoxes are the most direct way of inserting an illogical element into a logical structure. For the early Wittgenstein, tautology and paradox (contradiction) serve to delineate the two extremes of logical representation: "Contradiction is the outer limit of propositions, tautology is the unsubstantial point at their centre" (*Tractatus logico-philosophicus* 40).

34. Wilden critiques the digitalization of life from a sociopolitical angle, relating the loss of the real less to the inevitability of the "human condition" than to specific cultural developments in Western society: "I would be the last to deny the collective psychosis of our culture, but this split [of the subject] is by no means an irremediable adjunct to the 'human condition'" (460). Although Brown and Wilden take this return to imply a return to the natural body, in "Is it O.K. to Be a Luddite?" Pynchon evokes a vision that is directed into the future rather than the past. Trying to imagine the fantastic counterweight to postmodern culture, he imagines a cybernetic, fully digital monster that goes beyond the human condition: "If our world survives, the next great challenge to watch out for will come [. . .] when the curves of research and development in artificial intelligence, molecular biology and robotics all converge" (41). Wilden's project aims at a redefinition of the subject's relation to the real from within systems theory and Marxism, theories that promise a paradisiacal state of the "analog regained." For a discussion of *Gravity's Rainbow* in terms of systems theory, see also LeClair, *The Art of Excess*.

35. This lack of revelation follows Tchitcherine throughout the novel: "It happened first with the Kirghiz Light, and his only illumination then was that fear would always keep him from going all the way in. He will never get further than the edge" (GR 566).

36. For a reading of this passage in the light of conditioning and the Kirghiz Light episode see also Mendelson, "Gravity's Encyclopedia."

Chapter 7   ***Gravity's Rainbow:***
              Text as Film—Film as Text

> "Of course it happened. Of course it didn't happen."
> Thomas Pynchon, *Gravity's Rainbow*

> "War is cinema and cinema is War"
> Paul Virilio, *War and Cinema*

In this chapter, I trace Pynchon's transposition of his critique of digitality, control, and simulation from a *linguistic* to a *cinematic* level. This discussion deals—both structurally and thematically—with the cinematic character of *Gravity's Rainbow*, an aspect many critics have noted and commented on.[1] Charles Clerc in particular has dealt at length with the various ways in which film enters the novel in his exhaustive study "Film in *Gravity's Rainbow*," concluding that "Pynchon works film into the novel in a variety of ways. He introduces fresh, if occasionally contradictory, perceptions about the relationships of film and life.... He incorporates cinematic techniques into the texture itself so that the novel is like a movie. He relies upon cinema as a source for metaphors, images, symbols, and associations" (104). Clerc provides an almost complete account of the "supplemental usage of film" (104–5) in the article, and for detailed textual analyses I refer the reader to it. In what follows, I am more concerned with why Clerc might come to think that Pynchon's perceptions about film and life are occasionally contradictory, a conclusion based on a specific concept of subjectivity that informs his analyses, as well as on a lack of theoretical background concerning the structure of film. Although he provides the fullest and most detailed discussion of film in *Gravity's Rainbow* to date, his argument is weakest when he talks about the relation between film and literature, such as when he states that "fiction can handle differences of time; film has only one time: the present. On the other hand, the one principle most organic to film is space" (107). Similarly, he fails to differentiate between surface and superficiality when he argues that "the camera cannot penetrate into the inner being. Fiction thus has the advantage of exploring psychological states, of rendering attributes of thought. However, the reality of the camera's picture is certainly as real as the subject itself" (107). His final assessment that "it is thus quite possible to take the novel itself as film" (112) unduly equates their respective structures and actually runs counter to the lucidity of his detailed textual analyses.

In David Marriott's article "Moviegoing"[2] film has predominantly negative connotations. According to Marriott, Pynchon uses the cinema as both "symptom and symbol of a mass abdication of responsibility in which most people are both deceiver and deceived" (64). Filmic references, he argues, serve to provide specific, prefabricated, ideologically biased roles that alienate people from their "real" selves and insert them into culturally prefixed positions. Because Marriott, like Clerc, differentiates between a *cinematic* and a *real* self, the identification of real people with characters on the silver screen entails the *loss* of an initial, more natural and real self: "America . . . is a nation of cinemagoers who have abdicated the ability to discriminate between the simplified and neatly structured version of life to be found in the movies and the real world outside the cinema" (55). For Marriott, the only exceptions to this co-optation are a number of films and filmmakers that comment directly on this aspect of film, "rebels like Welles and Cocteau and Hellman whose films do not fulfill expectations. These filmmakers use the medium to question its own nature rather than reinforce its subtle deceptions" (75). Ultimately, what Marriott provides is a specific aesthetics and ethics of the cinema rather than a critique of the medium itself. In his view, the distinction between good and bad films is developed along the notion of self-reflexivity. Good films jolt the viewers out of their passivity and make them aware that they are watching a movie rather than the "real thing." The unquestioned assumption on which this structure rests, however, is that it is possible to distinguish between film and reality, that there is available a more primary, uncorrupted reality from which to critique film. Often, however, this very idea is questioned by "good" films. Pynchon's use of *Citizen Kane,* for example, specifically opens up questions of reality—of what remains of the self after all cultural material has been stripped off—and of the relation of the self and culture, the very question that makes the distinction between film and real life so problematic in the first place. Pynchon does not stop at positing an uncontaminated self that has to be saved from the movies. If such a self exists at all, it is only as a hallucination at the vanishing point of his texts.

Whereas Marriott unduly separates film and reality, McHoul and Wills actually conflate the two registers. Although this is certainly more useful than Marriott's approach, their generalizing, like Clerc's, comes dangerously close to simply covering up the issue: "It is almost impossible to resist the distinction between the cinematic and the real. However, this form of distinction is a virtually impossible one to make in the case of *Gravity's Rainbow*" (WP 45).

An investigation into the cinematic aspect of *Gravity's Rainbow* has to operate exactly in the space between these two approaches. It is necessary not to deal with the medium of film as either a cultural (Marriott) *or* a structural (McHoul and Wills) phenomenon but to show the interrelatedness of both aspects.

Within film studies, the latter aspect has been largely relegated to the semiotics of film, which developed out of a separation from the field of literary and linguistic studies and defined film along the asymmetry of linguistic and cinematographic systems of signification. Although the cinematic can be related to other art forms, such as theater and painting, it is the literary signifier that provides its most consistent "other."

What warrants a more detailed review of this semiology is that it is centered on exactly the problems that are of importance in Pynchon's texts. In particular, the apparently *natural* and *direct* representation of referents in film has become the focus of a highly controversial debate. More so than language and the literary signifier, film seems to be based on a *natural* bond between its images and the objects/referents they represent. This has to do with the fact that unlike language, film is not based on a "double articulation" and the digital abstraction inherent in an alphabetical system of representation (the topics of the previous chapter) but proceeds by an analog transfer of referents into images.

Whereas Umberto Eco questions the inherent metaphysics of this structure, developing a threefold articulation within a specifically *cinematographic* code with which it should be possible to reduce the image, like language, to a digitalized structure,[3] Roland Barthes, who shares with Eco the basic contention that no image is ever completely natural, does not believe in the possibility of digitalizing and codifying film. For him, the question is whether "analogical representation (the 'copy') [can] produce true sign-systems and no longer merely simply agglutinations of symbols. . . . Is an analogical—and no longer a digital—'code' conceivable?" (*Respon-*

sibility 21). Barthes's concept of the "obtuse meaning," in fact, leaves the purely filmic beyond analytic reach: "The filmic is what, in the film, cannot be described, it is the representation that cannot be represented. The filmic begins only where language and articulated metalanguage cease" (58). It is exactly what is outside of language, something "which we can locate theoretically but not describe" (59), because it cannot be defined according to digitalizable codes: "Between this object and its image, it is not at all necessary to arrange a relay, i.e., a code; of course, the image is not the reality, but at least it is its perfect *analogon* . . . *it is a message without a code*" (5).

It is a basic paradox of film that "the connoted (or coded) message develops . . . from a message *without a code*" (*Responsibility* 8). The filmic, then, is exactly that which differentiates film and the image from language. Although every spectator immediately translates the image into language, the filmic denotes what is lost within this process of translation, or, in Kristeva's terms, transposition.[4] In their indebtedness to both the word and the image, Pynchon's works present a *mise-en-abîme* of such transpositions.

Next to the development of this inherently cinematographic semiotics, and often traversing its terrain, a second discussion deals with film as a cultural force. Studies such as Kracauer's *From Caligari to Hitler* often echo similar discussions within literary theory, predominantly by Marxist critics such as Theodor Adorno[5] or George Lukacs. This *cultural* critique highlights the co-optation of the medium by ideological, fascist, and, later on, capitalist systems.

Both discussions, however, stress the fact that films are extremely illusionist. For better or worse, they lull the viewer into a sleeplike weariness and a state of daydreaming. Within the cultural discussion this weariness facilitates the workings of ideology, but it marks for the strictly structural discussion a specifically filmic quality that differentiates film from literary works, which evoke images in the reader as a secondary step and only after the passage through the complex and abstract structure of language. Furthermore, whereas literary images are different for every reader, because they are the result of a personal projection, the filmic image is prearranged and preselected. It is because of the apparent naturality and objectivity of these images that the viewer easily takes them for real.

In the study of film, these two approaches can never be fully separated. A crucial link between them is the notion of *perception*, which defines the parallel between the structure of film and the psychic structure of the spectator. Christian Metz deals with this relation in *Psychoanalysis and Cinema*.

Watching a film differs from other instances of spectatorship vis-à-vis art forms such as painting, theater, opera, and, one might add, reading, in that it "mobilises a larger number of the axes of perception" (43). This richness, however, is realized within a basically fictional, or simulatory, scenario: "The perceived is not really the object, it is its shade, its phantom, its double, its *replica* in a new kind of mirror" (45). Metz stresses the difference between the naturality of the strikingly realistic impression and the simultaneous irreality of the *mode* of presentation of this impression, whose fragility Walter Benjamin noted when he described the cinematic image as "a mute image, . . . flickering an instant on the screen, then vanishing into silence" (229).[6] Film thus provides a perceptual richness based on an "originary" lack. This structure relates it to Lacan's object *o*. In fact, film is a perfect model to show the oscillation between the irreality of the objects (and by extension, symbols)—mirrored in the irreality of the filmic images—and their reality, which is why Lacan's statement that the gaze "contain[s] in itself the *objet a* of the Lacanian algebra" (Lacan, *Fundamental Concepts* 76) is again a useful reference.[7] By representing its referents only in effigy, film opens up the register of desire, which regulates the subject's relation to the object *o*, especially in its relation to lack: "The lack is what it wishes to fill, and at the same time what it is always careful to leave gaping, in order to survive as desire. In the end it has no . . . real object . . . it pursues an imaginary object (a 'lost object') which is its truest object, an object that has always been lost and is always desired as such" (Metz 59). This lack is highlighted by the structure of film, which presents a complete simulation of its object but places this simulacrum in an irretrievably inaccessible space. If the cortex is seen as a screen, film actually reduplicates the perceptual process by representing its referents on yet "another screen":

> What distinguishes the cinema is an extra reduplication, a supplementarity and specific turn of the screw bolting desire to the lack . . . . The cinema only gives it [the given] in effigy, inaccessible from the outset, in a primordial *elsewhere,* infinitely desirable (= never possible), on another scene which is that of absence and which nonetheless represents the absent in detail, thus making it very present, but by a different itinerary. (Metz 61)

The apparent naturality of the image is thus countered by its equally intense unreality. This structure differentiates film from language, in which the medium itself is already highly abstract, so that the unreality of the content is already prefigured by the unreality of the medium. As early as

1933 Roman Jakobson remarked on this characteristic of film (Metz 194), which thus creates a perfect illusion of reality with completely unrealistic means. Film is "a vast simulation, a non-real real; a 'milieu' with all the structures of the real and lacking . . . only the specific exponent of real being" (141). Because of this structure, film is a perfect vehicle for opening up the two diverging trajectories within which desire operates: toward the reality within the lack and the lack within the reality.

Film, however, regulates desire not only along a structural axis but also along a *temporal* one, because "no sooner has . . . [the] eye grasped a scene than it is already changed" (Benjamin 238). Because it is swept along by the flux of images, there is no chance for desire to attach itself to a stable object. Any fetishistic position, which always entails a certain amount of stability, is thus forestalled. This aspect also adds to the illusionistic character of film and facilitates the viewer's insertion into the narrative structure. Much more than is the case with literary texts, the spectator is at the mercy of the filmic image and has to adapt his or her perception to the speed of the presented images, which makes it much harder to maintain a reflexive position.

Although film seems to be grounded firmly in the imaginary, the symbolic also shares an important aspect with film. It is along this parallel that the seemingly *natural, analog* characteristics of film are put into question, because the analog filmic images are nevertheless embedded in a digital, discontinuous structure that defines the succession in which they simulate continuous movement. In language, the subject sinks into the voids between the signifiers; in film, it falls into the void between the single images on the reel. In fact, Derrida's notion of *trace,* which guarantees the continuity of signification, works very much like filmic images. According to Derrida, the trace functions like the perception-memory, which ensures the illusion of continuity in film. The eye retains one image until it perceives the next one. This physiological inertia—the phi phenomenon—is another in the growing number of inertias operative in Pynchon's text. It ensures the illusion of a temporal and temporary identity of images, a "persistence of vision" (GR 422) that Derrida transposes to a "persistence of thought." Although *retention* describes the subjective aspect within memory, its "objective correlative"—the "inertia of language"—is the concept of the *trace:* "The appearing and functioning of difference presupposes an originary synthesis not preceded by any absolute simplicity. Such would be the originary trace. Without a retention in the minimal unit of temporal experience . . . no meaning would appear" (*Of Grammatology* 62). In Derrida's system the dissemination of meaning is grounded in this minimal unit(y) of retention.[8] The cinematic, "fake" continuity can thus be seen as analogous to psychic processes and the way meaning and subjectivity are created as continuous concepts. In both registers the result is an *animation*.

The perception of film and its "naturality" is based on this "temporal blur." A film sweeps the subject from image to image, shrouding over the invisible bars between frames and evoking the illusion of continuity. The (cinematic) differentiation between time as continuous movement/duration and a consecutive sequence of single frames/moments also defines the dialectics of Henri Bergson,[9] which open up in its full force the question of *experience/artificiality* and *perception/naturality*. Like sexuality, pure, unmediated, and dynamic perception is generally considered a completely natural process. Yet for the subject, this raw perception is always already filtered. Although "raw perception" is an integral and necessary part of experience, it cannot be isolated. As it is itself *without form,* it cannot even be defined. Like the real, it is out of discursive reach and functions as a hole within discourse: "from intuition one can pass to analysis, but not from analysis to intuition" (Bergson, *Metaphysics* 48).[10] Within experience, the initial sensory perception is no longer pure and dynamic but cut into discrete segments and digitalized, no longer unmediated but part of a symbolic system. Raw sensory perception is thus recuperable only *within* experience, marking exactly that part of experience that cannot be imagined. If, then, perception is always already mediated, the isolation of the part that is unimaginable within experience is in fact an ultimate abstraction, the abstraction from abstraction itself. Bergson's theory thus shares the logical and temporal structure that defines the concept of belatedness—in Lacanian terms, the logical and temporal supremacy of the symbolic over the real. It is according to this logic of belatedness that what is generally called natural, then, emerges as the most abstract term, whereas abstraction itself emerges as the most natural: "'Pure,' that is to say, instantaneous, perception is, in fact, only an ideal, an extreme" (*Matter and Memory* 240). Bergson therefore differentiates between *pure* and *concrete* perception: "This perception, which coincides with its object, exists rather in theory than in fact: it could only happen if we were shut up within the present moment. In concrete perception, memory intervenes" (218–19). He describes this double definition within the dichotomy of *abstract* and *lived* time: *temps* and *durée*. Lived time, *perceived* as dynamic, unmediated, and personal, can only be *experienced* as abstract time. It exists solely in relation to the organic, "real" subject, because it is this "self which endures" (*Metaphysics* 9). This duration is brought about by memory, which connects, groups, and conceptualizes various experiences.

Film operates exactly in this dichotomy of *temps* and *durée*. As an apparatus, it is based on a rigorous selection and serialization of single moments and positions on a temporal scale and thus is related to *temps*. Via this abstraction, however, it simulates movement and the continuity of *durée*. The experiments of Marey and Muybridge are a perfect hinge between these two definitions. In *Slow Learner,* Pynchon comments on this twofold structure in his desire for "not the still photograph of finished character but the movie, the soul in flux" (SL 23). Because of this characteristic, film is the most intricate and powerful artistic simulation machine of naturality, which it sustains but simultaneously questions by revealing the fluidity of lived time as an irrecuperable ideal.[11]

The structure of film contains and reflects these two positions. The desire for naturality is lodged in its illusionistic character, yet film can become this utopia only because it is created within a structure of abstraction and idealization to which it continually draws attention. As Metz has shown, film inherently "takes on" desire while "bolting it to the lack." While referring the subject continuously to the inhuman realm of the Lacanian real, it simultaneously highlights the workings of the symbolic and imaginary. It is within these parameters that Pynchon uses film in *Gravity's Rainbow*.

As a final point, any use and mention of film in literature, and vice versa, apart from having to take into account both aspects of film, must rely on a theory of translation. Every such translation from one medium into the other implies a *structural* transposition. Julia Kristeva deals with such transpositions in her study *Revolution in Poetic Language,* in which she maintains that the adaptation of meaning carrying forms cannot proceed without a deep distortion of the signifier and the signified, and that it is never the *same* form that "passes" from one art-form to the other. Always, "the *passage from one sign system to another* . . . involves an altering of the thetic *position*—the destruction of the old position and the formation of a new one" (59). It is a change that is connected both to the destruction of the old signifying system and to the establishment of a new one. Every transposition creates a new thetic position: "a break in the signifying process, establishing the *identification* of the subject and its object as preconditions of propositionality" (43). A thetic position, comparable to Bergson's concept of *temps,* is the precondition for signification. Through an arrest of the gliding of signification, it shapes and brings into form a specific relation between subject and object. It is the structure of this "bringing into form" that is changed in the process of transposition, the carrying over of a unit of signification from one system of articulation (e.g., writing) into another (e.g., film). It destroys the fixed identification within one system of articulation and reconstructs it within a new sign system. Transposition thus involves the reflexive use of previous discursive positions within new ones: "The term *inter-textuality* denotes this transposition of one (or several) sign system(s) into another; but since this term has often been understood in the banal sense of 'study of sources,' we prefer the term *transposition*" (59–60). All investigations into the insertion of "filmic" instances within literature ultimately have to account for the dynamics of this transposition, which is why the novel can never *become* film. Rather, a novel that uses filmic references and "poses as film" presents a field of constant transpositions and continual oscillations among various media, all of which, except writing, are simulated. Pynchon makes constant use of these shifts. In fact, *Gravity's Rainbow* often "illustrate[s] uses of the film script" (Clerc, "Film in *Gravity's Rainbow*" 105), a characteristic that invites a comparison with a fictional literary genre invented and theorized by Pier Paolo Pasolini, who envisions a script to which the film has never been made and that is thus "an autonomous script . . . which meticulously documents a conscious decision of the author—the decision for a narrative strategy" (205). This narrative strategy implies that "the reader should *primarily see the kineme*[12] *in the grapheme and thus think in images, to re-construct in his own mind the film to which the script refers as a work still to be realized*" (212). *Gravity's Rainbow*, which seems to be written with such an imaginary script in mind, gains filmic dimensions without providing the image material itself, yet in this structure, every word gains a double, oscillating status: "The word of the script is *simultaneously the sign of two different structures. . . . It belongs to two languages, which have different structures*" (Pasolini 212). This twofold definition renders the word fundamentally ambivalent. As with certain entities in physics, it can act as either particle—linguistic digitality—or wave—filmic analogy.

In dealing with the insertion of cinematic material into Pynchon's text, it is necessary to differentiate between various routes of entry. The most basic one is the text inserting itself "directly" into a filmic mode by making use of film as *film* rather than *apparatus*.[13] Such a strategy involves the description of scenes that evoke film images through their visuality. In fact, *Gravity's Rainbow* is immensely rich in visual detail, a *horror vacui* resulting from the translation of a complete visual image, and not only perceptual

160   Textual Analyses

foci, into textual parameters; its *textual* richness is thus the direct result of the *textual* richness of the movie image.

On the other hand, the text can use film indirectly, as an apparatus, by borrowing words and concepts such as "cut," "closeup," or "zoom" and so evoke film as a practice, as in the following: "Here's a medium shot, himself backlit, alone at the high window in the Grand Hotel, whisky glass tipped at the bright subarctic sky" (GR 142). Other images directly evoke cinematic framing, point of view, and camera positions. Katje, for instance "gazes at 45° to Slothrop" (GR 254). Pynchon often uses such devices, for instance, a subjective camera angle when Slothrop comes to lying on the grass after his fall from a tree, gazing up at the sky: "Presently the sky is obscured by faces of some General and Teddy Bloat, gazing curiously down" (GR 200). A third route of entry is the insertion of *movie references* into the text. In fact, as the various critical studies of Pynchon's use of film show, film is arguably the semantic field most often exploited in the book.

The immediate insertion into the filmic through the simulation of filmic visuality points toward *one* desire of the text. By trying to achieve filmic dimensions the text lures and inserts the reader more firmly into its narrative system, drawing him into a hypnosis, reinforcing what Moore calls the "dreamlikeness" of the novel and stressing its mimetic character. In contrast, the use of film as apparatus opens up the possibility of an indirect self-reflexivity. Rather than calling attention to the writing itself, which is the usual literary device used to jolt the reader from the textual, fictional universe into an extratextual, authorial position, the cinematic reference calls attention to the "text as film." Whereas the presence of a camera in a film points directly toward film as a medium and to its artificiality, the presence—even if indirect—of a camera in a text disguised as film points to a more general artificiality realized within the filmic aspect of the novel without touching the dissimulated text itself. Like the referent in a film, the writing survives only from within a position of lack. The "textual desire" for signification is not halted by a self-reflexive stop and is perpetuated beneath a secondary self-reflexivity. The two movements of direct and indirect reference thus point toward two simultaneous desires of and in the text: its desire to simulate reality and its desire to persist as a text.

Thematically, Pynchon almost invariably uses film within a "deconstructive" project, a practice that seems to undermine this line of argument because it also jolts the reader out of "mimetic space." His use of the soundtrack, for instance, serves predominantly to distance the reader from the "serious" plot, much like the use of music in Marx Brothers movies.

[margin note: tautological]

Even the love scenes, although heavily enmeshed in movie imagery, are carried "over the top," with the text refusing to fade out at the appropriate moment. Katje is first "melting toward him [Slothrop] as he topples in slow-motion toward her mouth" (GR 196). Later, "she has sunk to the deep bed, pulling him along, into down, satin, seraphic and floral embroidery" (GR 196). A highly visual and thus filmic image—a straight description of surfaces—makes up the scene. As in a conventional movie shot, the lovers recline on the bed, whose luxurious softness is emphasized by "down, satin, seraphic and floral," all denoting a specific textural quality. Within movie conventions, this carefully staged image must be followed by either a fade-out or a closeup of the two lovers' faces kissing. Pynchon, however, without any transition whatsoever, follows it with a graphic description that is a total contrast to the imagery built up before, switching the mode of description from impressionistic luxury to the technical directness of a porn movie. She is "turning immediately to take his erection into her stretched fork, [. . .] as they fuck she quakes" (GR 196).

Throughout the book, Pynchon stages such intricate games with and within movie conventions, structures, and references, in a constant assembly and disassembly of filmic modes.[14] This strategy creates an oscillating and unsettling narrative space in which thetic positions are continually transposed and shifted among various media, without ever reaching either a stable reality or representational stability. In fact, by using a filmic mode, the text strategically and fundamentally destabilizes its own mode of representation, precluding both final identifications and stable meanings. Simultaneously, it highlights its indebtedness to sign systems rather than to unmediated reality, so that *Gravity's Rainbow* is a mimesis of media events rather than reality. In this respect it mirrors consciousness, which is also made up of numerous layers of superimposed texts represented in various media and in which the "missing text," the one situated on the "other scene," is continually translated from one fictional scenario to the next.

In *Gravity's Rainbow* reality is always a "media event," and mimesis a "media mimesis," which is why the book can quite drastically exclude whole fields of historical material and data from its historical panorama. If it portrays World War II without depicting, and indeed, rarely even mentioning, combat action and, except for one brief scene, referring to concentration camps only in passing, one explanation for these exclusions is that, in his portrayal of war, Pynchon draws not so much on a "real war" as on movies, their conventions, genres, and the images of war they project, freely switching from one genre to the next in a constant transposition. In particular, the genre of wartime spy movies—a genre Pynchon uses constantly—does without exactly these two topics.

By using filmic models in his portrayal of reality, Pynchon dismantles a preconceived image of war not by contrasting it with "real" images but by dismembering and restructuring certain key scenes of secondary representations, seeing war as a fictional site as well as a media event. This is especially fitting, because, for those who did not "live" World War II, most of the entries in their image repertoire of this war undoubtedly come from the movies, and the war's reconstitution is always already a media event and a simulation, just as all reconstitutions of history are mediated ones. Our culture, however, seems to have a special mania for translating history into images, and movies are the most common filter through which we perceive our past. The way in which Pynchon describes the WW II scenario pays homage to this fact. Apart from being a collage and agglomeration of movie images, it makes use of newspaper items, encyclopedic entries, and virtually any other available text. Almost all its material is culturally mediated before it enters the text. For this reason, it creates an extra *mise-en-abîme* when protagonists wander into movie sets, meet actors as well as directors, and move in landscapes of real and fake movies. This double use of cinematic references should always be kept in mind; if Pynchon uses cinematic strategies within the narration, he is always filming "a film" and creating a new image repertoire from the fragments of an older one, putting reality at one remove.

The story of Gerhardt von Göll focuses most directly on this interplay between film and reality, linking the multiple definitions of a cinematographic world with questions of control.[15] The introduction of a character who is a film director already creates an extra complexity and ambiguity; in a book written largely within cinematic parameters, a fictional movie director creates a cinematic counterreality to the reality described in the book. While doing this, he comes to believe that it is his counterreality that created the reality around him in the first place.

Gerhardt von Göll, the "white knight of the black market" (GR 492) occasionally intersects Slothrop's wanderings through the Zone, although his exact whereabouts are seldom fully known. "He is the knight who leaps perpetually [. . .] across the chessboard of the Zone [. . . .] He could be anyplace. He is everywhere" (GR 376). His freedom of movement and mobility are the reasons for his nickname, "der Springer," the only chess piece able to transcend the two-dimensionality of the board and have an overall perspective of its figurations: "One *sees how* it fits, ja? learns patterns, adjusts to rhythms, one day you are no longer an actor, but free now, over on the other side of the camera [. . .] just waking up one day, and knowing that Queen, Bishop, and King are only splendid cripples, and pawns [. . .] condemned to creep in two dimensions, and no Tower will ever rise or descend—no: *flight has been given only to the Springer!*" (GR 494).

Von Göll, moving "in higher orbits" (GR 438), has this general overview, which ensures his dominance on the black market. His double definition as both filmmaker and marketeer stresses the relation between film and economy, art and the commodity system. Originally a film director, von Göll has turned marketeer to earn money for the production of his future films, which is the only way to keep financial and artistic control, the "only way to be sure of having final cuts" (GR 386).

One of von Göll's projects is footage of a fake "Schwarzkommando," which he shoots in the "White Visitation" as part of a complicated scheme to simulate a fake reality that will disorient the German secret service. At first glance, this seems yet another of Pynchon's fertile metaphors. Nonetheless, it is a strategy delineated in detail by Paul Virilio in *War and Cinema*,[16] in which he cites Amos Vogel's account of Leni Riefenstahl's film of the Reichstag as the *"creation of an artificial universe that looked entirely real"* (54). This conflation of film and reality on the level of a "real event" makes Pynchon's repetition of this conflation especially forceful. His decision to provide a mimesis of media events rather than of unmediated reality is actually the more realistic project, because the "original" war has already turned reality into a media event.

In *Gravity's Rainbow,* Etzel Ölsch, the architect of the "Mittelwerke," actually proposes to Hitler designs that are "visually in the groove [. . .] except that none of the buildings will stay up. They look normal enough, but they are designed to fall down [. . .] shortly after the last rivet is driven, the last forms removed from the newly set allegorical statue. This is Ölsch's 'deathwish' problem here" (GR 300). Later on in the book, Enzian fears an even more sinister connection vis-à-vis the ruins of the Jamf-Ölwerke: "This ex-refinery [. . .] is *not a ruin at all. It is in perfect working order.* Only waiting for the right connections to be set up, to be switched on . . . modified, precisely, *deliberately* by bombing that was never hostile, but part of a plan both sides—'sides?'—had always agreed on" (GR 520).

In the light of Virilio's depiction of the effects of the movie images on wartime reality, and the implosion of these terms into each other, this description takes on an extra meaning; in fact, he explicitly mentions Göbbels's "Theory of the Value of Ruins," in which the architect has "a cinematic function similar to that of the military commander—namely, the capacity to determine in a building *what is permanent and what is impermanent*. In the last analysis . . . to construct a building is to foresee the way in which it will be destroyed" (Virilio 55). As a result, the buildings would eventually turn into ruins resembling those of the Romans, a perfect example of the inherent death wish of Dr. Göbbels and a prefiguration of Pynchon's ruins.

In Virilio's study, whose acuteness has been belatedly and frighteningly proven by the Gulf War, war becomes a movie machine in which battles are fought not on real battlefields but on fields of perception: "In other words, war consists not so much in scoring territorial, economical or other material victories as in appropriating the 'immateriality' of perceptual fields" (7). The result is a vortex of film and reality: "The concept of reality is always the first victim of war" (33). The war zone becomes a movie set in which fictional landscapes and machinery are handled by equally fictional personnel actually "reminiscent" of Pynchon's "Schwarzkommando."

Perhaps the most bizarre instance of these simulations was Hitler's plan at the end of the war to let Veit Harlan shoot a film depicting an early German victory in Narvik—on location and with "real" soldiers. When the British learned about this "remake" project and promised to turn the filmed "real" battle back into a real "real" one, Hitler gave up the plan. Generally, however, the strategy of filmic simulation was widely used in the war.

> The Luftwaffe's bombers and reconnaissance aircraft were at once engines of destruction and engines of cinema, movie producers, as it were, filming not only the battlefield but also the territory of the United Kingdom itself . . . the Allies therefore decided to take part in the *mise en scène* of Hitler's newsreel and intelligence films. Their main technique was not classical camouflage but, on the contrary, overexposure. Enemy cameras were offered sight of scenery, matériel, troop movements—all part of the almost limitless repertoire of visual illusions in real space.
>
> At the crucial point when massive preparations were under way for the Normandy landings, the East Anglian countryside came to resemble an enormous film lot complete with Hollywood-style props. Men with imagination, such as the architecture professor Basil Spence, were assisted in their work of visual disinformation by a mass of painters, poets, theatre and cinema technicians. Famous studios like Shepperton near London went over to producing phoney ar-

moured vehicles or landing ships. . . . The sound-track was also well worked out, with all the care of a film-script. (Virilio 63–64)

Von Göll's "Schwarzkommando" project has a similar aim:

> Running time of the film is three minutes, 25 seconds and there are twelve shots. It will be antiqued, given a bit of fungus and ferrotyping, and transported to Holland, to become part of the "remains" of a counterfeit rocket-firing site in the Rijkswijksche Bosch. The Dutch resistance will then "raid" this site, making a lot of commotion [. . . .] Among ashes, charred clothing, blackened and slightly melted gin bottles, will be found fragments of carefully forged Schwarzkommando documents, and of a reel of film, only three minutes and 25 seconds of which will be viewable. Von Göll, with a straight face, proclaims it to be his greatest work. (GR 113)

In Virilio's "real-life" example, as well as in von Göll's fictional project, film is used to simulate a fake reality. Although there are also *forged texts* involved in von Göll's setup, the *forged footage* serves as a final device to give authenticity to the scenario. The naturality of movie images is used to provide an aura of reality. The reversal of this situation—history as film rather than film as history—is again provided by Pökler:

> Pökler does manage to tell a little about Laszlo Jamf, but keeps getting sidetracked off into talking about the movies, German movies Slothrop has never heard of, much less seen . . . yes here's some kind of fanatical movie hound all right—"On D-Day," he confesses, "when I heard General Eisenhower on the radio announcing the invasion of Normandy, I thought it was really Clark Gable, have you ever noticed? the voices are *identical*. . . ." (GR 577)

The realization that the Schwarzkommando—carefully realized fictions—do exist in reality, that the filmic reality is "literally true" (GR 276), makes von Göll believe in his capacity actually to create and thus simulate reality:[17]

> Since discovering that Schwarzkommando are really in the Zone, leading real, paracinematic lives that have nothing to do with him or the phony Schwarzkommando footage he shot last winter in England for Operation Black Wing, Springer has been zooming around in a controlled ecstasy of megalomania. He is convinced that his film has somehow brought them into being. "It is my mission," he announces to Squalidozzi, with the profound humility that only a Ger-

man movie director can summon, "to sow in the Zone seeds of reality." (GR 388)

Like Pierce Inverarity in *Lot 49,* von Göll stands for the instance of control in all these projects. His mind projects personal, phantasmatic images onto the screen, translating the phantasm first into real images and from there into reality in a structure reminiscent of Schopenhauer's concept of the world as will and representation. This enables von Göll to structure reality itself, to superimpose his will on and to assert his control over life's image material. In the case of the Schwarzkommando, it is literally the repressed that reappears in the real: "What is rejected from the symbolic register reappears in the real" (Lacan, "Desire" 38), a "return" that is a perfect image of "belatedness": "What we see in the return of the repressed is the effaced signal of something which only takes on its value in the future, through its symbolic realisation. . . . Literally, it will only ever be a thing which, at the given moment of its occurrence, *will have been*" (*Seminar I* 159). Through film, von Göll can bring into existence, and thus actually to life, the repressed of Western culture, which is itself of course never sure about its ontological status.[18] It is this almost mythic power that he wants to use for another project involving a group of Argentine anarchists, for whom he wants to film the life of Martin Fierro with the aim of bringing about a "real" counterhistory: "My images, somehow, have been chosen for incarnation. What I can do for the Schwarzkommando I can do for your dream of pampas and sky. . . . I can take down your fences and your labyrinth walls, I can lead you back to the Garden you hardly remember . . ." (GR 388).

The convergence of life and film is further enhanced by synthetic devices such as Imipolex G and Emulsion J., also invented by Jamf, which is able to "render the human skin transparent to a depth of half a millimeter, revealing the face just beneath the surface" (GR 387). Both of these symbolize the synthesization of natural objects in a further step toward a complete cinematic simulation.

If film can actually *create* reality, the movie director becomes the perfect *alter deus.* Nonetheless, the question of the naturality and authenticity of this reality, as well as the question of the integrity of the director, persists: "Will the soul of the Gaucho survive the mechanics of putting him into light and sound? Or will someone ultimately come by, von Göll or another, to make a Part II, and dismantle the dream?" (GR 388). Another of von Göll's films, *Alpdrücken,* is of special importance in this respect. It again aligns the implosion of film and reality with the motif of control and is an allegory of love in a fully controlled and simulated universe. It stars Margherita Erdmann and Max Schlepzig as a sadomasochistic couple. It is during its shooting that Bianca is conceived and after watching it that Pökler "conceives" Ilse: "I suppose you heard about how she [Margherita] got pregnant with Bianca. [. . .] You never saw *Alpdrücken*? In that one scene, after the Grand Inquisitor gets through, the jackal men come in to ravish and dismember the captive baroness. Von Göll let the cameras run right on. The footage got cut out for the release prints of course" (GR 461).

Without the actors realizing it, their "real" life is turned into film in this scene. Whereas Bianca is a movie-child because she is conceived after the *shooting*[19] of a scene, Ilse is one because she is conceived after the *watching* of the same scene, in a repetition of the original's sadomasochistic rituals:

> . . . yes, bitch—yes, little bitch—poor helpless *bitch* you're coming can't stop yourself now I'll whip you again whip till you *bleed*. . . . Thus Pökler's whole front surface, eyes to knees: flooded with tonight's image of the delicious victim bound on her dungeon rack, filling the movie screen—close-ups of her twisting face, nipples under the silk gown amazingly erect, making lies of her announcements of pain—*bitch!* she loves it . . . and Leni no longer solemn wife, embittered source of strength, but Margherita Erdmann underneath him, on the bottom for a change [. . . .] He had come out of the Ufa theatre on the Friedrichstrasse that night with an erection, thinking like everybody else only about getting home, fucking somebody, fucking her into some submission. [. . .] How many shadow-children would be fathered on Erdmann that night? [. . .] *That's how it happened. A film. How else? Isn't that what they made of my child, a film?* (GR 397–98)

The structure of projection that underlies this reaction brings into play the analogy between film and the psychic apparatus, as movie projections are quite literally turned into psychic ones. Both the transferral of movie images onto "real" people and the substitution of these images for live ones take place within the characteristic of film Metz comments on: to tie the desire for identification to a specific lack. This link presides over the scenario of constant displacements and missed encounters that are restaged during Slothrop's lovemaking to Erdmann in the original movie sets. The initial sadomasochistic scenario is reenacted, so that the circular structure of displaced desire and projections is finally closed:

> Slothrop puts the whip down and climbs on top, covering her with the wings of his cape, her Schlepzig-surrogate, his latest reminder of

> Katje ... and they commence fucking, the old phony rack groaning beneath them, Margherita whispering *God how you hurt me* and *Ah, Max* ... and just as Slothrop's about to come, the name of her child: strained through her perfect teeth, a clear extrusion of pain that is not in play, she cries, *Bianca*.... (GR 397)

In this passage, film and reality are inextricably amalgamated in a complicated whirl of missed identifications: Slothrop identifies Greta with Katje, while he functions for her as a reminder of Max Schlepzig (with whose passport he is actually traveling) and their child Bianca, whose loss she reexperiences in this passage.

The economy of sadomasochism holds these hierarchies of power in balance. In its economy, pain functions as the promise of a return to something real, the passage from the social and simulated to the organic and real body. Yet this perception of the real in (the *jouissance* of) pain remains imaginary and ends—at least for Pudding—in death. Lacan thematizes this imaginary character when he states that "at the outset of the sado-masochistic drive, pain has nothing to do with it. It is a question of a *Herrschaft* [mastery], of *Bewältigung* [mastering] ... a violence that the subject commits, with a view to mastery, upon himself" (*Fundamental Concepts* 183). Only after the internal reversal within the structure of sadomasochism, when the sadistic subject has reached the end of the trajectory of its drive, "the terminus" (183), and has arrived at the masochistic pole of its symmetry, does pain come "into play in so far as the subject experiences it from the other" (183). This shift explains why "sadism is merely the disavowal of masochism" (186). This sadomasochistic economy shows the degree of the entanglement of imaginary *jouissance* in "the *jouissance* of the other" (183) and the impossibility of real *jouissance*. This "ontological" impossibility, however, is supplemented in Pynchon by a critique of the growing erasure of the real *as* negativity. Consequently, although the promise of escape is inherent in Pynchon's text, sadomasochism is not presented as a positive phenomenon; rather, it is seen as the inevitable result of simulation. The sadomasochistic acts are not simply, as Joseph Slade maintains, "attempts by characters to break through the boundaries of the individual self and to reestablish the sense of community that an impoverished spirituality has forestalled" ("Religion" 189). Although real *jouissance* is ontologically impossible, the extreme scenarios of sadomasochism in Pynchon's text are the only "possible" bodily and direct answer to the growing textual overcoding of the subject and its body by a repressive simulatory system: the body's desperate, "real-ly" deadly answer to the erasure of the body and symbolic death in simulation. As in the Kirghiz Light episode, pain is the last refuge wherein the subject can experience the self, because pain falls out of simulatory operationality. Brigadier Pudding, for example, is "bound by nothing but his need for pain, for something real, something pure. They have taken him so far from his simple nerves. They have stuffed paper illusions [. . .] between him and this truth" (GR 234). His relation to Katje is the only escape from this fully mediated reality. It is only in his submission to her that he can experience "his failing body, his true body: undisguised by uniform, uncluttered by drugs to keep him from her communiqués of vertigo, nausea and pain . . . Above all, pain. The clearest poetry, the endearment of greatest worth . . ." (GR 235). The reference to paper and writing is a clear indication that sadomasochism is an attempt to reach back from the simulation in which, as Baudrillard states, "guilt, anguish and death . . . [have been] substituted [by] the total joy of the *signs* of guilt, despair, violence and death (*Simulations* 148; emphasis added) to a real act in which, as Pierre Janet maintains, "'the act of injuring and the act of being injured are joined in the behavior of the whole injury'" (GR 88). This concept, however, is in turn immediately questioned in regard to its "tragic" relation to and complicity with power structures: "Speaker and spoken-of, master and slave, virgin and seducer, each pair *most conveniently* coupled and inseparable" (GR 88; emphasis added). Pynchon's critique of sadomasochism as a system based on a more initial "simulation" also incorporates the family as the microcosm of the state: "Why will the Structure allow every other kind of sexual behaviour but *that* one? Because submission and dominance are resources it needs for its very survival. [. . .] It needs our submission so that it may remain in power. [. . .] I tell you, if S and M could be established universally, at the family level, the State would wither away" (GR 737).

Pökler is caught in a similar structure of pain and replacement. He actually turns Ilse, Bianca's "twin," who visits him as a "movie image" for their annual visits to Zwölfkinder, into a fetish, creating out of these unmoving, unreal images "something like the persistence of vision, for They have used it to create for him the moving image of a daughter, flashing him only these summertime frames of her, leaving it to him to build the illusion of a single child . . . what would the time scale matter, a 24th of a second or a year" (GR 422).

Ilse's reconstitution as a "continuous concept" is again both a cinematic and a psychic event. In the pun on the "persistence of vision"—not only the phi phenomenon but also the "continuity of a special vision" Pökler has of his daughter as an "identical," growing child—the *psychic* is correlated to the *cinematic* machinery: "This strange connection between the German mind and the rapid flashing of successive stills to counterfeit movement [. . . .] And now Pökler was about to be given proof that these techniques had been extended past images on film, to human lives" (GR 407). Fittingly, Pökler's last encounter with the simulated Ilse takes place in a fully simulated scenario, the Antarctic Panorama: "A few 'sled dogs' lay suffering in the shade of the dirty papier-mâché sastrugi, on plaster snow that had begun to crack. A hidden projector threw images of the aurora on a white scrim. Half a dozen stuffed penguins also dotted the landscape" (GR 420).

Although he is a figure of control, von Göll remains a highly ambiguous figure. On the one hand megalomaniac, on the other he seems to share the vision of a democratic use of films described by Benjamin: "Any man today can lay claim to being filmed. . . . Thus, the distinction between author and public is about to lose its basic character. . . . At any moment the reader is ready to turn into a writer" (231–32).

This dynamization of the functions of actor and director is possible only if the artistic medium is available for everybody. It must be on the market and economically accessible. This is the mythical future of which von Göll dreams: "Someday, when the film is fast enough, the equipment pocket-size and burdenless and selling at people's prices, the lights and booms no longer necessary, *then* . . . then . . ." (GR 527).[20]

Von Göll continually disrupts the official market system of the ultimate directors of reality. Like them, he is a figure of control, but unlike them, he is sufficiently chaotic, likeable, and irresponsible to remain a positive figure in Pynchon's ménagerie, a fact highlighted by his end at "Der Platz," (GR 686), a free and open territory and Säure's and von Göll's final whereabouts. Here von Göll's last project, *New Dope,* is shown, a film about a drug that has two specific characteristics—you cannot tell anybody how it feels to take it and you cannot remember where you got it. In a parallel to the S-Gerät's search for Slothrop, "it is the dope that finds *you,* apparently" (GR 745).

The last image, however, shows the reverse side of this chaotic playground. It shows von Göll in a nonsignifying delirium, which connects him both to many other positive figures in the book but also to their common Achilles heel, their "deathless" innocence and investment in imaginary *jouissance:* "Gerhardt von Göll on his camera dolly, whooping with joy, barrel-assing down the long corridors at Nymphenburg. (Let us leave him here, in his transport, in his innocence . . .)" (GR 750). Apart from the inevitable pun on transport, this ending evokes the "Corridor metaphysics" (GR 394) of *Last Year in Marienbad,* a film Pynchon might well have used to denote a completely self-contained, surreal signifying system without connection to any outer reality. If von Göll previously had used his powers on behalf of the "repressed," he is now "living inside fantasy," in a position that completely forecloses the signifier and the real—and thus lack and death— a state symbolized by the structure of reversal operative in *New Dope,* which shows "part of a reverse world whose agents run around with guns which are like vacuum cleaners operating *in the direction of life*—pull the trigger and bullets are sucked back out of the recently dead into the barrel, and the *Great Irreversible is actually reversed*" (GR 745; emphases added).

Whereas von Göll is *creating* counterrealities, Katje, like Greta Erdmann, is a *creature,* an actor whose moves are prearranged and choreographed by a director. She serves as a focus for questions not of the creation of reality but of modes of control within a prefabricated and simulated reality. Her position is always that of a victim, and it is because of her position as a completely controlled subject that her story is "the saddest of all" (GR 661). Whenever he is together with Katje, Slothrop is especially aware of the systems of control: "All in his life of what has looked free or random, is discovered to've been under some Control, all the time, the same as a fixed roulette wheel" (GR 209). These systems are also dealt with in filmic terms. Sir Stephen Dodson-Truck's role of observing Slothrop and his intimate relationship with Katje, for instance, actually turns him into a camera, an objective recording and surveillance machine: "'Th-they think I don't *care,* any more. "You can observe without passion." [. . .] Slothrop, we're all such mechanical men. Doing our jobs. That's all we are. Listen— how do you think I *feel?* When you're off with her after every lesson. I'm an impotent *man* [. . .] my "function" is to observe you. That's my function. You like my function? You like it? *Your* "function" . . . is, learn the rocket'" (GR 216).

When Slothrop asks whether Dodson-Truck actually watches Katje and him make love, Sir Stephen replies, "'What difference's it make? I'm the perfect man for it. Perfect. I can't even masturbate half the time [. . . .] Just a neuter, just a *recording eye*'" (GR 216; emphasis added). Here, with Sir Stephen as the perfect camera eye, observing and cold, the functionalization of human beings into machines is thematized. Observer and observed are both mere functions and variables within a complex network of control. It is in fact only after Slothrop decodes "Their" setup that he finally has an uncontrolled moment. When he looks out the window, "for ten extraordinary seconds there's nothing in his field but simple love for what he's seeing" (GR 221). This is immediately followed by a moment of uncontrolled sex: "It occurs to him he's naked and also, hmm, seems to be getting a hardon here, look out, Slothrop. And nobody here to note it, or speculate why . . ." (GR 221). It is symptomatically after this lovemaking that he becomes aware of the "real," deadly aspect of Katje, "watching her face turned ¾ away [. . .] the terrible Face That Is No Face, gone too abstract, unreachable [. . .] a noseless mask of the Other Order of Being, of Katje's being—the lifeless nonface that is the only face of hers he really knows" (GR 222).

This is a privileged moment because, like Mélanie in *V.*, the actress Katje is almost always all surface and defined throughout by her outer appearance: "Now she wears a white pelisse, with sequins all over, padded shoulders, jagged white ostrich plumes at the neckline and wrists. The tiara is gone: in the electricity her hair is new snowfall" (GR 194). In addition to clothes, makeup (which hides the "real face" in the same way that clothes hide the "real body") is included in these celebrations of visual surfaces: "She has her hair combed high today in a pompadour, her fair eyebrows, plucked to wings, darkened, eyes rimmed in black" (GR 224). All these evoke the cliché image of the beautiful female spy. It establishes Katje as an actor through the emphasis on her outer appearance, as well as through her definition as an agent who is in many senses also an actor and a *poseur*. She is an operative caught in a vast network of espionage, interference, infiltration, conditioning, control, and codification. Her story contains most of the book's grandiose and absurd schemes of message transmission and reality control. In the beginning of *Gravity's Rainbow*, Pirate Prentice gets a message about her via a V-2, requesting that she be picked up from Holland, where she has spied on Blicero. The coded message is written in Kryptosam, a substance that becomes visible only in contact with the specific receiver's semen and arrives together with the stimulus appropriate for the specific receiver.[21] Next, she is in London at Pirate Prentice's maisonette, secretly being filmed to serve as a stimulus for octopus Grigori. This, her first textual appearance, from the beginning defines her as "someone who is being filmed":

> In silence, hidden from her, the camera follows as she moves deliberately nowhere longlegged about the rooms [. . .] her hair not

bluntly Dutch at all, but secured in a modish upsweep with an old, tarnished silver crown, yesterday's new *perm* leaving her very blonde hair frozen on top in a hundred vortices, shining through the dark filigree. Widest lens-opening this afternoon, extra tungsten light laid on. [. . .] She's alone in the house, except for the secret cameraman and Osbie Feel. (GR 92; emphasis added)[22]

It is again a glitter of surfaces that is recorded by the camera, a rich texture of light reflexes and sparkling forms. The description goes on in these cinematic terms: "In close-up her skin, though nearly perfect, is seen to be lightly powdered and rouged, the eyelashes a touch darkened, brows reshaped a matter of two or three empty follicles . . ." (GR 93). A glimpse of an open oven reminds her suddenly of her Hansel and Gretel setup with Blicero. This reminiscence of death (the real) is fittingly described in cinematographic terms as a stopping of the "film of life": "The camera records no change in her face, but why does she stand now so immobile at the door? as if the frame were to be stopped and prolonged" (GR 93). Pynchon uses the portrayal of these surfaces to relate to an invisible, again deadly, inside in a correlation of the camera and the mirror as two "systems of identification":[23] "At the images she sees in the mirror Katje also feels a cameraman's pleasure, but knows what he cannot: that inside herself, enclosed in the *soignée* surface of dear fabric and dead cells, she is corruption and *ashes*" (GR 94; emphasis added).

Her assignment to play Domina Nocturna to Brigadier Pudding's masochistic desires and fantasies ties her in with the other sadomasochistic scenarios in *Gravity's Rainbow* and is her bleakest and darkest job (GR 233–36). After Pudding's death, she joins the Counterforce, recruited via another secret, codified message conveyed by film.[24] The remainder of the book shows her working for the Counterforce and trying to come to terms with her guilt and her "leukemia of soul" (GR 658), unable to die, to get out of the game, and with a "life sentence" suspended over her head. As Enzian tells her, "you are meant to survive. Yes, probably. No matter how painful you want to make it for yourself, still you're always going to come through. You're free to choose exactly how pleasant each passage will be. Usually it's given as a reward. I won't ask for what. I'm sorry, but you seem really not to know. That's why your story *is* saddest of all" (GR 662).

Katje, always acting on orders, is never sure of her freedom. Her life is a film of prearranged sequences and moves and contains no possibility of choice. Even within the Counterforce she is never sure as to the final instances of control and wonders whether the Counterforce is not itself only another entry in Their script. Within all these nets of control, however, she dreams of a "world of Reality she still believes in and will never give up hoping to rejoin someday" (GR 658).

Pynchon stages the relation between simulation and reality—between Katje as actor and her "real" personality—in black and white imagery to highlight its dualism and to show the dependence of the one on the other. This color symbolism also defines von Göll's films. As Margherita (Greta) Erdmann states, "The light came from above and below at the same time, so that everyone had two shadows: Cain's and Abel's, Gerhardt told us. It was at the height of his symbolist period. Later on he began to use more natural light, to shoot more on location" (GR 394).

Ultimately, these filmic "shades of gray" become a metaphor for reality in general: "The Double Light was always there, outside all film" (GR 429). Like the meeting when "paranoid meets paranoid" (GR 395), this double light creates "a moiré, a new world of flowing shadows, interferences . . ." (GR 395). Later, Pynchon takes up the subject again from the side of the megalomaniac von Göll, who, although he counts himself among the elite, states that "elite and preterite [. . .] move through a cosmic design of darkness and light, and in all humility, I am one of the very few who can comprehend it *in toto*" (GR 495); at this point, ironically, the "sky has begun to look less like a moiré" (GR 494).

The implosion of reality control and film control is highlighted by the fact that Katje occupies the same position within "Their" framework that Greta Erdmann occupied in von Göll's: "I knew he was a genius from the beginning. I was only his creature" (GR 393). But whereas von Göll can still be surprised about the reversal of cause and effect that his Schwarzkommando footage seems to have brought about and ends in a fantasy that actually reverses this sequence, "Their" project is the creation of reality and the system of cause and effect in the first place. In this relation, film does indeed function as a sinister force within *Gravity's Rainbow*, as the ultimate machinery of control and simulation.[25] Nonetheless, although it is used *by* "Them" (and film imagery is used to describe "Their" position of absolute control against a preterite "you": "Trapped inside Their frame [. . .] ass hanging out all over Their Movieola viewer, waiting for Their editorial blade" [GR 694]), it is also used *against* "Them," as for instance in the *Doper's Greed* or the Dillinger sequence. This double, ambiguous encoding of film as both danger and promise "overrides" its either purely positive or purely negative aspects. It is operative everywhere in the book, especially in its metaphorical relation to the rocket, which is itself similarly doubly encoded. Pynchon uses the structure of film, as well as the flight of the rocket, to discuss questions of reality and its perception. In this framework, film "carries" the discussion rather than providing an answer to it. The rocket and film are aligned via the concept of continuity, which is such a central topic in film studies.

From the beginning, the grid of time-space continuity on which the structure of cause and effect is based is rendered ineffective in *Gravity's Rainbow*. As I discuss in chapter 6, already with the first sentence, "a screaming comes across the sky" (GR 3), the book announces the disruption of this time-space continuity by the V-2 and the inauguration of a belated universe. Because the rocket travels faster than the speed of sound, it is only after it has hit somewhere *else* that its screaming can be heard by the survivors. In the opening section Pirate Prentice muses about this disconcerting fact: "He won't hear the thing come in. It travels faster than the speed of sound. The first news you get of it is the blast. Then, if you're still around, you hear the sound of it coming in" (GR 7). In an unattributed, anonymous remark inserted into a discussion between Spectro and Pointsman, this idea is again linked to the structure of film: "Imagine a missile one hears approaching only *after* it explodes. The reversal! A piece of time neatly snipped out . . . a few feet of film run backwards . . . the blast of the rocket, fallen faster than sound—then growing *out of it* the roar of its own fall, catching up to what's already death and burning . . . a ghost in the sky . . ." (GR 48).

The V-2's reversal of impact and sound of approach is a first instance in which a referent passes—like the trauma—through symbolic space without bothering to become a sign. By virtue of mere speed, the hermeneutic scene is overthrown. In *Fatal Strategies*, Baudrillard evokes a similar scenario, taking as his point of reference the ultimate border of the speed of light: "The speed of light is what protects the reality of things because it is what guarantees that the images we have of them are contemporaneous. All plausibility of a causal universe would disappear with a perceptible change of this speed. Everything would interfere, in total disorder" (18). Of course, things have already broken the sound barrier, such as the V-2, and are now, with the electronic media, notably TV, as fast as light: "This is what is happening today with electronic media, as the information starts to circulate everywhere at the very speed of light" (18). Already, the scenario is one of the schizophrenic "absolute proximity to and total instantaneousness with things." If the things moved even faster, "they would rub into us without our seeing them coming" (19).

Throughout *Gravity's Rainbow*, Pynchon evokes scenes in which this continuity is put out of order. In one passage, ironically one in which he almost mockingly provides the reader with a completely improbable chain of cause and effect within the labyrinths of his plots ("You will want cause and effect. All right" [GR 663]), he exemplifies this breaking up of the continuity of life by the story of the Polish undertaker, a "digital companion" (GR 663) who tries to get hit by lightning because he has heard of people being hit and surviving: "What stories *they* could tell!" (GR 663). Being hit by lightning can cause revelations: "Well, it's a matter of continuity. Most people's lives have ups and downs that are relatively gradual, a sinuous curve with first derivatives at every point. They're the ones who never get struck by lightning" (GR 664).

Because lightning causes the isolation of one instant within this gradual continuity, "the ones who do get hit experience a singular point, a discontinuity in the curve of life" (GR 664). Isolating this moment of change, the lightning reveals, in mathematical imagery, the vastness of the gap between one instant and the next—or, in film imagery, that between two frames: "Do you know what the time rate of change *is* at a cusp? *Infinity*, that's what! A-and right across the point, it's *minus* infinity! How's *that* for sudden change, eh?" (GR 664). It is indeed the gap between two infinities that is opened up by this isolation. Such an isolation results in a mapping of and possibility of passage between two worlds. After the return, the world "will *look* like the world you left, but it'll be different. Between congruent and identical there seems to be another class of look-alike that only finds the lightning-heads. Another world laid down on the previous one and to all appearances no different. Ha-*ha*! But the lightning-struck know, all right! Even if they may not *know* they know" (GR 664).

The isolation of one specific moment reveals the whole concept of continuity as illusory. In relation to the problematics of subjectivity, this opens up the question of the continuity of the self's identity. Pynchon's use of film touches on exactly these problems. Life is broken up into separate images, single frames, and then artificially reanimated.

> Three hundred years ago mathematicians were learning to break the cannonball's rise and fall into stairsteps of range and height, Δx and Δy, allowing them to grow smaller and smaller, approaching zero as armies of eternally shrinking midgets galloped upstairs and down again. [. . .] This analytic legacy has been handed down intact—it brought the technicians at Peenemünde to peer at the Askania films of Rocket flights, frame by frame, Δx by Δy, flightless themselves . . .

film and calculus, both pornographies of flight. Reminders of impotence and abstraction. (GR 567)

Bergson already had related this infinitesimal structure, in which the mind splits up a continuous movement into discrete moments, to the structure of film: "But the points in time [*temps*] . . . of the moving object are only snapshots, which our mind takes of the continuity of movement and duration [*durée*]" (*La Pensée* 7). The intellect produces "stills" of a prior but irrevocably lost continuity. Film, in turn, reverses the process by creating the illusion of continuity from the succession of these stills. This continuity, however, can never be "real," because the succession of images is prearranged and leaves no possibility of a real and natural development: "In theory, the film on which the positions of a completely pre-arranged system are represented might be running at any speed, without anything being changed" (12).

This is exactly what happens during the rerun of history described in *Gravity's Rainbow*, in which the mythical depopulation of America that should reestablish its virgin freedom is again—as with *New Dope*—described as a film running backward.

> Ghosts of fishermen, glassworkers, fur traders, renegade preachers, hilltop patriarchs and valley politicians go avalanching back from Slothrop here, back to 1630 when Governor Winthrop came over to America on the *Arbella*, flagship of a great Puritan flotilla that year, on which the first American Slothrop had been a mess cook or something—there go that *Arbella* and its whole fleet, sailing backward in formation, the wind sucking them east again, the creatures leaning from the margins of the unknown *sucking in* their cheeks, growing crosseyed with the effort [. . .] as the old ships zoom out of Boston Harbor, back across an Atlantic whose currents and swells go flowing and heaving in reverse . . . a redemption of every mess cook who ever slipped and fell when the deck made an unexpected move, the night's stew collecting itself up out of the planks and off the indignant shoes of the more elect, slithering in a fountain back into the pewter kettle as the servant himself staggers upright again and the vomit he slipped on goes gushing back into the mouth that spilled it. . . . (GR 203–4)

The only "real" duration within this film is the fact that "the spooling off of the film corresponds to a specific duration of our inner life" (Bergson,

La Pensée 12). The difference is thus between "an evolution and a spooling-off" (13). Film creates the illusion of duration and evolution, so that the plot seems to develop naturally, although it is of course prearranged and prefigured by a succession of stills—and "something static that is strung together with something else that is static will never create a true duration" (7). The same is true for modern simulation, in which movement results from the realization of an underlying infinitesimal mathematical matrix.

As Moore states, "film yields a sort of mechanical imitation or parody of the world's raw continuity (87), and its continuous process of breaking up and reassembling is the ultimate subject of Pynchon's investigation. Godard's statement that "cinema is truth, twenty-four times a second" is thus balanced by the realization that a second of this truth contains twenty-four positions of "barred" movement. Twenty-four times each second the image is disrupted and broken, stuttering in the way infinitesimal calculus is also the stuttering of a continuous trajectory. This stuttering is taken up by the text, in which ellipses continually break up the "natural movement" of the narrative voice.

The disintegration of Slothrop incorporates all these themes. Slothrop, Clerc says, "is the single character who seems most deeply immersed in the images and patois of cinema" ("Film" 129); he is a "thinking, walking, sleeping conglomeration of many movie beings" (130). His final disintegration, seemingly unrelated to film, is in fact the climax of cinematic structures. "Slothrop, as noted, at least as early as the *Anubis* era, has begun to thin, to scatter" (GR 509). This disintegration has been "the basis or pivot of much controversy and interpretation regarding the implications of Slothrop's disappearance for the role of the 'self' in the modern novel" (Schaub, *Ambiguity* 75). On the one hand, it has been interpreted as a final textual dispersion: "Scattering is a difficult stage in the freak's journey because it also plays a positive role in throwing off the rigidities of the System—it plays the role of 'deconstruction'" (Olderman 219). On the other hand, it has been interpreted as a vitalistic metamorphosis: "Slothrop returns to nature without understanding. Such a transformation is sterile" (Slade, "Religion" 177). In the light of its cinematic structure it takes on yet another meaning. The dispersion is from the beginning presented in terms of "integrals." Slothrop is losing his personal density, which is "directly proportional to temporal bandwidth" (GR 509), which in turn is "the width of your present, your *now*. It is the familiar 'Δt' considered as a dependent variable. The more you dwell in the past and in the future, the thicker your bandwidth, the more solid your persona. But the narrower your sense of Now, the more tenuous you are" (GR 509). The more one lives every moment—every "still"—the less one is able to define oneself and the more one has to face the raw continuity of the real. The description of this dispersion shows very clearly what de Man means when he states that "selfhood is not a substance but a figure" (*Allegories* 170).

The vitalistic interpretation refers mainly to Slothrop's ending as a "crossroad": "And now, in the Zone, later in the day he became a crossroad [. . . .] Slothrop sees a very thick rainbow here, a stout rainbow cock driven down out of pubic clouds into Earth [. . .] and his chest fills and he stands crying, not a thing in his head, just feeling natural . . ." (GR 626). Rather than implying a simple, unmediated return to perception, however, the scattering process involves the scattering of personality and the entry into a state of pure sensation that actually *excludes* subjectivity: "In the mode of pure sensation, everything is 'outside' everything else; there is nothing but outside differences and no integration is possible" (de Man, *Allegories* 231). Pure perception and the loss of self fall together and can be re-created only by the anonymous narrative voice: "He has become one plucked albatross. Plucked, hell—*stripped*. Scattered all over the Zone. It's doubtful if he can ever be 'found' again, in the conventional sense of 'positively identified and detained'" (GR 712).

This scattering opens up the issues of a natural state but also functions as a critique of the operational reason inherent in simulatory systems. As in the Kirghiz Light episode, the problem touches again on the *interrelatedness* of the concepts of subjectivity/culture and nature rather than the *cancellation* of the former in the utopian image of a purely natural existence: "There is no good reason to hope for any turn, any surprise *I see-it*, not from Slothrop. [. . .] Forgive him as you forgave Tchitcherine at the Kirghiz Light" (GR 509–10). Slothrop's final disintegration can be read only within the space created by these "mutually exclusive" parameters: "He's been changing, sure, changing, plucking the albatross of self now and then [. . .] but the one ghost-feather his fingers always brush by is America. Poor asshole, he can't let her go. She's whispered *love me* too often to him in his sleep, vamped insatiably his waking attention with [. . .] incredible promises" (GR 623).

The relation of subject and culture is the axis around which Slothrop's disintegration revolves; by plucking at his self, he is simultaneously plucking away at that which defines him: his history, language, and culture, all the forces of Pavlovian conditioning that have "created" him.

As he does in *Lot 49*, Pynchon describes the ego as a purely cultural creation: "Discontinuities [. . .] alienation—whatever's analogous, in a social sense, to the development of an independent ego by the very young child" (GR 206). Only in very privileged moments—such as Mondaugen experiences in the desert—can this ego be annulled. Mondaugen's "electro-mysticism" (GR 404), in fact, evokes the idea of a "journey without hysteresis": "Think of the ego, the self that suffers a personal history bound to time, as the grid. [. . .] Signals—sense-data, feelings, memories relocating—are put onto the grid, and modulate the flow. We live lives that are waveforms constantly changing with time, now positive, now negative. Only at moments of great serenity is it possible to find the pure, the informationless state of signal zero" (GR 404).[26]

Again as in *Lot 49*, America stands for the subject's deepest determinations, because it hosts its desires and promises their fulfillment: "The Man has a branch office in each of our brains, his corporate emblem is a white albatross, each local rep has a cover known as the Ego, and their mission in this world is Bad Shit" (GR 712–13).

Slothrop's culture stands for the symbolic and imaginary instances that define him as a subject, as well as for the agencies that have been erected to cope with the subject's initial loss and lack. The symbolic universe is bound inextricably to this lack, which can be dissolved only by dissolving the subject. The disintegration of the subject is thus the promise of the cancellation of lack. The subject disintegrates out of the symbolic and the imaginary into the real, from the "thought identity" (Lacan, *Séminaire VII* 41) of the secondary processes to the "perceptual identity" (40) of the primary processes, the "zero signal" between "personal identity and impersonal salvation" (GR 406).

In this shift, cultural signification gives way to a "crying" that for Juranville gathers "all the elements of the death-drive" (231).[27] After countless impersonations, disguises, and other "rhetorical" gestures, Slothrop is reduced to his body, "finding in every bone and cabbage leaf *paraphrases* of himself" (GR 625; emphasis added). This anthropomorphization of nature within the passage has to be read inversely to the naturalization of man. Nature can only be put "under erasure": n̶a̶t̶u̶r̶e̶. In fact, the "*jouissance-*effects" in the descriptions of the epileptic, the sailor and the "saint, the clairvoyant, the paranoid and the dreamer" in *Lot 49*, as well as of the point O in the hysteresis loop, of the Kirghiz Light, of the Polish undertaker, of Mondaugen in the desert and of Slothrop as a crossroad in *Gravity's Rainbow*, all problematize a "naturality under erasure."

It is in relation to this erasure that the relation between the body and the text (the real and the symbolic) is most pertinent. Unlike Pavlov, Lacan understands the materials of the "real" less as biological givens than as signifiers: "Nature provides . . . signifiers, and these signifiers organize human relations in a creative way, providing them with structures and shaping them" (*Fundamental Concepts* 20). Human reality is made up from the ensemble of these materials. Although they are strictly excluded from representation, their effects within the imaginary and the symbolic make for the specifically ambiguous nature of human space. They denote the seam between the symbolic and the real. Every part of the body, for example, can "alternatively or simultaneously be taken as a letter (signifier) or as an object" (Leclaire 81). In this oscillation, the *biological* body is aligned with the *speaking* body, an alignment that provides yet another instance of belatedness, because the speaking, symbolic body actually "precedes" the biological, real one: "The first [speaking] body produces the second [biological] one, by incorporating itself in it" (Lacan, "Radiophonie" 61). The biological body is the "first of all that which can carry the mark, suitable to inscribe it into a chain of signifiers" (61); these signifiers turn the biological body into a "game-table" (77). The first body takes the second body partially out of the realm of the living, a double trajectory Lacan expresses by a pun on "corpse": "the body in which language lives, which language *corpsified*" (61).[28] Accordingly, symbolic *jouissance* precedes the impossible real *jouissance*. In accordance to this concept, the movement toward naturality and *jouissance* described in the scene does not imply a utopian or regressive move, because Slothrop remains at the border of the symbolic and the real: although his description already defines him as part of the latter, his grammatical existence still defines and thus "retains" him as part of the former. It is the fictional text itself—as a vehicle of symbolic rather than real *jouissance*—that installs itself as a screen between the subject and the real. What the text thus shows is that language, as a descriptive medium, "precedes" the real *jouissance* and naturality described by it.

On the fictional level, Slothrop, like the Polish undertaker, has broken through the continuity of a life, of which he, like Katje, is never sure whether it is a prearranged film or a real evolution. Here, change is seen for what it really is: a hole, or black bar, in which the subject, which normally bridges these gaps by gliding from signifying unit to signifying unit, dissolves. Because this structure is universal, Pynchon can combine various images that are all based on this structure: the flight of the rocket, film, or even "this singular point at the top of a lady's stocking, this transition from silk to bare skin and suspender! [. . .] there is a cosmology: of nodes and cusps and points of osculation, mathematical kisses . . . *singularities!* [. . .] In each case, the change from point to no-point carries a luminosity and enigma at which something in us must leap and sing, or withdraw in fright" (GR 396).

In this passage the flight of the rocket, infinitesimal calculus, and the passage from silk to bare skin are all combined and defined within the common binary structure of "point to no-point," the abstract structure that underlies perception and film, as well as infinitesimal calculus. In *Gravity's Rainbow,* the numerous ellipses serve as another symbol of these "holes in representation."

This ending, however, is only the first in a number of endings, which are presented as stills, or very short pieces of film. It is precisely the shift from real to symbolic *jouissance* that presides over these final mentionings of Slothrop, in which he is turning more and more into a grammatical category. In fact, Slothrop's dispersion is described in three stages, first on the level of the plot, then through an absence, and, as a final step, *through these* to fiction, the "writing of absence." First, Slothrop is mentioned in an interview with the Counterforce: "Some called him a 'pretext.' Others felt that he was a genuine, point-for-point microcosm" (GR 738). Then, in conversation, Seaman Bodine is "looking straight at Slothrop . . . being one of the few who can still see Slothrop as any sort of integral creature any more" (GR 740), while at a party of village idiots, "it appears that some part of Slothrop ran into the AWOL Džabajev one night [. . . .] Some believe that fragments of Slothrop have grown into consistent personae of their own" (GR 742). Again, his face is supposed to appear on the cover of a rock album, although it is impossible to make out which of the musicians he might be, and the only reference to him is a *printed credit:* "Harmonica, kazoo—a friend" (GR 742). In another allusion shortly before, an anonymous narrative voice again stakes *life* against *death:* "'Dying a weird death,' Slothrop's Visitor by this time may be scrawled lines of carbon on a wall [. . .] 'the object of life is to make sure you die a weird death. To make sure that *however it finds you,* it will find you under *very weird* circumstances'" (GR 742). His last two mentionings, however, are especially interesting. The first is actually a *negative* one that describes him by his absence:

> "An apple tree by the road is in blossom. The limbs are wet with this morning's rain, dark and wet. Sitting under it, with anyone else but Slothrop, is a barelegged girl, blonde and brown as honey. Her name is Marjorie. Hogan will come home from the Pacific and court her,

but he'll lose out to Pete Dufay. She and Dufay will have a daughter named Kim [. . . .] It will all go on, occupation or not, with or without Uncle Tyrone." (GR 744)

The second mention, appropriately, is a *fictional* one. After a description of the decrepit surroundings of "Hick's Garage," Pynchon evokes Slothrop for a last time: "*If* Slothrop wants to get home from here, he has to slide into a pathway [. . . .] But [. . .] it *may be* too late to get home" (GR 744; emphases added). Here, in a movement comparable to the merging of V. and *V.*, the fictionality of Slothrop and the fictionality of the text merge.

The natural Slothrop cannot persist because he exists out of time. Again and again, he is resurrected in a newly erupting signification or projection. Rather than the "real self" that Marriott posits, there is only continuous dissolution and reassembly. No real self can be saved from the movies, because the self is always already cinematic. One cannot escape the cinematic structuration of life and its inherent falsification. As soon as there is life, there is falsification and misapprehension. Film and life are congruent, because perception and film are based on a similar structure. There is no escape from this initial break; only death will return the individual to the real, the world's raw continuity.

My discussion has shown that the concept of film is used to carry various topics in *Gravity's Rainbow*: control, escape from control, the narrative dissimulation of the text, the rewriting of history, and the discussion of subjectivity. A final evaluation of film along only one of these various axes would be a distortion, because the use of multiple viewpoints and voices, which makes up so much of the book's structure, also operates in relation to the incorporation of film. Rather than being merely a part of the content and plot of the novel, it is the underlying complex metaphorical matrix along which various rhetorical positions are developed.

A final investigation, however, has to put the use of film in relation to writing. Simulating film, the text opens up the question of illusion and reality in its full force from within its own mode of presentation. Filmic writing marks the text's desire toward itself and its own textuality. The insertion of a specifically filmic mode stages and plays out this desire in its most concise and effective form. On the one hand, the filmic makes up much of the text itself and as such supports the textual signifying system by providing a great part of the signifying material. On the other hand, the filmic quality of the text undermines the written word, because the writing poses as something it is not. This double definition has to do with a textual self-denial operative in the book on various levels. Many instances in *Gravity's Rainbow*—such as the Kirghiz Light episode—express the text's questioning of its own mode of signification and show the suspicion of writing against itself.

The filmic as part of the book's signifying system is thus held in two diverging structures. On the one hand, it *adds* to the signifying material and provides the word with precisely that mode of signification it lacks, adding to the text something that is "outside" language because "language—in so far as it is a primarily digital instrument syntactically complex enough to transmit certain kinds of information with considerable precision—is incapable of properly representing the rich and ambiguous semantics of analog communication" (Wilden 24). Like "speech, gesture and touch" in the Kirghiz Light episode, film provides the text with an extra, atextual, richness, "redeeming" the digitality of language and the lack-of-being, the structure that the gaps between the signifiers introduce into life. In reference to Lacan, Wilden describes these holes as "the 'gaps' which digital communication and signification necessarily introduce into the analog continuum of 'life,' 'relation,' and 'meaning.' . . . [They] correspond to a kind of hole or 'lack in being' introduced into being BY LANGUAGE ITSELF" (25).

On the other hand, the filmic takes away part of the presence of the written word. Yet this lack is again *retrieved* by the written word, because writing is still the medium that supports the filmic, although it does so from a position of lack. Beneath the filmic disguise, the text persists from within the strategic lack of its own presence. The "written filmic" thus combines the two realms of meaning and signification: "The analog is pregnant with MEANING whereas the digital domain of SIGNIFICATION is . . . somewhat barren" (Wilden 163). Within Pasolini's double definition of the word as a *grapheme* and a *kineme*, the word gains a double status. It is part of language, and thus capable of mediation and self-reflexivity, as well as part of the imaginary, which is analog, and thus "meaningful," but which cannot reflect on itself: "There is no metalevel within the Imaginary (which is analog in form, and thus cannot comment on itself, as language and digital communication can)" (94). The "written filmic" is thus constantly oscillating between "digital distinctions [which] introduce GAPS into continuums . . . [and] analog differences, such as presence and absence, [which] FILL continuums" (186).

This structure, however, is incorporated into another framework concerning the use of film imagery to present the artificiality of both subjectivity and meaning in the *content* of the novel. On the one hand, through its hallucinatory clarity, the filmic *adds* a specifically imaginary register to the symbolic, the combination of which provides a strong platform against which the real can be played out, yet it is along the lines of this relation to the real that the tragedy of consciousness turns into the tragedy of writing and film, because Pynchon stresses that even the analog medium of film is based on a discontinuous structure of gaps and holes, a structure ultimately mirrored in the binarism of the unconscious and consciousness. On this level, *both* media deal with the tragic situation of consciousness dreaming of a state in which it is absent. It is the real that Pynchon denotes by the world's raw continuity. Positing film as an abstraction and parody of this real implies that reality is always already mediated by our perception of it and that the life of the subject is always phantasmatic. A "vitalistic reading" of Slothrop's ending stresses the real—the subject's biological needs and its body—and refers to a subject that has lost its definition within the symbolic and imaginary registers, one that has returned to an "inhuman," purely biological, and natural being and still continues as a subject. Such a reading is reminiscent of Norman O. Brown's utopianism; like Wilden, Brown believes in the possibility for humanity to return from culture to nature: "But if man has revolted from nature, it is possible for him to return to nature and heal himself" (*Life* 84). Symptomatically, Brown looks for such a return in the idea of an unrepressed "Absolute Body" (93), and thus a state of existence "before" the split of the unconscious and consciousness, which is "constituted by . . . 'primal repression'" (Wilden 451). Interestingly, in the "id" to which Brown wants to return, as in the analog realm, "there is no negation, only affirmation and eternity" (Brown 175).[29] Although he was doubtless influenced by Brown, in his writing Pynchon seems much less optimistic, continually stressing that the aporia of the human condition is exactly that the subject cannot regain a naturality it has irretrievably lost at birth—the first splitting of unity and the birth of subjectivity—except in death, the ultimate return to the "country of the real."

The real, then, denoting the specific interface between subject and object, life and death, and mind and body, can be treated only by the symbolic and the imaginary. In Pynchon's correlation of film and reality, the filmic is active in both vectors theorized by Metz, the affirmative desire—the identification of the subject within the imaginary and the symbolic—and the desire directed *against* these false identifications and toward the irretrievable but desired unity and continuity. The filmic in *Gravity's Rainbow* thus serves as an artificial buffer that language inserts between itself and its self-destruction, lodging the desire for its own annihilation into a virtual space: the "written filmic." The result is the possibility of writing about the destruction of language in the most direct form without, as Burroughs does, actually destroying the signifying material itself.

The final convergence of writing and consciousness is mirrored in the text's formal dispersal, which proceeds parallel to Slothrop's at the end of the book. Like Slothrop's, this dispersal is only partial and is a *fragmentation* rather than a *destruction*. It is a textual de-montage by which the natural flow and continuity of the narrative is broken up into single stills. Like Slothrop's, the text's "bandwidth" becomes thinner and thinner. This scattering figurizes the desire for and impossibility of a real *jouissance* in and of the text. Simultaneously, however, in this very cancellation, the text evokes the *"jouissance* of the signifier," the symbolic *"jouissance* of the Other." In this final parallel the text reveals itself as an *abstraction*. In this complex figure it acknowledges its abstract structure while simultaneously voicing a desire to escape from it.

Notes

1. Beyond those discussed in the text, see Thomas Moore, "A Decade of *Gravity's Rainbow,* the Incredible Moving Film"; Thomas Schaub, *Pynchon: The Voice of Ambiguity* 70; Scott Simmon, "Beyond the Theatre of War: *Gravity's Rainbow* as Film"; John Stark, *Pynchon's Fictions;* David Cowart, *Thomas Pynchon* 62; and Brian McHale, "'You Used to Know What These Words Mean': Misreading *Gravity's Rainbow.*"

2. Besides "Moviegoing," see also Donald Larsson, "The Camera Eye: 'Cinematic' Narrative in *U.S.A.* and *Gravity's Rainbow,*" in which he states that "most of Pynchon's references to film have negative connotations" (103). As a result, Pynchon's narrative technique is ultimately "*anticinematic*" (104).

3. See Umberto Eco, *Einführung in die Semiotik* 250–62. For a discussion of analog and digital structures see also Anthony Wilden, *System and Structure: Essays in Communication and Exchange.*

4. For more on her use of this term, see Kristeva, *Revolution in Poetic Language.*

5. Film is one of the arenas in which Adorno and Horkheimer, in *Dialectic of Enlightenment,* trace cultural co-optation. Any *real* amusement would have to deny this co-optation and return to a subversive, absurd, and complicated form of art, which Adorno sees realized in some of popular culture, in which Pynchon's writing is so enmeshed: "In some revue films, and especially in the grotesque and the

funnies, the possibility of this negation does glimmer for a few moments" (142). Adorno's critique is directed against the general theory of the sign: the better language sinks into the message, the more words turn from "real" carriers of meaning to signs without "qualities," the more purely and more *transparently* the message is communicated, the more impenetrable the signs become.

6. "For the first time—and this is the effect of the film—man has to operate with his whole living person, yet forgoing its aura. For aura is tied to his presence; there can be no replica of it" (Benjamin 229).

7. See also my discussion of the gaze in chapter 4.

8. The trace is a minimal memory of language. Any differential structure, such as language, has to be based on at least two terms that must be defined in relation to each other. Yet a simultaneous presence of two terms seems to imply unity, as well as an agency that can hold and synthesize these two terms, which would again imply an originary synthesis. It is to make a synthesis possible without implying an originary unity that Derrida takes recourse to the concept of the trace. Unlike Lacan, who similarly relies on this concept, Derrida relates this trace not so much to a subject's memory as to a memory of language itself.

9. For a discussion of Bergson's theory of film in the light of recent theory see Gilles Deleuze, *Cinema 1: The Movement-Image,* and *Cinema 2: The Time Image.* In *Cinema 1,* Deleuze attempts a classification of the movie image within Bergsonian references. His main device is to introduce a camera consciousness, which is reminiscent of his earlier machinic unconscious: "The shot . . . acts like a consciousness. But the sole cinematographic consciousness is not us, the spectator, nor the hero; it is the camera—sometimes human, sometimes inhuman or superhuman" (20).

10. On Pynchon and Bergson see James Earl, "Freedom and Knowledge in the Zone."

11. Any hermeneutic position that defines the human individual within a dichotomy of body and mind will inevitably create this image, in which mind is always the final perspective point. A stress on the bodily aspect would, in contrast, try to minimize the importance of the abstraction machine and to evade its modifications and selections. It is Bergson's aim, however, to reconcile these two aspects, and for that aim he proposes his own "poetics." Although "our intellect, when it follows its *natural* bent, proceeds on the one hand by solid perceptions, and on the other by stable conceptions" (*Metaphysics* 66; emphasis added), it can still create "fluid concepts" (69). To do this, "the mind has to do violence to itself, has to reverse the direction of the operation by which it habitually thinks, has perpetually to revise, or rather to recast, all its categories" (69). Bergson's aim is thus ultimately to liquify the intellect and its language.

12. Pasolini sees the sign as "simultaneously verbal (phoneme), written (grapheme) and visual (kineme)" (207).

13. This is what McHoul and Wills call use and mention of cinema. Rather

than trying to keep these two registers apart, however, they stress that "it becomes impossible to distinguish cinematic use from cinematic mention. What remains is a levelling of the distinction, a flattening that we are calling *material typonomy*" (WP 54).

14. Within his use of the filmic mode, Pynchon inserts literary metaphors: "Bloat, on the other hand, sits perfectly sober, mustache unruffled, regulation uniform, watching Slothrop closely. His companion Ghislaine, tiny and slender, pin-up girl legs, long hair brushed behind her ears falling all the way down her back, shifts her round bottom in the sand, writing marginal commentaries around the text of Bloat" (GR 188). Other textual instances are interwoven closely with visual images: "He gets back to the Casino just as big globular raindrops, thick as honey, begin to splat into giant asterisks on the pavement, inviting him to look down at the bottom of the text of the day, where footnotes will explain all" (GR 204). Furthermore, just as there are references to specific films and actors, there are countless literary intertextual references.

15. For discussions of Pynchon's use of German film see Brian Edwards, "Mixing Media: Film as Metaphor in Pynchon's *Gravity's Rainbow*"; David Cowart, "Cinematic Auguries of the Third Reich in *Gravity's Rainbow*"; and Sherrill E. Grace, "Fritz Lang and the 'Paracinematic Lives' of *Gravity's Rainbow*."

16. For further references to Virilio and Pynchon see Friedrich Kittler, "Medien und Drogen in Pynchons Zweitem Weltkrieg."

17. For a discussion of the simulated reality of the Schwarzkommando see my "Digging for the Truth: Archaeology and the End of History."

18. See also Lawrence C. Wolfley, "Repression's Rainbow: The Presence of Norman O. Brown in Pynchon's Big Novel": "the repressed, reified as black tribesmen, return literally" (879).

19. Virilio also remarks on the parallel between the technical structure of a film and a gun, commenting on Marey as the inventor of the "chronophotographic rifle [which] was . . . both precursor of the Lumière brothers' camera and direct descendant of the Colt revolvers and cylindrical guns" (*War and Cinema* 68). This parallelization defines both epistemes throughout their history: "In the space of a hundred and fifty years, the target area had become a cinema 'location,' the battlefield a film set out of bounds to civilians" (11). Pynchon also plays on this double meaning of shooting: "making the unreal reel / By shooting at it, one way or the other—" (GR 689).

20. Clerc sees in this premonition a bleak outlook: "Film will be so ubiquitous everybody will be using it; people will be leading staged lives; the control of directors will be expanded; life will have become like the movies" ("Film" 116). This view implies, as for Marriott, a "real self" that one has to save from these movies.

21. Note also the "echo" of Pavlovian conditioning. For the use of Kryptosam, "developed by IG Farben," a "thorough knowledge of the addressee's psychosexual profile would seem of invaluable aid" (GR 71). Luckily, "like every young man

growing up in England, he [Pirate Prentice] was conditioned to get a hardon in the presence of certain fetishes, and then conditioned to feel shame about his new reflexes. Could there be, somewhere, a dossier, could They (They?) . . . have managed to monitor everything he saw and read since puberty . . . ?" (GR 71–72).

22. "Perm" puns on the title of the second part of *Gravity's Rainbow,* which also deals with "a perm," if understood metonymically for Katje herself.

23. This film project is closely related to the one concerning the Schwarzkommando. In fact, the two operations are connected by their common use of a film projector: "At 'The White Visitation,' because of erratic funding, there is only one film projector. Each day [. . .] after the Operation Black Wing people have watched their fraudulent African rocket troops, Webley Silvernail comes to carry the projector [. . .] to the inner room where octopus Grigori oozes sullenly in his tank" (GR 113).

24. While roaming through the empty White Visitation, Katje finds a stack of film reels and a projector. Some of the films are of her, used for Grigori's conditioning, but then she comes to *Doper's Greed,* a movie in which two cowboys discuss questions of reality. The two have been held up by a midget sheriff; the film shows their discussion about the "reality" of that sheriff, in which the cowboys debate whether he was real or only a "*joint* hallucination" (GR 534), another of Pynchon's "bad puns."

25. In relation to writing, film, and control see also the work of William Burroughs, perhaps the most filmic in contemporary literature. Like Pynchon, Burroughs sees reality as a film: "There is no true or real 'reality'—'Reality' is simply a more or less constant scanning pattern . . . we accept as 'reality'" (*Nova Express* 61). This scanning pattern "has been imposed by the controlling power . . . a power primarily oriented towards total control" (61). In *Nova Express* he describes the fight over a "Reality Studio" in the control of "their universe of Fear Death and Monopoly" (15). Burroughs's answer to this prerecorded reality is a radical silence: "Apomorphine. . . . A powerful variation of this drug could deactivate all verbal units and blanket the earth in silence" (47). His *Naked Lunch* is also very similar to Pynchon's work and shows a similar attitude toward bureaucracy, silence, and death. Images of "the Zone" (155) and of Dillinger's death (227) even suggest a direct influence on *Gravity's Rainbow.* The main difference between Burroughs's and Pynchon's writing lies in their differing stances toward the signifier. Whereas Burroughs actually attempts to destroy the signifier in his cut-ups, fold-ins, and collages, which he has theorized in *The Third Mind,* Pynchon leaves the network of signifiers intact. In this respect, Burroughs is nearer to Kristeva's idea of the semiotic and its relation to Freudian foreclosure, which, while "establishing the sign, subject, and judgement . . . points *at the same time* toward the repeated scissions of a-symbolized living matter and toward the inorganic . . . [and] sends the signifying body back to biological a-significance and finally to death" (Kristeva 160).

26. See also Leni's attempt to explain things to Pökler: "She even tried, from

what little calculus she'd picked up, to explain it to Franz as Δt approaching zero, eternally approaching, the slices of time growing thinner and thinner, a succession of rooms each with walls more silver, transparent, as the pure light of the zero comes nearer." To this, the pragmatic Pökler replies, "'Not the same, Leni. The important thing is taking a function to its limit. Δt is just a convenience, so that it can happen'" (GR 159).

27. See also Wilden's description of crying—although in the sense of shedding tears—as a purely analog mode of communication: "Although language, compared with crying, would seem to offer a huge gamut of possibilities of 'explaining what you mean,' it is semantically and structurally much more limited than crying as a form of communication. Language takes time, but for the child, crying says EVERYTHING AND ALL AT ONCE" (24).

28. "The reader should recognize in the metaphor of the return of the inanimate . . . that margin beyond life that language gives to the human being by virtue of the fact that he speaks, and which is precisely that in which such a being places in the position of a signifier, not only those parts of his body that are exchangeable, but this body itself (Lacan, *Écrits* 301).

29. "There seems to be a relation between the absence of zero and the absence of negation in the analog machine" (Wilden 178). For a further reference to the problem of lack, suture, and the hole/zero, see Brian Rotman, *Signifying Nothing*.

Chapter 8   *Gravity's Rainbow:*
            The Fatal Word

> "At last: something real."
> Thomas Pynchon, *Gravity's Rainbow*

The theme of life "under the shadow of death," which had already been evoked by "Slothrop's Visitor," is brought into focus for a last time by the launching of the 00000. From the very first sentence, in which it "screams" into representational space, the V-2 quite literally spells death. Its impact, for instance, is described in linguistic terms as "a Word, spoken with no warning into your ear, and then silence forever" (GR 25), while it is itself a "Word that rips apart the day . . ." (GR 25). In this denomination, the "meeting with the rocket" literally comes to stand for the "meeting with the real," which implies the termination of selfhood and the possibility of a revelation without the interference of the signifier.

Nevertheless, Lacan's theory of language shows that the meeting with the real can be reconstructed only within language: "The letter kills, but we experience this only through the letter" (*Écrits* 848, French ed.). Even a direct *naming* of death can never escape this mediation. In fact, because of death's position as an absence within language, its naming can evoke death only while simultaneously putting it at bay. As Hermann Lang states, "By creating a sign of itself within language as an absence, death simultaneously represses itself" (287). It is this inevitable relation of language to death, and vice versa, that makes it impossible for human life to fully close in on itself, either "dialectically or mathematically" (303). As Gödel's theorem shows about mathematics and the propositions that constitute it, something always "falls out" of the system of "human life" and cannot be described by it. In the human arena, this term is the real.

These dynamics of language and death (or the immortal/atemporal text and the mortal subject), however, are constantly threatened in Pynchon's texts by a simulatory "operational death" (GR 566). In these "rationalized forms of death—death in the service of the one species cursed with the knowledge that it will die . . ." (GR 230), the tragedy of self-consciousness is linked to sociocultural, simulatory registers, which exclude a "real" death in the same manner in which simulation excludes the real *in toto*. Along with death, the realms of dream and psychoanalysis—as well as art—are excluded, which is why Pynchon calls this exclusion a suicide, which "in its pathology, in its *dreamless version of the real*, the Empire commits by the thousands every day, completely unaware of what it's doing . . ." (GR 129; emphasis added).[1] By excluding any reference to real death, operational death destroys language and art simultaneously. Because the vision of the deathless and dreamless artificial world that Pynchon evokes in *Gravity's Rainbow* is again beyond psychoanalysis, it is comparable to Baudrillard's. In both, a similar exclusion of "real" death paradoxically turns the whole "operational metropolis" (Baudrillard, *L'Échange symbolique* 196)—or as Brown calls it, "Nekropolis" (286)—into a "culture of death" (GR 176). Like Baudrillard and Pynchon, Brown sees that modern culture—especially Protestant culture—has become, through the exclusion of the body—and thus the real and death—a pure manifestation of Thanatos: "The recognition of life as death-in-life reflects and crystallizes an immense withdrawal of libido from life . . . in the Protestant era life becomes a pure culture of the death instinct" (216). Like Pynchon, Brown and Baudrillard trace this exclusion back to questions of power and power structures, which, "in the last instance, rest on the manipulation and the management of death" (*L'Échange symbolique* 201). Ironically, the promise of life and the power over it ultimately legitimate a power structure that uses the fear of death—which it has instigated in the first place—to control its populace, so that "to abolish death is our phantasm, which spreads out in all directions" (225). It is because this power is in itself purely operational that it cannot integrate "real" death. Like Pynchon, Baudrillard describes this power as an enterprise, or "firm": "Eros in the service of death, the whole cultural sublimation is *a long detour towards death* . . . all of this is right, but right for *our* culture—an enterprise of death which tries to abolish death and therefore piles death upon death, and which is obsessed with death as its own termination" (233; emphasis added). The exclusion of real death by a simulatory culture leads to a sterile life: "So generation after generation of men in love with pain and passivity serve out their time in the Zone, silent, redolent of faded sperm, terrified of dying, desperately addicted to the comforts others sell them, however useless, ugly or shallow, willing to have life defined for them by men whose only talent is for death" (GR 747).

In this passage, Pynchon can describe simulated life as *silent* and *sterile,* because once organic chemistry has been replaced by inorganic, or better transorganic, simulatory chemistry, the "erotic" chemistry between people is replaced by sterile fetish structures.

In *Gravity's Rainbow,* Father Rapier, as a devil's advocate, preaches the ultimate vision of hopelessness, the "terrible possibility [. . .] that They will not die" (GR 539)—a real possibility because in simulatory society, power has been de-personalized into a Foucauldian scenario of anonymous power structures. The realization that the "Critical Mass" (GR 539) has been exceeded puts under erasure any nostalgic wish for a return to a "time before": "Once the technical means of control have reached a certain size, a certain degree of *being connected* one to another, the chances for freedom are over for good" (GR 539). Accordingly, Father Rapier states that "to affirm Their mortality is to affirm Return. I have been pointing out certain obstacles in the way of affirming Return" (GR 540). As always, Pynchon's implicit "humanism" and "nostalgia" have to be read as rhetorical positions.

The only possible means to escape this death-in-life is, again ironically, the V-2, whose speed brings about the destruction of the space in which operational control and power operate. By reversing cause and effect, it renders the system's rational modes of protection useless: "They have lied to us. They can't keep us from dying, so They lie to us about death. A cooperative structure of lies. [. . .] Before the Rocket we went on believing, because we wanted to. But the Rocket can penetrate, from the sky, at any given point. Nowhere is safe. We can't believe Them any more" (GR 728).

At this point, however, the twin definition of the rocket—represented by the 00000 and the 00001—comes into play. Even while in one of its aspects the rocket promises escape and life, in the other, it implies (the simulation of) death—as in "V. in love"—in a final marriage of human and machine, which is only fitting, for "our modern idea of death is defined by . . . that of the machine" (Baudrillard, *L'Échange symbolique* 243). In *Gravity's Rainbow* this death is invested with desire through Imipolex G, in what Schwab has called a "simultaneous machinization of the body and the anthropomorphization of the machine" (174). The simulation of desire, the term that in Lacanian theory mediates between language and death, closes the circle of the simulation of the Lacanian scene. Death, language, and the body—as well as desire, which regulates their interplay—are finally all simulated when Gottfried and the 00000 are "mated to each other, Schwarzgerät and next higher assembly" (GR 751). Linked to the rocket by a shroud of Imipolex G, Gottfried carries Slothrop's conditioning to its ultimate conclusion: "The soft smell of Imipolex, wrapping him absolutely, [. . .] doesn't frighten him. It was in the room when he fell asleep so long ago, so deep in sweet paralyzed childhood [. . . .] Now it is the time to wake, into the breath of what was always real" (GR 754).[2]

Himself an "erotic category" (GR 758), Gottfried in the "bridal" (GR 754) room of the 00000 is a final image of the death wish of modern man and society, a death wish that can be described not in Freudian terms but only in Baudrillardian ones. Gottfried and the rocket become the phantasmagoric simulations of the sexual scene. Gottfried has a "giant white fly: an erect penis buzzing in white lace, clotted with blood or sperm. Deathlace is the boy's bridal costume" (GR 750). The 00000 is the steel virgin, the final incarnation of V., the artificial, steel "womb into which Gottfried returns" (GR 750): "His bare limbs in their metal bondage writhe among the fuel, oxidizer, live-steam lines, thrust frame, compressed air battery, exhaust elbow, decomposer, tanks, vents, valves . . . and one of these valves, one test-point, one pressure-switch is the right one, the true clitoris, routed directly into the nervous system of the 00000" (GR 751).

Because technological and human terms have become interchangeable in this passage, the rocket engine's "deep cry of combustion," which mirrors the screaming on the first page, can come to denote the 00000's desire, which is itself locked from the beginning into a structure of denial—in technological terms, gravity: "This ascent will be betrayed to Gravity. But the Rocket engine, the deep cry of combustion that jars the soul, promises escape. The victim, in bondage to falling, rises on a promise, a prophecy, of Escape. . . . Moving now toward the kind of light where [. . .] Everything is where it is, no clearer than usual, but certainly more present" (GR 758).

The final two passages of *Gravity's Rainbow*, headlined "Ascent" and "Descent," crystallize the last binary positions of the novel. It is only at the zero point, with ascent and descent canceling each other out, that the 00000 and Gottfried can escape the Derridean play of differences and the war of conflicting and competing forces. Only then can it be that "everything is where it is, no clearer than usual, but certainly more present." Again, this utopian presence is a rhetorical one. The suspension of the forces of the world, for which gravity is a metonymical stand-in, is the price to be paid for presence. For Gottfried, as for all of Pynchon's characters, this presence is linked to death, as well as to a final revelation. At some point, for instance, Roger Mexico also has "the leading edge of a revelation, blinding, crescent, at the periphery of his brain" (GR 631). Pynchon deliberately links this logocentric revelation to social simulation and the negative aspects of the rocket by implying that Slothrop is a "sensitive" only because of the Pavlovian conditioning he has gone through in his youth: "There is in his history, and likely [. . .] in his dossier, a peculiar sensitivity to what is revealed in the sky. (But a *hardon?*)" (GR 26).

Comparable and parallel to Slothrop's scattering process, and rendered in similar film imagery, this final moment of the book describes the rocket's own loss of self, the momentary escape from its "twin shadows." This passage describes the penultimate "*jouissance* effect" in *Gravity's Rainbow*. Symptomatically, it is simultaneously the moment at which the parameters that define the 00000 and the 00001 finally become interchangeable. In the topography defined by the Möbius strip it is precisely the point or moment of the "twist" or the "cut," whose function is here similar to and related to the cinematic "cut," for this moment falls together with Gottfried's death, before which his "film of life" passes before his eyes, with the spool constantly "catching" (GR 758–60). The text thus repeats on the level of content its own dispersion, which starts with the text, like Gottfried's film of life, beginning to disperse into single frames, from "The Low-Frequency Listener" (GR 681) onward.

Like all singularities, however, this one is also bound to fall back into duality and into the play of differences, although in itself, as a final Δt, it is timeless: "The moving vehicle is frozen, in space, to become architecture, and timeless. It was never launched. It will never fall" (GR 301). Pökler experiences this timelessness in even the first tryouts of the rocket: "The time base has lengthened, and slowed: the Perfect Rocket is still up there, still descending" (GR 426).

Death-in-life can thus be escaped only with the rocket, which is itself related to real death. Yet the question remains of whether there is a middle term along which escape from this fatal choice might be possible. From the beginning, love (Togetherness) serves as such an option in Pynchon's writing, because in the utopian space of love, the structures of operational simulation are put out of operation. Nevertheless, Pynchon's scenarios of love all contain their own undoing within them. On a cultural level, these ironized scenarios describe Baudrillard's idea of "symbolic exchange."

Baudrillard's and Lacan's differing interpretations of the death drive and the repetition compulsion define exactly the two levels operative in Pynchon's writing, which encompasses *both,* relating Baudrillard's to the *vision* (the realm of rhetoric) and Lacan's to the *reality.* Baudrillard's evocations of a "symbolic" and of a strategy of the object/referent are both similarly visionary, utopian positions, from which Lacan's "insistence of the real" is seen as the structural effect of the separation of two parts, namely, life and death and subject and object, the very binarism overridden by "love." Roger Mexico and Jessica's love, for instance, is staked against the culture of death symbolized by the war and an attempt at "mindless pleasures": "Every assertion the fucking War has ever made—that we are meant for work and government, for austerity: and these shall take priority over love, dreams, the spirit, the senses and the other second-class trivia that are found among the idle and mindless hours of the day . . ." (GR 177). Pynchon describes this romantic scenario in the same way in which he describes the utopia of a "private language" in the love story of Enzian's father and mother. Here, it is the complete merging of two image repertoires that becomes the utopia of "Togetherness": "You go from dream to dream inside me. You have passage to my last shabby corner, and there, among the debris, you've found life. I'm no longer sure which of all the words, images, dreams or ghosts are 'yours' and which are 'mine.' It's past sorting out. We're both being someone new now, someone incredible . . ." (GR 177).

Yet Pynchon is careful to ironize this utopia immediately. The next sentence takes back all the pathos and inscribes the scene into a fictional mode: "His act of faith. In the street the children are singing: 'Hark, the herald angels sing: Mrs. Simpson's pinched our King . . .'" (GR 177).

In Lacan, *language* inaugurates the realm of digitality and oppositionality, and with that, the repetition compulsion. As Baudrillard states, "The reality of nature . . . its 'materiality' is the result of the separation of man and nature. . . . Even the reality of the body, its material status, is only the result of the separation of a mental [*spirituel*] principle" (*L'Échange symbolique* 205). Baudrillard argues that the same move that defines life as human defines the real as dead, a concept Baudrillard sees as a specifically Western (and specifically historical) idea, because not all cultures (and not all periods) "produce the idea of lifelessness" (234). Wilden also comments on this cultural aspect of digitality: "The internalization of the digital . . . engenders a SPLITTING OF THE SUBJECT into mind and body, reason and emotion, self and other, male and female" (92).

In *Gravity's Rainbow,* which is less optimistic than Wilden about the possibility of a reversal and thus a return to the analog, the hallucinatory and therefore doubly fictionalized experiences of Lyle Bland evoke the scenario of such a living real. In his "archaeological" mental journeys he "imagines that he has been journeying underneath history: that history is Earth's mind, and that there are layers, set very deep, layers of history analogous to layers of coal and oil in Earth's body" (GR 589). Similarly, he meets "presences [. . .] members of an astral IG, whose mission [. . .] is past secular good and evil" (GR 589–90). When asked why he still "keep[s] saying 'mind and body?' Why make that distinction?" (GR 590), Bland answers, "Because it's hard to get over the wonder of finding that Earth is a living critter, after all these years of thinking about a big dumb rock to find a body and a psyche" (GR 590). As he does in the Kirghiz Light episode, Pynchon links this natural realm to organic chemistry, while in the cultural realm organic combinations are broken up, synthesized, and operationally simulated. Here, they are "taken up again by the coal-tar Kabbalists of the other side, [. . .] teased apart, explicated to every last permutation of useful magic, centuries past exhaustion still finding new molecular pieces, combining and recombining them into new synthetics—'Forget them, they are no better than the Qlippoth, the shells of the dead'" (GR 590).

Although they evoke the utopia of a living world pervaded by love, Bland's journeys are fictions, and the subject has to refer back to the "text of the world," the puns, the "Kute Korrespondences" of language in which one might approach a more real experience:

> The rest of us, not chosen for enlightenment, left on the outside of Earth, at the mercy of [. . .] Gravity [. . .] must go on blundering inside our front-brain faith in Kute Korrespondences, hoping that for each psi-synthetic taken from Earth's soul there is a molecule, secular, [. . .] over here—kicking endlessly among the plastic trivia, finding in each Deeper Significance and trying to string them all together like terms of a power series hoping to zero in on the tremendous and secret Function whose name [. . .] cannot be spoken. (GR 590)

Like Bland, and in a similarly rhetorical framework, Baudrillard imagines the earth as a mindbody, which is why, like Bland's hallucinated mindbody, Baudrillard's symbolic *"puts an end to the real"* (*L'Échange symbolique* 204). As the promise of the closure of the breach between human and world, thinking and being, Baudrillard's symbolic can come to function as the utopian dream of the subject. In the last instance, it is a utopia that ends oppositionality as such: "an order of reversibility" (220) without oppositionality, "an immediate and not phantasmatic actualization of symbolic reciprocity" (220).³

Yet Pynchon continually destroys such visions of reciprocity. In particular, the novel's end, which links for a last time the motifs of writing, death, and silence (as well as writing and film), shows that Pynchon is a fantastic *and* a humanist writer. It presents a flash-forward to the 1970s. Now, however, in the most obvious time loop in the novel, the "screaming [that] comes across the sky" (GR 3) is that of a rocket above a contemporary (at least at the time of publication) movie theater in Los Angeles, which presents the final Δt of the novel. A "belated rocket" has come from the past to destroy the present. Simultaneously, in a twist again reminiscent of a Möbius strip, the "textual" rocket seems to have transcended the book's interior narrative space and to have become a "real" rocket, no longer a textual concept but now a referent—although this transition does of course take place in a fictional space.

> The rhythmic clapping resonates inside these walls, which are hard and glossy as coal: Come-*on! Start*-the-*show!* Come-*on! Start*-the-*show!* The screen is a dim page spread before us, white and silent. The film has broken, or a projector bulb has burned out. It was difficult even for us, old fans who've always been at the movies (haven't we?) to tell which before the darkness swept in. The last image was too immediate for any eye to register. [. . .] And it is just here, just at this dark and silent frame, that the pointed tip of the Rocket, falling nearly a mile per second, absolutely and forever without sound, reaches its last unmeasurable gap above the roof of this old theatre, the last delta-t. (GR 760)

The narration now, for the first time, includes both the reader and the text (book) itself in a virtual space that is neither textual nor "real," and as such is reminiscent of the equivocal space created by the text for the staging of *its* annihilation via film. It is now used to stage Gottfried's, the text's, and the reader's annihilation in a highly ambiguous narrative space. It is exactly here that the interplay of *writing* and *film* is at its most acute. The final passage combines once again the dominant motifs of the cinematic structure, the rocket, infinitesimal calculus, and the structure of animated stills. In a process parallel to Gottfried's annihilation, the "textual film" breaks, opening up the frightening possibility of "perceiving perception." And this perception, running *below* experience, is indeed "a film we have not learned to see . . . it is now a closeup of the face, a face we all know—" (GR 760). It is a nice irony that this last image, which could well be the fantastic Medusa's head, is an image we have *not* learned to see, whereas Pynchon's use of film throughout the rest of the book relies on classical images we *have* indeed learned to see. With this closeup, the novel freezes into atemporality. It is within this final gap in the infinitesimal succession of images that the rocket reaches *its* last Δt. Like the rocket itself, meaning is forever "suspended." Yet, as de Man has stated, this suspension does not imply "disinterested play, but always a threat or a challenge" (*Allegories* 208), exactly the two motifs that define the rocket in *Gravity's Rainbow*. The rocket will never fall, because the gap between points a—the tip of the rocket—and b—the roof of the theater—will become continually smaller, a paradox also defined within mathematical calculus, so that, as in Zeno's paradox, a final convergence is mathematically and "logically" impossible.

With a frightening logic reminiscent of Bergson's image of film as a "pre-arranged succession of images," the film and the book terminate, with the text re-creating and simulating Slothrop's final scattering process, his fall into the gaps between the signifiers. The final image of the book thus denotes again the structure of dispersal and the insistence of the real within the realms of the imaginary and the symbolic. Pynchon brings his readers to the very edge of this real but leaves them "forever suspended" within signification, with a hint of the promise of unity (*jouissance*)—a promise, however, that is immediately balanced by the presence of death. This is the final "*jouissance*-effect" in *Gravity's Rainbow*. It describes the moment of the ending of the textual scattering parallel to Slothrop ending as a grammatical category. As I noted already, it is a moment that involves both *text* and *reader*. As in *Lot 49*, in which Pierce is faced with the fact that "the bouncing would stop," now

> there is time, if you need the comfort, to touch the person next to you, or to reach between your own cold legs . . . or, if song must find you, here's one They never taught anyone to sing, a hymn by William Slothrop, centuries forgotten and out of print, sung to a simple and pleasant air of the period. Follow the *bouncing ball*." (GR 760; emphasis added)

The song that follows gives one last image of the ambivalent, anthropomorphic space in and "of" *Gravity's Rainbow*. It is neither fully real nor fully symbolic and imaginary, neither human nor unhuman, neither inside nor outside, but both:

> There is a Hand to turn the time,
> Though thy Glass today be run,

> Till the Light that hath brought the Towers low
> Find the last poor Pret'rite one . . .
> Till the Riders sleep by ev'ry road,
> All through our crippl'd Zone,
> *With a face on ev'ry mountainside,*
> *And a Soul in ev'ry stone.* . . . (760; emphasis added)

Notes

1. In another context, this pathology is described as "a perfect mechanism" (GR 48), evoking the pathological perfection of the sociopolitical machine.

2. See also Slothrop's realization that "once something was done to him, in a room, while he lay helpless . . ." (GR 285).

3. The myth of this symbolic forms the "other" to the modern myth of the unconscious and psychoanalysis, with its inscription of death into the psyche via the concept of the death drive, the repetition compulsion, and their relation to Eros: "In a cycle of repetition, death continually destroys the constructive, linear or dialectical teleology [*finalités*] of the Eros" (Baudrillard, *L'Échange symbolique* 230). The idea that somehow, biologically, the organism strives toward death results in the fact that "death becomes . . . the object of a perverse desire" (226).

Chapter 9   *Vineland:*
             Everything under Control

"a merciless nostalgia . . ."
Thomas Pynchon, *Vineland*

"Between us and the real, there is the truth."
Jacques Lacan, *Le Séminaire XVII*

"Every woman adores a Fascist."
Sylvia Plath, *Daddy*

When *Vineland* came out in 1990, the first thing that struck most reviewers was a change of mood and tone. Brad Leithauser detected a "moving note of sweet inconclusion" in its ending (7), Frank Kermode made out an "almost sentimental rhetoric" (3), Christina Koning commented on its "curiously elegiac feel," while one of the most positive reviewers, Salman Rushdie, actually saw "some faint possibility of redemption, some fleeting hints of happiness and grace" (1). None of these are characteristics that—prior to the publication of *Vineland*—anyone would have expected from a new book by Pynchon.

The second opinion most reviewers shared was that the book presented a step backward rather than forward. Leithauser saw in it "a return to what was weakest in his patchy novella, *The Crying of Lot 49*" (7) and noted an "indestructible nostalgia" (10). His judgment about its humor is metonymic for his overall evaluation of the book: "We've heard it all before" (8). In a similar vein, Kermode diagnosed a "fairly simple nostalgia" (4) and the "re-emergence of . . . [earlier] themes in a manner even more bitter but also less guarded by irony, less cogent" (3).[1]

It is true that Pynchon's writing in *Vineland* is less directly invested in the pleasure principle and *jouissance* than it is in his other works, more symbolic than imaginary and thus more aware of the "insistence of the signifier." Less concerned with the pure *play* of the signifier and the portrayal of intricate systems of simulation, it is also the least Derridean or Baudrillardian and the most Lacanian of Pynchon's books. This shift had already been announced by Pynchon's closing statements in the introduction to *Slow Learner* and involves his attempt to ground his writing less in abstract systems than in the subject, "the life we all really live" (SL 21). In *Slow Learner,* Pynchon actually comes close to denouncing the completely textualized universe of "Under the Rose," whose landscapes he lifted from a Baedeker, a strategy that in his own evaluation created a purely textual environment without "some grounding in human reality" (SL 18).

As a result of this shift, in *Vineland* Pynchon no longer handles conflicts on a predominantly abstract level, with the characters reflecting specific theoretical and structural positions, but transposes them into the psychic space of the protagonists. Although this is a curiously idiosyncratic and somewhat unpopular move in a time in which "cyberpunk" is the latest literary fashion, Pynchon's evaluation of his early work as "fancy footwork" (SL 21) rather than the "real thing" and his statement that "education too [. . .] keeps going on forever" (SL 23) attest to the fact that for Pynchon, if not for the critics, *Vineland* is a step forward. In fact, in that it is written in a simpler and more direct style—in which, however, it expresses a darker universe—one might consider *Vineland* the first work of Pynchon's "late period."

In one sense, however, it is quite natural that *Vineland* should be a step backward, because it is a retrospective, a concept that can clarify a number of the book's characteristics. As a retrospective, it is related to death and absence and consequently, pervaded with a sense of loss, nostalgia, and mourning. Furthermore, it has the character of a reunion. Just as a retrospective assembles once again the dispersed work of an artist, the reunion portrayed at the end of the book brings together a cast of characters who have been out of touch. This idea of a reunion even goes beyond the confines of *Vineland.* Although in previous works Pynchon has occasionally taken figures over from one book to the next, the reunion here with characters from other books, such as Takeshi from *Gravity's Rainbow* and Mucho Maas from *Lot 49,* is a first clue that *Vineland* is a retrospective not only of an era but simultaneously of Pynchon's own work.

In the opening scene, in which Zoyd prepares for his annual "transfenestration," Pynchon already creates a densely allusive space in which constant echoes of his earlier work reverberate. The process of transfenestration itself, for instance, evokes a detail from the opening scene of *V.*, in which a "potential berserk stud[ies] the best technique for jumping through a plate glass window" (*V.* 10), whereas the image of "blue jays [. . .] *screaming* down out of the redwoods" evokes the opening of *Gravity's Rainbow* (*Vineland* 4; Emphasis added. Further citations are abbreviated as VL). Furthermore, the sign of the "Cucumber Lounge"—"a huge green neon cucumber with blinking warts, cocked at an angle that approached, within a degree or two, a certain vulgarity" (VL 12)—presents (very appropriately, as the following discussion shows) a male version of the "Echo Courts" sign in *Lot 49*, whereas Zoyd's choice of clothes, "a party dress in a number of colors that would look good on television" (VL 4), is a structural parallel to Mucho Maas's pronunciation of Oedipa's name as "Edna Mosh": "It'll come out the right way [. . .] I was allowing for the distortion on these rigs, and then when they put it on tape" (*Lot 49* 139).

It comes as no surprise, therefore, that not only characters but most of the leitmotifs of his earlier work are present in *Vineland*. Again, for instance, Pynchon presents an irredeemably fallen, "spilled [. . . and] broken world" (VL 267) in which an original unity is irredeemably lost. Within this world, he then traces the development toward more and more fragmentation and impurity. DL, for instance, although she has been given to understand that "she would discover that all souls, human and otherwise, were different disguises of the same greater being—God at play" (VL 121), has to realize that this promise will never be kept, because her ninja education is only a profane version of the "original purity of ninja intent" (VL 126–27), which, like the magic of the "Masonic rituals" in *Gravity's Rainbow* (GR 588),[2] has been "subverted, made cruel and more worldly, bled of spirit [. . .] once greater patterns now only a string of encounters [. . .] none with any meaning beyond itself [. . .] not the brave hard-won grace of any warrior, but the cheaper brutality of an assassin [. . .] this is for all the rest of us down here with the insects [. . .] this is our equalizer, our edge" (VL 127). What her teacher, Inoshiro Sensei, prepares her for is not transcendence but the fatal "entanglement in the world" (VL 180).[3]

The motif of an apocalyptic intrusion is taken up by the story of Takeshi, who, with another echo of Pynchon's work, "had come to value and watch closely in the world for *signs and symptoms*, messages from beyond" (VL 147–48; emphasis added). Again, as in *Gravity's Rainbow*'s tale of the Herero's history of "lost messages" (GR 520), this intrusion is related to some sort of "forever missed" message. In his dream, for instance, the blue jays that

Zoyd hears on the roof when he wakes up "had been carrier pigeons from someplace far across the ocean, landing and taking off again one by one, each bearing a message for him, but none of whom, light pulsing in their wings, he could ever quite get to in time" (VL 3).

For Zoyd, these messages are either forever "too soon" or simply withheld: "It was like being on 'Wheel of Fortune,' only [there was . . .] no tanned and beautiful Vanna White [. . .] to wish him well, to flip over one by one letters of a message he knew he didn't want to read anyway" (VL 12–13). While he is looking for Frenesi, Zoyd actually locates these messages, such as those on a parking lot that "the local weather had been writing gullies across [. . .] for years" (VL 9), into the very space occupied by the unconscious: that *"between perception and consciousness"* (Lacan, *Fundamental Concepts* 56):

> "Where is she?"
> "Keep tryin' to find out. Try to read signs, locate landmarks, anything that'll give a clue, but—well the signs are there on street corners and store windows—but I can't read them."
> "It's some other language?"
> "Nope, it's in English, but there's something between it and my brain that won't let it through." (VL 40)

Some of these messages, finally, are related to a direct meeting with the "head of the Medusa." Frenesi, for instance, has the "leading edge of a revelation" of such an object of anxiety in a scene that juxtaposes the world of dreams to that of reality: "Often, through some dense lightning-shot stirring of night on night, she would be just about to see Its face when her waking mind would kick in and send her spreading awake into what should have been the world newly formatted, even innocent, but from which, as it proved, the creature had not after all been banished, only become, for a while, less visible" (VL 202).

Pynchon's most elaborate joke on these messages is the "mysterious obliteration of a research complex belonging to the shadowy world conglomerate Chipco" (VL 142) by a "gigantic animal footprint" (VL 142). In the story of the "imminent unthinkable descent" (VL 144), which turns out to be a helicopter whose "underside its crew [. . .] had playfully disguised [. . .] as a monster's sole" (VL 145), Pynchon ironically plays out the mystery and ineffability of the real's intrusion into reality against its ironic, profane "real intrusion."

A further motif that reemerges in *Vineland* is that of simulation. Early on, Pynchon describes the moment when the TV crew is waiting to film Zoyd jumping through the window with a pun on the staged character of the event: "At last all was set" (VL 11); this aspect of the action as a media event is further highlighted by the fact that the window through which Zoyd jumps is not "real" but a simulated stunt window made from "clear sheet candy" (VL 12). All through *Vineland,* in fact, Pynchon describes reality as a "tubal fantasy," in an implosion of cause and effect, watcher and watched, "as if the Tube were suddenly to stop showing pictures and instead announce, 'From now on, I'm watching you'" (VL 340).

As in *Lot 49,* it is a letter that marks the beginning of a new "era" in *Vineland,* yet the delivery of the letter that informs Frenesi of her new position is directly linked to this implosion of TV and reality. While she watches a rerun of "CHiPs," a police show whose two leads are for her male icons of authority that provide her with masturbatory stimulus, she experiences the intrusion of TV into real life, the "primal Tubefreek miracle" (VL 84). With the deliberate pun on "screen," Pynchon describes the interface between reality and simulation: "Through the screen [door], broken up into little dots like pixels of a video image, only squarer, was this large, handsome U.S. Marshal, in full uniform, hat, service .38, and leather beltwork, with an envelope to deliver. And his partner, waiting down beside the car in the latening sunlight, was *twice* as cute" (VL 84).

Ultimately, TV becomes the membrane that simultaneously connects and separates the realms of life and death. When Weed Atman dies, for instance, he cannot pass into death because "the soul newly in transition often doesn't like to admit—indeed will deny quite vehemently—that it's really dead, having slipped so effortlessly into the new dispensation that it finds no difference between the weirdness of life and the weirdness of death" (VL 218). This similarity is caused by the fact that through TV, life is already pervaded with a mediated, fake death. TV, "with its history of picking away at the topic with doctor shows, war shows, cop shows, murder shows, had trivialized the Big D itself. If mediated lives [. . .] why not mediated deaths?" (VL 218).

As it does in *Lot 49,* TV in *Vineland* stands for the vision of a closed-off space, both representational and political, which renders as strictly rhetorical the question of whether "the United States still lingered in a prefascist twilight, or whether the darkness had fallen long stupefied years ago, and the light they thought they saw was coming only from millions of Tubes all showing the same bright-colored shadows" (VL 371).

The passage into more and more complete, operational simulation is again one into death-in-life, which is negotiated, as in *V.* and *Gravity's Rainbow*, over the subject's body, with the simulatory power coming to control and replace "anything that could remotely please any of your senses" (VL 313). DL's reclaiming of her body, her "returning to herself" (VL 128), should therefore be read as a revolutionary act against a simulatory system that turns the body not only of the individual but of the whole of America into "the scabland garrison state the green free America of their childhoods even then was turning into" (VL 314).[4]

Finally, there is the difference between *digital* and *analog* systems. The computer that destroys Frenesi's and Zoyd's files is the most extensive digital environment in *Vineland*, reducing lives to "weightless, invisible chains of electronic presence or absence" (VL 90), but Pynchon develops the shift predominantly along the difference between TV and film, as well as the development of rock and roll from "the highest state of the analog arts all too soon to be eclipsed by digital technology" (VL 308). When Van Meter sees Jaco Pastorius's act of removing the frets from his bass guitar as an attempt at "the restoration of a premodal innocence in which all the notes of the universe would be available to him" (VL 224), this is only one of many nostalgic evocations of a sixties "epiphany" (VL 224) of unity and continuity, with the continuity of the musical scale a parallel to the continuity of the movie image. In *Vineland*, the sixties in general stand for this "slower-moving time, predigital, not yet so cut into pieces, not even by television. It would be easy to remember the day as a soft-focus shot" (VL 38).

It thus seems true that we have heard it all before, or put positively, that like many great writers, Pynchon writes the same book over and over again, a gesture that can be related both to the topology of the Möbius strip and to a certain "repetition compulsion." Rather than deal with these variations of old, familiar themes, however, I will try to trace what is *new* in *Vineland*. This aspect concerns its portrayal of the relationship between power, language, reality, history, *jouissance*, and death. In fact, power is the central theme of *Vineland*, a book that constantly asks how political power operates and what its effects are.[5]

Foucault, whose theory of power presides for long stretches over the poetics of *Gravity's Rainbow*, sees power as an anonymous "technology" (*Discipline* 215): a global network of infinitely complex and ramose power relations into which the subject is inscribed.[6] This network and the position of the subject within its discursive space are made up of "discursive formations" that are created and controlled by "the System," Foucault's term for what Pynchon calls "Them" or "the Firm." Foucault's analysis shows the inevitability and fatality of the subject's inscription into power. Although he does not exclude the subject, the fact that he proceeds from the idea of a fully textualized subject, whose position is defined in textual rather than "transcendental . . . [or] psychological" (*Archaeology* 55) registers, makes for a specific anonymity of Foucauldian power, in what he describes as a scenario in which an evil and anonymous force presides over a helpless subject.[7] Accordingly, Foucault's final vision of this space is of a closed system of infinite control:

> The ideal point of penality today would be an indefinite discipline: an interrogation without end, an investigation that would be extended without limit to a meticulous and ever more analytical observation, a judgment that would at the same time be the constitution of a file that was never closed, the calculated leniency of a penalty that would be interlaced with the ruthless curiosity of an examination. (*Discipline* 227)

Such a scenario perfectly defines the state of things at the beginning of *Vineland*. The fact that the real action starts only when this infinite network of control breaks down, however, shows that in *Vineland*, Foucault's theory of power functions only as a frame.

Whereas with Foucault power is *everywhere,* with Baudrillard it is *nowhere*. In *Forget Foucault* Baudrillard directly criticizes Foucault's theory of power by defining power as a mutual and personal challenge and seduction that operates over a void, in a social field in which power itself—as defined in Foucauldian terms—is already dead: "This universal fascination with power . . . is so intense because it is a fascination with a *dead* power" (61).

Although both of these extremes are implicit in *Vineland*'s portrayal of power, rather than focus on the subject's tragic inscription within power or the ultimate emptiness of the term, Pynchon foregrounds the *complicity* between the subject and power. Whereas the characters of *Gravity's Rainbow* are portrayed as pieces in a cosmic chess game, those in *Vineland* are themselves players. Sasha, for instance, sees injustices "more directly, not as world history or anything too theoretical, but as humans, usually male, living here on the planet [. . .] committing these crimes [. . .] against other living humans" (VL 80).

It is the complicity between "the System" and the subject within a sexual and thus symbolic agenda that informs the poetics of *Vineland* and relates it to Lacan's theory of power, which, symptomatically, Lacan developed during the student revolt in France. For my investigation, this theory provides a final structure in which the subject is aligned with the signifier and in which the ontological breach between the subject and the world is linked to sociopolitical strategies of positioning the subject in relation to this breach. It encompasses both the poetological and political aspects of Pynchon's writing through the common reference to the signifier, because both aspects are based on the law of language, which "has been the law . . . since the first words of recognition presided over the first gifts" (Lacan, *Écrits* 61). This symbolic law underlies the moves and positions of the subject within discursive/social space. It comprises "the law of desire," which defines the (textual) detour every subject has to take because direct access to real *jouissance* is impossible. As I discussed in part 1, for Lacan, "castration means that *jouissance* must be refused, so that it can be reached on the inverted ladder . . . of the Law of desire" (324). Through castration, the "law of desire" is aligned with lack, because desire comes into being as the result of an initial loss for which the phallus, in its definition as the "bar . . . which strikes the signified" (288), is the ultimate signifier.

Lacan describes the various positions the subject can take in relation to the symbolic law via a kind of discursive machine, the matheme of the "four discourses"—those of the master, of knowledge,[8] of the hysteric, and of the analyst. These "radical" (*Séminaire XVII* 19) discourses denote four modes of social/symbolic action. They are defined by four terms—

S_1 (the master signifier)
S_2 (knowledge)
$\$$ (the subject)
a   (surplus *jouissance;* the object *o*)

—which rotate over four places, with each quarter-turn describing one of the discourses (see figure 2).

Roughly, the position of the agent denotes in whose name and under whose auspices the discourse is held; the position of the other, its addressee; that of the production, its result; and that of the truth, its latent organizing principle.

In Lacan's formalization of the discourse of the master, the positions are as follows:

$$\text{impossibility}$$

$$\frac{S_1 \longrightarrow S_2}{\$ \longleftarrow a}$$

Figure 2.

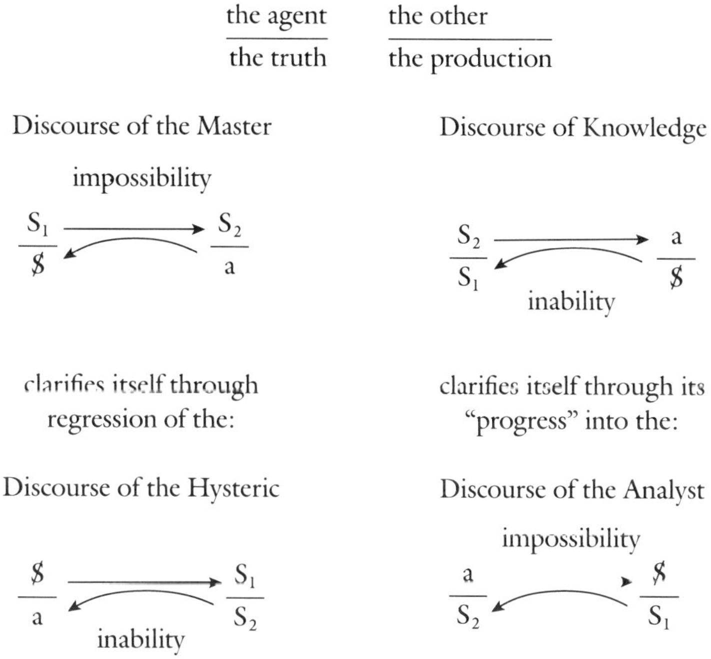

$$\frac{\text{the agent}}{\text{the truth}} \quad \frac{\text{the other}}{\text{the production}}$$

Discourse of the Master

impossibility

$$\frac{S_1}{\$} \longrightarrow \frac{S_2}{a}$$

Discourse of Knowledge

$$\frac{S_2}{S_1} \longrightarrow \frac{a}{\$}$$
$$\text{inability}$$

clarifies itself through
regression of the:

clarifies itself through its
"progress" into the:

Discourse of the Hysteric

$$\frac{\$}{a} \longrightarrow \frac{S_1}{S_2}$$
$$\text{inability}$$

Discourse of the Analyst

impossibility

$$\frac{a}{S_2} \longrightarrow \frac{\$}{S_1}$$

Here, S_1 is in the position of the agent. It denotes an (arbitrarily chosen) signifier that is singled out from the already existing "battery of signifiers," the "Other." This signifier, simply by being privileged in relation to the network of differences provided by language and thus "in opposition to difference," becomes the law and, as such, the perspective point for all other signifiers: "The first words spoken . . . stand as a decree, a law, an aphorism, an oracle; they confer their obscure authority upon the real other. Take just one signifier as an emblem of this omnipotence . . . and you have the unbroken line *(trait unaire)* which . . . alienates th[e] subject in the primary identification that forms the ego ideal" (*Écrits* 306). The master occupies the position of this unary signifier, which does not have a signified, for a signified comes into being only from the position of S_2, the binary signifier. As a result of this "retrogression," S_1 becomes a signified in itself.[9]

As the $\$$ defines itself in the space and differences between two or more signifiers, it is constituted by the multiple relations and tensions between S_1 and S_2. Ideally, these relations compose Derrida's "poetic space," a space for which the postcard is his symbol. When, however, as in the discourse of the master, S_1 comes to *dominate* S_2 (in psychoanalytic terms, becoming the ego ideal), free dissemination is arrested, in the sense of both *stopped* and *taken into custody*, a pun that perfectly captures the birth of power through the domination of S_2 by S_1. Similarly, S_1 "orders" S_2 in the sense of both *structuring* it and *giving commands*. The discourse of the master describes a scenario in which S_1 has assumed mastery over S_2, which, in the position of the other, has become its "slave." In the position of the production is the object *o* (surplus-*jouissance*), the residue of the initial splitting of the subject: the "cause of desire" (*Encore* 85) that instigates the repetition compulsion, which in turn charts out the detour desire takes to participate in *jouissance:* "With the advent of *desire* . . . all of the affective drive is displaced into the object. But the object, no longer a means but an end, never satisfies, becoming instead the source of repeated, futile . . . attempts to satisfy desire" (MacCannell 166).[10] In the sociopolitical framework of the discourse of the master, the objects *o*, which are produced *by* the slave but *for* the master,[11] manifest the "surplus-*jouissance*," a term coined to parallel Marx's "surplus value." This surplus-*jouissance* is what "make[s] the [human] machine run" (Lacan, "Radiophonie" 86). In this way, Lacan reads Marx's theory *with* desire: "The *Mehrwert* [*surplus value*], that's the *Marxlust* [*Marx jouissance*], the surplus-jouissance of Marx" (87).

The master, identifying fully with (the law of) S_1, is in a position "which masks the division of the subject" (*Séminaire XVII* 118). As a result, he "acts 'as if' he knew what he wants, as if he was no split subject; he seems 'unequivocal' in his orders and 'believes' in it" (Lipowatz, *Diskurs* 141). He can, however, participate in the object *o* only via the go-between of the slave.[12] As the slave is in this position only because of the master's threat of death, the "absolute Master" (Lacan, *Écrits* 26), and "cannot find pleasure without death intervening" (Lipowatz, *Diskurs* 141). He projects this ment without death intervening" (Lipowatz, *Diskurs* 141). He projects this death, which he cannot accept for himself, into the outside, a scene whose violence Pasolini has described in detail in *The 120 Days of Sodom:* "The inability to accept the lack leads to the attempt to project it 'into the outside.' . . . This lies at the origin of what is called 'power.' . . . Power masters, excludes or destroys its objects (including the 'I')" (*Diskurs* 144–45). $, the barred subject, is therefore in the position of the repressed truth because "the conditions for the master's existence [lie] in the mis-recognition of the nature of the split subject, whose ambiguity is latent and hidden from him" (142).

The economy of the discourse of the master, which is also that of politics, leads to an imaginary impasse also operative in the Hegelian master-slave conflict, which "seems . . . to lead to a dead end" (Lacan, *Seminar I* 223), an aspect that has already been important in my discussion of the binary character of the sociopolitical space portrayed in *Lot 49:* "The discourse of the master has developed itself fully, to speak its final word in the discourse of the capitalist, with its curious *copulation* with science" (*Séminaire XVII* 126; emphasis added).[13] The impossibility that defines the discourse of the master is thus that of reciprocity because it can merely sustain "the reality of the only phantasm" ("Radiophonie" 97): only one can be the master. In *Vineland,* this position is held by Vond. Vond is not only an unrestricted master, however; he is also the result of the discourse of knowledge, best exemplified by that of the university—another link to *Vineland*—which is complementary to that of the master.

$$\frac{S_2 \rightarrow a}{S_1 \leftarrow \$}$$

inability

Here, S_2 (knowledge) has shifted into the position of the agent, whereas the object *o* (surplus-*jouissance*) has shifted into the position of the other. In this discourse, the objects (*o*) of knowledge, as well as, by extension, the "student," are "cleansed" of their relation to desire and thereby turned into "dead," neutralized objects that S_2 can then order, form, homogenize, and dissect, a process Wilden links to the ideology of digitality: "Through the digitalization of the Real and through the myth of 'pure' digital knowledge, the scientific discourse alienates itself in the reification of the lost object" (473). Unlike the discourse of the master, the discourse of knowledge professes to be completely neutral, a claim through which it, however, like that of the master, excludes every manifestation of lack, especially that manifested in sexual difference and the reality of death; its knowledge is never libidinal or subjective.

Through these exclusions, it produces an ordered, stable body of knowledge, which is why it is also operative in all discourses of morality, bureaucracy, the police, the Protestant ethic, capitalism, rationalization, and organization—all the forces and forms of mastery that continuously threaten the subject in Pynchon's work. Although it professes to be completely neutral, S_1—in the guise of the "great authors" whose knowledge it presumes to spread and who function as its unquestioned "authorities"—is in the position of its repressed truth. The discourse cannot abolish but only repress this master signifier. It is, in fact, exactly from this repressed position that the discourse is sustained and from which the idea(l) of a neutral science is revealed as an illusion. In *Gravity's Rainbow*, this master signifier is symbolized by "The Book" (GR 47), which contains Pavlov's, the "Master's" (GR 140), writings. Pointsman's own sad and sterile existence is a *memento* that in the discourse of knowledge, $\$$ is in the position of the production, which means that it is from this discourse that the barred subject is produced: science is "an ideology of the subjection of the subject" (Lacan, "Radiophonie" 89). Like Pointsman, Vond is a victim, because he is caught in the complicity of these two discourses: "The discourse of knowledge is the accomplice of the discourse of the master, because it proclaims the mastery of knowledge . . . the disavowal of difference. It is therefore impossible that the discourse of knowledge is a way out of the discourse of the master" (Lipowatz, *Diskurs* 182). The inability that defines this discourse is the inability to live up to its underlying law, that of S_1.

Whereas the relation between the discourse of the master and that of knowledge defines Vond, the relation between him and Frenesi is defined through the relation of the discourse of the master to that of the hysteric. Ultimately, and that is one of the tragedies thematized by *Vineland*, the discourse of the master is *produced* by that of the hysteric:

$$\frac{\$ \rightarrow S_1}{a \leftarrow S_2}$$

inability

Here, $\$$ poses the question about its "split"—the incompatibility of *being* and *thinking*—to a subject/signifier that it puts into the position of mastery/knowledge. Because $\$$ cannot accept the split, the object *o* (surplus-*jouissance*), which symbolizes and manifests this split, is in the position of the repressed truth. Rather than accept its relation to the object *o* and thus to lack, $\$$ looks for and demands unity and harmony (real *jouissance*), constantly voicing its unhappiness about its split. These complaints are directed toward a master signifier, or "idealized father" (*Séminaire XVII* 107), whom $\$$ demands to produce a knowledge (which is why S_2 is in the position of production) that will answer $\$$'s question, because "the lack of the object experienced in the real results in its being placed somewhere else, in the imaginary" (Juranville 83). Here, S_1 is put into the position of this phantasmatic unity: the position of the Thing. This positioning thus shows the entanglement of imaginary *jouissance* in the "*jouissance* of the other." Because S_1 is only arbitrarily chosen, it is ultimately the hysteric's question that produces the desire to know in the master. This is why the hysteric's question is also the birth of science. Yet the difficulty in providing an "acceptable" answer to the hysteric's question "can lead to the renunciation of the question itself, which establishes the discourse of the master" (Lipowatz, *Diskurs* 191) because it is the master himself (S_1) who comes to represent knowledge. The discourse of the hysteric thus *produces* and also *unveils* the structure of the discourse of the master, yet it remains in complicity with it, because the master, who embodies unity for the hysteric, becomes the ultimate object of desire. Like Frenesi, the hysteric wants a master "over which she reigns. She reigns and he does not rule" (Lacan, *Séminaire XVII* 150), which is a tragic contradiction in terms. Here, the inability of the discourse has to do with the subject's "inability to know." This inability "produces its discourse" in the first place. The second inability is the resulting inability "to come to life through desire" ("Radiophonie" 97).

The fourth discourse, that of the analyst—which I claim presides over *Vineland*'s poetics—is the reverse of the discourse of the master. It does not (attempt to) provide a "mystical insight into freedom for the subject, no 'redemption' or 'liberation' from death . . . and the difference of the sexes, but much more an acceptance of its history, which is impossible in the other discourses" (Lipowatz, *Diskurs* 226).

Here, $\$$, which is repressed in the discourse of the master, is made the object of the discourse:

$$\text{impossibility}$$

$$\frac{a \longrightarrow \$}{S_2 \longleftarrow S_1}$$

In this discourse, power relations are minimized. It is the only one in which an acceptance of lack is possible, and thus also "true knowledge," the truth of castration and sublimation in which "truth" and "desire" are linked. It is dominated by the object o (surplus-*jouissance*) and its relation to the $\$$. In this discourse, knowledge is produced in the position of truth, *through the intervention of the analyst*, who functions as a "subject-supposed-to-know" (*Séminaire XVII* 217). As such, he is in the position of the master signifier, because "there is the necessity that, within knowledge, something produces itself which has the function of the master-signifier" (218), yet he is only a "father surrogate" and thus not a "real" master, because he is aware of the fact that "any statement of authority has no other guarantee than its very enunciation . . . no metalanguage can be spoken. . . . And when the Legislator (he who claims to lay down the Law) presents himself to fill the gap, he does so as an impostor. But there is nothing false about the Law itself, or about him who assumes its authority" (*Écrits* 310–11).[14]

The result of the discourse is a specifically "analytic" truth, a "half-saying" (*Séminaire XVII* 39) that acknowledges that the "signifier is stupid" and, as a result of this, that "there is no knowledge which isn't either illusion or myth" ("Radiophonie" 84), a shift taken up in *Vineland's* final passages, in which "reality" is gradually replaced by dreams and myths, which begin to puncture mimetic space, turning the mimesis of reality into a mimesis of psychic space. As in *Gravity's Rainbow*, the text begins to disintegrate, yet in *Vineland* it is a disintegration not into the gaps between the signifiers but into dream, mythological, and thus psychic space, as for instance in the story of the *woge* (VL 186–87). This disintegration runs counter to the exclusion of precisely these realms by modern culture: "As modern civilization ruthlessly eliminates Eros from culture, modern science ruthlessly demythologizes our view of the world and of ourselves" (Brown 303). The impossibility of the discourse of the analyst is a positive one—namely, that of "truth" itself, the realization that "the Thing . . . is a myth" (Juranville 99) and that a myth ultimately "does not explain anything" (*Séminaire VII* 172). For both Pynchon and Lacan, it is appropriately within the ambiguous and oscillating scenarios of dreams and myths that the character of truth as an inevitable half-truth becomes apparent. Because of this oneiric ambiguity, which Lacan actually identifies with "desire" (*Fundamental Concepts* 176), interpretation is "often founded on an enigma" (*Séminaire XVII* 40). Ultimately, what "the discourse of analysis shows is the idea that . . . meaning is make-believe" (*Encore* 74). Only in this discourse, in which knowledge and, by extension, the unconscious "only support [themselves] by presenting [themselves] as impossible, in order to confirm [themselves] as real (. . . real discourse)" ("Radiophonie" 77), does the subject accept "being as illusion." In their various alignments, the four discourses perfectly illustrate the saying that "knowledge is power." Whereas the discourse of the master and that of the hysteric cover the field of power, those of knowledge and the analyst cover that of knowledge. Only in the discourse of the analyst, however, are the fields of power and knowledge aligned with the subject's acceptance of the lack-of-being.

Lacan's theory of the four discourses provides an archaeology of power from within the law of the unconscious. The four discourses describe theoretically—as *Vineland* does fictionally—a dynamic field in which power, knowledge, desire, and the subject come to occupy varying positions and constantly define each other: "The different discourses are different modi of dealing with the lack . . . they do not presuppose an inner homogeneity of the subjects in question and there is *no* polarity between 'strong,' self-assured and self-controlled subjects and 'weak' ones . . . in all cases the subjects remain split . . . complex rather than simple" (Lipowatz, *Verleugnung* 123).

From a Lacanian perspective it becomes clear that what Foucault describes in *Discipline and Punish* is the gradual shift from a politics of the discourse of the master to one of the discourse of knowledge, in which the shift from direct punishment to discipline and penalization describes the passage of the subject from slave to a disciplined and normalized surface of knowledge, whereas Baudrillard's theory shows a universe in which the discourse of knowledge has taken full control over all other discourses.

The most obvious carrier of political power is the discourse of the master, whose first appearance marks the birth of "Western individuality"—exactly the moment of origin that Pynchon constantly questions but also returns to, as for instance in the description of Slothrop's disintegration. The historical emergence of Western subjectivity "means the beginning of the . . . de-mythologizing of the world and the subjects. . . . It also has to do with the creation and dissemination of the first forms of domination and private property, the free and 'unhappy' individuality, the radicalization of the question about the meaning of life and death" (Lipowatz, *Diskurs* 129). Today, however, the discourse of the master is amalgamated with the discourse of knowledge. In fact, for the future, Lacan envisions everything pointing "towards a procession of what [he] define[s] as the discourse of knowledge . . . an increase of its administration. That is the discourse of the master, but intensified with obscurantism" ("Radiophonie" 88).

As in *Gravity's Rainbow,* the most important hinge between power and the subject in *Vineland* is the economy of sadomasochism, the sexual machine in and by which power is produced. Although sadomasochism is the most common "perversion" in Pynchon's work, because it mirrors the perversion of culture in general, in *Vineland* it becomes the *central* concern. In the following I use Lacan's formalization of the four discourses as a theoretical grid within which this structure can be read.

In *Vineland,* sadomasochism is introduced by the ironic *vignette* of Millard Hobbs, the "Marquis de Sod," whose career is from the start bound up with the implosion of a simulated media reality and reality itself. Originally an actor hired to do TV commercials for the lawn-care service "The Marquis de Sod," Hobbs is mistaken by "people out in the non-Tubal world [. . .] for the real owner [. . .] and Millard, being an actor, started believing them" (VL 46). Eventually, he takes over the business with money earned from his appearances in the commercials, which he then changes into "micromovies" (VL 47) in which the Marquis "whips the lawn into shape,"

> each grass blade in extreme close-up being seen to have a face and little mouth, out of which, in thousandfold-echoplexed chorus, would come piping, "More, more! We love eet!" The Marquis, leaning down playfully, "Ah cahn't *'ear* you!" Presently the grass would start to sing the company jingle, to a, by then, postdisco arrangement of the *Marseillaise*—
>
> A lawn savant, who'll lop a tree-ee-uh,
> Nobody beats Mar-
> Quis de Sod! (VL 47)

In the pun on "beating," Pynchon playfully suggests an alignment of the structures of capitalism and sadomasochism. With this tableau he introduces the economy of sadomasochism, which will define, in less comic and more lethal terms, the relationship between Frenesi and Vond, in which Vond dreams of domination ("one day he would order her down on her knees in front of all these cryptically staring children, put a pistol to her head, and give her something to do with her smart mouth" [VL 273]) while Frenesi dreams of submission ("beaming a significant look at a cop in riot gear [. . .] while one hand [. . .] appeared to brush with its fingertips the underside of the barrel of his assault rifle" [VL 114]). Their complicity within the sexual register of sadomasochism is made very clear when Zoyd is forced by Vond to watch Frenesi enter his car, "to watch him then seize her hair [. . .] to guide her head below the roofline and into the padded shadows, though not exactly to notice the way her neck was bent, the anticipation, the long erotic baring of nape, as if willingly, for some high-fashion leather collar . . ." (VL 304).

A similar complicity between victim and victimizer is evoked when Frenesi tells DL about her experiences with Thorazine in Vond's reeducation camp, a drug used earlier by Steve Edelman in *Gravity's Rainbow* (GR 753):

"I wanted them to come and hold me down, stick needles in me, push things up my ass [. . .] the workin' stiffs [. . .] were digging it just as much as I was" (VL 261).

The economy of sadomasochism can be elucidated by superimposing it on the relation between the discourses of the master and the hysteric. Vond, as the perfect result of the complicity of the discourse of the master and that of knowledge, is, like Weissmann/Blicero in *Gravity's Rainbow*, a leader with an almost symptomatic, charismatic aura about him: "Brock's supernatural luck [. . .] a pure white light surrounding Brock entirely" (VL 272). Like every true master, he represses that he is an $, so that it can only emerge in "true dreams" to haunt him:

> The careful product of older men, Brock [. . .] carried with him a watchful, never quite trustworthy companion personality, feminine, underdeveloped, against whom his male version, supposedly running the unit, had to be equally vigilant. In dreams he could not control, in which lucid intervention was impossible, dreams that couldn't be denatured by drugs or alcohol, he was visited by his uneasy anima in a number of guises, notably as the Madwoman in the Attic. (VL 274)

This repression is the reason for the nightmares in which Vond experiences sexual intercourse as deadly. In the sexual economy in which the death of the individual is staked against the life of the species, it is appropriately only the latter aspect that is important for him:[15] "In nightmares he was forced to procreate with women who approached never from floor or ground level but from steep overhead angles, as if from someplace not on the surface of Earth [. . . .] He understood, in some way impossible to face, that each child he thus produced, each birth, would be only another death for him" (VL 276–77). These dreams show Vond's involvement in the structure of castration. Although he normally represses the fact that "having" the phallus does not mean to "be" the phallus, these dreams manifest his fear of castration.

As in his other works, Pynchon relates the discourse of the master and that of knowledge to a male position, which is why Vond's repressed anima is female. The head ninjette Rochelle, for instance, tells Takeshi of the myth of Lilith and how men "dragged us all down into this wreck they'd made of the Creation, all subdivided and labeled" (VL 166), a world ordered into "'good' and 'evil,' where before women had been content to just be" (VL 166). This subdivided and labeled world is exactly that created by the discourse of knowledge. Within another framework, Baudrillard provides a description of this operational world that could well have been written by Pynchon, (cf. his letter to Hirsch): "the obsession peculiar to our culture with 'instancing' and instrumentalizing all things. Just as it is absurd to separate in other cultures the religious, the economic, the political" (*Forget Foucault* 23). One part of Vond, Vond as the "careful product of older men," stands for this neutral and dead knowledge. Frenesi, on the other hand, with her dreams of universal love and harmony, is caught in the hysteric's position and thus "hystericized" by and in a phallocratic, Western society whose "patriarchal order tends to make masters of men and hysterics of women" (Ragland-Sullivan, *Philosophy of Psychoanalysis* 305). Frenesi dreams of the idea of unity as the absence of oppositionality, "a mysterious people's oneness, drawing together toward the best chances of light, achieved once or twice that she'd seen in the street, in short, timeless bursts, all paths, human and projectile, true, the people in a single presence, the police likewise simple as a moving blade" (VL 117).

The tragic moment of *Vineland* is related to the fact that this position, rather than providing a "counterforce" to the discourse of the master, is its perfect accomplice, which clarifies Pynchon's ambivalence about such "counterforces." Frenesi herself experiences this desire for and thus complicity with a master as a fatality,

> a helpless turn toward images of authority, especially uniformed men [. . .] as if some Cosmic Fascist had spliced in a DNA sequence requiring this form of *seduction* and initiation into the dark joys of social control [. . .] the dismal possibility that all her oppositions, however just and good, to forms of power were really acts of denying that dangerous swoon that came creeping at the edges of her optic lobes every time the troops came marching by, that wetness of attention and perhaps ancestral curse. (VL 83; emphasis added)

Pynchon relates this complicity to the difference between real and imagined life. What Frenesi wants to recover in Vond is exactly the "master who does not rule"; his impossible film version. Ironically—and tragically—she imagines this master as a "child" to be saved rather than the idealized father she desires:

> Someplace [. . .] was the "real" Brock, the endearing adolescent who would allow her to lead him stumbling out into light she imagined as sun plus sky, with an 85 filter in, returning him to the man he should have grown into [. . .] Yet if there was anything left to believe, she

must have in the power even of that weightless, daylit commodity of the sixties [love] to redeem even Brock, amiably, stupidly brutal, fascist Brock. (VL 216–17)

Like both sadism and masochism, the discourse of the master and that of the hysteric find their basis in a disavowal that language fundamentally splits the subject. Both negate the lack, the "second death" brought by symbolization, the death that "brings life" (308) and that stands in opposition to the real, biological death, the one "which is brought by life" (308). In the discourse of the master the subject negates this "second death" by identifying completely with S_1, the master signifier that stands for the initial murder of the thing, so that the master identifies completely with the subject who "renders himself master of the thing, precisely in so far as he destroys it" (*Seminar I* 173). It is because of this identification that "primal masochism should be located around this initial negativation, around this original murder of the thing" (174). Like the sadist, the master projects the death he cannot accept for himself into the outside, because he is caught in the illusion that by doing so, he can throw back "the pain of existence . . . onto the Other, only . . . he does not realize that in this manner he also changes into an 'eternal thing' [*objet*]" (*Écrits*, French ed., 778).

The hysteric subject's disavowal is even more direct, resulting in its willful adoption of the slave's position and thus its identification with the master signifier. In this perverse alignment, each derives pleasure *through* the other. While the victim/hysteric desires the pleasure (*jouissance*) of the victimizer/master, the "sadist himself occupies the place of the object, but without knowing it, to the benefit of another, for whose *jouissance* he exercises his action as sadistic pervert" (*Fundamental Concepts* 185).

The result of this complicity is a game of mutual identifications that are often held in a state of immobility and balance by gazes and in which, "in the mirage of play, each identifies himself with the other" (*Seminar I* 215), an imaginary setup Lacan describes in detail in "Kant avec Sade" (*Écrits*, French ed., 765–90). In the sadomasochistic relationship pleasure (*jouissance*) and death are always deferred, because both master and victim ultimately derive their pleasure within its economy: "The sadistic relation can only be sustained in so far as the other is on the verge of still remaining a subject. . . . The sadistic relation implies, in fact, that the partner's consent has been secured—his freedom, his confession, his humiliation" (*Seminar I* 214–15).

In Frenesi and Vond's relationship, the camera symbolizes the fascination of this—in the Lacanian sense—imaginary deadlock. Film also defines Vond's (the master's) "real" world and Frenesi's (the hysteric's) "utopian and imaginary" one: "The two separate worlds—one always includes a camera somewhere, and the other always includes a gun, one is make-believe, one is real" (VL 241). Ultimately, Pynchon lays the blame for the revolution's failure on the belief in a filmic utopia and the childishness and innocence of this belief: " 'We were running around like little kids with toy weapons, like the camera really was some kind of gun, gave us that kind of power. Shit. How could we lose track like that, about what was real? [. . .] Who'd we save? The minute the guns came out, all that art-of-the-cinema handjob was over' " (VL 259).

Pynchon stages the convergence of Frenesi's and Vond's worlds on the campus of "The College of the Surf" during a carnevalesque, Bakhtinian student revolt that Vond subsequently breaks up. This revolt frames the fatal climax to the relations of Frenesi, Vond, and Weed Atman,[16] the "innocent" (VL 216) mathematics professor who has more or less inadvertently become one of the leaders of the student revolt.

In a perfect parallel to her relation to Vond, whom Frenesi first sees through the "safety of her viewfinder" (VL 116) and by whom she is from the first moment fascinated ("he could feel how she focused in on him, him alone—the lines of force" [VL 200]), Frenesi relates to Atman sexually and through the camera: "And oh how Frenesi, that throbbing eye, was lingering on him, and presently, in time to the music, zooming in and out every chance she got on Weed's crotch" (VL 210). Soon she is traveling back and forth between Atman and Vond, whom she meets for "regular trysts in the waterbed suite of a motor inn" (VL 211). It is during one of those meetings that the relation between Frenesi, Vond, and Atman is brought into the open. Fittingly, this takes place during a gathering storm, which functions as yet another of Pynchon's scenarios of impending doom and the break of an enigmatic and frightening force into reality: "Outside, from a remote camera, the sky was the underside of a beast" (VL 212). Vond tells her that she—more particularly, her body—is "the medium Weed and I use to communicate" (VL 214), the channel through which they relay their imaginary hatred of each other. The sexual and symbolic (or rather, imaginary) registers overlap when Vond tells Frenesi not to shower after they have made love, for after she subsequently makes love to Atman, Vond can tell her: "You were coming in his face and he was tasting me all the time" (VL 214).

It is during this apocalyptic scene that Frenesi realizes she will betray the revolution. The reason is that she wants to bring out the child she suspects hidden behind Vond's fascist facade, a child that she feels needs to be saved and redeemed by her love. Nevertheless, in the timeless moment in which the storm holds "the city down like prey, trying repeatedly to sting it into paralysis" (VL 216), she is confronted already with the ultimate impossibility of such a redemption. When she thinks he is sleeping she attempts to talk to the hidden, childlike Vond by figuratively entering his dreams. Vond is always awake, however, and, like the white metropolis in *Gravity's Rainbow*, forever dreamless: "She leaned in to whisper to him her heart's overflow, and saw in the half-light that what she'd thought were closed eyelids had been open all the time. He'd been watching her. She let out a short jolted scream. Brock started laughing" (VL 217). Another clue to the degree of Vond's repression is that the atmospheric intrusion is for him nothing but "a commercial, as if the Beast opposite the city were a coming attraction he had grown overfamiliar with" (VL 212).

Vond, like Pointsman in *Gravity's Rainbow*, is a believer in a purely physiological and thus machinic universe, a "devotee of the thinking of pioneer criminologist Cesare Lombroso" (VL 272), from whom he takes not only the idea of phrenology but also that of misoneism, the "hatred of anything new" (VL 273), which, as in *Gravity's Rainbow*, turns people into machines, linking control to stasis and thus to a pure manifestation of the death drive. Yet it is Frenesi who breaks up Vond's careful exclusions of change, enigma, and desire. Whereas Lombroso files revolutionaries as "geniuses, enthusiasts, fools, rogues, and followers," Frenesi is "the unforeseen sixth, the one without a label" (VL 273), Vond's "mystery revolutionary/stimulus," and as such is the nodal point that denotes Vond's own ultimate, repressed complicity with the revolution, and thus his "humanity." Both Zoyd and Vond, in fact, are similarly haunted by Frenesi. Whereas Vond has "to find a girl to project Frenesi's *ghost* onto" (VL 278; emphasis added) after she has left him, Zoyd, in a similarly phantasmatic manner, masturbates after the break-up of their marriage, hallucinating her presence and image and thus becoming "apprentice *ghostly* peeper" (VL 60; emphasis added). Masturbation, in fact, perfectly captures the tragic scene of sex with a ghost, a reference that will become important later on. In fact, Frenesi comes to symbolize not only the "object of desire" but also desire as such, especially in its relation to death and *jouissance:* "its [desire's] frenzy [*frénésie*] mocking the abyss of the infinite, the secret collusion with which it envelops the pleasure of knowing and of dominating with *jouissance*" (Lacan, *Écrits* 166–67). In this reference, it is inspiring also that Rushdie sees in Frenesi's name an anagram of *free* and *sin*. In that both Zoyd and Vond fantasize her, Frenesi comes—like desire itself—to pass through and mediate the realms of both *innocence* and *guilt*. In that she also represents for them the *lack* in and of desire, however, she also embodies the absence that pervades both Zoyd and Vond, in the sense in which Lacan states that the bar ($) pervades both the positions of power and nonpower. Although occupying different positions, everybody is caught up in the same structure. Only the Foucauldian anonymous forces that preside over even Vond escape this structure. Fittingly, they are "the Real Ones" (VL 276) who live in a "real" realm without human parameters. As in *Gravity's Rainbow,* they "aren't even sadists. . . . There's just *no passion at all* . . ." (GR 216).

Together with Atman's death—the actual moment of betrayal—the moment of the conception of betrayal is the "primal scene" and thus the central moment in *Vineland*. It describes the loss of *free,* unmediated innocence. While closing off the natural realm, it simultaneously opens up the cultural realm of the double and the mirror. In a manner similar to what happens in Lacan's mirror stage, Frenesi becomes her own ghost. The fact that her life becomes a movie she watches highlights the fact that it becomes a piece of art(ifice). The moment thus describes a general and complex, ultimately sexual betrayal, which involves the passage from nature to culture, from the real to reality/fiction/simulation, and within these registers, to the birth of subjectivity and the signifier/writing. It is, in fact, closely linked to the ultimate fall into knowledge and human reality brought about by the "original *sin*":

> She was walking around next to herself, haunting herself, attending a movie of it all. If the step was irreversible, then she ought to be all right now, safe in a world-next-to-the-world that not many would know how to get to, where she could kick back and watch the unfolding drama. No problem anymore with talk of "taking out" Weed Atman, as he'd gone turning into a character in a movie, one who as a bonus happened to fuck like a porno star . . . but even sex was mediated for her now—she did not enter in. (VL 237)

Whereas Frenesi is the hinge between innocence and guilt and actively betrays, Atman is the innocent victim who is being betrayed. Yet his world, like Frenesi's, is overlayed with Vond's—although inadvertently and passively—because Vond has him brainwashed: "We gave him some reality [. . .] no worse than going to the dentist. Till after a while he could begin to see our side" (VL 240). The process, which is quite reminiscent of Slothrop's

Vineland: Everything under Control   223

conditioning in *Gravity's Rainbow,* is performed by Dr. Larry Elasmo and is once again related to paper, writing, and bureaucracy: "There was a recurring message, one too deep for Weed, always about paper" (VL 228). Elasmo, an interface between dentist and psychiatrist, whose "dental cases" (VL 228) are actually "mental" ones, "had been authorized in those days to send people, Weed included, a form that required them to come to his offices at a certain time" (VL 227):

> It was some long, ongoing transaction, carried on, like dentistry, in a currency of pain inflicted, pain withheld, pain drugged away, pain become amnesia [. . .] sometimes Ilse, the hygienist, stood waiting by a door into a corridor, leading, he knew, to a bright high room with a tiny window at the top, impossibly far away, some blade of sky . . . she was holding something   something white and . . . he couldn't remember. . . . (VL 228)

Pynchon describes the growing convergence of the worlds of Vond, Frenesi, and Atman by means of the convergence of the camera and the gun with which Atman is killed and that McHoul and Wills would certainly see as *Vineland*'s major "material typonomy." He establishes this overlapping of the two worlds *over* the gun by a pun again reminiscent of Virilio's alignment of cinema and war. When Zoyd talks to Hector Zuñiga, he says, "When you said cuttin' and shootin' I didn't know you were talkin' about film" (VL 52). In fact, the convergence proceeds like a slow zoom on the gun, whose first appearance is truly cinematic. Oscillating between real object and cinematic ghost, it is in a position reminiscent of Metz's cinematic object: "All at once there it was, perfectly in focus, complexly highlighted, mythical, *latent* and *solid* at the same time" (VL 240; emphases added).

Frenesi, the "courier of death" (VL 241), plants the gun in Rex's bag (VL 229). On one level, the gun links sexuality, power, and death: "Men had it so simple. When it wasn't about Sticking It In, it was about Having The Gun, a variation that allowed them to Stick It In from a distance" (VL 241). Nonetheless, Frenesi still innocently dreams of a more cinematic truth of the gun, the "almost [. . .] supernatural term in the story" (VL 243). Somehow, she feels, film should be able to reveal the underlying, *real* truth, of which everything else has only been an insubstantial, unreal ghost:

> Her impulse was to deny [t]his simple formula, to imagine that with the gun in the house, the 24-frame-per-second truth she still believed

> in would find some new, more intense level of truth [. . . .] Light this little 'sucker here about eight to one, soften the specular highlights, start in on a tight close-up . . . draw back, incorporating the lovely, deadly thing in the master shot of tonight's gathering, transfiguring the frame, returning at last to the invisible presences and unavoidable terms of which all she had up till now lit and made visible had only been ghosts. . . . . (VL 241–42)

The motif of ghosts presides over the convergence of the two worlds, and thus of the *real* and *reality, death* and *life*.[17] Of course, a gun is predestined for such a position, because its function is quite literally to bring about the passage from life to death. Both a real and a cinematic object, it functions as the threshold or dividing line between these realms. This medial position makes it the *almost supernatural* term of the story and relates it to the "fantastic," which is a similar "dividing line" (Todorov 27) and as such is similarly related to the concept of the gap, a common reference in which the motifs of language, the real, death, and the unconscious merge. As the phantasmatic "return of the repressed" within the Möbius strip of representational space, the fantastic becomes another framework in which the passage from the real to reality can be read. Pynchon himself deals with the Freudian aspects of the fantastic in "Is it O.K. to Be a Luddite?" Commenting on *The Castle of Otranto*, he describes Alfonso as being "assembled from pieces [. . .] which fall from the sky [. . .] relentless as Freud's slow return of the repressed" (40).

Of course, the fantastic elements of Pynchon's work have been commented on; in fact, Douglas Fowler states that "the core of his [Pynchon's] fiction is always fantastic and always the same" ("Pynchon's Magic" 53),[18] whereas Meikle comments on the motif of "transcendence gained at the cost of individual dissolution" ("Other Frequencies" 291) in his comparison of Pynchon and Lovecraft. Although the idea of "transcendence gained" lays too much emphasis on the "other side," and neglects the ultimate impossibility of the meeting with the real, Lance Olsen's Derridean interpretation of the fantastic explicitly relates it only to "this side." In an article with the misleading title of "Deconstructing the Enemy of Color: The Fantastic in *Gravity's Rainbow*," Olsen reads *Gravity's Rainbow* as a "deconstructive fantasy" (84) that makes use of the fantastic as "the mode of discourse chosen as a vehicle for the postmodern consciousness" (75). Olsen argues that "fantasy becomes the literary equivalent of deconstructionism" (76), because it provides the scenario for the "endless displacement of 'meaning,' the blocking of conceptual closure" (76–77). In a final convergence, "fantasy and deconstructionism—a bizarre freeplay among texts, a delight in possibility, a joyous affirmation of kinesis, an invitation to narrative and cultural illegality" (84)—become one and the same. Although Olsen professes to deal with the fantastic, however, what he actually talks about is fantasy/the marvelous. Even though Olsen's concept of fantasy doubtlessly covers one aspect of Pynchon's work, it is certainly not the fantastic one, which is not a nexus between texts but the dividing line/gap between text and nontext, life and death, rationality and irrationality, empiricism and metaphysics.

The fantastic has a number of interfaces with the sublime, which is in turn related to the "sublimity" of the object *o* and the relation of fiction to the ultimate enigmaticity of this object, which can never fully represent the "always already" lost absolute object. Although it sustains the fantasy—and thus the text—it is merely the representative of the absolute object, the "referent 'outside of language' . . . the referent of all of that through which language never says what it 'wants to say'" (Žižek, *Die Missverständnisse* 71). If through *sublimation* an object is elevated to the "dignity of the Thing" (Lacan, *Séminaire VII* 133)—that is, to the discursive representative of the absolute object—it becomes *sublime*. These sublime objects *o* in turn "lure the subject to the same position as *das Ding*" (119). In this position, the subject experiences an "imbalance that arises in the fantasy when it decomposes" and "periods of irruption, of subjective disorganization which occur when something in the fantasy wavers and . . . the imaginary limits between subject and object change" ("Desire" 22).[19] Both terms (the fantastic and the sublime) thus describe a fundamentally paradoxical and ambivalent structure. As in the fantastic, in the sublime "pleasure derives from pain" (Lyotard 77), or better, from fear, the fear that "has no 'object' . . . its object is the lack, which is neutralized by the symbol" (Lipowatz, *Diskurs* 118). On the fictional level, this fear is pleasurable, because the subject's meeting with the real—the absolute object ("through" the Thing)—is only *staged*. Both terms, furthermore, deal with threshold experiences and bring language to its limit (etymologically, *sublime* derives from *sub limes*, "just under the threshold or border") because they try to express "ideas of which no presentation is possible" (Lyotard 78). Both also deal with nature as something separated from humanity, which is why their aesthetics are *monstrous* rather than *beautiful*,[20] which in turn is why Pynchon's revelations are always "frightful." The sublime, then, is the interface between representation and the absolute object, which it can never reach and which remains enigmatic. This precarious balance between *sublimity* and *stupidity* is a main topic of *Vineland,* in which one can detect a shift from the first to the second. This has to do with the poetological shift of emphasis to the discourse of the analyst, which is the only one that "holds" itself by supporting itself "through the dimension of stupidity" (Lacan, *Encore* 17), in so far as stupidity is "a dimension in the exercise of the signifier" (24). In contrast, the other three discourses attempt to escape stupidity, "aim[ing] always at the least stupidity, at the sublime stupidity, because *sublime* wants to say the most elevated point of that which is low" (18).

In this respect, *Vineland* highlights the symbolic relation of writing to the sublime, in which the real is always already symbolic. Sublimation, in fact, means to bring the absolute object to the level of the signifier, where it is represented by the Thing. Through sublimation, "the signifier introduces the human being into the real, simultaneously arousing and disappointing desire" (Juranville 282). Here, "writing itself, the 'letter,' is the presence of the signifier in the real" (283). As such, "it is *writing* . . . which accomplishes a negation of finitude and death, but to which one only gains entrance if one enters into death oneself. This new structure, the phenomenon of which is writing, one can call sublimation" (277). In this respect, "sublimation allows, by tracing the letter across the page which offers the empty space, to support . . . the suffering which is imposed by the inevitable lack of the Other" (286–87). Despite its fantastical elements, which highlight the imaginary aspect of the relation between the subject and the real, it is ultimately this presence of the signifier—in its conjunction with stupidity—that presides over *Vineland*'s poetics.

Lyotard, who sees the sublime as the aesthetic form in which modern art "finds its axioms" (77), differentiates between a modern and a postmodern form of the sublime, which almost uncannily evokes Derrida's two modes of interpretation. "The emphasis can be placed on the powerlessness of the faculty of presentation, on the nostalgia for presence felt by the human subject. . . . The emphasis can also be placed on the increase of being and the jubilation which result from the invention of new rules of the game" (Lyotard 79–80). It is fittingly within another reference to the concept of the gap that Lyotard aligns these two modes: "The nuance which distinguishes these two modes may be infinitesimal; they often coexist in the same piece . . . and yet they testify to a difference (*un différend*) on which the fate of thought depends . . . between regret and assay" (80).[21]

If the fantastic and sublime is related to the experience of separation and of a gap, then it is only appropriate that Pynchon should use film imagery to describe Atman's death. Much like Gottfried's death in *Gravity's Rainbow*, it is defined as a falling through the gaps between film frames. Life and film converge completely when, during a screening of the shooting scene years later, it is possible to see on the film "some silvery effluent, vacating his [Atman's] image, the real moment of his passing. He had just time enough to say Frenesi's name before the frame went twisting and flying off his face" (VL 246). The general confusion and the changing of film rolls prevent the filming of the actual shooting, so that there are only the voices. Howie "missed the actual moment, although shapes may have moved somewhere in the frame, black on black, like *ghosts* trying to return to earthly form" (VL 246; emphasis added).

The passage aligns the threshold experience of the fantastic and sublime, film imagery, ghosts, and the idea of the gap. The notion of the gap, symbolized by the "falling out of representation" of the actual happening, is also what relates the scene to the structure of language—and thus of the unconscious. In a manner similar to that in which the moment of death and betrayal falls into the time between two "takes," the unconscious falls into the timeless gap—in filmic terms, the "cut"—between the real and reality, the unspecularizable absolute object and the object *o*, which is the specular image that "lends its clothes" (*Écrits* 316) to this absolute object. The cut denotes the "uncanny" difference between these objects. This is why the abyss, which in Kant functions as the sublime image *par excellence,* is understood no longer figuratively but literally as the (structural) abyss between two signifiers—the gap of the real. Pynchon's use of film imagery illustrates the unrepresentability of the moment of the meeting of the real and reality, a motif that also characterized his use of film in *Gravity's Rainbow*. In *Vineland* he uses film to dramatize the insufficiency of the apparatuses of representation to "catch" the unconscious through the reference to the fantastic and the sublime, each of which denotes "a conflict between . . . the faculty to conceive of something and the faculty to 'present' something" (Lyotard 77). As with Zoyd's "lost messages," the imagery Lacan uses to describe the unconscious almost directly mirrors Pynchon's: "The primary process—which is simply . . . the unconscious—must, once again, be apprehended in its experience of rupture . . . in that non-temporal locus . . . another space, another scene" *(Fundamental Concepts* 56). It lies between "perception and consciousness."

The real image is outside the human realm. This is perfectly captured by the fact that both cameras present at the shooting miss the actual moment of Atman's death. The unconscious and fantastic—the meeting with the real—can be reconstructed only retroactively through the *failure* of the representational machine: "Whereas the parts of the real image . . . can never be seen, those places where the apparatus seizes up, where it blocks up . . . that is the unconscious" (Lacan, *Seminar I* 158).

The unconscious, which can be apprehended only in the stuttering of language, will be forever something that will be realized in the symbolic, a "belatedness" that defines the tragedy of the unconscious and repression. Because of this deferral—the impossibility of a complete *"anamnesis"* (Brown 60)—everything always happens "forever too soon."

Appropriately, the scene closes with the description of Atman's death "in retrospect," in a passage in which the two worlds are finally mapped onto each other. Again, Pynchon expresses this overlapping by puns, a strategy that also characterized the poetics of *Lot 49*. Within the frame of the fantastic and the sublime, the "high magic to low puns" is an especially apt vehicle to describe the passage from transcendence to the signifier: "That's when Frenesi *killed* the light, that's how the *shot* ended, in a close-up of one of Rex's gleaming eyeballs, with the light she was holding reflected on it round and bright, and in the backscatter [. . .] Frenesi herself, dark on dark, face in wide-angle distortion, with an expression that might, Prairie admitted, prove unbearable" (VL 247; emphases added).

Atman's experiences on "the other side" continue and conclude the movie imagery in which his death is described. In the same manner in which his death falls into the gap between two film frames, his reentry into life is also a "filmic" process, "finding a new body to be born into—seeking out men and women in the act of sex, looking for a just-fertilized egg, slipping to and fro with needful dim others in a space like a bleak smoke-tarnished district of sex shows and porno theaters, looking for the magical exact film frame through which the dispossessed soul might reenter the world" (VL 364).

Because he cannot forget the injustices, he returns to life as a ghost who is still "obsessed with those who've wronged [him], with their continuing exemption from punishment . . ." (VL 365). In fact, he has the recurring dream of being carried through the country on a train, laid out "on some bed of ice" (VL 365), watched over by two companions—maybe his parents—who try "to find a local coroner willing to perform an autopsy [. . .] and reveal to the world at last [his] murder [. . . and] murderers" (VL 365).[22] In this image of the preterite forever haunting America's railroads—an image reminiscent of America's tradition of carrying its dead presidents by train through the country to their burial place—*Vineland* again evokes a Foucauldian scenario of an anonymous power. When talking to Prairie, Atman states, "Used to think I was climbing, step by step, right? toward a resolution—first Rex, above him your mother, then Brock Vond, then—but that's when it begins to go dark, and that door at the top I thought I saw isn't there anymore, because the light behind it just went off too" (VL 366). Yet this anonymous scenario is constantly overruled by the question of complicity, as in the discussion about the possibility that Vond is either (1) "a rebel cop, with his own deeply personal agenda," or (2) "only following the orders of a repressive regime based on death" (VL 366). *Vineland* is ultimately about the impossibility of choosing one version, because the alternatives are in complicity with each other.

The extended parallel between the word—a presence made of an absence—the ghost, a similar "presence of an absence," and the object *o*, a final presence of an absence, makes Pynchon's poetics in *Vineland* the fantastic and sublime poetics of "the ghost of language." This ghostly realm is most fully embodied in the Thanatoids, who provide a link to the story of Atman in that he returns as a Thanatoid at the end of the novel. When he returns, he is both alive and dead, but whereas Thanatoids are still "officially alive," Atman is "officially dead." The Blackstream Hotel, in which the '84 Thanatoid Roast is held, is a symbol of the interface between the two realms. It lies in a landscape that is believed "to draw [the two worlds] closer, nearly together, out of register only by the thinnest of shadows. In the century since the place was built, tales of twilight happenings had accumulated" (VL 220).

"'Thanatoid' means 'like death, only different'" (VL 170). Thanatoids "limit themselves [. . .] to emotions helpful in setting right whatever was keeping them from advancing further into the condition of death" (VL 171). They see themselves merely as "victims [. . .] of karmic imbalances—unanswered blows, unredeemed suffering, escapes by the guilty—anything that frustrated their daily expeditions on into the interior of Death" (VL 173), injustices that they carry, like symptoms, "right out on their bodies—written down for—all to see" (VL 174). In former times, "Karmic Adjustment" promised a direct revenge, most drastically death, whereas today, in a culture in which simulation has taken over completely, justice is enmeshed in complex bureaucratic and capitalist structures that forever defer death, a shift reminiscent of Foucault's shift from a direct, carnivalesque punishment to an endless, all-embracing social discipline and of Brown's contention that "death is the reality with which human beings, infants and adults, cannot come to terms" (38). In fact, Brown argues that "only if Eros—the life instinct—can affirm the life of the body can the death instinct affirm death, and in affirming death magnify life" (109). As I showed in the previous chapter, in modern culture especially, "the incapacity to accept death turns the death instinct into its distinctively human and distinctively morbid form" (284). Paradoxically, it is the constant deferral and negation of death that makes reality so deadly. In earlier times, "death was the driving pulse—everything had moved as slowly as the cycles of birth and death, but this proved to be too slow for enough people to begin, eventually, to provide a market niche. There arose a system of deferment, of borrowing against karmic futures. Death, in Modern Karmic Adjustment, got removed from the process" (VL 174–75).

This creeping adjustment, in which endless and fruitless negotiations are necessary to balance out injustices, is a sterile process with a merely simulated and fully coded death drive against which Pynchon sets the quite literal and real death drive of the highway surfers, the "motorhead valley roulette" (VL 37), in which the idea is to drive full speed into the "tule fogs." This is a suicide wager in which real pleasure (*jouissance*) is produced by staking the pleasure principle against a real death. Like the surfer, the drivers "shared the *terrors* and *ecstasies* of the passive, taken rider" (VL 37; emphases added). The idea is "to enter the pale wall at a speed meaningfully over the limit, to bet that the white passage held no other vehicles, no curves, no construction, only smooth, level, empty roadway to an indefinite distance—a motorhead variation on a surfer's dream" (VL 37).

Although in moments such as this *Vineland* evokes a "childlike" world, it is generally the most "grown up" of Pynchon's books. This thematic and stylistic change has to do with a theoretical position that is itself thematized in the book, because it is a book about the tragedy of growing up, as well as the tragedy of childhood, two positions that Pynchon describes as equally "untenable." *Vineland's* ultimate tragedy is that whereas growing up entails the loss of innocence from *within*, staying a child entails the loss of innocence from *without*, because as a child one is inevitably co-opted by the dominant culture.[23] *Vineland* constantly thematizes this fateful complicity of innocence with power, which is contained in the double aspect of innocence as both "childlike" (positive) and "childish" (negative).

In one sense, both the discourse of the master and that of the hysteric are secretly those of children: "The secret that life is soldiering, that soldiering includes death, that those soldiered for, not yet and often never in on the secret, are always, at every age, children" (VL 216). Both "repress" the $, a fact that becomes very clear when Vond's repression is aligned with Frenesi's "postpartum depression" after Prairie's birth. For Zoyd, who has deliberately "dropped just a quarter of a tab of acid on the chance of glimpsing something cosmic that might tell him he wouldn't die" (VL 285) and who sees the child "looking right at him with a vast, an unmistakable recognition" (VL 285), this first gaze is a promise of a continuity beyond the binary structure of life and death. "At the moment, oh God, God, she knew him, *from someplace else*" (VL 285). Yet for Frenesi, it heralds only her inability to enter the role of a mother. In this "postnatal depression" (a term that might come to describe life in general), it is fittingly the ghost of Vond, with his own fear of procreation, who comes to haunt her: "With his own private horrors further unfolded into an ideology of the mortal and uncontinued self, Brock came to visit, and strangely to comfort, in the half-lit hallways of the night, leaning darkly in above her like any of the sleek raptors that decorate fascist architecture" (VL 286–87).

Most obviously, Vond is near her because there is no third position in the structure of sadomasochism. In fact, the idea of a mother is diametrically opposed to the image of woman in the sadomasochist structure. A child endangers its economy because it would force Frenesi to grow up, to overcome her imaginary relation to *jouissance* and to stop being a child herself. Frenesi's depression results precisely from her inability to enter that role: "No amnesia, no kind leaching bath of time would ever take from her memories of descent to cold regions of hatred for the tiny life, raw, parasitic, using her body through the wearying months and now still looking to control her [. . . .] Where was the clean new soul, the true love, her own promised leap into grown-up reality?" (VL 286).

Vond, in turn, can perpetuate his position of power because he recognized the young revolutionaries' "need only to stay children forever, safe inside some extended national Family" (VL 269).[24] His position is maintained because the revolutionaries are "children longing for discipline" (VL 269). Because she has remained a child, Frenesi has "been privileged to live outside of Time, to enter and leave at will, looting and manipulating, weightless, invisible" (VL 287), a description that evokes the weightlessness of computer lives. It is when she becomes a mother that she realizes that "time had claimed her again, put her under house arrest, taken her passport away. Only an animal with a full set of pain receptors after all" (VL 287).

In the present of the story, 1984, the protagonists struggle with their reentry into reality and history and their acknowledgments of the "reality principle": "At the unreadable whim of something in power, [they] must reenter the clockwork of cause and effect" (VL 90). Since the failed campus revolt at the end of the sixties, they have lived "in some time-free zone" (VL 90) whose "falsely deathless parameter" (VL 293) has kept them insulated and out of touch with changes and reality. Symptomatically, when Zuñiga reenters Zoyd's life, death is the first thing he mentions: "Hey, all right fuckhead, try this—*you are goín to have to die?* Yeah-heh-heh, remember that? Death!" (VL 32). Similarly, Zuñiga reminds Zoyd that "all o'you are still children inside, livín your real life back then. Still waitín for that magic payoff" (VL 28).

Co-opted by and enveloped in power, Frenesi has lived in a children's world, with a freedom

> granted to a few, to act outside warrants and charters, to ignore history and the dead, to imagine no future, no yet-to-be-born, to be able simply to go on defining moments only, purely, by the action that filled them. Here was a world of simplicity and certainty no acidhead, no revolutionary anarchist would ever find, a world based on the one and zero of life and death. Minimal, beautiful. The patterns of lives and deaths.... (VL 71–72)

Because it is a world "bought" by her initial betrayal, however, its insulation is punctured by the ghosts who haunt her—most prominently Atman—and through them by the phantom of death. In fact, "the past was on her case forever, the zombie at her back, the enemy no one wanted to see, a mouth wide and dark as the grave" (VL 71).

Whereas Frenesi's ghosts are connected to her guilt, the innocent Zoyd, who has never entered the political struggle directly, nevertheless is haunted, like Frenesi before him, by the ghost of a cosmic unity, a dream he attempts to make true with the help of drugs that, significantly, permit real *jouissance* through a "fading of subjectivity" and, like the "motorhead valley roulette," through a transgression of the law: "And these acid adventures [which entail such realizations as that everything is connected and that 'he wouldn't die'], they came in those days and they went, some we gave away and forgot, others sad to say turned out to be fugitive or false" (VL 285). In this light, he is the ultimate image in the book of "fatal innocence." When he meets Mucho Maas on his way to Vineland, their reminiscing about the "good old days" and the way the state interfered in them evokes a similar discussion in *Gravity's Rainbow* (728ff.).

> "I knew. . . ."
> . . . "Uh-huh, me too. That you were never going to die. Ha! No wonder the State panicked. How are they supposed to control a population that knows it'll never die? When that was always their last big chip, when they thought they had the power of life and death. [. . .] They just let us forget. Give us too much to process, fill up every minute, keep us distracted, it's what the Tube is for [. . .] they have us convinced all over again that we really are going to die." (VL 313–14)

It is this state-controlled, deadly, and adult culture from which Zoyd wants to protect Prairie, a culture in which "man loses contact with his own body, more specifically with his senses, with sensuality and with the pleasure-principle" (Brown 238). After the visit to Mucho, Zoyd plays pinball, with Prairie seated on the glass of the pinball machine, an image that describes within it the difference between childlike innocence and the polymorphously perverse pleasure principle and adulthood and the reality principle (which Brown defines as sublimated and thus desexualized, Apollonian, patriarchal, and fetishistic). Pynchon provides a perfect image of real *jouissance* when he describes how Prairie at this age "liked to lie face down on the glass, kick her feet, and squeal at the full sensuous effect, especially when bumpers got into prolonged cycling or when her father got manic with the flippers [. . . .] 'Enjoy it while you can,' he muttered at his innocent child, 'while you're light enough for that glass to hold you'" (VL 314).[25]

All of *Vineland*'s main characters share a longing and nostalgia for their lost childhood and innocence, or, as Pynchon expresses it in "Is It O.K. to Be a Luddite?" "the same profound unwillingness to give up elements of faith, however 'irrational,' to an emerging technopolitical order" (41). Van Meter "had been searching all his life for transcendent chances exactly like this one the kids took so for granted, but whenever he got close it was like, can't shit, can't get a hardon, the more he worried the less likely it was to happen . . ." (VL 223), whereas Frenesi "wanted, would have given up all the rest for, a chance to go back to when she and Sasha had talked hours, nights, with no restraints, everything from penis folklore to Mom, where do we go to when we die" (VL 292). *Vineland,* more than Pynchon's other works, highlights and simultaneously questions this nostalgia. The tragedy is that this innocence, like the messages Zoyd never gets to in time, is "like a time machine departing for the future, forever too soon for Zoyd" (VL 55). Unlike the adults, children symbolize a state without consciousness. As with the comic-book heroes of *Gravity's Rainbow*, "'too late' was never in their programming" (GR 752). Yet, as in *Gravity's Rainbow*, in which even the comic book heroes come too late, such a childlike state is rigorously questioned in *Vineland*.

Vineland also shows that revolutions are started in the name of the pleasure principle, or real *jouissance*: "The perverse desire to break the law and the disavowal of the Name-of-the-Father seems to lie at the core of every revolution and thus to contain in it the fatality of its failure" (Lipowatz, *Verleugnung* 222).[26] The fate of Frenesi's revolution is precisely the fate of a revolution started under this muse, yet Prairie's story shows that every revolution implies a *rotation* rather than a *reversal*: "The concept of a quarter-turn evokes the revolution, but certainly not in the sense in which revolution is subversion. On the contrary, what turns . . . is destined . . . to evoke re-turn" (*Encore* 41). This is precisely the movement caught in the spiral ending that, as in *Lot 49*, closes the book.

The closure of one cycle is complete when Zuñiga plans a movie, starring Frenesi, that he hopes will re-create "all those long-ago political wars, the drugs, the sex, the rock an' roll, which th' ultimate message will be that the real threat to America, then and now, is from th' illegal abuse of narcotics" (VL 51). This reversal and closure, however, opens up another rotation, this time related to Prairie and thus to a new generation.

At the end of her quest, Prairie is as reluctant to meet its "goal" as Oedipa is in *Lot 49*. Like Oedipa's quest, Prairie's search for her mother is always a search through mediated space, because all the images she has of her mother are fragments of film or stories. Actually, like the film images themselves, Frenesi is a ghost that haunts her. Simultaneously, however, Prairie also haunts Frenesi: "When I get very weird, I go into this alternate-universe idea, and wonder if there isn't a parallel world where she decided to have the abortion [. . .] and what's really happening is that I'm looking for her so I can haunt her like a ghost" (VL 334).

When she finally meets her mother, the reality is somewhat of a letdown in relation to the fantastic dimensions of the ghost image. What she sees is "a woman about forty, who had been a girl in a movie, and behind its cameras and lights, heavier than Prairie expected" (VL 367). Yet her meeting with Vond, which is what ultimately relates her to her mother, is again darker, more mysterious and ambiguous: "What was creepy, the heart of creep-out, lay back down the road behind her, in, but not limited to, the person, hard and nearly invisible, like quartz, of her pursuer, Brock Vond" (VL 108).

When Vond tells her during their final showdown that he is her real father, she reacts with the same mixture of derision and flirtation that her mother did when she first met Vond. (VL 201) Although she dismisses Vond's claim, saying, "you can't be my father, Mr. Vond [. . .] my blood is type A. Yours is Preparation H" (VL 376), after his "withdrawal" from the sky, she feels a curious emptiness: "He had left too suddenly. There should have been more [. . .] 'You can come back,' she whispered, waves of cold sweeping over her, trying to gaze steadily into a night that now at any turn could prove unfaceable. 'It's OK, rilly. Come on, come in. I don't care. Take me anyplace you want'" (VL 384).

When he does not return, "her flirting [becomes] more obvious" (VL 384). It seems that she shares her mother's "ancestral curse," but Vond's time is up. Like Zuñiga's film, Vond's death marks the ending of the cycle, and he passes into the realm of ghosts along the "Ghost's Trail leading to Tsorrek" (VL 379), the "world of the dead" (VL 186), where the exiled ghosts are "not chanting together but remembering, speculating, arguing, telling tales, uttering curses, singing songs, all the things voices do, but without ever allowing the briefest breath of silence. All these voices, forever" (VL 379). While the ruin of his body remains on the surface, Vond's spirit enters this underground limbo in which the disembodied voices replace "life." Symptomatically, Vond's withdrawal is a result of the fact that "suddenly, some white male far away must have awakened from a dream" (VL 376); the predominance shifts from the "one phantasm" of the discourse of the master to that of knowledge, simulation, and the "reality principle" of the budget.

The "re-turn" of the revolution is described in Prairie's relation to Ché, with whom she has a friendship similar to the one between Frenesi and DL. That this new scene is one of a fully simulated and tubal world only underscores the shift. In fact, her grandmother remembers that already as a child Prairie "wanted to climb inside the television set" (VL 368) when watching "Gilligan's Island." Ironically, it is Justin, Frenesi's other child, who inhabits this world most fully. A friend in kindergarten has already told him "to pretend his parents were characters in a television sitcom. 'Pretend there's a frame around 'em like the Tube, pretend they're a show you're watching. You can go into it if you want, or you can just watch, and *not* go into it'" (VL 351).

The battlefield of this new scene is no longer the campus but the artificial, postmodern, fully plasticized mall. It is a scene where, as in the development of rock and roll, "revolution [is] blending into commerce" (VL 308). Prairie's fight is therefore always between "herself" and her "tubal version." When she sees the embodiment of the image of the "new child" instigated by TV, for instance, Prairie feels like "exiled royalty" (VL 327): "On the Tube she saw them all the time, these junior-high gymnasts in leotards, teenagers in sitcoms" (VL 327). These images are the dream of a fully simulated, deathless, and eternally young woman/child, the perfect semiotic simulation. When Ché and Fleur try on some stolen lingerie and play centerfold, becoming deathless "surfaces" onto which cultural messages are coded, Prairie thinks "strangely" of "her dad, and how much he would have enjoyed the display" (VL 332). This codification is actually related to the simulation of desires and stimuli, a simulation expressed by a pun on cultural and TV programming. When Ché wears black and red, she becomes a representative of "Night and Blood [. . .] it's like they's *programmed* for it or somethin'" (VL 332; emphasis added), but when she wears something pink or white, "her street plausibility's all shot to hell" (VL 332). Whereas Ché tends toward the image of depravity, however, Prairie—who has to be persuaded to enter the game at all and then wears something in precisely these colors—tends toward innocence, but an innocence that is doubly coded. It evokes the freedom of the lost prairies, but, as her meeting with Vond shows, it is an innocence that is in constant danger of being co-opted.

This complicity is again not only treated on the level of content but also operative in *Vineland*'s mode of writing, which is in constant complicity with the myths and forms of the simulations of reality, especially television, a strategy that again defines language as the ultimate ambivalent object *o*. From the start, *Vineland* is filled with references to movies and TV series, both real and imaginary—mostly science fiction, horror movies, TV game shows, cop shows, sitcoms, and cartoons. Besides simply mentioning film and TV, the writing also makes use of the structures of several cinematic genres: the docudrama, when the story of the Hollywood blacklistings is retold; the horror movie, which defines the Thanatoid subplot; the karate movie, which defines the parameters of DL's world; the war movie, which is a model for Vond's raid on Vineland; the Mafia movie, which is related to Ralph Wayvone; and the monster movie, which defines Takeshi's relation to the "unrelenting forces." Similarly, the writing uses TV models such as the sitcom, which defines most of the humor of the book. *Vineland* thus acknowledges, thematically as well as structurally, that literature (as well as criticism) is never innocent, "never merely an agent of resistance against networks of power-serving knowledge; rather, it is one of that network's most seductive manifestations" (Bersani 116).

Vineland's main theme is the *complicity* of the subject and power. As in Lacan's four discourses, the subject is caught at the nexus of several force fields, in which it is suspended simultaneously. In fact, *Vineland* presents a "figure" of this discursive moiré, aligning the subject with three "fundamental passions" (Lacan, *Seminar I* 271), love, hate, and ignorance. On the final pages, the development of the relationship of Takeshi and DL, which might lead to a "literally mindless joy" (VL 180) exactly because it is mediated through death—"the Vibrating Palm, or Ninja Death Touch" (VL 131), during the application of which DL wears contact lenses "taken from the eyes of a dead person" (VL 152)—gives rise to the following question:

> whether the Baby Eros, that tricky little pud-puller, would give or take away an edge regarding the unrelenting forces that leaned ever after the partners into Time's wind, impassive in pursuit, usually gaining, the faceless predators who'd once boarded Takeshi's airplane in the sky, the ones who'd had the Chipco lab stomped on, who despite every Karmic Adjustment resource brought to bear so far had simply persisted, stone-humorless, beyond cause and effect, rejecting all attempts to bargain or accommodate, following through pools of night where nothing else moved wrongs forgotten by all but the direly possessed, continuing as a body to refuse to be bought off for any but the full price, which they had never named. (VL 383)

In this passage, which might be read as a rewriting of the one from Emerson that Jess recites annually (VL 369), Pynchon transforms Emerson's declarative belief in an ultimate justice into a question. It is only within this question that Eros—the principle counter to Thanatos—is evoked in the book for the first time, which is why Rushdie could speak of a "faint possibility of redemption." Whereas Thanatos separates—a negativity perfectly captured in the world of the Thanatoids—Eros denotes "the universal presence of a power binding subjects together" (*Seminar I* 112), and whereas Thanatos negates, "affirmation . . . belongs to Eros" (295). The relation between Eros and Thanatos is that "between love and hate" (180). As in *The Night of the Hunter*, however, "the tendency to union—Eros tends to unite—is only ever apprehended in its relation to the contrary tendency" (*Seminar II* 79), which is why Eros is also "the presentification of lack"

(*Séminaire XVII* 87) and can be read only in complicity with its opposite. In *Gravity's Rainbow,* the rocket "binds" these two forces. In its launching, "Eros and Thanatos, the act of love and the act of death, [are] finally and colossally made one" (Fowler, *Reader's Guide* 58).²⁷

It is this economy of love and hate that is questioned in the passage, its very form as a question introducing the third fundamental passion, ignorance. In his *Seminar I* Lacan gives a figure of this structure, which can serve as a figure of the fictional universe of *Vineland,* as well as Pynchon's other novels. It is a six-sided diamond, a crystal that symbolizes "human space."

◇

In it, the "surface of the real" (*Seminar I* 271) separates (and links, since all of the planes have hinges with the others) the realms of *being* and *nothingness, life* and *death*. On the upper pyramid, the three realms of the symbolic, the imaginary, and the real are aligned in a complex/complicit triadic structure that defines human reality in three directions: "at the junction of the imaginary and the real . . . [there is] hate" (271). The imaginary and violent scenarios of Pynchon's novels—in *Vineland,* the sadomasochistic setup, but also the revolution presided over by the "pleasure principle"—are inscribed into this plane. "At the junction of the symbolic and the imaginary . . . [there is] love" (271), the possibility of which occasionally flashes through the relationship between DL and Takeshi, which evokes "an ethics of *justice* as resistance against socio-political mastery *and* an ethics of *love* as resistance against the perverse mastery of . . . endless, wild desire" (Lipowatz, *Verleugnung* 233). Finally, "at the junction of the real and the symbolic . . . [there is] ignorance" (*Seminar I* 271). This is the plane on which writing is inscribed, the "stupid" medium that makes the passage from *real* to *reality* possible in the first place, "because words, symbols, introduce a hollow, a hole, thanks to which all manner of crossings are possible" (271), but which is also the medium that opens up the gap between being and thinking—the real and the signifier—in the first place and defines the object *o* as a sublime object. Brown also comments on this double definition: "*Animal symbolicum* is the animal which has lost its world and life, and which preserves in its symbol systems a map of the lost reality, guiding the search to recover it" (167). Pynchon's work shows the subject's incessant detour through the textual space of this map. However, whereas Brown and Wilden still believe in the possibility of a return, Pynchon evokes the frightening scenario of the "primal experience—a child away from home too late at night" (LeClair 57).

The twofold structure of language as both promise and denial presides over the endings of all Pynchon's novels: Stencil in his metonymic flight to Stockholm, following "the frayed end of another clue" (*V.* 452); Profane and Brenda being carried by sheer momentum "toward the edge of Malta, and the Mediterranean beyond" (*V.* 455); Oedipa in her continued search through symbolic space; Slothrop, for whom "it may be too late to get home" (GR 744); and finally, first Zoyd and then Desmond, "wagging his tail, thinking he must be home" (VL 385)—all are described as subjects who are, in both real and symbolic space, forever "almost home."

Notes

1. Since the publication of *Critique* 32, no. 2 (1990), which is dedicated to *Vineland*, the evaluation has not changed significantly. David Cowart's "Attenuated Postmodernism: Pynchon's *Vineland*" sees *Vineland* as indebted "less to indeterminate postmodernist 'play' than to totalizing modernist 'purpose'" (68). N. Katherine Hayles, in "'Who Was Saved?' Families, Snitches, and Recuperation in Pynchon's *Vineland*," states that *Vineland* is "innocuously sentimental but has an ironic undertow" (77). Edward Mendelson, in "Levity's Rainbow," comes closest to my reading when he states that "*Vineland* adopts the nostalgic wish of its early chapters precisely in order to expose the delusion and fantasy of those wishes later" (44).

2. In fact, the passages are almost identical: "The magic in these Masonic rituals is very, very old. And way back in those days, it *worked*. As time went on, and it started being used for spectacle, to consolidate what were only secular appearances of power, it began to lose its zip. But the words, moves, and machinery have been more or less faithfully carried down over the millennia, through the grim rationalizing of the World, and so the magic is still there, though latent, needing only to touch the right sensitive head to reassert itself" (GR 685).

3. In this context, see also Weissmann's Tarot in *Gravity's Rainbow*: "What will come: The World" (GR 747).

4. In this context, the "ad hoc arrangements" of the Counterforce in *Gravity's Rainbow* in its fight against this simulatory system, in which it stakes *jouissance* against the law, are evoked through the name of the revolutionary group, "All Damned Heat Off Campus, or ADHOC" (VL 208).

5. Interestingly, this shift is paralleled in Pynchon criticism. See especially the recent re-politicization of Pynchon in Madsen and in Paul Maltby. Madsen argues that, although the subject is "a product of cultural discourses" (37) and "cultural

ideology" (44), Pynchon's allegories allow one "to see the strategies of cultural repression" (59) and "reveal the operations of absolutist ideologies" (114). Especially, "an openness to belief structures other than those of cultural orthodoxy, saves the self from the tyranny of the socially determined signifier" (70). This—maybe somewhat optimistic—idea that an escape from the social (and, perhaps even more problematical, from the signifier) is possible is also advocated by Maltby in his treatment of Pynchon as an "adversarial" (11) postmodernist. For Maltby, "Pynchon's anti-quest formally signifies the impossibility of enlightened or intellectual growth in a culture characterized by a deficit of meaning" (136). As in Madsen, the escape is into unorthodoxy, here especially anti-eurocentrism, anarchism, naturism, and the clown-freak mentality. For Madsen as well as for Maltby "Pynchon's mode of writing, in stressing ambiguity and uncertainty, 'liberates' the signifier" (Madsen 146).

6. "It seems to me that power must be understood in the first instance as the multiplicity of force relations immanent in the sphere in which they operate and which constitute their own organization; as the process which, through ceaseless struggles and confrontations, transforms, strengthens, or reverses them" (Foucault, *The History of Sexuality, vol. 1* 92). Most generally, power is the name given to a complex strategic situation in a society.

7. In this respect see also Maltby's discussion of Virilio's concept of endocolonization, which shares many aspects of Foucault's theory of power: "the 'pacification' and total administration of one's own population by means of intensive military-policing" (Maltby 176).

8. Although Lacan calls this discourse the "discourse of the university," I will, for reasons of clarity, refer to it as the "discourse of knowledge."

9. This "signifier One is not just any signifier. It is the signifying order" (Lacan, *Encore* 131). As such, this "master-signifier is what ensures the unity of the *copulation* of the subject with knowledge" (130; emphasis added).

10. In that the object *o* cannot provide the fulfillment of desire, it comes to symbolize the inevitable "rest" of and in desire. As this rest-object, it delineates the margin between desire and *jouissance:* "the object *o* can be enunciated as 'plus-de-jouir' [surplus-*jouissance*], but it is not 'object of jouissance'" (Juranville 227). See also Ragland-Sullivan, who sees the *plus-de-jouir*—which she gives as "Desire cum lack" (*Philosophy of Psychoanalysis* 226)—as the concept in which "*jouissance* and Desire meet" (271). In this context, compare also the phenomenon of the "rest" in my discussion of the Kirghiz Light passage in chapter 6.

11. Lacan uses Hegel's "master-slave conflict" to describe this aspect of the discourse of the master: "Indeed, beginning with the mythical situation, an action is undertaken, and establishes the relation between pleasure [*jouissance*] and labour. A law is imposed upon the slave, that he should satisfy the desire and the pleasure [*jouissance*] of the other" (*Seminar I* 223). The term thus links the fields of

work, *desire*, and *knowledge*, because, like every material object that is produced, knowledge is an object of desire rather than necessity.

12. "*Jouissance* comes easily to the slave, and it will leave the work in bondage" (Lacan, *Écrits* 308).

13. In this respect see also Lacan's matheme of the discourse of the capitalist:

$$\frac{\$_1 \rightarrow S_2}{S_1 \leftarrow a}$$

(from *Lacan in Italia*; quoted in Widmer 144). In this discourse the object o is—as in the discourse of the master—in the position of production. The positions of S_1 and $, however, are reversed.

14. Authority differs from power in that it is related to what a person says, whereas what is generally called power—especially political power—has more to do with who is in a position to speak. Whereas power uses a dead, imaginary, unambiguous, empty, and fetishized language that kills desire, authority uses a symbolic language that produces differences and ambiguity. And whereas power is grounded in a law, authority is based in a subject.

15. Foucault sees sex as a means "to compensate for the passing away of living beings and to provide the species as a whole with the eternity that could not be given to each individual. . . . For Aristotle and Plato alike, the sexual act was at the point of junction of an individual life that was bound to perish—and from which, moreover, it drew off a portion of its most precious resources—and an immortality that assumed the concrete form of a survival of the species" (Foucault, *Sexuality and Truth*, 2: 133–34).

16. Apart from the obvious reference to drugs, see also Fahringer in *Gravity's Rainbow*: "*Atmen* . . . *atman* . . . not only to breathe, but also the soul, the breath of God . . ." (GR 454).

17. One thing that *Vineland* shows, in fact, is how important the ghost motif has been throughout Pynchon's work. In *Lot 49*, Oedipa looks for the ghosts of Pierce and Driblette, and *Gravity's Rainbow* is populated by a whole array of people from "the other side." More importantly, its main metaphor, the rocket, is itself "a ghost in the sky" (GR 48).

18. See also his introduction to *A Reader's Guide to "Gravity's Rainbow,"* as well as Marc W. Redfield, "Pynchon's Postmodern Sublime."

19. Because within simulation the real has been replaced by the imaginary, in a simulatory framework there must be a "synthetic sublime," which is formed according to the culture from which it emerges, the "sublime (object) of ideology." The culture simulates sublime moments that are accepted as natural, such as the sublimity of technology or the sublimity of capitalism, in both of which fear is foreclosed together with the real. Through the closure of representational space the space of psychosis is opened up, which is directed toward exactly the foreclo-

sure of the lack within the signifier and the resulting foreclosure of "fear." The end point of this development is the total (and thus totalitarian) fantasy in which reality closes in on itself. The program is "to exist in a world totally fabricated by man, i.e. to live *inside* fantasy" (Koolhaas 6). This seems to promise the fulfillment of desire through the "annihilation" of the real.

20. See Terry P. Caesar, "'Beasts Vaulting among The Earthworks': Monstrosity in *Gravity's Rainbow.*'"

21. For Lyotard, it is ultimately a question of form that decides between the two aspects. A truly postmodern work would deny itself "the solace of good forms" (Lyotard 81).

22. See also Bianca's dream in *Gravity's Rainbow:* "She dreams often of the same journey: a passage by train, between two well-known cities [. . .] dictating her story. She feels able at last to tell of a personal horror, tell it clearly in a way others can share" (GR 471).

23. Consider the following: "In a corporate State, a place must be made for innocence, and its many *uses*. In developing an *official version of innocence*, the culture of childhood has proven invaluable" (GR 419; emphases added).

24. Compare Lacan during "Impromptu at Vincennes": "the aspiration to revolution has but one conceivable issue, always, the discourse of the master. That is what experience has proved. What you, as revolutionaries, aspire to is a Master. You will have one!" (*Television* 126).

25. Note also the relation between "to enjoy" (*jouir*) and "to play" (*jouer*).

26. See also Kristeva, who aligns *jouissance* with revolution, relating *jouissance*, however—unlike the revolutionaries in *Vineland*—inextricably to the law of the signifier and the phallic symbolic: "the semiotization of the the symbolic . . . represents the flow of jouissance into language" (*Revolution* 79).

27. It would be inviting, in fact, to read the parabola of the rocket's flight in the light of Lacan's reading of Freud's "drive," especially in its conjunction of sex (*jouissance*) with death. Lacan, who describes the movement of the drive as a "movement outwards and back" (*Fundamental Concepts* 177), in fact seems to follow Freud—who actually uses technical terms such as "thrust" (*Schub*) to designate the parabolic path of the drive—when he describes it in directly ballistic terms: "the loop turns around itself, it is a missile" (182).

Conclusion: Writing the Real

In all his works, Pynchon proceeds from the idea of a completely textualized universe, in which the position of the subject directly depends on its position within discursive networks. As a result, the relation between language and subjectivity is essential to any interpretation of Pynchon's work. Lacan's psychoanalytic theory and his theory of language provide a basis for such an interpretation.

Rather than giving a straightforward presentation of a Lacanian subject, however, Pynchon presents the reader with a subject that is suspended between the two rhetorical extremes of *naturality* and *simulation*.

This procedure accounts for Pynchon's deconstructive readings of psychoanalysis. According to the different rhetorical perspectives, for instance, femininity on the one hand is the privileged site of machinizations, whereas on the other it denotes the promise of naturality. Both the completely simulated and the natural scenes are fictions between which the fundamentally split subject is constantly oscillating and in which, as de Man states, "the very pathos of the desire (regardless of whether it is valorized positively or negatively) indicates that the presence of desire replaces the absence of identity" (*Allegories* 198).

In Pynchon, therefore, the terms *naturality, identity,* and *self-presence* have to be read as operative within a deconstruction of this logocentric scene. In an "eternally repeated pattern of regression," the deconstruction of "a system of relationships always reveals a more fragmented stage that can be called natural with regard to the system that is being undone" (*Allegories* 249). De Man's contention that "the entire assumption of a nonverbal realm governed by needs may well be a speculative hypothesis that exists only . . . *for the sake of* language" (210) certainly applies to Pynchon's work.

The subject is defined within the interplay of these positions. Because of their rhetorical and therefore *open* structure, the three references of Lacan, Derrida, and Baudrillard constantly both complement and deconstruct one another, a fact that any reading should take into account. Together, they compose the kaleidoscopic space in which the subject's forever missed encounters with the real are staged. Within the thematic structure of Pynchon's works, each of the references can be assigned a specific field. Whereas the Lacanian reference has a specifically ontological character, focusing on the subject's relation to death and desire, the Derridean one deals predominantly with epistemological questions and is defined within a textual register. The Baudrillardian reference, finally, deals predominantly with sociopolitical and sociocultural questions.

Ultimately, these references converge on the question of the text itself and account for the motif of textual autodestruction that operates in Pynchon's work on almost every level. It can be followed in the constant movements of language toward the borders of the symbolic. Everywhere in Pynchon, the text voices its "desire" to terminate itself.

The idea of the center focuses on this desire and refers to the differentiation between Lacanian concentricity and Derridean dissemination. In the dynamics of the center the forces of centralization and centrifugality are balanced. In *Gravity's Rainbow*, therefore, whereas "Holy-Center-Approaching is soon to be the number one Zonal pastime" (GR 508), simultaneously, "separations are proceeding. Each alternative Zone speed[ing] away from all the others, in fated acceleration, red-shifting, fleeing the Center. [. . .] The single root lost" (GR 519). This twofold movement marks the center as a fundamentally equivocal term, an impossible perspective point of discursive space, comparable to the real, which is similarly "impossible." The Zone—as the space in which human reality unfolds—and The Center both define and exclude each other. Pynchon deliberately connects these dynamics to the motif of writing, in which a similar twofold dynamics is at work. During a meeting with Slothrop, Squalidozzi states that although "in the days of the gauchos, my country was a blank piece of paper [. . . we] cannot abide that *openness* [. . .] that anarchic oneness of pampas and sky . . ." (GR 264). Pynchon employs metaphors of the writing process to express the inevitability of cultural inscriptions and portrays the human scene as one of obsessive writing in which emptiness—or in literary terms, silence—cannot be endured: "We are obsessed with building labyrinths [. . . .] To draw ever more complex patterns on the blank sheet" (GR 264).

Pynchon continually highlights the problematic relation of writing to questions of subjectivity. Certainly in *Vineland*, but also already, if less conspicuously, in *Gravity's Rainbow*, this relation is connected to children and their world of "mindless pleasures" (GR 270)—a perfect definition of "real *jouissance*"—which evoke Brown's utopia of a regained childhood: "Our repressed desires are the desires we had, unrepressed, in childhood; and they are sexual desires" (23). Brown believes that, although "the history of childhood is the history of an organism caught in an ever widening sequence of dualisms" (116), it is possible to regress toward this childhood and its innocent, polymorphously perverse play through a return to the body. In fact, he sees art as one route back: "art as pleasure, art as play, art as the recovery of childhood" (65). Pynchon, however, shows the dangers these innocent children are in and the way in which art and language are always co-opted and guilty. Pointsman, for instance, with his purely operational language—"a language without a libidinal (erotic) component" (Brown 71)—is obsessed with children on whom he can "operate": "new children, painless, egoless for one pulse of the Between . . . tablet erased, new writing about to begin, hand and chalk poised in winter gloom over these poor human palimpsests shivering under their government blankets, drugged, drowning in tears and snot of grief so real, torn from so deep that it surprises, seems more than their own . . ." (GR 50).

Pointsman dreams of inscribing sterile litanies of cultural conditioning and simulation directly on the surface of the childrens' bodies, in an image that again inextricably links the motifs of writing and the body: "How Pointsman lusts after them, pretty children. Those drab undershorts of his are full to bursting with need humorlessly, worldly to use their innocence, to write on them new words of himself [. . .] how seductively they lie ranked in their iron bedsteads, their virginal sheets, the darlings so artlessly erotic . . ." (GR 50).

In the double reference to bedsheets and sheets of paper, the passage assembles the motifs of simulation, sexuality, power, control, and writing. The children stand for the timeless moment of egolessness; Pointsman, for the simulations of cultural power he projects and writes onto their bodies. Although his aggression has its roots in a sexual register, it is a perverse one that turns the children into fetishes.

Pynchon describes these inscriptions—the birth of the textual subject—less within the framework of a Derridean "free-play" than as a site on which a constant battle is fought over the body and the mind of the subject, providing an archaeological historiography of this site similar to Foucault's. As the subject becomes a palimpsest, history becomes a table of representation. Slothrop's desk, from which my study departed, is a perfect image of the "rhetorical chaos" of this space.

Seen in this way, Pynchon's writing becomes a truly literary deconstruction of the notion of selfhood within a project sketched out by de Man: "Within the epistemological labyrinth of figural structures, the recuperation of selfhood would be accomplished by the rigor with which the discourse deconstructs the very notion of the self" (*Allegories* 173). On a purely poetological level, this is also a deconstruction of the text: *the recuperation of writing would be accomplished by the rigor with which the discourse deconstructs the very notion of writing.*

One of the chief strategies Pynchon uses for these mutual deconstructions is the constant undercutting of the text's statements through an ironization that creates a kaleidoscopic discursive space and that, according to de Man, is the "systematic undoing . . . of understanding" (*Allegories* 301). It is a final, tragic irony that the space of cultural inscription is also the space in which art and writing unfold. The innocent children are "artlessly erotic." Pynchon's poetics is perhaps best described by the ambiguous valorization of art that this image contains.

Works Cited

Abernethy, Peter. "Entropy in Pynchon's *The Crying of Lot 49*." *Critique* 14.2 (1972): 18–33.

Adams, Henry. *The Education of Henry Adams: An Autobiography*. Cambridge, Mass.: Riverside, 1961.

Adams, Michael V. "The Benzene Uroboros: Plastic and Catastrophe in *Gravity's Rainbow*." In James Hillman, ed., *Spring 1981: An Annual of Archetypal Psychology and Jungian Thought*, 149–61. Dallas: Spring, 1981.

Adorno, Theodor, and Max Horkheimer. *Dialectic of Enlightenment*. Trans. J. Cumming. London: Verso, 1979; *Dialektik der Aufklärung*. Frankfurt am Main: Fischer, 1969.

Baader, Gerhard. "Das Leben Iwan Petrowitch Pawlows" [The Life of Ivan Petrovitch Pavlov]. In Pawlow, *Iwan Petrovitch Pawlow: Die bedingten Reflexe*. München: Kindler, 1972.

Bakhtin, Mikhail. *The Dialogic Imagination*. Trans. C. Emerson and M. Holquist. Austin: University of Texas Press, 1981.

Barthes, Roland. "The Death of the Author." In *Image, Music, Text*, 142–48. Trans. S. Heath. New York: Hill & Wang, 1977.

———. "Objective Literature: Alain Robbe-Grillet." In *Two Novels by Robbe-Grillet: "Jealousy" and "In the Labyrinth,"* 11–25. Trans. R. Howard. New York: Grove, 1965.

———. *The Pleasure of the Text*. Trans. R. Miller. New York: Hill & Wang, 1975; *Le Plaisir du texte*. Paris: Seuil, 1973.

———. *The Responsibility of Forms*. Trans. R. Howard. New York: Hill & Wang, 1985; *L'Obvie et l'obtuse*. Paris: Seuil, 1982.

———. *S/Z*. Trans. R. Miller. New York: Hill & Wang, 1974; *S/Z*. Paris: Seuil, 1970.

Baudrillard, Jean. *For a Critique of the Political Economy of the Sign*. Trans. C. Levin. St. Louis: Telos, 1981; *Pour une critique de l'economie politique du signe*. Paris: Gallimard, 1972.

———. *L'Échange symbolique et la mort*. Paris: Gallimard, 1976.

———. *The Ecstasy of Communication*. Trans. B. Schutze and C. Schutze. New York: Semiotext(e), 1988; *L'autre par lui-même*. Paris: Galilée, 1987.

———. *The Evil Demon of Images*. Trans. P. Patton and P. Foss. Sydney: Power Institute, 1987.
———. *Fatal Strategies*. Trans. P. Beichtman and W. G. J. Niesluchowski. New York: Semiotext(e), 1990; *Les Stratégies fatales*. Paris: Grasset et Fasquelle, 1983.
———. *Forget Foucault*. Trans. P. Beichtman, L. Hildreth, and M. Polizzotti. New York: Semiotext(e), 1987; *Oublier Foucault*. Paris: Galilée, 1977.
———. *In the Shadow of the Silent Majorities*. Trans. P. Foss, P. Patton, and J. Johnston. New York: Semiotext(e), 1983.
———. *Simulations*. Trans. P. Foss, P. Patton, and P. Beichtman. New York: Semiotext(e), 1983.
Bell, Daniel. *The Coming of Post-Industrial Society*. New York: Basic, 1973.
Benjamin, Walter. "The Work of Art in the Age of Mechanical Reproduction," *Illuminations: Essays and Reflections*, 217–51. Trans. H. Zahn. New York: Schocken, 1968; *Gesammelte Schriften, Band 1.2*, 431–508. Ed. R. Tiedemann and H. Scheppenhäuser. Frankfurt am Main: Suhrkamp, 1974.
Bergson, Henri. *An Introduction to Metaphysics*. Trans T. E. Hulme. New York: Knickerbocker Press, 1912.
———. *Matter and Memory*. Trans. N. M. Paul and W. S. Palmer. New York: Zone, 1991.
———. *La Pensée et le mouvant*. Paris: Quadriga, 1990.
Berressem, Hanjo. "Digging for the Truth: Archaeology and the End of History." In E. Lehmann and E. Reckwitz, eds., *Crisis and Conflict: Essays on Southern African Literature*, 117–31. Essen: Die Blaue Eule, 1990.
———. "Even Signs Must Burn: Jean Baudrillard and the Reemergence of the Object." *Subjects/Objects* 4 (1986): 72–84.
———. "Godolphin, Goodolphin, Goodol'phin, Goodol'Pyn, Good ol' Pym: A Question of Integration." *Pynchon Notes* 10 (1982): 3–17.
———. "A Short Note on Pynchon's Sources for 'The Firm.'" *Pynchon Notes* 15 (1984): 77–79.
Bersani, Leo. "Pynchon, Paranoia, and Literature." *Representations* 25 (1989): 99–118.
Bloom, Harold, ed. *Thomas Pynchon*. New York: Chelsea House, 1986.
Brown, Norman O. *Life against Death: The Psychoanalytical Meaning of History*. Middletown: Wesleyan University Press, 1959.
Burde, Wolfgang. *Strawinsky*. Mainz: Goldmann, 1982.
Burgin, Victor. *The End of Art Theory*. Atlantic Highlands, N.J.: Humanities Press International, 1986.
Burke, Edmund. *A Philosophical Enquiry into the Origin of our Ideal of the Sublime and Beautiful*. London: Routledge and Kegan Paul, 1958.
Burroughs, William S. *The Job*. New York: Grove Press, 1970.
———. *Naked Lunch*. New York: Grove Press, 1959.
———. *Nova Express*. New York: Grove Press, 1964.

Burroughs, William S., and Brion Gysin. *The Third Mind*. New York: Viking, 1978.
Caesar, Terry P. "'Beasts Vaulting among the Earthworks': Monstrosity in *Gravity's Rainbow*." *Novel* 17.2: 158–70.
Clerc, Charles, ed. *Approaches to "Gravity's Rainbow."* Columbus: Ohio State University Press, 1983.
———. "Introduction." In Charles Clerk, ed., *Approaches to "Gravity's Rainbow,"* 3–30. Columbus: Ohio State University Press, 1983.
———. "Film in *Gravity's Rainbow*." In Charles Clerk, ed., *Approaches to "Gravity's Rainbow,"* 103–51. Columbus: Ohio State University Press, 1983.
Cooper, Peter. *Signs and Symptoms: Thomas Pynchon and the Contemporary World*. Berkeley: University of California Press, 1983.
Cowart, David. "Attenuated Postmodernism: Pynchon's *Vineland*." *Critique: Studies in Contemporary Fiction* 32.2 (1990): 67–76.
———. "Cinematic Auguries of the Third Reich in *Gravity's Rainbow*." *Literature/Film Quarterly* 6.4 (1978): 364–70.
———. *Thomas Pynchon: The Art of Allusion*. Carbondale: Southern Illinois University Press, 1980.
Culler, Jonathan. *On Deconstruction: Theory and Criticism after Structuralism*. Ithaca: Cornell University Press, 1982.
Debord, Guy. *Society of the Spectacle*. Exeter: Rebel, 1987; *La Societé du spectacle*. Paris: Buchet-Chastel, 1967.
Deleuze, Gilles. *Cinema 1: The Movement-Image*. Trans. H. Tomlinson and B. Habberjam. Minneapolis: University of Minnesota Press, 1986; *Cinéma 1: L'Image-Mouvement*. Paris: Minuit, 1983.
———. *Cinema 2: The Time Image*. Trans. H. Tomlinson and R. Galeta. Minneapolis: University of Minnesota Press, 1989; *Cinéma 2: L'image-temps*. Paris: Minuit, 1985.
Deleuze, Gilles, and Felix Guattari. *Anti-Oedipus: Capitalism and Schizophrenia*. Trans. R. Hurley, M. Seem, and H. R. Lane. Minneapolis: University of Minnesota Press, 1983; *L'Anti-Oedipe*. Paris: Minuit, 1972.
———. *A Thousand Plateaus: Capitalism and Schizophrenia*. Trans. B. Massumi. Minneapolis: University of Minnesota Press, 1987; *Mille Plateaux*. Paris: Minuit, 1980.
De Man, Paul. *Allegories of Reading: Figural Language in Rousseau, Nietzsche, Rilke, and Proust*. New Haven: Yale University Press, 1979.
———. *Blindness and Insight: Essays in the Rhetoric of Contemporary Criticism*. Minneapolis: University of Minnesota Press, 1983.
Derrida, Jacques. *Chôra*. Paris: EHESS, 1987. 265–96.
———. "Deconstruction and the Possibility of Justice." *The Cardozo Law Review* 11.5–6 (1990).
———. *Dissemination*. Trans. B. Johnson. Chicago: University of Chicago Press, 1981; *La Dissémination*. Paris: Seuil, 1972.

———. *Of Grammatology*. Trans. G. C. Spivak. Baltimore: Johns Hopkins University Press, 1976; *De la Grammatologie*. Paris: Minuit, 1967.

———. "Letter to a Japanese Friend." In D. Wood and R. Bernasconi, eds., *Derrida and Différance*, 1–8. Warwick: Parousia, 1985.

———. *Margins of Philosophy*. Trans. A. Bass. Brighton: Harvester, 1986; *Marges de la philosophie*. Paris: Minuit, 1972.

———. "No Apocalypse, Not Now: Full Speed Ahead, Seven Missiles, Seven Missives." *Diacritics* 14.2 (1984): 20–31.

———. *The Post Card: From Socrates to Freud and Beyond*. Trans. A. Bass. Chicago: University of Chicago Press, 1987; *La Carte postale: De Socrate à Freud et au-delà*. Paris: Flammarion, 1980.

———. "Pour l'amour de Lacan," *Lacan avec les philosophes*, 397–420. Paris: Albin Michel, 1991.

———. *La Voix et le phénomène*. Paris: Presses Universitaires de France, 1967.

———. *Writing and Difference*. Trans. A. Bass. Chicago: University of Chicago Press, 1978; *L'Écriture et la différence*. Paris: Seuil, 1976.

Earl, James. "Freedom and Knowledge in the Zone." In Charles Clerk, ed., *Approaches to "Gravity's Rainbow,"* 229–50. Columbus: Ohio State University Press, 1983.

Eco, Umberto. *Einführung in die Semiotik [An Introduction to Semiotics]*. München: W. Fink, 1972.

———. *The Open Work*. Trans. A. Cancogni. London: Hutchinson Radius, 1989.

———. *The Role of the Reader*. Bloomington: Indiana University Press, 1984.

Eddins, Dwight. *The Gnostic Pynchon*. Bloomington: Indiana University Press, 1990.

Edwards, Brian. "Mixing Media: Film as Metaphor in Pynchon's *Gravity's Rainbow*." *Australian Journal of American Studies* 1.3 (1982): 1–15.

Fisher, David H. "Introduction: Framing Lacan." In Edith Wyschogrod, David Crownfield, and Carl A. Raschke, eds., *Lacan and Theological Discourse*. Albany: SUNY Press, 1989.

Foucault, Michel. *The Archaeology of Knowledge*. Trans. A. M. Sheridan Smith. New York: Random House, 1972; *L'Archéologie du savoir*. Paris: Gallimard, 1969.

———. *Discipline and Punish: The Birth of the Prison*. Trans. A. Sheridan. New York: Random House, 1979; *Surveiller et Punir; Naissance de la prison*. Paris: Gallimard, 1975.

———. *The History of Sexuality, vol. 1: An Introduction*. Trans. R. Hurley. New York: Vintage/Random House, 1978; *Histoire de la sexualité, 1: La Volonté de savoir*. Paris: Gallimard, 1976.

———. *The History of Sexuality, vol. 2: The Uses of Pleasure*. Trans. R. Hurley. New York: Vintage Books/Random House, 1985; *Histoire de la sexualité, 2: L'Usage des plaisirs*. Paris: Gallimard, 1984.

———. *The Order of Things: An Archaeology of the Human Sciences.* New York: Vintage Books, 1970; *Les Mots et les choses.* Paris: Gallimard, 1966.

———. "Preface." In Deleuze and Guattari, *Anti-Oedipus: Capitalism and Schizophrenia,* xi–xxiv. Trans. R. Hurley, M. Seem, and H. R. Lane. Minneapolis: University of Minnesota Press, 1983.

———. "What Is an Author?" *Textual Strategies,* 141–60. Ed. and trans. Josué V. Harari. London: Methuen, 1979.

Fowler, Douglas. "Pynchon's Magic World." *South Atlantic Quarterly* 79.1 (1980): 51–60.

———. *A Reader's Guide to Pynchon's "Gravity's Rainbow."* Ann Arbor: Ardis, 1980.

Freud, Sigmund. *The Standard Edition of the Complete Psychological Works.* 24 vols. Ed. and trans. James Strachey. London: Hogarth, 1953–74; *Studienausgabe.* Ed. M. Mitscherlich, A. Richards, and J. Strachey. Frankfurt am Main: Fischer, 1969.

Gondek, Hans-Dieter. *Angst, Einbildungskraft, Sprache* [*Fear, Imagination, Language*]: *Kant, Freud, Lacan.* Munich: Boer, 1990.

Grace, Sherrill E. "Fritz Lang and the 'Paracinematic Lives' of *Gravity's Rainbow.*" *Modern Fiction Studies* 29.4 (1983): 655–70.

Graff, Gerald. *Literature against Itself: Literary Ideas in Modern Society.* Chicago: University of Chicago Press, 1979.

Granon-Lafont, Jeanne. *La Topologie Ordinaire de Jacques Lacan.* Paris: Point Hors Lignes, 1985.

Grosz, Elizabeth. *Jacques Lacan: A Feminist Introduction.* London: Routledge, 1990.

Guattari, Felix. *Molecular Revolution.* Trans. R. Sheed. Harmondsworth: Penguin Books, 1984. Compiled from *Psychanalyse et traversalité* (Paris: Maspero, 1972) and *La Révolution moléculaire* (Paris: Recherches, Séries "Encre," 1977).

Hayles, N. Katherine. "'Who Was Saved?' Families, Snitches, and Recuperation in Pynchon's *Vineland.*" *Critique* 32.2 (1990): 77–92.

Hite, Molly. *Ideas of Order in the Novels of Thomas Pynchon.* Columbus: Ohio State University Press, 1983.

———. "Review of Cooper, Peter L., 'Signs and Symptoms.'" *SubStance* 44/45 (1985): 32–34.

Hogan, Patrick Colm. "Introduction: The Repression of Lacan." In Patrick Colm Hogan and Lalita Pandit, eds., *Criticism and Lacan: Essays and Dialogue on Language, Structure, and the Unconscious.* Athens: University of Georgia Press, 1990.

Hohmann, Charles. *Thomas Pynchon's "Gravity's Rainbow": A Study of Its Conceptual Structure and of Rilke's Influence.* New York: Peter Lang, 1986.

Hume, Kathryn. *Pynchon's Mythography: An Approach to "Gravity's Rainbow."* Carbondale: Southern Illinois University Press, 1987.

Jameson, Fredric. "Imaginary and Symbolic in Lacan: Marxism, Psychoanalytic Criticism, and the Problem of the Subject." In Shoshana Felman, ed., *Literature*

and Psychoanalysis, 338–95. Baltimore: Johns Hopkins University Press, 1982.
Juranville, Alain. *Lacan et la philosophie.* Paris: Presses Universitaires de France, 1984.
Kellner, Douglas. *Jean Baudrillard: From Marxism to Postmodernism and Beyond.* Cambridge: Polity Press, 1989.
Kermode, Frank. "That Was Another Planet." Review of *Vineland. London Review of Books* 12 (8 Feb. 1990).
Kittler, Friedrich. "Medien und Drogen in Pynchons Zweitem Weltkrieg" [Media and Drugs in Pynchon's World War II] In D. Kamper D. and W. van Reijen, eds., *Die unvollendete Vernunft: Moderne versus Postmoderne [Unfinished Reason: Modernity versus Postmodernity],* 240–59. Frankfurt am Main: Suhrkamp, 1987.
Klinkowitz, Jerome. *Literary Subversions: New American Fiction and the Practice of Criticism.* Carbondale: Southern Illinois University Press, 1985.
———. *The Self-Apparent Word: Fiction as Language/Language as Fiction.* Carbondale: Southern Illinois University Press, 1984.
Koning, Christina. "Vineland the Good." Review of *Vineland. Guardian Weekly* (18 Feb. 1990).
Koolhaas, Rem. *Delirious New York: A Retroactive Manifesto for Manhattan.* London: Thames and Hudson, 1978.
Kracauer, Siegfried. *From Caligari to Hitler.* Princeton: Princeton University Press, 1947.
Kristeva, Julia. *Revolution in Poetic Language.* Trans. M. Waller. New York: Columbia University Press, 1984; *La Révolution du langage poétique.* Paris: Seuil, 1974.
Kroker, Arthur, and David Cook, eds. *The Postmodern Scene: Excremental Culture and Hyper-Aesthetics.* New York: St. Martin's Press, 1986.
Lacan, Jacques. "Desire and the Interpretation of Desire in Hamlet." Trans. J. Hulbert. In Shoshana Felman, ed., *Literature and Psychoanalysis: The Question of Reading: Otherwise.* Baltimore: Johns Hopkins University Press, 1982.
———. *Écrits.* Paris: Seuil, 1966.
———. *Écrits: A Selection.* Trans. A. Sheridan. New York: Norton, 1977.
———. *Encore: Le séminaire livre XX: Encore.* Paris: Seuil, 1975.
———. "Radiophonie." *Scilicet* 2/3 (1970): 55–99.
———. *The Four Fundamental Concepts of Psycho-Analysis.* Trans. A. Sheridan. New York: Norton, 1978; *Le Séminaire livre XI: Les quatre concepts fondamentaux de la psychanalyse.* Paris: Seuil, 1973.
———. "Intervention on Transference." Trans. J. Rose. In Juliet Mitchell and Jacqueline Rose, eds., *Feminine Sexuality.* New York: Norton, 1985.
———. *Schriften* II [*Writings*]. Excerpts from *Écrits.* Trans. N. Haas, F. Kaltenbeck, F. A. Kittler, H-J. Metzger, M. Metzger, and U. Rütt-Förster. Olten: Walter Verlag, 1980.
———. *Le Séminaire livre VII: L'Éthique de la psychanalyse.* Paris: Seuil, 1986.
———. *Le Séminaire livre XVII: L'Envers de la psychanalyse.* Paris: Seuil, 1991.

———. *The Seminar of Jacques Lacan Book I: Freud's Papers on Technique 1953–54*. Trans. J. Forrester. Cambridge: Cambridge University Press, 1988; *Le Séminaire livre I: Les Écrits techniques de Freud*. Paris: Seuil, 1975.

———. *The Seminar of Jacques Lacan Book II: The Ego in Freud's Theory and in the Technique of Psycho-analysis 1954–55*. Trans. S. Tomaselli. Cambridge: Cambridge University Press, 1988; *Le Séminaire livre II: Le Moi dans la théorie de Freud et dans la technique de la psychanalyse*. Paris: Seuil, 1978.

———. "Seminar on 'The Purloined Letter.'" Trans. J. Mehlman. In John P. Muller and William J. Richardson, eds., *The Purloined Poe: Lacan, Derrida, and Psychoanalytic Reading*, 28–54. Baltimore: Johns Hopkins University Press, 1988.

———. "Le Sinthome: Le Séminaire XXIII," *Ornicar?* 6/7/8 (1976) and 9/10/11 (1977).

———. "Television." *Télévision: A Challenge to the Psychoanalytic Establishment*. Trans. Denis Mollies, Rosalind Krauss, and Annette Michelson. Ed. Joan Copjec. New York: Norton, 1990.

Lang, Hermann. *Die Sprache und das Unbewußte: Jacques Lacans Grundlegung der Psychoanalyse* [*Language and the Unconscious: Jacques Lacan's Foundation of Psychoanalysis*]. Frankfurt am Main: Suhrkamp, 1986.

Larsson, Donald. "The Camera Eye: 'Cinematic' Narrative in *U.S.A.* and *Gravity's Rainbow*." In Peter Ruppert, ed., *Ideas of Order in Literature and Film*, 94–106. Tallahassee: University Press of Florida, 1980.

LeClair, Tom. *The Art of Excess: Mastery in Contemporary American Fiction*. Urbana: University of Illinois Press, 1989.

Leclaire, Serge. *Démasquer le réel: Un Essai sur l'objet en psychanalyse*. Paris: Seuil, 1971.

Leithauser, Brad. "Any Place You Want." Review of *Vineland*. *New York Review of Books* (15 March 1990): 7–10.

Leland, John. P. "Pynchon's Linguistic Demon: *The Crying of Lot 49*." *Critique* 16.2 (1974): 45–53.

Levine, George, and David Leverenz, eds. *Mindful Pleasures: Essays on Thomas Pynchon*. Boston: Little, Brown, 1976.

Lévi-Strauss, Claude. *Tristes Tropiques*. Trans. J. Weightman and D. Weightman. Harmondsworth: Penguin, 1973; *Tristes Tropiques*. Paris: Librairie Plon, 1955.

Lipowatz, Athanasius. *Diskurs und Macht: Jacques Lacans Begriff des Diskurses* [*Discourse and Power: Jacques Lacan's Concept of the Discourse*]. Marburg/Lahn: Guttandin & Hoppe, 1982.

———. *Die Verleugnung des Politischen: Die Ethik des Symbolischen bei Jacques Lacan* [*The Disavowal of the Political: The Ethics of the Symbolic in Jacques Lacan*]. Weinheim and Berlin: Quadriga, 1986.

Lyotard, Jean-François. *The Postmodern Condition: A Report on Knowledge*. Trans. G. Bennington and B. Massumi. Minneapolis: University of Minnesota Press, 1984.

MacCannell, Juliet Flower. *Figuring Lacan: Criticism and the Cultural Unconscious*. Lincoln: University of Nebraska Press, 1986.
McHale, Brian. *Postmodernism*. New York: Methuen, 1987.
———. "'You Used to Know What These Words Mean': Misreading *Gravity's Rainbow*." *Language and Style* 18.1 (1985): 93–118.
McHoul, Alec, and David Wills. *Writing Pynchon*. Urbana: University of Illinois Press, 1989.
McLuhan, Marshall. *The Mechanical Bride*. London: Routledge and Kegan Paul, 1967.
———. *The Medium Is the Massage*. New York: Bantam, 1967.
———. *Understanding Media*. London: Sphere Books, 1964.
Madsen, Deborah L. *The Postmodern Allegories of Thomas Pynchon*. New York: St. Martin's, 1991.
Maltby, Paul. *Dissident Postmodernists: Barthelme, Coover, Pynchon*. Philadelphia: University of Pennsylvania Press, 1991.
Mangel, Anne. "Maxwell's Demon, Entropy, Information: *The Crying of Lot 49*." *TriQuarterly* 20 (1971): 194–208.
Mankiewicz, Herman J., and Orson Welles. *The Citizen Kane Book*. New York: Bantam, 1974.
Marriott, David. "Moviegoing." *Pynchon Notes* 16 (1985): 46–77.
Meikle, Jeffrey, L. "The Culture of Plasticity: Observations on Contemporary Cultural Transformation." *Amerikastudien* 28 (1983): 205–18.
———. "'Other Frequencies': The Parallel Worlds of Thomas Pynchon and H. P. Lovecraft." *Modern Fiction Studies* 27 (1981): 287–94.
Mellard, James M. *Using Lacan, Reading Fiction*. Urbana: University of Illinois Press, 1991.
Mendelson, Edward. "Gravity's Encyclopedia." In G. Levine and D. Leverenz, eds., *Mindful Pleasures: Essays on Thomas Pynchon*, 161–95. Boston: Little, Brown, 1976.
———. "Levity's Rainbow." Review of *Vineland*. *The New Republic* (6 July 1990).
Metz, Christian. *Psychoanalysis and Cinema: The Imaginary Signifier*. Trans. C. Britton, A. Williams, B. Brewster, and A. Guzzetti. London: Macmillan, 1982; *Le Signifiant imaginaire: Psychanalyse et cinéma*. Paris: Union Générale d'Éditions, 1977.
Miller, J. Hillis. "The Critic as Host." *Deconstruction and Criticism*, 217–53. New York: Seabury, 1979.
Miller, Jacques-Alain. "A and *a* in Clinical Structures." In *Acts of the Paris–New York Psychoanalytic Workshop*. New York: Schneidermann, 1986.
Mitchell, Juliet, and Jacqueline Rose, eds. *Feminine Sexuality*. New York: Norton, 1985.
Moore, Thomas. "A Decade of *Gravity's Rainbow*, the Incredible Moving Film." *Michigan Quarterly Review*, 22.1 (1983): 78–94.

Moulthorpe, Stuart. "Strobe's Stimulus." *Pynchon Notes* 24–25 (1989): 71–79.
Muste, John. "The Mandala in *Gravity's Rainbow*." *Boundary* 2 9 (Winter 1981): 163–79.
Olderman, Raymond M. "The New Consciousness and the Old System." In Charles Clerk, ed., *Approaches to Gravity's Rainbow*, 199–228. Columbus: Ohio State University Press, 1983.
Olsen, Lance. "Deconstructing the Enemy of Color: The Fantastic in *Gravity's Rainbow*." *Studies in the Novel* 18.1 (1986): 74–86.
Pasolini, Pier Paolo. "Das Drehbuch als 'Struktur, die eine andere Struktur sein will'" [The Script as a 'Structure That Wants to Be Another Structure']. *Ketzererfahrungen: "Empirismo eretico: Schriften zu Sprache, Literatur und Film."* [*Experience of a Heretic: Writings about Language, Literature and Film*]. Trans. R. Klein. Frankfurt am Main: Hanser, 1979; *Empirismo eretico*. Milan: Garzanti, 1972.
Pearce, Richard, ed. *Critical Essays on Thomas Pynchon*. Boston: Hall, 1981.
Plater, William M. *The Grim Phoenix: Reconstructing Thomas Pynchon*. Bloomington: Indiana University Press, 1978.
Poe, Edgar Allan. "The Narrative of Arthur Gordon Pym." *The Complete Tales and Poems of Edgar Allan Poe*. New York: Modern Library, 1983.
———. "The Murders in the Rue Morgue." *The Complete Tales and Poems of Edgar Allan Poe*. New York: Modern Library, 1983.
———. "The Purloined Letter." *The Complete Tales and Poems of Edgar Allan Poe*. New York: Modern Library, 1983.
Postman, Neil. *Amusing Ourselves to Death*. New York: Penguin, 1985.
Profit, Marie-Claude. "The Rhetoric of Death in *The Crying of Lot 49*." Trans. M. S. Langford. *Pynchon Notes* 10 (1982): 18–36; "La Rhétorique de la mort dans *The Crying of Lot 49*." *Delta* (1979): 155–74.
Pynchon, Thomas. *The Crying of Lot 49*. New York/London: Bantam/Jonathan Cape, 1967. First published by Lippincott (Philadelphia), March 1966.
———. *Gravity's Rainbow*. New York/London: Viking/Jonathan Cape, 1973.
———. "Introduction." In Richard Farina, *Been Down So Long It Looks Like Up to Me*, v–xiv. Harmondsworth: Penguin, 1983.
———. "Is It O.K. to Be a Luddite?" *The New York Times Book Review* (28 Oct. 1984).
———. *Slow Learner: Early Stories*. Boston/London: Little Brown/Jonathan Cape, 1984.
———. *V*. New York/London: Bantam/Jonathan Cape, 1964. First published by Lippincott (Philadelphia), March 1963.
Qazi, Javaid. "Pynchon in Central Asia: The Use of Sources and Resources." *Rocky Mountain Review* 34.4 (1980): 229–42.
Quilligan, Maureen. "Thomas Pynchon and the Language of Allegory." In Harold Bloom, ed., *Thomas Pynchon*, 111–37. New York: Chelsea, 1986.

Ragland-Sullivan, Ellie. "*Hamlet*, Logical Time and the Structure of Obsession." *Newsletter of the Freudian Field* 2/2 (Fall 1988): 29–45.

———. *Jacques Lacan and the Philosophy of Psychoanalysis*. Urbana: University of Illinois Press, 1987.

———. "The Magnetism between Reader and Text: Prolegomena to a Lacanian Poetics." *Poetics* 13 (1984): 381–406.

———. "The Sexual Masquerade: A Lacanian Theory of Sexual Difference." In Ellie Ragland-Sullivan and Marc Bracher, eds., *Lacan and the Subject of Language*. New York: Routledge, 1991.

Redfield, Marc W. "Pynchon's Postmodern Sublime." *PMLA* 104.2 (1989): 152–62.

Robbe-Grillet. *Snapshots and Notes toward a New Novel*. Trans. B. Wright. London: Calder and Boyars, 1965; *Pour un nouveau roman*. Paris: Minuit, 1962.

———. *Two Novels by Robbe-Grillet: "Jealousy" and "In the Labyrinth."* Trans. R. Howard. New York: Grove, 1965. Compiled from *La Jalousie* (Paris: Minuit, 1957) and *Dans le labyrinthe* (Paris: Minuit, 1959).

Rose, Jacqueline. *Sexuality in the Field of Vision*. London: Verso, 1986.

Rotman, Brian. *Signifying Nothing: The Semiotics of Zero*. New York: St. Martin's, 1987.

Rushdie, Salman. "Rushdie on Pynchon: Invisible Man's Triumphant Return." Review of *Vineland*. *International Herald Tribune* (13/14 Jan. 1990).

Saussure, Ferdinand de. *Course in General Linguistics*. Trans. W. Baskin. New York: McGraw-Hill, 1966.

Schaub, Thomas H. "Mythologies New and Old: Hume and Current Theory." *Pynchon Notes* 18–19 (1986): 110–15.

———. *Pynchon: The Voice of Ambiguity*. Urbana: University of Illinois Press, 1981.

Schwab, Gabriele. *Entgrenzungen und Entgrenzungsmythen: Zur Subjektivität im modernen Roman* [*Subjects without Selves: Subjectivity and Aesthetics of Response in Modern Fiction*]. Stuttgart: Franz Steiner, 1987.

Seed, David. "The Central Asian Uprising of 1916." *Pynchon Notes* 11 (1983): 49–53.

———. *The Fictional Labyrinths of Thomas Pynchon*. London: Macmillan, 1988.

Simmon, Scott. "Beyond the Theatre of War: *Gravity's Rainbow* as Film." In Richard Pearce, ed., *Critical Essays on Thomas Pynchon*, 124–39. Boston: Hall, 1981.

Slade, Joseph. "Religion, Psychology, Sex and Love in *Gravity's Rainbow*." In Charles Clerc, ed., *Approaches to "Gravity's Rainbow,"* 153–98. Columbus: Ohio State University Press, 1983.

———. "Thomas Pynchon: Postindustrial Humanist." *Technology and Culture* 23.1 (1982): 53–72.

Stark, John O. *Pynchon's Fictions: Thomas Pynchon and the Literature of Information*. Athens: Ohio University Press, 1980.

Tanner, Tony. *City of Words: American Fiction 1950–1970*. London: Jonathan Cape, 1971.

———. *Thomas Pynchon*. London: Methuen 1982.
Todorov, Tzvetan. *The Fantastic: A Structural Approach to a Literary Genre*. Ithaca: Cornell University Press, 1975.
Tölölyan, Khachig. "Criticism as Symptom: Thomas Pynchon and the Crisis of the Humanities." *New Orleans Review* 5 (1979): 314–18.
———. "Seven on Pynchon: The Novelist as Deconstructionist." *Novel* 16 (1983): 165–72.
———. "War as Background in *Gravity's Rainbow*." In Charles Clerk, ed., *Approaches to Gravity's Rainbow*, 31–67. Columbus: Ohio State University Press, 1983.
Ulmer, Gregory. *Applied Grammatology: Post(e)-Pedagogy from Jacques Derrida to Joseph Beuys*. Baltimore: Johns Hopkins University Press, 1985.
———. *Glassary*. Lincoln: University of Nebraska Press, 1986.
Virilio, Paul. *War and Cinema: The Logistics of Perception*. Trans. P. Camiller. London: Verso, 1989; *Guerre et cinéma 1: Logistique de la perception*. Paris. L'Etoile, 1984.
Weber, Max. *The Protestant Ethic and the Spirit of Capitalism*. New York: Scribner's, 1958.
Weisenburger, Steven. *A "Gravity's Rainbow" Companion: Sources and Contexts for Pynchon's Novel*. Athens: University of Georgia Press, 1988.
Widmer, Peter. *Subversion des Begehrens. Jacques Lacan oder Die zweite Revolution der Psychoanalyse* [*The Subversion of Desire: Jacques Lacan, or the Second Revolution of Psychoanalysis*]. Frankfurt am Main: Fischer, 1990.
Wilden, Anthony. *System and Structure: Essays in Communication and Exchange*. London: Tavistock, 1972.
Wittgenstein, Ludwig. *Tractatus Logico-Philosophicus*. Trans. D. F. Pears and B. F. McGuinness. London: Routledge, 1974; *Tractatus logico-philosophicus: Logisch-philosophische Abhandlung*. *Annalen der Naturphilosophie* (1922).
Wolfley, Lawrence C. "Repression's Rainbow: The Presence of Norman O. Brown in Pynchon's Big Novel." *PMLA* 92 (1977): 873–89.
Žižek, Slavoj. "Die Missverständnisse des Metonymismus" [The Misunderstandings of Metonomy]. *Der Wunderblock: Zeitschrift für Psychoanalyse* [*The Magic Writing Pad: Journal of Psychoanalysis*] 10 (1983): 50–76.
———. *The Sublime Object of Ideology*. London: Verso, 1989.
———. "Why Lacan Is Not a 'Post-structuralist.'" *Newsletter of the Freudian Field* 1/2 (1987): 31–39.

Index

00000, the: and Imipolex G, 125; as counter-rocket to the 00001, 131; firing of, 191, 193–95. *See also* Rocket; 00001

00001, the: as counter-rocket to the 00000, 131, 193; as the 00000's "other side," 195. *See also* Rocket; 00000

Absolute object, 225–27. *See also* Object, lost

Addiction, 133–34, 139, 141

Aggressivity: and the mirror stage, 17; and real *jouissance*, 21; and society, 113

Allegory: of horizontality, 10; the rocket as, 39n4; postmodern, 41n16; *V.* as, 81n29; of belatedness, 91–92; of textuality, 108; of America, 112; of the signifier, 115n5; hysteresis as, 128; of reading, 132; alphabetical language as, 141; Alpdrücken as, 167; and Pynchon's poetics, 240n5

Ambassadors, The: and Lacan, 79–80n25

Amnesia, 223, 231

Analgesia, 134

Analogicity: television and film, 85; pictogram and algebra, 106; and Chinese epistemology, 118n20; and language, 140–41; and the aqyn's song, 144; and sociopolitics, 149n34; and film, 153–54, 156, 159; film and writing, 184–185; and crying, 190n27; and negation, 190n29; and Lyle Bland, 197; in *Vineland*, 206. *See also* Digitality

Analyst: Dupin as, 93; discourse of the, 208–9, 213, 214, 226. *See also* Discourse of the analyst

Anamnesis: and Norman O. Brown, 228

Anamorphosis: and libido, 18; and *The Ambassadors*, 79–80n25. *See also* Lacan; Paranoia

Anarchism: and the Zone, 126, 130; and Martin Fierro, 166; and Frenesi, 232; and Pynchon's poetics, 240n5, 244

Anodyne, 134

Apocalypse: and language, 23; and Baudrillard's polemics, 50n8; pentecostal 55, 114; and Takeshi, 203; and Frenesi, 220

Aristotle, 241n15. *See also* Foucault

Artaud, Antonin, 40n10

Atemporality: of the text, 25, 88, 192, 199; of Mélanie as object, 70

Athetical, the, 33. *See also* McHoul/Wills

Aufhebung, Hegelian: and Derrida, 31; defined, 39n3; and Baudrillard, 50n8. *See also* Cancellation

Authority: phallic, 71; Frenesi's complicity with, 205, 218; and Lacan's four discourses, 209, 212, 214, 241n14

Automaton: language as, 24–25; and Bongo-Shaftsbury, 57; and the body, 58; and Mélanie, 63–65, 67, 71–73; and Stravinsky's *Petruschka*, 78n11

Baedeker, 202
Bakhtin, Mikhail: and carnival, 76n2, and the polylogue, 147n20; and "The College of the Surf" uprising, 220
Ballard, J. G., 57
Barthes, Roland: and "The Death of the Author" 3–4; and Robbe-Grillet, 11n8; and the text as fetish, 75; and the filmic, 153–54
Baudrillard, Jean, 2, 11n3; and Pynchon's notion of subjectivity, 39, 244; replacement of the real by simulation, 42–45; and Pynchon's poetics, 46; and the fantastic, 46–47; and paranoia *vs.* schizophrenia, 47, 109; and Möbius space, 48–49; and *V.*, 53; deconstructive reading of psychoanalysis in *V.*, 58–59, 62, 69–70, 72–73, 78n10, 79n18; and the cybernetic landscapes in *Lot 49*, 84–86; and textualization of the world, 95; and entropy, 103; and power, 111, 113; and McLuhan, 115n3; and plastics, language and simulation in *Gravity's Rainbow*'s Kirghiz Light episode, 135–41; and sadomasochism, 169; and speed, 175; and ooooo and operational death, 192–97; and death drive, 200n3; and *Vineland*, 202; and power, 207, 215; and discourse of knowledge, 217
Beatles, 98
Been Down So Long It Looks Like Up to Me, 29n15
Belatedness (*Nachträglichkeit*): and unconscious, 18, 228; and real, 23; translated, 28n6; logic of in Pynchon, Lacan, Derrida, and Baudrillard, 48–49; "Bordando el Manto Terrestre" as allegory of, 91; and trauma, 121; and Mexico's map, 123; and Imipolex G,

125; and Schwarzgerät, 129; and Zone, 130; and text, 131; and Bergson, 157; and Virilio, 164; and the repressed, 166; and V-2, 175, 198; and biological and speaking body, 181. *See also Nachträglichkeit*
Benjamin, Walter, 155–56, 170, 187n6
Bergson, Henri, 157–58, 177, 187nn9, 10, 11, 199. *See also* Temps; Durée
Birth of Venus: and Mantissa, 55
Blade Runner, 82
Blow Up, 82
Borromean knot, 17
Botticelli, 55; "Strip Botticelli," 85
Braid-cutter, 69, 80n26
Brown, Norman O.: and the return to a natural body, 149n34, 185, 233, 238; and power, 192; and Eros, 214; and death, 228–30; and language, 245
Bureaucracy, 7; of war, 8; and chemistry, 140; in Burroughs, 189n25; and discourse of knowledge, 211; and Atman's conditioning, 223; karmic, 229
Burke, Edmund, 29n20
Burroughs, William S.: and the hieroglyph, 117n19; and cinematic writing, 186, 189n25

Cancellation, Hegelian: and Derrida, 31; defined, 39n3; and fear of castration, 62; Derridean reading of, 77n7. *See also Aufhebung*
Castle of Otranto, The, 224
Champollion, Jean François: and Freud, 117n20
Chemistry: and synthesis, 120; in Kirghiz Light passage, 133–35, 137–140, 142; organic *vs.* inorganic, 193, 197

Chora, 48
Citizen Kane: and *Lot 49*, 83–85, 152; and detective novel, 93; Pierce as, 110; and Slothrop, 129
Cocteau, Jean, 152
Cogitans, 2
Colonization: and female body, 67; and tourism, 72; and media, 85; and Kirghiz Light episode, 133; and Hereros, 147n21
Complementarity: of theoretical systems, 2, 244; of poetics, 6, 30; of readings, 9–10, 82, 88, 139
Complicity: of knowledge and representation, 3; of subject, language and power, 6, 120, 137, 169, 207, 212–13, 216–19, 221, 229–30, 236–38; textual, 9, 147n18; of sex and the inanimate, 65; of language and fetishization, 72, 75; of pictogram and algebra, 105
Condensation: and metaphor, 41n19, 107–8; and dream, 65. *See also* Displacement
Conditioning, Pavlovian, 6; Slothrop's, 119–20, 122–24, 127–30, 132, 139, 179, 194–95, 223; in Kirghiz Light passage, 133, 136–37, 139, 141, 147n16, 150n36; and Katje, 172; and Kryptosam, 188–89n21; and Gottfried, 194–95; and Atman, 223; and Pointsman, 245
Control, 5, 6; and Foucault, 76n2, 207; and Baudrillard, 78n10; and Derrida, 88; and synthesis, 120, 130, 133–37, 141–42; and film, 151, 162–63, 166–67, 170–72, 174, 183; and Burroughs, 189n25; and death, 192, 193; and *Vineland*, 206, 207, 218, 233; and Pointsman, 245
Counterforce: and *Lot 49*, 113; and

Gravity's Rainbow, 120, 173–74, 182; and *Vineland,* 218, 239n4
Cybernetics, 5; and science, 77n6; and *Lot 49,* 83–84; and death, 116–17n15; and *Gravity's Rainbow,* 120; and body, 128; and language, 139, 149n28
Cyberpunk: and *Vineland,* 202
Cyberspace, and meeting of machine and subject, 57; and *Lot 49,* 83, 86–87

Dali, Salvador, 107
De-territorialization: and the Zone, 120, 126
Death-in-life, 192–93, 195, 206
Death drive: and entropy, 102–4, 116n14; and language, 140, 180; interpreted by Baudrillard and Lacan, 195; and control, 221; and motorhead valley roulette, 230
Decadence: in *V.,* 53, 58, 78n12; and language, 140
Deconstruction: and Pynchon, 1, 12n10, 243–46; as athetic, 33; American, 37; and de Man, 37–39; and psychoanalysis, 58; of detective novel, 93; and Pynchon's use of film, 160. *See also* Derrida
Delirium: and Pynchon's poetics, 26, 46; and Baudrillard, 47; and reading, 79n19; Oedipa's, 107; and McLuhan, 115n3; and von Göll, 170
De Man, Paul: and deconstruction, 37–39, 243–46; and psychoanalysis, 41n18; selfhood as figure, 179. *See also* Rhetorics
Demand: defined, 17–19, 128; and *jouissance,* 21; and love, 60, 212; and Pynchon's characters, 106. *See also* Desire; Need
Demon, Maxwell's, 99–100

Derrida, Jacques, 1–2, 4; and Pynchon's text, 6, 12n10, 244–45; and subjectivity, 11n3; and textual *jouissance*, 21; and detour, 27; and deferral, 28n6, 89; and writing 30, 39n2; and material typonomy, 31; and interpretation, 32; and repetition, 33; dissemination and literary text, 34; and silence, 35; and desire, 35–36; and American deconstruction, 37; and de Man, 38–39; and power structures, 42; and simulation, 45; and Möbius space, 48–49; and textual machine 56, 74, 77n7, 139; and poetic language, 86–88, 210; Derridean reading of *Lot 49*, 101, 104; and hieroglyphic script, 105–6, 117n18; and silence, 142; Derridean reading of *Gravity's Rainbow*, 143; and film/trace 156, 187n8; and rocket, 194; and *Vineland*, 202; and fantastic, 224, 226

Descartes, René: Lacan's rewriting of, 2–4; Cartesian space, 48, 80

Desire: defined, 18–20; law of, 21, 208; Lacanian *vs.* Derridean notion of, 35; Mélanie's, 60–61, 63; and hieroglyph, 106; and Pavlovian conditioning, 128–29; and language, 139; of text, 145, 160, 183, 243; and film, 155–56, 158; simulation through Imipolex G, 193; of the ooooo, 194; and interpretation, 214; Frenesi as figure of, 222; and simulation, 236; and deconstruction, 243–44. *See also* Demand; Need

Desiring-machines, 77n8

Detour: and Lacan, 19, 25, 27, 128, 210; and Derrida, 32, 35, 101; and narcissism, 63; and text, 75, 208, 238; and Baudrillard, 192

Différance: and Derrida, 31–34; between theories of Derrida and Lacan, 36; and digitality, 139. *See also* Derrida

Digitality: and fetish, 62; and phallic economy, 72; and brain, 74; and film *vs.* television, 85; and pictogram *vs.* algebra, 106; and language, 120, 139, 140–41, 184, 196; and aqyn's song, 144; and sociopolitics, 149n34; and film, 151, 153–54, 156; and perception/experience, 157, 159, 176; in *Vineland*, 206; and discourse of knowledge, 211. *See also* Analogicity

Discourse of the master, 208–11; and political power, 215, 235, 242n24; and sadomasochism, 217, 219, 230

Discourse of the hysteric, 208–9, 212–13; and sadomasochism, 217, 219, 230

Discourse of knowledge, 208–9, 211–12; and political power, 215, 217, 235

Discourse of the analyst, 208–9, 213–14; and Pynchon's poetics, 226

Discourse of the capitalist, 241n13

Displacement: and fiction, 23; and Derrida, 35, 224; and metonymy, 41n19, 65, 107; in Pynchon's text, 69–70; post as agency of, 86; and Mucho's letter, 96; in sadomasochism, 167. *See also* Condensation

Dissemination: of meaning, 6; and writing, 29n19; and Derrida, 32–36, 40n12, 41n16, 42; and Baudrillard, 45; and fictional text, 75, 115; and landscape in *Lot 49*, 83; and poetic language, 86–88; and Driblette and Mucho Maas, 97–98; and Oedipa, 104; and simulation, 140; and trace, 157; and discourse of the master, 210; and Pynchon's poetics, 244. *See also* Derrida

Duchamp, Marcel, 107

Dupin, C. Auguste, 93

Durée: and film, 157–58, 177. *See also* Bergson, Henri

Écriture: and allegory, 41n16
Ego: and mirror stage, 17; and object, 19; and *jouissance,* 21; and the real, 23–24; and Baudrillard, 45; and Profane, 54; and Mélanie, 69; and Oedipa's mirror stage, 89–92, 95, 98; and entropy, 102; and paranoia, 110; and aggressivity, 113–14; and passions, 115n6; and its loss, 145; and Slothrop's scattering, 179–80; and ego ideal, 209; and children, 245
Elect, the: and *Lot 49,* 111; and the Zone, 126; and film, 177. *See also* Preterite
Eliot, T. S., 82
Emerson, Ralph Waldo, 237
Emulsion J., 166
Enlightenment, the: and simulation, 43; *Dialectic of Enlightenment,* 49n4, 186n5
"Entropy": reading of, 16–17, and entropy, 25; and Henry Adams, 76n1; and Stravinsky, 78n11
Entropy: social, 54, 83; and Narcissus, 94; in *Lot 49,* 99–103, 113, 116n10; and hysteresis, 128; and language, 129
Epileptic, the: and revelation, 104; and *jouissance,* 180
Epiphany: and the real, 23; in *Vineland,* 206
Erasure, under: the subject, 3; the real and the body, 58, 168–69; the origin, 89, 193; detective novel, 93; alphabetical script, 117n18; metaphysics, 122–23; the Zone, 130; preliterate society, 143; nature, 180
Eros, and Thanatos: and the real, 22; and conditioning, 122, 124; and Pynchon's poetics, 132; and masochism, 147n16; and power, 192; and death drive, 200n3; and modern civilization, 214; and death, 230; and *Vineland,* 237–38

Ethics: Derridean, 33; of film, 152; Protestant, 211; Lacanian, 238
Exile: language as, 19; interpretation as, 32; and the Zone, 131; and death, 235; and Prairie, 236

Fantastic, the: and *jouissance,* 22; and Pynchon's poetics, 26, 28–29n13, 82, 149n34; and Baudrillard, 47; and *Lot 49,* 106, 109, 114; and the rocket, 124, 198–99; in *Vineland,* 224–29, 234
Fariña, Richard, *Been Down So Long It Looks Like Up to Me,* 29n15
Fetish/ism, 6; and Mélanie, 57, 59–63, 66–74, 78nn10,13,14, 79nn17,24, 80n26; and fictional text, 74–75; and Imipolex G, 137–38; and film, 156; and Ilse, 169; and conditioning, 188–89n21; and chemistry, 193; and reality principle, 233; and language, 241n14; and simulation, 245
Figure, rhetorical: and material typonomy, 39; and substance, 41n19; V. as, 81n29; selfhood as, 179; and deconstruction, 246. *See also* De Man, Paul
Film: and *Citizen Kane,* 83–84; and TV, 84–85; critical reception of Pynchon's use of, 151–53; semiotics of, 153–59; and the poetics of *Gravity's Rainbow,* 160–62, 183–86; and von Göll, 162–71; and Katje, 171–74; and V-2, 174–78; and Slothrop's disintegration, 178–83; and Burroughs, 189n25; and Gottfried's death, 195; and Frenesi, 219–20, 222–24; and fantastic, 227–28; complicity of writing with, 236
Foreclosure (*Verwerfung*): of death, 103, 139, 171; of signifier, 109, 128, 171; of nature and the real, 139, 171,

264   Index

Foreclosure (*Verwerfung*) (*continued*) 241–42n19; and Burroughs/Kristeva, 189n25; of fear, 241–42n19
"Fort-Da," 25, 139
Foucault, Michel: and subjectivity, 3; and table of representation, 7, 11n6; and archaeology, 8; critique of Derrida and Lacan, 35; and punishment, 55, 76n2, 215; and power, 193, 206–7, 222, 229, 240n6,7; and sexuality, 241n15; and Pynchon's poetics, 245
Freud, Sigmund: Pynchon's reading of, 6; and the real, 24; and belatedness, 28n6; and "Under the Rose," 44; Pynchon's deconstructive reading in *V.*, 57–60, 64–67, 69–71, 73–74, 79nn20,24, 80n26; and *Lot 49* and *Citizen Kane*, 83; and projection, 97; and death drive, 101–3, 194; and hieroglyphic script, 105, 117n20; and condensation and displacement, 107; and pain of existence, 134; and psychic inertia, 146n8; and Eros and Thanatos, 147n16; and foreclosure, 189n25; and return of the repressed, 224; and drive, 242n27

Gaze: as object *o*, 69, 155; and eye, 79–80n25; of camera, 83; and sadomasochism, 219
Ghost: (un)holy, 55; and dream, 65; and phallic scene, 67; and revelation, 100; and rocket, 175; and film, 177; and love, 196; in *Vineland*, 221–24, 227–28; language as, 229; and guilt, 231–32; Frenesie as, 234; Vond as, 235; and Pynchon's poetics, 241n17
Godard, Jean-Luc, 178
Gödel, Kurt, 191

Harlan, Veit, 164
Hegel, Georg Wilhelm Friedrich: and absolute knowledge, 31, 50n7; and cancellation, 39n3; Derridean reading of, 77n7; and hieroglyphic script, 105, 117n18; and master-slave conflict, 211, 240–41n11
Heisenberg, Werner Karl, 134
Hellman, Monte, 152
Hermeneutics: and dissemination, 36; and speed, 175; and Bergson, 187n11
Hieroglyph: and linguistics, 105–6, 117n18; and Burroughs, 117n19; and Lacan, 117–18n20
Historiography: Foucault and Pynchon's poetics, 8, 245; and *V.*, 53
Hitler, Adolf, 163–64
Holbein, Hans, 79–80n25
Holy-Center-Approaching, 26, 244
Homeostasis: and entropy, 25, 101–2; and Chinese epistemology, 117–18n20
Homme-machine, 71
Homosexuality, 70, 80n26
Humboldt, Freiherr von, Wilhelm, 105
Hyperreal: and simulation, 43, 48; and Lacan's three orders, 45; and fetishism, 78n10
Hysteresis: and Pavlovian conditioning, 127–28; and Mondaugen, 180
Hysteric. See Discourse of the Hysteric
Hysteron proteron, 121

Icon: *Citizen Kane* as cultural, 83; Pierce as cultural, 89; iconic communication, 144; of authority, 205
Id (*Es*), 185
Ideogram, 105, 117–18n20
Ideology: and Baudrillard, 42, 113; and film, 152, 154; of digitality, 211; and science, 212; of individuality, 231;

and Pynchon's allegories, 239–40n5;
the sublime object of, 241n19
Ignorance: as fundamental passion,
237–38
Imaginary: in Lacanian theory, 17–21,
23, 26–27, 28n7; Baudrillard's rewriting of, 44–45, 48; and Wilden,
50n6; and interpretation, 50n12; and
Mélanie, 66, 68–69; and machine,
77n6; and *Lot 49*, 83, 86, 98; and mirror stage, 90–92; and Poe's theory of
ratiocination, 93; and myth of Narcissus, 95; and entropy, 102; and analog,
106; and cultural aggressivity, 111–13;
and the Zone, 126; and demand, 128;
and game of odd and even, 148n26;
and film, 155–56, 158, 184–85; and
sadomasochism, 168, 219–20; and
jouissance, 170, 231; and Slothrop's
disintegration, 180–81, 185; and text,
199; in *Vineland*, 202; and discourse of
master/hysteric, 211, 213, 219–20; and
fantastic, 225–26; and alignment with
symbolic and real, 238; and simulation,
241n19
Imipolex G: as material typonymy, 31;
and Pavlovian conditioning, 125; and
simulation, 137–38; irregularities in
Pynchon's use of, 146n6; and film, 166;
and rocket, 193, 194
Implosion: of Eros and Thanatos, 22;
of language and the real, 44; of real
and imaginary space, 48; and autoabolition of culture, 50n8; of personal
and general history, 53; of subject
and fetish, 68; of animate and inanimate, 70–71; of television and reality,
85–86, 216; of sexual scene, 114; and
McLuhan, 115n3; and revelation, 131;
and Imipolex G, 137; of war and film,
163; of film and reality, 166, 174; of
cause and effect, 205
Induction, 122, 124–25, 127, 146n10
Inertia: and Pavlovian conditioning, 124,
127; of language, 129; psychic, 146n8;
and phi-phenomenon, 156
Inhibition, 124
Insistence of the real: and Lacan, 18;
and McHoul/Wills, 39; and ending of
Gravity's Rainbow, 199
Intertextuality: and transposition, 159;
and *Gravity's Rainbow*, 188n14
Intuition: and Descartes, 2; and Derrida,
30; and Poe, 93; and Hegel, 117n18;
and Bergson, 157

Jakobson, Roman, 156
Janet, Pierre, 124, 169
Jouissance: defined, 20–22, 28n9,11;
and fantastic, 28–29n13; and writing, 29n19; textual, 35, 87, 103; and
metonymy, 41n19; machinic, 56, 86;
and death, 104; and pain, 168; and
innocence, 170; alignment of real
and symbolic *jouissance*, 181–82; and
Pynchon's poetics, 186; and *Vineland*, 201, 206; and law of desire,
208; surplus *jouissance*, 210, 212, 213,
240n10; and sadomasochism, 219;
and Frenesi, 221, 231; and motorhead valley roulette, 230; and Zoyd,
232; and Prairie, 233; and revolution,
234, 239n4; and master-slave conflict,
240n11, 241n12; and play, 242n25;
and Kristeva, 242n26; and drive,
242n27; and mindless pleasures, 245
Jouissance effect: and fantastic, 22; and
epileptic, 180; and rocket, 195, 199

Kant, Immanuel, 219, 227

Kekulé, von Stradonitz, Friedrich August, 135–36
Kineme: as used by Pasolini, 159, 187n12; and Pynchon's poetics, 184
Kracauer, Siegfried: *From Caligari to Hitler,* 154
Kristeva, Julia: and transposition, 154, 158; and the semiotic, 189n25; and *jouissance,* 242n26
Kryptosam, 172, 188n21

Lacan, Jacques: rewriting Descartes, 2–3; barred subject, 15–16; and "Entropy," 16–17; and paranoia, 17; and the real, 17–18; and desire, 18–20; and *jouissance,* 20–21, 28n11, 240n10; and "The Small Rain," 22–23; and meeting with the real, 23–25; and "Entropy," 25; and Pynchon's poetics, 26–27, 132; and writing and sublimation, 29n19; and Derrida, 30–41; and Baudrillard, 42–50; and poetics, 50n12; and mirror stage of Profane and Stencil, 53–54; and machine, 56–57, 76–77n6; and poetics of *V.,* 58; and fetishism, 59–61, 65–66, 69–71; and text as fetish, 74; and gaze, 79–80n25, 155; and Oedipa's mirror stage, 90–95; and puns, 96; and vanishing of "the Other," 98; and entropy, 99–101; and death, 104; and hieroglyph, 105–7; and metaphor and metonymy, 108–9; and aggressivity, 113–14, 115–18 *passim;* and Pavlovian conditioning, 128–29; and digitality of language, 139–41, 184; and game of odd and even, 148–49n26; and cybernetics, 149n28; and film, 157–58; and Schwarzkommando, 166; and sadomasochism, 168, 219–22; and Slothrop's disintegration, 180–81; and death, 191; and launching of the 00000, 193–95; and repetition compulsion, 196; and *Vineland,* 201–02; and Zoyd's lost messages, 204; and matheme of four discourses, 207–15, 241n13, 242n24; and fantastic, 225–228; and alignment of the real, imaginary, and symbolic, 237–38; and master-slave conflict, 240–41n11, 241n12; and Pynchon's poetics, 243–44
Lack. *See* Object *o*
Lack-of-being: explained, 16–17; and desire, 19; and gaze, 69, 79–80n25; and film, 184; and the discourse of analyst, 214
Last Year in Marienbad, 171
Law-of-the-machine, Name-of-the-machine, 71
Leibniz, Gottfried Wilhelm, 105
Lesbianism, 67–69, 80n26
Lévi-Strauss, Claude, 143, 149n32
Logocentrism: and Derrida, 30; and de Man, 38–39; Pynchon's rhetorical logocentrism, 48, 54, 97, 127–28, 139, 143, 195, 243; and psychoanalysis, 57; and Mélanie, 59; and Poe, 93; and code, 99–100; and hieroglyph, 105–6
Lovecraft, H. P., 114, 224
Luddites, 149n34, 224, 233
Lyotard, Jean-François: and sublime, 225–27, 242n21

Machiavelli, Niccolò: and Foucault, 76n2
Machine: and subject, 56, 171; and female body, 67, 74; molar, 68, 73; and language, 74–75, 76–77n6, 77n7, 77–78n9, 102, 139, 141; dreamless, 75; *jouissance* of, 86; and textual *jouissance,* 87; Nefastis's, 99; body as, 101–2; and rocket, 193; and film, 170; of surveillance, 171; sociopolitical, 200n1; and Lacan's four discourses, 208; sado-

masochism as a sexual, 215; universe as, 221
Mandala, 146n2
Mannequin: and Mélanie, 63; as simulation of body, 72–73; and Stravinsky, 78n11; as narcissistic object, 79n21
Marey, Etienne Jules, 158, 188n19
Marxism: and Baudrillard, 42; and Wilden, 149n34; and film studies, 154; and discourse of the master, 210
Marx Brothers, 160
Masochism: and family, 147n16; economy of, 168; and Brigadier Pudding, 173; and discourse of the hysteric, 219
Master signifier, 214, 240n9
Master-slave conflict: and discourse of the master, 211, 240–41n11
Matheme: of four discourses, 208, 241n13
Maxwell, James Clerc, 99–100, 116n12
McHoul, Alec, and David Wills: Derridean reading of Pynchon, 11n1, 30–39; and *V.*, 54, 74–75; and *Lot 49*, 86, 97, 100–101, 104; and *Gravity's Rainbow*, 153, 187–88n13; and *Vineland*, 223
McLuhan, Herbert Marshall: *The Medium Is the Massage*, 79n18; and television, 84–86; and Narcissus, 94; and hieroglyph, 105; and Baudrillard, 115n3; and Burroughs, 117n19
Medusa, 23, 29n20, 199, 204
Merchant of Venice, The: and Lacan, 101
Metalanguage: and Lacan, 16, 132, 214; and Barthes, 154
Metamorphosis: and life, 136; Slothrop's, 178
Metaphor and metonymy: and repetition, 25, 41n19, 117n17; and Profane and Stencil, 53–54; and Oedipa, 107–8; and simulation, 141

Metz, Christian: and cinematic apparatus as fetish, 78n13; semiotics of film, 154–56, 158, 167, 185, 223
Mimesis: and simulation, 84, 135; and film, 160; of media events, 161, 163; of psychic space, 214
Mindbody, 128, 197
Mirror stage, 17; and simulation, 45; and Stencil and Profane, 54; and Mélanie, 66, 69–70, 79n21; and Oedipa, 89–92; and Dupin, 93; of culture, 94; and aggressivity, 113; and Frenesie, 222
Misreading: and Derrida, 37; and literary criticism, 49
Möbius strip: reorganization of time and space, 47–48, 50n9, 106; and belatedness, 121; and the Zone, 125, 131; and subjectivity, 127; and rocket, 195, 198; and Pynchon's poetics, 206; and return of the repressed, 224
Modern Times, 56
Molar machines: and subject, 56, 77n8; and *V.*, 68; and body, 73
Molecular machines: and subject, 56, 77n8
Mourning: for center, 32; for lost bodily totality, 101; and nostalgia, 202
Muybridge, Eadweard, 158
Myth: and coincidence, 54; of Narcissus, 94–95; and aqyn's song, 144; of Baudrillard's symbolic, 200n3; of lost messages, 145; of purely digital knowledge, 211; and *Vineland*'s poetics, 214; of Lilith, 217; of simulation, 236; of master-slave conflict, 240–41n11

Nachträglichkeit (belatedness): and unconscious, 18; and lost object, 20; translation, 28n6. *See also* Belatedness
Name-of-the-Machine, Law-of-the-Machine, 71

Name-of-the-Father, 42, 71, 234. *See also* Lacan

Narcissism: and imaginary *jouissance*, 21; and Mélanie, 63, 79n21, 80n26; and mirror stage, 90–91; culture of, 94–95, 111–13

Narcissus, 94–95

Need: defined, 18; and Pavlovian conditioning, 128–29; and sadomasochism, 169; and sadism, 245. *See also* Demand; Desire

Negentropy, 101, 103

Neurosis: and Pavlovian conditioning, 129

Night of the Hunter, The, 237

Nijinsky, Vaslav, 78n11

Nostalgia: of psychoanalysis, 65; and Pynchon's poetics, 139, 193, 201–2, 206, 233, 239n1; and sublime, 226

Object, lost: defined, 19–20; and desire, 35; and simulation, 78n10; and *Citizen Kane*, 83; and film, 155; and digitality, 211

Object *o*: defined, 20; and Pynchon's poetics, 26–27; and material typonomy, 31; and "objects *o[perational]*," 45–46; and phantasm, 48; and gaze, 69, 79–80n25; and *objet-machine petit "a,"* 77n9; and phantom limb, 101; and film, 155; as surplus *jouissance*, 208, 240n10; and Lacan's four discourses, 210–13; and sublime, 225, 227, 229; language as, 236, 238; and discourse of the capitalist, 241n13

Objet-machine petit "a," 77n9

Odd and even, 148n26

Olsen, Lance, 224–25

120 Days of Sodom, The, 210

Ontotheology, 32

Other: defined, 16–17, 29n18; and demand, 21; and phallus, 60; vanishing of, 98, 101; Trystero as, 112; magical, 114; and discourse of the master, 209. *See also* other; Object *o*

other: and demand, 21; and Mélanie's mirror stage, 68–70; and tourism, 72; vanishing, 98, 101; Trystero as, 112; literature as film's, 153; and discourse of the master, 210. *See also* Other; Object *o*

Other-as-audience, self-as-audience, 68

Pain: phantom, 101; and addiction, 134, 223; of existence (*Not des Lebens*), 134, 219; and sadomasochism, 167–69, 192; and sublime, 225; and Frenesie, 231; painless children, 245

Parabola: as material typonomy, 31; and drive, 242n27

Paranoia: and Pynchon's poetics, 17; and reality, 17, 90; and schizophrenia, 47–48; and criticism, 49; and mirror stage, 90–94; and projection, 97; and entropy, 101; and delirium, 107, 142, 144; and psychosis, 109; and simulation, 110; and Pierce, 111; and "We-system," 113, 120; critical reception of in Pynchon's writing, 116n7; and Slothrop, 121; and conditioning, 124, 146n11; and simulation, 136–37; and film, 174; and *jouissance* effects, 180

Pasolini, Pier Paolo, 159, 184, 187n12, 210

Pavlov, Ivan Petrovich: and conditioning, 119–33, 146–47; and Lacan, 181; and "The Book," 212

Penalization: and Foucault, 76n2, 207, 215

Phallus: as symbol of desire, 21, 208; and *jouissance* beyond, 28n11; phallic and symbolic *jouissance,* 29n19; law of, 32; and fetishism, 59–61, 67, 71, 74; and simulation, 62–63, 72; and psychoanalysis, 64–65; phallic code, 66; as signifier, 78–79n16; and female alienation, 79n17; Pynchon's "phallocratic" writing, 147n18; "having" vs. "being" phallus, 217; phallocratic society, 218; and Kristeva, 242n26

Phantasm: and mirror stage, 17; and lost object, 20; and real *jouissance,* 21; and Derrida, 33; and real, 48, 92, 101; and Stencil, 54; and *Lot 49,* 82; and film, 85, 185; and Mucho Maas, 98–99; and V-2, 124; and von Göll, 166; and death, 192; and Gottfried and rocket, 194; and Baudrillard's notion of symbolic, 198; and discourse of the master, 211, 235; and discourse of the hysteric, 213; and Zoyd, 221; and fantastic, 224

Phi phenomenon: and trace, 156; and Ilse, 170

Phrenology, 221

Pictogram. *See* Ideogram

Plastics: and V., 74; and Schwarzgerät, 129; and simulation, 134–138, 140, 148n25, 197, 236

Plato, 241n15

Pleasure principle: and entropy, 102–4, 116n14; and simulation, 141; and Pynchon's poetics in *Vineland,* 201; and Prairie, 233; and revolution, 234, 238. *See also* Reality principle

Plus-de-jouir, 240n10. *See also* Surplus *jouissance*

Poe, Edgar Allan: and theory of ratiocination, 93; *Narrative of Arthur Gordon Pym,* 106; Lacan's and Derrida's reading of "The Purloined Letter," 115n5

Polymorphous perversity: of signifier in Pynchon's writing, 6; and Derrida's notion of poetic language, 87; and Prairie, 233; and art, 254

Post-histoire, 123

Post Card, The: and *Lot 49,* 88; as symbol of poetic space, 88, 210

Poststructuralism: and Pynchon, 1–2, 11–12n9; and subjectivity, 5

Preterite: and the elect, 111, 126, 174; and Slothrop, 129; and Weed Atman, 228. *See also* Elect

Projection. *See* Paranoia

Prosthesis: prosthetic reading strategy, 32; and Oedipa, 101, 104

Protestant culture: and *Lot 49,* 88; and Thanatos, 192; ethics of, 211

Psychosis: and Oedipa, 109–10; and Western society, 149n34; and simulation, 241–42n19

Pun: e/jaculations, 28n11; Pynchon's low puns, 67, 146n10, 97, 228; and Pynchon's poetics, 108, 197; defined, 96–97; odious awry, 97; mathematical, 99; and Oedipa, 100; and dreamer, 107; DT, 109; butadiene, 138; persistence of vision, 169; transport, 171; corpse, 181; joint hallucination, 189n24; screen, 205; beating, 216; cuttin' and shootin,' 223; "killed" and "shot," 228; programming, 236

Puritanism, 8; and robot, 73; and Trystero, 112; and America, 177

"Purloined Letter, The": Lacan's seminar on, 40n7, 78n15, 115n5, 148n26; and theory of ratiocination, 93

Pynchon's poetics: and rhetorical deconstruction, 5, 17, 106, 119, 122, 132, 243–46; and insistence of the real, 18,

Pynchon's poetics (*continued*)
199; and Lacanian poetics, 22, 26; and Baudrillardian poetics, 46; rhetorical deconstruction of psychoanalysis, 57–58; deconstruction of detective novel, 93; kaleidoscopic character of, 132; and Lacan's four discourses, 208; and discourse of the analyst, 226

Ratiocination, Poe's theory of, 93
Real, the: defined, 17–18; characteristics, 20–24; and Pynchon's poetics, 26–27, 199, 243–46; and *Hamlet*, 29n14; and *différance*, 34–35; and de Man, 38–39; and simulation, 43–49, 78n10, 84–86, 241–42n19; abolition of, 55; under erasure, 58; and fetish, 66; reality as grimce of, 90; Oedipa's encounter with, 92–93; and symbolic, 94; prose of, 106; and delirium, 107; history of, 130; real text, 131–32, 145; real space, 132; and art, 138; game of odd and even, 148n26; and cybernetics, 149n28; and film, 155–156; and pain, 168; and body, 181; as interface between world and subject, 185; and death, 191–92; and discourse of knowledge, 211; and discourse of the hysteric, 212; and "the Real Ones," 222; and ghosts, 224; and writing, 226; and filmic cut, 227; and alignment with imaginary and symbolic, 238–239
Reality principle: and entropy, 102, 104; and simulation, 141; and Frenesie, 231–32; and Prairie, 233; of budget, 235. *See also* Pleasure principle
Rebus: dream as, 117–18n20
Reflex: hardon, 123; conditioned, 128–29, 188–89n21; reflex arc, 146n10

Regression: of meaning, 87; and inheritance, 112; and deconstruction, 243
Remanence, 127
Repetition compulsion: defined, 25–26, 29n18; and Derrida, 33; and Pynchon's poetics, 196, 206; and Baudrillard, 200n3; and object *o*, 210
Residual induction, 127
Resinification, 135, 148n25
Retention, 156–57. *See also* Trace; Derrida, Jacques
Re-territorialization, 126
Retrospective, *Vineland* as, 202
Revolution: and simulation, 46, 50n8; and media, 115n3; and DL, 206; and Frenesie, 220–21, 231–32; and *jouissance*, 234, 238; and Prairie, 235–236; and Counterforce, 239n4; and discourse of the master, 242n24
Rhetorics: and material typonomy, 31; and de Man, 37–39, 97; and Baudrillardian theory, 46; and hieroglyph, 106; and Pynchon's poetics, 119, 122, 132, 143, 243–46
Robbe-Grillet, Alain, 9–10
Robot: and *V.*, 53; and machine, 56, 68; and Mélanie, 72–73; and V-1 and V-2, 125; and robotics, 149n34
Rocket: as leitmotif, 8; trajectory as a material typonomy, 31; as allegorical "figura," 39n4; and Slothrop's Pavlovian conditioning, 122–125, 146n10,12; and Zone, 130–31; and "real text," 145; and Enzian, 147n19; and Slothrop, 171; and film, 174–76, 181–82; meeting with, 191; launching of the 00000, 193–95; and logic of belatedness, 198–99; and Eros and Thanatos, 238; as ghost, 241n17; and drive, 242n27

Rosebud: as mystery signifier, 83. *See also Citizen Kane;* Welles

$, and Lacan, 16; and Derrida, 36; and Lacan's four discourses, 208–9, 211–13, 231; and Vond, 217; and Frenesie, 222; and discourse of the capitalist, 241n13

S_1: and Lacan's four discourses, 208–13; and discourse of the master, 219; and discourse of the capitalist, 241n13

S_2: and Lacan's four discourses, 208–13; and discourse of the capitalist, 241n13

Sadism: economy of, 168, 219; and "the Real Ones," 222

Sadomasochism: economy of, 167–169; and Katje, 173; and Frenesie and Vond, 215–17, 219, 231, 238

Saussure, Ferdinand de: and hieroglyphic script, 105; and chess metaphor, 138

Schizo, 3

Schizophrenia: and paranoia, 47; and Profane and Stencil, 54; utopia of, 59; and Oedipa, 109; and Counterforce, 120; and conditioning, 124; and simulation, 175

Schopenhauer, Arthur, 166

Schrift (Writing): and Oedipa, 115

Schwarzgerät: and Imipolex G, 125; and logic of belatedness, 129, 170; and Gottfried, 194

Schwarzknabe, 119

Schwarzkommando: and "True Text," 131, 145; and Enzian, 133; and film, 163–66, 174, 189n23

Sign-signal: and Derrida's notion of poetic language, 87

Silence: Lacan's notion of, 22–24; Derrida's notion of, 35; Mélanie's, 66; and the real, 92, 141–42, 144–45; and conditioning, 128; and nature, 145; and Burroughs, 189n25; and rocket, 191; and Pynchon's poetics, 198, 244; and Vond's death, 235

Simulation, 6; theory of, 43–48, 50n7, 78n10; and *V.*, 53, 72–75; and Mélanie, 57–59, 61, 63, 65–66, 71; and media, 84–86, 204–6, 216; Pierce as, 89; and information, 103; and schizophrenia, 109; and reality, 110–11, 114; and McLuhan, 115n3; and conditioning, 120, 131; and plastics, 134–36; and Imipolex G, 137–38; and language, 139–41, 143, 145; and film, 151, 155–56, 158–60, 162–71, 174, 178–79; and filmic writing, 183–84; and death, 192–95, 229–30; and chemistry, 197; and *Vineland*, 202; and Frenesie, 222; and Prairie, 235–36; and psychosis, 241–42n19; and Pynchon's poetics, 243, 245

Slow Learner: and death, 22; and silence, 23; and entropy, 25; McHoul/Wills's reading of, 36; and simulation, 45; and Pynchon's poetics, 158, 202

"The Small Rain," 22

Soma, 21

Spacing, 117n18

Sphinx, 44

Stimulus: and Slothrop's Pavlovian conditioning, 123–25, 128–29, 137, 139, 141, 146n10; Katje as, 172; and CHiPs, 205; Frenesie as, 221; Prairie as, 236

Stravinsky, Igor, 78n11

Stucco, 135. *See also* Plastics

Stupidity of the signifier, 108, 214, 226, 238

Subject-supposed-to-know, 213

Sublimation: and death, 192; and discourse of the analyst, 213; and sublime,

272   Index

Sublimation (*continued*)
225–26; and reality principle, 233
Sublime: and object *o*, 27, 238; and Burke, 29n20; and Pynchon's poetics, 46; and fantastic, 225–229; and ideology, 241n19
Superego, 114
Surplus *jouissance:* and object *o*, 208, 210–13, 240n10. *See also Jouissance*
Symbolic: logic of, 17; and unconscious, 18; and desire, 19, 21; its ontological failure, 24; as automaton, 25, 75, 76–77n6; and writing, 27, 29n19; and the real, 28n9; and Name-of-the-Father, 42; and theory of ratiocination, 93; and vanishing of the "Other," 98; and death drive, 102–4; and hieroglyph, 106, 117–118n20; and delirium, 107; and Zone, 131; and digitality, 141, 144; and game of odd and even, 148n26; and film, 156–58; and V-2, 175; and Slothrop's scattering, 180–181; and *Vineland*, 202; and law of desire, 208; and sublime, 226; and alignment with the imaginary and the real; 238–39
Synthesis. *See* Control

Technology: male technologies, 55; and penalization, 76n2; and simulation, 86; postal, 88; and digitality, 206; sublimity of, 241–42n19
Telecommunications, 88
Teleology: of death, 22; of Eros, 200n3
Telephone: and *Lot* 49, 84; and Oedipa, 89, 99, 114; and entropy, 116n11
Television: and Fergus, 74; and simulation, 84–86; and speed, 175; and Zoyd, 203, 205; and Frenesie, 205; and Weed Atman, 205; and fascism,

205; and film, 206; and Millard Hobbs, 216; and power, 233; and Prairie, 235–36
Temps. *See* Durée
Terror: of schizophrenia, 47; and postal technology, 88; and motorhead valley roulette, 230
Thanatos. *See* Eros
Thermodynamics, second law of, 103
Thetic: and Derrida, 33; and Kristeva, 158, 161
Thoth, 99
Thrust (*Schub*), 242n27
Tinguely, Jean, 56
Todorov, Tzvetan, 224
Togetherness, utopia of, 17, 195, 196
Tourism, 72
Trace: and the real, 27; Derrida's notion of, 48, 156, 187n8; and signifying chain, 88
Transgression: and *jouissance*, 21; and symbolic, 25, 35, 103; and simulation, 43; of the law, 232
Transmarginality: and Pavlovian conditioning, 124–25, 146n4
Transposition: and Kristeva, 154, 158–59, 161
Trauma: of symbolization, 25; and logic of belatedness, 121, 175; and conditioning, 130
Trompe-la-mort, 34
TV. *See* Television
Typonomy, material: explained, 31; and language, 34; and Pynchon's texts, 36; and substance *vs.* figure, 38–39; and film, 187–88n13; gun as, 223

Ultraparadoxical phase, 124, 146n5
Uncanny, the: and deconstructive reading, 37; and notion of cut, 227

"Under the Rose" and simulation, 43–44; and decadence, 53; and meeting with the real, 55; and automata, 57; and Pynchon's poetics, 202

V-1, 123, 125

V-2, 120, 122–23, 125, 128, 130–32, 138; and Katje, 172; and logic of belatedness, 175; and death, 191, 193. *See also* 00000; 00001; Rocket

Vheissu: and meeting with the real, 55

Video: and reality, 205

Virilio, Paul, 163–65

Void: and real/unconscious, 17, 55, 99; and Thing, 20; between signifiers, 24, 109; as transcendental signifier, 40n8; and Pierce, 89; and "Bordando el Manto Terreste," 91; below symbolic, 94; and phantom limb, 101; and Oedipa, 110; and film, 156; of power, 207

Voyeurism: and Mélanie, 68; and striptease, 79n17

Waiting for Godot, 18

Want-to-be, 28n1. *See also* Lack-of- being

War: and Slothrop's desk, 8; and discourse, 35; and war machine, 55; as a laboratory, 125; its destructions, 126, 130; as a media event, 161–65, 188n19; and culture of death, 196; and television, 205; and war movies, 236

Wasteland: semiotic, 5; *The Waste Land*, 82

We-system, They-system, 113

Weber, Max, 73

Welles, Orson: and *Lady from Shanghai*, 79n23; and *Citizen Kane*, 83–85, 93, 152

Wiener, Norbert, 116–17n15

Wills, David. *See* McHoul

Wittgenstein, Ludwig, 55, 100, 149n33

Writing-effect: the real as, 27

Writing-machine: and Derrida's notion of poetic language, 87

Zeno's paradox, 199

Zone: dynamics of, 26, 244; and Pavlovian conditioning, 120–21, 125–26, 128, 131–32; and Oedipal situation in, 147n16; and von Göll, 162, 166; and Slothrop's scattering, 179; and Burroughs, 189n25; and simulated death, 193; our crippl'd Zone, 200; Frenesi in her time-free zone, 232

HANJO BERRESSEM teaches American literature at the University of Aachen. He has published numerous articles on contemporary critical theory, cultural theory, modern literature, and art history.